The Way of Selflessness

A Practical Guide to Enlightenment Based on the Teachings of the World's Great Mystics

Joel Morwood

Center for Sacred Sciences
Eugene, Oregon

Published by

Center for Sacred Sciences
Eugene, Oregon, USA
www.centerforsacredsciences.org

Founded in 1987, the Center for Sacred Sciences is a non-profit spiritual organization whose mission is as follows:

1. To demonstrate that, despite their outer (or exoteric) differences, the world's great religious traditions share an inner (or esoteric) Truth testified to by their mystics.
2. To help develop a new worldview in which the Truth realized by the mystics and the truths of modern science can be seen as compatible ways of understanding the same underlying Reality.
3. To foster and maintain a community of spiritual practitioners who wish to follow the teachings and practices of the mystics of all the great traditions, presented in generic, contemporary terms.

Printed in the United States of America

Cover and page design by Lina Van Brunt, Van Brunt/West Design

Cover photo by Jack Yousey

Index by Kathleen Simpson

ISBN 978-0-9620387-2-3

For my wife, Jennifer, light of my life.

Acknowledgements

Special thanks are due to John Richardson for suggesting that I write this book, Mora Dewey for laying out and formatting a preliminary version of the manuscript and to Vip Short for supervising its printing; Thomas McFarlane for his extensive editorial comments; Sheila Craven, Maggie Free and Karen Fierman for editing and proofreading; Therese Engelmann and Valerie Stuart for their financial support; and all of the members of the Center for Sacred Sciences' practitioners' groups who provided invaluable advice and suggestions after working with an earlier draft of this book.

Contents

Preface

Know, O noble brother, that while the paths are many, the Way of Truth is single.

— Ibn al-`Arabi (Muslim)

During a particularly dark period in my life, when I despaired of ever finding happiness, I happened to stumble on some of the writings of the mystics—men and women who claimed to have discovered a universal and liberating Truth about the ultimate nature of Reality. What I found so striking about their testimonies was that, unlike the works of other philosophers and theologians, whose ideas seemed always to conflict, the mystics' accounts of this Reality were remarkably similar. And this was true despite the fact that they had lived in very different times and places, and come from very different religious traditions. Listen, for example, to one of the authors of the Hindu Upanishads, some of which date back to the eighth-century BCE:

> As rivers flowing towards the ocean find their final peace and their name and form disappear, even so the wise become free from name and form and enter into the radiance of the Supreme Spirit who is greater than all greatness... In truth who knows God becomes God.[1]

Now, compare this to how the eleventh-century Muslim poet Abdullah Ansari of Herat describes what happened to him:

> The rain drop reached the sea and found therein its mellowing,
> Just as the star was effaced by the daylight,
> Whoever reached his Lord and Master (Mawlā) has attained
> his true "self."[2]

Four hundred years later, the Christian mystic Teresa of Avila had this to say of her "union with God":

> Here it is like rain falling from the heavens into a river or spring; there is nothing but water there and it is impossible to divide or separate the water belonging to the river from that which fell from the heavens. Or it is as if a tiny streamlet enters the sea, from which

> it will find no way of separating itself, or as if in a room there were two large windows through which the light streamed in: it enters in different places but it all becomes one.[3]

And here's what the contemporary Tibetan master Dudjom Lingpa writes about the end of the Buddhist path:

> It is like a drop of water blending with the ocean and becoming the ocean without altering it, or space within a vase blending with the space outside, extending freely throughout space without its being altered.[4]

Another difference between the mystics and ordinary philosophers and theologians was that, instead of trying to convince the reader of the truth of their ideas through argument, the mystics insisted that anyone willing to undertake the appropriate spiritual disciplines and practices could discover it directly for themselves. Thus, among Sufis (the mystics of Islam), seekers who reach the end of the path are called *al-muhaqqiqun,* which means "verifiers." This is because, as the thirteenth-century Sufi shaykh (master), Ibn al-`Arabi, declares,

> Knowledge of mystical states can only be had by actual experience, nor can the reason of man define it, nor arrive at any cognizing of it by deduction.[5]

So, too, the anonymous author of the two fourteenth-century Christian classics *The Cloud of Unknowing* and *The Book of Privy Counseling* writes,

> You will not really understand all this until your own contemplative experience confirms it.[6]

And here's how the seventh-century Hindu sage Shankara sums up this insistence on empirical confirmation:

> From the lips of your teacher you have learned of the truth of Brahman as it is revealed in the scriptures. Now you must realize that truth directly and immediately. Then only will your heart be free from any doubt.[7]

In this respect, mysticism is not unlike a science. In science, theories can be verified by observations gained through various kinds of experiments. So, too, the teachings of the mystics can be verified by insights and experiences gained through various kinds of practices—which is precisely what I myself did.

Slowly but surely I began to engage in practices of meditation, keeping precepts, cultivating love and compassion, and conducting self-inquiry. At first, I thought of all this more as a hobby—something to do in my spare time. But, eventually, walking a spiritual path became the priority of my life. I abandoned my career, friends, and family in search of the Truth to which all the mystics seemed to point. And yet, no matter how hard I tried or how far I traveled, that Holy Grail continued to elude me. Finally, after I had given up all hope of attaining my goal, it happened. In a cheap motel room on the night of August 13, 1983, I Awoke to a Reality at once far more astonishing and, at the same time, far more simple than anything I could have ever imagined. Here is part of what I wrote shortly thereafter:

> I jump up, turn on the light, and look around. Sure enough, I no longer see through a glass darkly. The veil has been lifted and the glass has cleared—no, more than cleared—it has vanished! I see the Kingdom, and now I am laughing wildly, because the great joke of it all is that this exalted Kingdom I have been searching for in such anguish and despair is none other than the very room I have been sleeping in, with its dirty, cinder block walls, frayed curtains, and horribly grungy, blue-green rug! I could have shouted! I could have danced! I could have done anything for that matter, because it really didn't matter. It didn't even exist and never had. I was free.[8]

In the years that followed a number of students sought my help with their own spiritual quests. In 1987 we established the Center for Sacred Sciences—a small organization dedicated to studying mystical teachings and engaging in mystical practices. This book is an outgrowth of that work. In it you will hear the voices of many mystics from very different traditions, but it is not meant to be an argument for the validity of their claims. Rather, it is meant to be a manual of instruction, a step-by-step guide for anyone who wishes to walk this path and find out for themselves if what the mystics say is true. To this end I have tried to distill out the most universal principles and the most essential practices taught by mystics of all the great traditions. I have also tried to restate them in more generic terms, suitable for modern seekers, whether they belong to an established tradition or not.

How to Use This Book

There are several ways to approach the teachings contained in this book. Some of you may wish to read through the entire text and only then, if you are so moved, go back and actually do the practices. Others may want to start practicing from the very beginning. Either way is fine. However, because many of the earlier practices lay the foundations for later ones, it is important to undertake them in the order they are presented, practicing each one until you have gained some familiarity with it before moving on to the next. Then, at any point along the way, you can always return to a particular practice in order to deal with a particular problem you've encountered on your path.

So then the question is this: How long does it take to become familiar with a practice? The answer depends on a great many factors, such as how much previous experience you've had with the same or similar practices; how much time per day you have to devote to a practice; how strong your motivation is;

and what sort of guidance you receive. Most practices are designed either to help you attain specific states of consciousness or specific insights and experiences. Thus, you should continue with any practice you take up until you have reaped at least some of its actual fruit.

The same applies to questions about how long the path as a whole takes to complete. Perhaps the shortest one on record was that of the seventh-century Chinese Zen master Hui-Neng. As the story goes, he was an illiterate woodcutter, delivering a load of firewood to an inn. While standing in the courtyard, he heard a Buddhist guest chanting a verse from the *Diamond Sutra* and, suddenly, his mind opened up! At the opposite end of the spectrum, it took my own teacher, Franklin Merrell-Wolff, twenty-five years to reach the end of his journey. In point of fact, no one can predict how long anyone's path is going to take, nor does it really matter, for as Merrell-Wolff writes,

> I felt, and feel, that no cost could be too high as the price of its attainment, and I find that this testimony is repeated over and over again in mystical literature.[9]

Many of my students studied an early draft of this book in the context of our weekly practitioners' groups and said they found the community setting very helpful. Not only does it provide an opportunity to share experiences and have questions answered but, as is well known in mystical traditions, the support of spiritual brothers and sisters is of immense psychological and spiritual benefit. This is why, for instance, the *sangha* or spiritual community is considered to be one of the Three Jewels of Buddhism (along with the teachings and a teacher). It's also why the Sufis have a saying: *Travel with a friend.* So, if you don't have access to a circle of practitioners already using this book, you may want to consider forming one of your own.

In any case, whether you are starting out alone or in the company of fellow seekers, I hope the teachings and practices described in the pages to come will enrich your own path and make it more productive.

Before we begin, however, it may be helpful to get an overview of just where we are going and the various ways to get there.

The Way of Selflessness

Part I: *Overview of the Way*

CHAPTER 1

The Truth that Makes You Free

> *If you continue in my word, you are truly my disciples; and you will know the truth, and the truth will make you free.*
>
> — Jesus of Nazareth

When Jesus told his followers that the Truth would make them free, some objected that they had never been slaves to any man. Jesus, however, made it clear that the freedom he was talking about was not political but spiritual. It was freedom from sin and, by implication, sin's wages, which are suffering and death.[10] But that's not all. On other occasions he assured them that, not only was it possible to become free of suffering and death, they could also attain the kind of real, abiding happiness we all dream of, for as he told the Samaritan woman he met at a well,

> Everyone who drinks of this water will be thirsty again, but those who drink of the water that I will give them will never be thirsty. The water that I will give will become in them a spring of water gushing up to eternal life.[11]

Most Christians down through the centuries have interpreted such teachings to mean that if you believe Jesus is the Son of God, and you lead a good life, then after you die you will go to heaven where there will be no more suffering and no more death. But this is not the only way these teachings have been understood. Christian mystics have insisted that if you really knew the Truth Jesus was referring to, you would become free of suffering and death and find eternal happiness right now, in this very life. Thus, the fourteenth-century saint Catherine of Siena exclaims:

> Oh, how blessed is this soul who while still in her mortal body enjoys the reward of immortality![12]

And here is how the thirteenth-century mystic Meister Eckhart describes such a person:

> This man lives in one light with God, and therefore there is not in him either suffering or the passage of time, but an unchanging eternity.[13]

Similarly, the seventeenth-century monk Brother Lawrence says this of himself:

> Even if I were capable of suffering, it would be from not having any suffering at all.... My tranquility is so great that I fear nothing.[14]

Now such claims sound so incredible that we are apt to dismiss them as being, at best, wild exaggerations and, at worst, the ravings of religious lunatics. The trouble is, Christian mystics are not the only ones who have made them. In fact, virtually identical testimonies have been given by mystics of all the great traditions. The majority of Muslims, for example, hold beliefs about a post-mortem existence similar to those of Christians. But the Sufis maintain that you don't have to wait until after death to enter paradise, because as Ibn al-`Arabi explains,

> The Paradise which is pre-destined for those who will come to it in the next life is before your eyes already, this very day.... You are there now . . . but you do not know it.[15]

So, too, the thirteenth-century Jewish Kabbalist Abraham Abulafia writes,

> When the imaginary, lying apprehension is negated, and when its memory is razed from the hearts of those who feel and are enlightened, death will be swallowed up forever.[16]

In the East, of course, death is not seen as a one-time event. According to the Hindu tradition, the individual soul or *jiva* is born and dies again and again, until it finally accumulates enough good *karma* to attain *moksha* (liberation) from this whole miserable cycle of reincarnations. Hindu mystics, however, have always insisted that there is a way to become *jiva-mukta*—that is, one who is "liberated in this life." Thus, we read in the Upanishads,

> When a man knows God, he is free: his sorrows have an end, and birth and death are no more.[17]

Liberation from cyclic existence or *samsara* and the attainment of *nirvana* is also the goal of Buddhist mystics. The Buddha himself summarized this in his *Four Noble Truths*, which constitute the basis for all the rest of his teachings. These are as follows:

1) Life is suffering.

2) Suffering has a cause.

3) Suffering can be ended.

4) There is a path to the end of suffering.

And finally, here's what the legendary Taoist sage Chuang Tzu says of someone who has become one with the *Tao* or Way:

> A man like this rides the clouds and mists, straddling sun and moon, and wanders beyond the four seas. Even life and death have no effect on him![18]

So while, on first hearing, the very idea that suffering and death can be abolished and abiding happiness attained in this life seems absurd, the fact that so many mystics from such vastly different times, places, and cultures have attested to just this possibility should give us pause. Perhaps, instead of dismissing their claims out of hand, we should dig a little deeper to see just how they could actually be true.

What Causes Suffering

Let's go back to the Buddha's Second Noble Truth which states that suffering has a *cause*. Because if suffering has a cause, then it seems reasonable to suppose that, by eliminating this cause, we can eliminate suffering.

Now normally we think that the cause of our suffering lies outside of ourselves in the things that happen to us. Consequently, we keep trying to alter our external circumstances. To fend off poverty, for instance, we try to accumulate wealth. To avoid illness, we take vitamins, go on diets, and try to exercise more. To alleviate loneliness, we work at maintaining relationships with family, friends, and lovers. To escape boredom, we watch TV, go to movies, or attend sporting events. But suppose that, in adopting these strategies, we are only addressing the superficial causes of suffering and not its *root* cause. Suppose the root cause of suffering lies not in the external world, or even in our physical bodies, but within our own hearts and minds.

To see how this might be the case, suppose you woke up one morning to find your car had been stolen during the night. This would probably cause you a good deal of suffering. If you didn't have insurance, it would put a sizable dent in your pocketbook. And even if you did have insurance, you would still be faced with the inconvenience of having to make out a police report, file an insurance claim, and shop for a replacement.

But now, suppose you woke up one morning to find your neighbor's car had been stolen. Would that cause you the same amount of suffering? Almost certainly not. If you were acquainted with your neighbor, you might spend a few minutes commiserating with him or her, and you might also be a little concerned that such a theft had occurred so close to home. But chances are you wouldn't experience anywhere near the degree of suffering you would if your own car had been stolen.

What a comparison of these two scenarios demonstrates is that it is not the bare *fact* of a car being stolen that causes you to suffer, because in both cases cars were stolen. The real cause of your suffering is that you have formed an *attachment* to your car. But if your neighbor's car is stolen, it causes you much less suffering, because the only *attachment* you have to your neighbor's car is a vicarious one, based on whatever bond of sympathy you two share. Moreover, if you picked up the newspaper and read about a car being stolen from someone you had never met, you might fret for a moment about the crime rate going up but, aside from that, you wouldn't experience any suffering at all. Why? Because you have formed no attachment whatsoever to a car that belongs to a complete stranger.

So then why do we get attached to things in the first place? If you examine your own life, you will almost certainly find that you only get attached to things you *desire*. To give another example, let's say you are a coffee lover who stumbles across a beautiful old coffee mug in an antique store. Even though it is quite expensive, you decide to splurge and buy it anyway. From then on, every morning you sip your coffee from this mug and so over the years you build up a very strong attachment to it. One morning, however, you drop the mug and it shatters into a dozen pieces. No doubt, losing that mug would cause you considerable suffering.

But now suppose that your aunt Tilly gives you an ugly green soup tureen as a wedding present. Most of the time you keep it hidden away in a closet, bringing it out only on those occasions when she comes to visit. Then, suppose one day the tureen breaks. Not only would that not cause you any suffering, you would probably be glad to be rid of it.

So, what's the difference between these two scenarios? In the first one you had an intense *desire* for the coffee mug, but in the second you had *no* desire for the tureen. Consequently, when the mug breaks you suffer, but you experience no suffering when the tureen breaks.

Notice, also that an attachment can be based on an *aversion* which, although it may have a different feeling-tone, is actually a kind of negative desire. Thus, to have an aversion for sickness is really the flip side of having a desire for health. If you didn't care whether you were healthy or not, getting sick wouldn't cause you any suffering.

Now all this may sound pretty obvious—especially when we are dealing with simple desires, aversions, and attachments involving only material objects. Still, it is important to understand clearly that *we only suffer when we are attached to something, and we only get attached to things that we desire*, because this same principle applies even in the most complex situations. For instance, you may be stuck in a marriage you feel has stagnated. Part of you dreams of getting a divorce and starting a new, more rewarding life. But another part of you is still attached to the safety and comfort that your marital routines provide. In this kind of situation, your suffering results not from any single desire or attachment, but from being caught in a whole web of conflicting desires and attachments.

What's more, desires and attachments don't always involve possessions or people. They can be more psychological in nature. For instance, many people are attached to mental images they have of themselves. In such cases, suffering arises when there is a discrepancy between a person's self-image and how their lives actually unfold. If, say, you are attached to an image of yourself as being inordinately good at your job, then chances are whenever you make even some minor mistake, you will suffer inordinate humiliation. The point is, no matter how complex our lives become, whatever suffering we experience can still be traced back to some form of attachment which, in turn, is always based on some kind of desire. If there is no desire, there can be no attachment, and if there is no attachment, there can be no suffering.

But although suffering depends on desire and attachment, the presence of these two factors alone is still not sufficient to guarantee that suffering will actually arise. There is something else that we must take into consideration—something which is built into the very nature of the world—and that is that everything is impermanent. If things were not impermanent, then the fact that we desired and formed attachments to them would not be a problem. We could just go on accumulating all the things we wanted without ever experiencing any suffering from their loss. As we all know, however, this is not the case. Cars, coffee mugs, jobs, people—everything we desire and get attached to eventually breaks down, wears out, and ceases to exist.

Moreover, not only are all the things we desire and get attached to impermanent, but we, ourselves, are impermanent. We, ourselves, are doomed to die someday. Therefore, even if it were possible to get all the things we ever wanted, and even if it were possible to hold onto them for as long as we lived, in the end we would still have to forfeit them at the time of our death. So, it is not just that we get attached to things we desire that causes our suffering, but also the fact that all these things are impermanent.

Now, normally we don't like to think about the fact that everything is impermanent, and we especially don't like to think about our own impermanence. One reason for this is that there doesn't seem to be anything we can do about it. "Okay," we say, "everything is impermanent. That's just the way things are. So we might as well try to make the best of it: eat, drink, and be merry, for tomorrow we die, as the old saying goes."

But is impermanence really the *root* cause of our suffering? Because if it is, then, given that impermanence is an unalterable fact of our world, there is simply no way to end suffering, and attain true, abiding happiness in this life. The mystics, however, claim that our suffering has an even deeper cause—one that is not quite *so* obvious, or perhaps we should say one that is so obvious we habitually overlook it. And since this is where the mystics' teachings start to depart from the way we ordinarily view things, let's hear what they themselves have to say. Listen, for example, to the Hindu sage Shankara:

> The ego-sense is deep-rooted and powerful.... It creates the impression that "I am the actor, I am he who experiences." This impression causes our bondage to rebirth and death.[19]

And you'll find this same teaching given by mystics of all traditions. Here's how the twentieth-century Tibetan Buddhist master Bokar Rinpoche puts it:

> The fundamental dysfunction of our minds takes the form of a separation between I and other. We falsely grasp at an "I" on which attachment grafts itself at the same time as we conceive of an "other" that is the basis of aversion.[20]

Likewise, the Christian author of *The Cloud of Unknowing* writes,

> Every man has plenty of cause for sorrow but he alone understands the deep universal reason for sorrow who experiences *that he is*.[21]

The contemporary Sufi master Javad Nurbakhsh sums it up this way:

> As long as you are 'you', you will be miserable and impoverished.[22]

According to these mystics, then, it is not the simple fact of impermanence that causes our suffering. In order for suffering to occur, there has to be some self to experience it. If there were no self, there would be no suffering. If, for instance, you were to drop this book on the floor, it wouldn't experience any suffering. In fact, there is nothing you could do to this book—cut it, burn it, tear it apart—that would cause it to suffer in any way. And why? Because you are quite certain the book has no self. Consequently, although attachment, desire, and impermanence are all important *contributing* factors to the generation of suffering, what the mystics say is that, at an even deeper level, suffering depends on the presence of some self, capable of being a suffer-*er*.

But while the presence of some self may be crucial to the experience of suffering, is it really its root cause? Because if it is, then again there doesn't seem to be anything much we can do about it—except perhaps commit suicide. And even if suicide could put an end to suffering (which mystics of all traditions emphatically deny), this still cannot bring us the kind of true abiding happiness that mystics also claim it is possible to attain. Therefore, we have to dig deeper and ask this: Does suffering have a cause even more fundamental than the experience of being a separate self—a cause which perhaps we *can* do something about? And, of course, the mystics' answer to this is yes. Here is how the first-century Buddhist philosopher Nagarjuna explains it:

> The root of suffering is clinging, the root of clinging is craving, and the root of craving is ignorance.[23]

Notice that the first part of Nagarjuna's statement recapitulates what our own analysis has already revealed—namely, that the immediate cause of suffering is clinging (attachment), and that this, in turn, is based on craving (desire). But then he goes on to say that craving is based on ignorance. In other words, the only reason we desire and get attached to things is because there is something of which we are ignorant. And once again, you'll find this teaching in all mystical traditions. Thus, Shankara writes,

> The mind is filled with ignorance, and this causes the bondage of birth and death.[24]

The thirteenth-century Sufi poet Jalaluddin Rumi also insists that our suffering is based on ignorance or *heedlessness* as he calls it, and illustrates this with the following metaphor:

> Up to your knees in the stream's water, you are heedless of yourself
> and seek a drink from this person and that.[25]

And, of course, when Jesus declares that knowing the Truth will make us free from suffering and death, he is implying that our ignorance of this Truth is what causes us to experience them.

How Ignorance Can Cause Suffering

Now, to claim that ignorance is the root cause of all our suffering may sound strange, so let's take a moment to see how ignorance can be the cause of any kind of suffering. First of all, we usually think of ignorance as the *absence* of some type of knowledge or skill. For instance, in our culture, if a person lacks an education, it is very difficult to get a well-paying job. But when mystics talk about *ignorance*, they mean something a little different. As Shankara says, this kind of *spiritual* ignorance "fills our minds." In other words, the problem isn't so much that we lack knowledge, but that the knowledge we do possess is in some way false and so deceives us.

This is something we can experience in everyday life. Suppose, for example, you have a severe stomachache. You go to the doctor who runs a series of tests. In a couple of days the results come back, and the doctor informs you that you have incurable cancer. No doubt, this would cause you a tremendous amount of suffering. You would be overwhelmed by a host of horrific emotions—shock, grief, anger, fear.

Now, suppose a week later the doctor calls back and says there has been a terrible mistake. Your test results got mixed up with someone else's. You don't have cancer after all! The only thing wrong with you is a little indigestion caused by eating too much Polish sausage. Imagine the relief you would experience. In an instant, all your suffering would vanish to be replaced with feelings of elation, joy, and bliss! And why? Simply because you learned the truth about your situation. What had caused your suffering wasn't anything real to begin with. It was only a delusion that had temporarily *filled your mind*.

This scenario comes much closer to what mystics mean when they say that ignorance is the root cause of suffering. Not only do we fail to recognize the truth of our situation, but we are actually deluded by false knowledge—or, better yet, by false perceptions, because this kind of ignorance is not just conceptual. It involves a complete misapprehension of ourselves and the world. And what exactly is the nature of this misapprehension? It is that our experience of being a separate self—which as we have just seen is a necessary condition for suffering—is, in reality, a delusion. According to the mystics no such entity really exists.

In Buddhism, this is summed up in the teaching of *anatta,* which in Pali means literally "no self" (*an* = no, *atta* = self). Here's how contemporary Buddhist scholar Walpola Rahula explains it:

> According to the teaching of the Buddha, the idea of self is an imaginary, false belief which has no corresponding reality.[26]

Likewise, Shankara declares that

> [The appearance of] an individual soul is caused by the delusion of our understanding, and has no reality. By its very nature, this appearance is unreal. When our delusion has been removed, it ceases to exist.[27]

Ibn al-`Arabi agrees:

> Know that you are an imagination, as is all that you regard as other than yourself an imagination.[28]

And St. Catherine of Siena writes,

> In self knowledge, then, thou wilt humble thyself; seeing that, in thyself, thou dost not even exist.[29]

It is important to note that, when mystics claim that there is no self, they are not saying that such things as thoughts, memories, emotions, sensations—all the phenomena which most people think of as constituting themselves—don't appear in consciousness. What they are saying is that the boundary which encloses these phenomena and marks them off as a separate entity has no true existence. It is an imaginary creation, much like the boundaries which separate one country from another. We humans find it useful to draw such boundaries, but this still doesn't make them *real* features of the terrain. They are imaginary lines which we project onto our environment. And, according to the mystics, the same thing applies to the boundary we draw between 'self' and 'world.' It, too, is very useful but no less imaginary than, say, the border between the United States and Canada.

It is our ignorance of this fact, then, that gives rise to the delusion that some self actually exists. And when we believe that a self actually exists, we identify with everything inside the boundary which defines it—i.e., all the phenomena that constitute what we call a body-mind. But if 'I' am identified with a body-mind, then when the body-mind is hungry, 'I' feel hungry. And when the body-mind feels pain, 'I' feel pain. Likewise, the body-mind's emotions are experienced as 'my' emotions, so when fear or sorrow arise, they become 'my' fear and 'my' sorrow. And when confused or disturbing thoughts are present, then 'I' feel confused and disturbed. In other words, because we believe we are a separate self, we take all these phenomena *personally*. We experience them as happening to some *one*—some *victim* 'in here' who suffers as a result.

So to sum all this up, what the mystics claim is that, although the immediate causes of our suffering are the self's desires for and attachments to ephemeral things, the *root* cause stems from our ignorance of the fact that, in reality, no such 'self' exists! Consequently, in order to be free of suffering, what we need to do is dispel our ignorance, for as Shankara says,

> As long as we perceive things falsely, our false perception distracts us and makes us miserable. When our false perception is corrected, misery ends also.[30]

And the way to correct this "false perception" is, as Jesus said, simply to Realize the Truth of our situation. Here's how Bokar Rinpoche explains it in Buddhist terms:

> What is suffering? What is death? In reality, they do not have any existence. They appear within the framework of the manifestations produced by the mind wrapped up in an illusion, just as they appear in a dream.... In the emptiness of mind, there is no death. No one dies. There is no suffering and no fear.[31]

Or as Javad Nurbakhsh says so succinctly,

> Because the sufi has no self, there is no pain for him to bear.[32]

But this is only half the story—and the negative half at that! It only tells us how suffering can be ended. It does not tell us anything about the mystics' second, more positive claim—namely, that we can actually attain the kind of true, abiding happiness we all long for so deeply. To find out how this could be possible, we have to ask a different question: If we are not separate selves, then who or what are we *really*? Because what the mystics also claim is that knowing who or what we really are is the key to discovering this happiness.

Chapter 2

Who Are You, Really?

That Thou Art

— The Upanishads (Hindu)

The phrase *Tat tvam asi,* or "That thou art," first proclaimed by the *Upanishads,* lies at the heart of Hindu mysticism. But what does it mean? "Thou" stands for *Atman,* which refers to your *true* Self, as opposed to the separate 'self' you imagine yourself to be; "That" stands for *Brahman,* the Ultimate Reality of everything that is. So, if you asked the Hindu mystics who or what you really are, their answer would be this: You are none other than the Ultimate Reality Itself!

But if you then asked what exactly this Ultimate Reality is, not one of them would be able to tell you. Why? Because, as the Upanishads themselves declare,

> [Brahman] is immeasurable, inapprehensible, beyond conception, never-born, beyond reasoning, beyond thought.[33]

If you asked a Buddhist what it is to know who you *really* are, you might get an answer like this from Tibetan master Dudjom Lingpa:

> It is simply understanding correctly one's own true nature as the fundamental nature of reality.[34]

Notice, this is almost identical to the answer given by the Upanishads: Your true nature is the Fundamental Nature of everything. But then if you asked Dudjom Lingpa what that Fundamental Nature is, he couldn't tell you, because, as he also says,

> [That] nature is free of ultimately defining characteristics that can be expressed in words, beyond metaphorical approximation and devoid of any status as some entity that could actually be demonstrated.[35]

Similarly, if you asked a Taoist sage who or what you really are, he would answer that you are one with the *Tao,* or Way, which refers to the Ultimate Reality underlying all phenomena. But as for what the Way Itself is, he couldn't tell you because, according Lao Tzu, the fabled founder of Taoism,

> The Way that can be spoken of
> Is not the constant Way.[36]

When Jesus was asked who *he* really was, he answered, "The Father and I are one"[37]—which is to say, "I am one with the Ultimate Reality that is God." Now, although most Christians believe *only* Jesus is one with God, Christian mystics have claimed that God constitutes everybody's true being. This is why Meister Eckhart says,

> Some simple people think that they will see God as if he were standing there and they here. It is not so. God and I, we are one.[38]

But if you were to ask Meister Eckhart who or what God is, he couldn't tell you because, as he explains,

> God is "above names" and ineffable.[39]

Finally, if you asked a Sufi like Ibn al-`Arabi who or what you really are, he would answer that you are

> not other than the divine Identity Itself, as also no [determined] being, now or in the future, is other than His Identity; He is the Identity.[40]

As for this Divine Identity, however, nothing can truly be said of It, for as Ibn al-`Arabi also says,

> No eye perceives It, no limit encompasses It, and no demonstration (*burhān*) gives knowledge of It.[41]

So, if you asked any of these mystics from any of these traditions about your true nature, they would all give you the same answer: They would all declare that your true nature is Ultimate Reality Itself. But as to what this Ultimate Reality actually *is,* not one of them could tell you, and neither can I. This, in fact, is what the word *mysticism* means. It comes from the Greek root, *mustes* or "closed mouthed." *Mustes* is also etymologically related to *mute*—i.e., someone who cannot speak—which is very appropriate when applied to mystics. It is not that they have some deep dark secret they are intentionally withholding from you. It's that they *cannot* tell you. They cannot tell you because the nature of Ultimate Reality is quite literally *unspeakable.*

Why Reality is Unspeakable

So why should this be the case? Why can't the nature of Ultimate Reality be defined in words? The answer has to do with the nature of words themselves. Whenever we use a word, we distinguish one thing from another by indicating a boundary. For instance, if I say, "This is a book," what I am really saying is, there is some boundary which separates a certain aspect of my experience—this 'book'—from all the other aspects of my experience.

This is true not only of words that signify concrete objects, like books, but also of more abstract words that signify different classes of phenomena. For instance, if I say "This cushion is blue," I am placing it within a *class* of objects that can be distinguished from other *classes* of objects that are red, or green, or yellow. And if I say that the statement "the earth is round" is *true*, I am distinguishing it from another class of statements about the earth—such as "the earth is flat"—which are *false*. The point is, words always refer to some form of distinction, and whenever we have a distinction, we have a boundary which, in turn, automatically produces a duality. This is true even if I only use one word. Even if I simply give something a name, I still end up with a duality consisting of whatever falls *inside* the boundary indicated by the name, and everything else that falls *outside* of it. And, of course, the more words I use, the more dualities I end up with. Consequently, the world described by words and language is unavoidably a world of dualities.

Now we normally take these dualities to be real because we normally take the distinctions and boundaries which our words indicate to be real. This is especially true of those *physical* boundaries which seem so clearly to separate things like tables from chairs, and trees from stars. Whenever we talk about such things we think our words simply describe objects that already exist out there in the universe.

But suppose this isn't true. Suppose our language doesn't just *describe* boundaries that already exist. Suppose it actually *creates* them. Suppose it is not just the boundary between 'self' and 'world' that is imaginary, as the mystics claim, but that *all boundaries whatsoever are imaginary*. Suppose it is our own minds that create these boundaries and then project them onto a Reality whose fundamental nature is *nondual*. Well, this is precisely what the mystics say. In the Buddhist *Lankavatara Sutra*, for example, we read this:

> False-imagination teaches that such things as light and shade, long and short, black and white are different and are to be discriminated; but they are not independent of each other; they are only different aspects of the same thing, they are terms of relation not of reality. Conditions of existence are not of a mutually exclusive character; in essence things are not two but one.... All duality is falsely imagined.[42]

So, too, Shankara writes,

> No matter what a deluded man may think he is perceiving, he is really seeing Brahman and nothing else but Brahman. He sees mother-of-pearl and imagines that it is silver. He sees Brahman and imagines that it is the universe. But this universe, which is superimposed upon Brahman, is nothing but a name.[43]

And Meister Eckhart declares,

> If we will see things truly, they are strangers to goodness, truth and everything that tolerates any distinction, be it in a thought or in a name, in a notion or just a shadow of distinction. They are intimates of the One that is bare of any kind of multiplicity and distinction.[44]

Rumi employs a series of poetic images to convey the same nondual message:

> I sought round the world for "others" and reached certainty: There are no others.
> The buyers are all a single buyer, the bazaar has but one aisle....
> The whole world is indivisible, the whole world's harp has but one single string.[45]

So again, all these mystics agree: *All* boundaries are imaginary—not just the one which separates us from the world, but even boundaries that seem to separate concrete, physical objects from each other. All of them are products of our imagination, which we then superimpose upon a nondual Reality, so that it *appears* to be divided into a multiplicity of 'things.' And it is this appearance of multiplicity that prevents us from seeing that the true nature of everything—including ourselves—is nondual.

It is important to note, however, that mystics are not saying boundaries themselves are the problem. On the contrary, boundaries are extremely useful. If we could not distinguish between a tiger and a mouse, we would be in a lot of trouble. The real problem is that our minds get so habituated to seeing the world divided by these boundaries that we forget they are imaginary, and begin to treat them as though they actually existed 'out there' somewhere. To put it technically, we *reify* them—i.e., take the boundaries to be real. As a result, we start living in an *as if* reality, a metaphorical world which in the East they call *maya* or delusion.

So when mystics make statements such as "all dualities are falsely imagined" and "the universe is nothing but a name," they are not implying that we should get rid of boundaries. They are simply calling attention to our deluded way of perceiving a Reality whose ultimate nature is nondual.

But there is even a problem with this way of putting it, because if I say, "Ultimate Reality is nondual," this excludes the dualities created by imagining boundaries and distinctions. But if nonduality excludes duality, then nonduality ends up being dualistic, and is, therefore, in a sense false. A common analogy mystics use to try to clarify this paradoxical relationship between nonduality and duality is to compare it to the relationship between an ocean and its waves. Even though we can distinguish different kinds of waves—big ones, small ones, choppy ones, curling ones, etc.—they are really all just forms of the water which constitutes the ocean. So, if you venture out in a boat and actually try to locate the boundaries which seem to separate the waves from each other, you won't find any, because they only exist in your mind. In reality, ocean, waves, and water are all One.

Eventually, however, this analogy, too, breaks down, because we normally experience water as a substance, which has specific properties and attributes that can be distinguished from other substances with different properties and different attributes. But the Ultimate Reality to which mystics bear witness is not a substance. It has no specific properties or attributes. Consequently, it's not a 'thing' among other 'things' which can be pointed out and described in words. In fact, even to say "Ultimate Reality cannot be described in words" is self-contradictory, because I am using the words "Ultimate Reality" to describe Ultimate Reality, while simultaneously denying that this can be done.

Now, mystics themselves are under no illusions about the paradoxical nature of their teachings. They know full well words can never communicate Ultimate Reality. Their real purpose is to inspire and guide our quest to discover this Reality for ourselves. Thus, the Buddha of the *Lankavatara Sutra* declares,

> These teachings are only a finger pointing toward Noble Wisdom.... They are intended for the consideration and guidance of the discriminating minds of all people, but they are not the Truth itself, which can only be self-realized within one's own deepest consciousness.[46]

Similarly, Rumi writes,

> The only profit of speech is that it may cause you to seek and incite your desire. The goal is not realized through speech itself.[47]

For mystics, this applies even to their tradition's most sacred scriptures. Here, for example, is what Dionysius the Areopagite, a fifth-century Christian mystic, says about the descriptions of God found in the Bible:

> The reason for attributing shapes to that which is above shape, and forms to that which is beyond form, is ... the feebleness of our intellectual power which is unable to rise at once to spiritual contemplation, and which needs to be encouraged by the natural and suitable support and upliftment which offers forms perceptible to us of formless and supernatural contemplations.[48]

Describing the Indescribable

So what are some of the ways mystics have tried to describe "that which is above shape" and "beyond form?" The most universal way (and usually regarded as the most esoteric) is known as the *via negativa* or the way of negation—of which we have already encountered some examples at the beginning of this chapter. Buddhists in particular have favored this form of expression, partly because they know how easily our minds fall prey to imagining a 'thing' whenever a positive term for the Ultimate Reality is employed. For instance, when most people hear the word *God*, it automatically conjures a picture in their minds of some Big-Daddy-in-the-Sky. To avoid this, Buddhists have traditionally eschewed theistic language. Instead, they prefer to use terms such as *shunyata*, commonly translated as "emptiness" or "voidness," to indicate not only the true nature of our 'selves,' but of all 'things.' This teaching by Lama Yeshe, a twentieth-century Tibetan master, is typical:

> We and all other phenomena without exception are empty of even the smallest atom of self-existence, and it is this emptiness (*shunyata*) that is the ultimate nature of everything that exists.[49]

But while "emptiness" is specifically a Buddhist term, mystics of other traditions have also used the way of negation to convey their highest teachings about Reality. In Hinduism, for example, one of the most common formulas for speaking of Brahman is *neti neti*—"not this, not that." This is because, as Shankara explains:

> Brahman is without parts or attributes. It is subtle, absolute, taintless, one without a second. In Brahman there is no diversity whatsoever.[50]

Likewise, Ibn al-`Arabi writes this of the Absolute:

> Its reality cannot be conceived.... It is God. The utmost knowledge we can have regarding Him is the negative qualities, such as, "There is nothing like Him, "Your Honoured Lord is free from the qualities which they attribute to him."[51]

According to Ibn al-`Arabi, then, the Reality which underlies all things is Itself "empty of all things." Or to put it another way, despite the various Divine Names which are attributed to Him, God is actually a *no*-thing. This is also precisely the way Christian mystics have understood the Ultimate Reality, for as Dionysius says of what he calls the "nameless Cause of all being,"

> It is within our intellects, souls and bodies, in heaven, on earth, and whilst remaining the same in Itself, It is at once in, around and above the world, super-celestial, super-essential, a sun, a star, fire, water, spirit, dew, cloud, stone, rock, all that is; yet It is *nothing*.[52]

But although the *via negativa* avoids some of the pitfalls inherent in trying to characterize Ultimate Reality in words, it still contains a number of serious drawbacks of its own. For one thing, it doesn't give us much of a clue as to how this Reality relates to us personally. And yet if this Reality is, indeed, the

Truth of who we really are, then it cannot be all that remote from our everyday experience. On the contrary, it must be a *no-thing* that is somehow always present as an essential component of whatever we are doing, thinking, feeling, or perceiving.

The second drawback is that, by themselves, negative expressions fail to communicate any sense of the incomparable value which discovering this Reality might hold for us. If all we are going to find out at the end of a mystical path is that everything is "selfless," "empty," and "nothing," why bother to travel it? In order to counter-balance such nihilistic impressions mystics have also found it necessary to employ the *via positiva*, or the way of affirmation—especially in their more practice-orientated teachings. So let us explore some of the positive expressions mystics have used when trying to speak about Ultimate Reality.

Consciousness and Reality

Among Hindus, one of the most common ways of describing Ultimate Reality goes back to the Upanishads, which declare it to be the "Pure Consciousness of conscious beings." Here's how Shankara describes it:

> It [Brahman] is pure, absolute consciousness, the eternal reality. Such is Brahman, and "That art Thou".[53]

Now notice that Shankara is not saying Brahman is some sort of Supreme Being who *has* consciousness. Rather Brahman *is* Consciousness Itself. There is no Brahman apart from Consciousness and no Consciousness apart from Brahman. The two terms are synonymous. Moreover, this Consciousness is none other than the very consciousness that is illuminating your own mind, right now—which is why Shankara, along with the Upanishads, insists that Brahman is identical to Atman, your true Self.

Of course, *Consciousness* is not the actual word used in the Upanishads or by Shankara. It is an English translation of the Sanskrit, *chit*. And mystics of other traditions have used equivalent terms that we can also translate by our word *Consciousness*.

In Arabic there is apparently no single word that can be translated as *consciousness*. However, the Qur'an says repeatedly that Allah is "the Seeing and the Hearing." No doubt, ordinary Muslims take this to mean that Allah is the Supreme Being who sees and hears everything that goes on in the universe. But these words can also be taken to mean that Allah *is* Seeing itself and *is* Hearing itself—which is precisely how Sufis like Ibn al-`Arabi *do* take it. Moreover, this interpretation is reinforced by a *hadith* (saying of Muhammad) in which Allah specifically declares that He is the hearing and seeing of his servants. This is what Ibn al-`Arabi is referring to when he insists,

> He [Allah] is identical with the attributes and members of the servant, for He said, "I am his hearing." Thereby He attributed hearing

> to the entity of the existent thing which hears, while He ascribed it to Himself. But there is no Existent Being save He. So it is He who hears, and He is the hearing. So also is the case with the other faculties and perceptions. They are nothing but He.[54]

Now, when Ibn al-`Arabi talks about "hearing," and "the other faculties and perceptions," isn't he really talking about what we would call *consciousness*—that power of awareness which allows us to perceive and know whatever it is we perceive and know? And when he says that this awareness is none other than Allah Himself isn't this the same as saying that Allah is Consciousness Itself? In fact, this is precisely how one of today's foremost Sufi scholars, William Chittick, characterizes his teaching. "God" for Ibn al-`Arabi, Chittick writes, "is sheer Being, utter Plentitude, pure Consciousness."[55] And since, as Ibn al-`Arabi himself says, there are no beings other than God, this means that we ourselves must also be "sheer Being, utter Plentitude, pure Consciousness."

If we read the Christian mystics, we won't find the word *consciousness* in their vocabulary either. The reason is that, although *consciousness* is a Western word, it is also a relatively modern one, which only gained widespread currency after the seventeenth century. The historical timing here is significant, because this was precisely the period during which traditional religious terms such as *spirit* and *soul* were being nudged out of fashion by the new materialist paradigm just beginning to captivate the minds of educated Europeans. *Consciousness*, then, is really a kind of secular substitute for these older words which had been used to explain and express the same basic mystery—namely, what it is to be alive and *aware*. When we read in the Book of Genesis, for instance, that God gave Adam life by breathing His *Spirit* into him, we can understand this in modern terminology to mean that our own consciousness originates in the Divine Consciousness. Likewise, St. Augustine writes that, distinct from all objects, there is

> the light by which the soul is illumined, in order that it may see and truly understand everything, either in itself or in the light. For the light is God himself ... in whose illumination it [the soul] is enabled to see all the objects that it sees and understands in itself.[56]

Isn't he referring to what we would call the "light of consciousness," which Augustine here equates with God Himself? So again, while we almost never find Christian mystics before the modern period using the word *consciousness*, the sense of what they were trying to communicate is the same.

Even Buddhists have often found it necessary to employ positive expressions for Ultimate Reality—if only to make it clear that when they talk about "emptiness" they don't mean some kind of total vacuity. Here, for example, is how Dudjom Lingpa explains it:

> Emptiness does not constitute an inert void, but is subtly lucid, free of sullying factors, like a polished mirror in which anything at all can arise—this is mirror-like pristine awareness.[57]

Notice that the positive expression he chooses to characterize Ultimate Reality is "pristine awareness." This translates a Tibetan term *rigpa,* which is also sometimes rendered as "primordial awareness." In a similar fashion, Zen teachers often speak of "Big Mind," "Buddha Mind," or "One Mind." Thus, the ninth-century Zen master, Huang Po, writes,

> All the Buddhas and all sentient beings are nothing but the One Mind, besides which nothing exists.[58]

Once again, all these phrases are really synonymous with "Pure Consciousness," or "Consciousness Itself."[59]

Perhaps for Westerners the biggest problem with using *Consciousness* to describe Ultimate Reality is that the term comes with a lot of built-in materialist assumptions which dominate our culture. As a result, we tend to have all sorts of preconceptions about what consciousness is, and our relationship to it. For instance, most of us were taught that consciousness is something which is produced by and located in our physical brains. As such, it is something we "possess" and, therefore, can "lose." It is also something that all human beings (as well as other higher organisms) possess. Consequently, there are a great many consciousnesses in the world.

Moreover, according to the materialist worldview, all the contents of consciousness—sights, sounds, smells, tastes, tactile sensations—are caused by contact with objects outside of consciousness. Even the so-called subjective contents of consciousness—thoughts, memories, plans, feelings—are actually caused by processes in our brains which themselves exist outside of consciousness. Thus, consciousness and its contents have no real existence of their own. They're all mere *epiphenomena* or by-products of matter.

However, if we examine consciousness carefully, we find there are a number of problems with this materialist view. For one thing, no one has ever been able to explain exactly how the brain, which is composed of matter, can generate something like consciousness, which seems to be completely immaterial. If consciousness were material, it would, by definition, have at least some physical properties. But what properties can we attribute to consciousness? What color is it? Does it have any form, size, or shape? Does it have a taste, smell, or texture? Can we determine how much it weighs?

We can also ask whether consciousness really is located in our brains. If we look at our actual experience, the reverse is apparently true. Brains are located in consciousness, because that is where we always find them. But if we operate on a person's brain and peer inside, we will never find any 'thing' called consciousness. So it seems that, empirically speaking, while brains always appear *in* consciousness, consciousness never appears *in* brains. In fact, we can question whether consciousness can be located anywhere at all. For instance, if consciousness is, indeed, located in our brains, then how far beyond them does it extend? Fifty feet? Fifty miles? Fifty light years? This is a particularly interesting question to ask yourself on some clear night when you are outside, gazing up at the stars. Are they not *in* consciousness? And what about space itself? Is consciousness located in space, or is space located in consciousness? If space is located in consciousness, then consciousness itself has no location.

One of the hardest things for Westerners to question is the assumption that consciousness is something we possess and can lose. It seems so obvious, for instance, that when you fall into a deep sleep, you are *un*conscious of what is occurring around you. Moreover, this seems to be confirmed by other people who, when you wake up, tell you things like, "You don't know what has happened because you were unconscious." If, however, you pay close attention to the whole process of falling asleep and waking up, chances are you will find that what you actually experience is a break in the continuity of the *contents* of consciousness. When the contents of consciousness disappear, you take this to mean that consciousness itself has disappeared. But is this really the case? Have you ever actually *experienced* unconsciousness? Wouldn't this be a contradiction in terms? Is not consciousness the one component or dimension of all your experience that is *never* absent? Perhaps this notion of "losing consciousness" is simply an imaginary construct which allows you to maintain a sense that the world has a continuous, objective existence?

We can also examine the notion that there are multiple consciousnesses in the universe. If this is true, then where is the boundary between them? Where does your consciousness end and mine begin? Have you ever experienced more than one consciousness? Has anyone ever experienced more than one consciousness? If not, then why assume that more than one exists?

This brings us to the last and most profound question about consciousness—namely, is there really an objective world "out there" somewhere beyond it? If there is a world outside of your consciousness, how do you know it exists? Have you ever experienced anything *apart* from consciousness—trees, mountains, chairs, people, rivers, stars? In fact, we can ask the same question about the 'self' who is supposed to possess this consciousness. Don't all the things you regard as comprising yourself—thoughts, emotions, bodily sensations, memories—arise and pass *in* Consciousness? Perhaps, it is not you that has consciousness, but consciousness that has you!

In future chapters we will introduce a variety of contemplative experiments designed to help us explore these questions in much greater depth and detail. The point of raising them here is simply to put us on guard against taking for granted any materialist assumptions that we may be harboring about the nature of consciousness, because such preconceptions will distort our understanding of what the mystics mean when they use this term. For them, Consciousness is not an epiphenomenon of matter. On the contrary, what we call material 'things' are epiphenomena of Consciousness. This is why they claim it is Consciousness, and not matter, which constitutes the ultimate nature of Reality.

From a mystical perspective, the great advantage of employing the term *Consciousness* for Ultimate Reality is that, not only is it "empty" of any thingness (and therefore consistent with the mystics' use of the *via negativa*), but it also points in a positive way to an all-pervasive dimension of experience with which we are already intimately familiar. So, by equating Consciousness with the Ultimate Reality, mystics are actually giving us an instruction on how to start exploring this Reality in our own everyday lives. But it still does not answer this question: How will realizing that your true nature is Consciousness Itself bring you any closer to attaining the kind of abiding happiness we all long for?

Actually, what mystics claim is not that realizing your true nature will *bring* you happiness, but that you will discover you are *already* happy. Why? Because Consciousness Itself *is* Happiness Itself! This aspect of Ultimate Reality is perhaps the hardest to communicate in words, simply because the kind of Absolute Happiness we are talking about transcends anything we can experience as long as we remain trapped in delusion. Nevertheless, there are times in our lives when reflected rays of this Happiness do pierce through the veils of our ignorance, as for instance when we are transported out of our everyday selves by great love or bliss. That's why, in order to convey some hint of the kind of Happiness that constitutes our true nature, mystics have often compared it to these kinds of ecstatic states.

Love and Bliss

In Hinduism, for example, one of the most common formulas for describing Brahman is *Sat-Chit-Ananda* which means Being-Consciousness-Bliss. Here is how the twentieth-century mystic Anandamayi Ma explains it:

> When trying to express Him by language, He becomes imperfect. All the same, in order to use words, he is spoken of as *Sat-Cit-Ānanda* (Being-Consciousness-Bliss). Because He Is there is Being; and because He is Knowledge itself, there is Consciousness; and to become conscious of that Being is indeed Bliss. To know the essence of Truth is bliss. This is why He is called *Saccidānanda*, but in reality He is beyond bliss and non-bliss.[60]

Buddhists often use the term *Dharmakaya* or Truth-Body to indicate the most fundamental aspect of Ultimate Reality. In Tibetan Buddhism the Truth-Body is described as the inseparable union of Emptiness and Bliss out of which all phenomena manifest. Here is how the twelfth-century nun Machig Ongjo expresses her own Realization of this:

> The distinguishing factor of all phenomena is emptiness. Spontaneous liberation is the Great Bliss itself. It is the Dharmakaya, beginningless, beyond name and words. I know this only because of the guru's kindness. The natural state, spontaneity, arises by itself. This is the bliss of knowing myself as not separate.[61]

In many traditions, Love and Bliss are considered to be the motivating force behind the Formless Consciousness's manifestation in and as the world of forms. Thus, in the Upanishads we read,

> Brahman is bliss: for FROM BLISS ALL BEINGS HAVE COME, BY BLISS THEY ALL LIVE, AND UNTO BLISS THEY ALL RETURN.[62]

Ibn al-`Arabi puts it this way:

> The movement that is the coming into existence of the Cosmos is a movement of love. This is shown by the Apostle of God in the saying [which God communicated to him], "I was an unknown treasure, and longed to be known," so that, but for this longing, the Cosmos would not have become manifest in itself.[63]

And Dionysius the Areopagite insists,

> We must dare to say, for the sake of Truth, that the very Cause of the universe Himself, because of his beautiful and good love of everything, through the exceeding greatness of His loving goodness, becomes as it were transported out of Himself in His Providence for all beings.[64]

Now again, the great danger in using words like bliss and love is that they prompt us to conceive of the Ultimate Reality as some kind of anthropomorphic Super Self who experiences emotions the same way we do. This is because normally we assume there must be some self that has emotions. But is this really true—particularly when it comes to emotions of love and bliss? For example, our most intense experiences of bliss often occur when we completely "lose ourselves" in some all-consuming activity like singing, dancing, or sex. Likewise, our capacity for love is directly proportional to our capacity to disregard our own self-interests for the sake of others. Thus, for mystics, Perfect Love and Bliss indicate not the presence of some 'self'—whether human or divine—but rather its absence. Brahman does not experience bliss, Brahman is Bliss. God does not *feel* love, God *is* Love. It is precisely because, in their purest manifestation, love and bliss are expressions of self-less-ness that these terms can serve as powerful pointers to that aspect of both the Ultimate Reality and our own true nature which, once discovered, marks the end of our search for Happiness.

So perhaps we can sum all this up by saying that the full answer that mystics give to the question, who are you really? runs something like this: In reality, you are not some limited, finite entity, ego, or self that undergoes birth, suffering and death. This whole dualistic experience of 'I' and 'other', 'subject' and 'object', 'self' and 'world' is imaginary, maya, a delusion, founded on sheer ignorance. In Reality, you are Consciousness Itself (known in various traditions as "Allah," "Brahman," "Buddha-Mind," "God," "Tao"), which is empty of all 'thingness' and, therefore, no-thing—but a no-thing in which all things, selves, and worlds endlessly appear and disappear in a Great Cosmic Drama. Moreover, precisely because this Consciousness-that-you-are is completely Selfless, not only is it free of all suffering, its nature is Perfect Happiness, eternal Bliss, and overflowing Love.

This, then, is the "Truth that makes you free." But there is a catch. The only way to know this Truth for yourself is through a special mode of cognition called *Gnosis* or, more popularly, *Enlightenment*. It is this to which we must now turn our attention.

CHAPTER 3

Enlightenment

Then the breakthrough suddenly comes, and with that they [spiritual seekers] penetrate their own nature, the nature of others, the nature of sentient beings, the nature of evil passions and of enlightenment. . . . The great matter of their religious quest is completely and utterly resolved. There is nothing left. They are free of birth and death.

— Hakuin (Buddhist)

What Enlightenment Is Not

Normally, we think of knowledge as something that can be acquired in one of three ways. The first is through reasoning and logic, which gives us conceptual knowledge. The purest form of conceptual knowledge is found in mathematics whose truths are arrived at by a process of logical deduction. For example, if you take the axioms of Euclid's geometry to be true, they yield the Pythagorean theorem. The Pythagorean theorem states that the square of the hypotenuse of a right triangle is equal to the sum of the squares of its other two sides. This is something that can be proved by reason alone. You do not have to go out and measure a bunch of right triangles to determine if it's true. So the Pythagorean theorem is a purely conceptual form of knowledge, and it expresses a purely conceptual truth. But the Truth which mystics talk about is not a conceptual truth, and it cannot be grasped by any sort of reasoning process. Thus, the Upanishads say of Brahman,

> He comes to the thought of those who know him beyond thought,
> not to those who imagine he can be attained by thought.[65]

And in the Lankavatara Sutra we are told that Enlightenment

> is an exalted state of inner attainment which transcends all dualistic thinking and which is above the mind-system with its logic, reasoning, theorising, and illustrations.[66]

Similarly, Ibn al-`Arabi writes,

> After those who had faith in God came to know Him through considerative proofs, their rational faculties saw that God still asks them to know Him. So they came to know that there is another knowledge of God which is not reached by way of reflection.[67]

This is why the sixteenth-century Christian mystic St. John of the Cross says,

> Accordingly, to reach union with the wisdom of God, a person must advance by unknowing rather than by knowing.[68]

Mystical Truth cannot be grasped by concepts for the same reason that Ultimate Reality cannot be communicated in words. Both are nondual and thus transcend all forms of distinction. Conceptual truths, on the other hand, depend on distinctions. In fact, making a distinction between A and not-A constitutes one of the cornerstones of logic. This is why all attempts to formulate the nondual Truth revealed by Enlightenment in logical terms result in one of those paradoxes for which mystics are so famous. Here, for example, is the way Nagarjuna describes what the Buddha discovered upon attaining his Enlightenment:

> Everything is true, nothing is true; everything is both true and not true; everything is neither true nor not true. This is the teaching of the Buddha.[69]

And this is how Ibn al-`Arabi characterizes what he calls the "Reality of realities":

> If you say that this thing is the [temporal] Universe, you are right. If you say that it is God who is eternal, you are right. If you say that it is neither the Universe nor God but is something conveying some additional meaning, you are right. All these views are correct, for it is the whole comprising the eternal and the temporal.[70]

So, too, the fifteenth-century Christian mystic Nicholas of Cusa writes this to God:

> I have found the abode wherein You dwell unveiledly—an abode surrounded by the coincidence of contradictories. And [this coincidence] is the wall of Paradise, wherein You dwell. The gate of this wall is guarded by a most lofty rational spirit; unless this spirit is vanquished the entrance will not be accessible. Therefore, on the

other side of the coincidences of contradictories You can be seen—but not at all on this side.[71]

The second way we usually think of knowledge being acquired is through experience. For example, I used to live in Los Angeles, so if you ask me, "Do you know Los Angeles?" I will answer, "Oh, yes, I know Los Angeles very well." Of course, this sort of knowledge also includes some concepts, like knowing the names of the major streets, and being able to give directions on how to get to important places. But when I say, "I know Los Angeles," what I really mean is I have an *experiential* knowledge of that city, and not merely some book-knowledge I might have acquired from a travel guide.

Now, experiential knowledge is closer to Gnosis or Enlightenment than conceptual knowledge and, in fact, mystics often describe Gnosis as if it were some kind of experience. But, while Gnosis or Enlightenment has something of the *immediacy* and *directness* of experiential knowledge, strictly speaking, it is *not* an experience. For one thing, all experiences are ephemeral. They fade with time. So even when I say, "I know Los Angeles," I am not actually referring to an on-going experience I have of that city, but to something which has already passed and is now only a memory. The Truth which Gnosis reveals, however, is *not* ephemeral. It does *not* fade with time.

The third way we have of acquiring ordinary knowledge is through science, or more properly the scientific method, which gives us *scientific* knowledge. Now, strictly speaking, the scientific method does not actually constitute a "third" way of knowing. It is simply a method for testing conceptual knowledge against experiential knowledge in a particularly rigorous manner. This is what has allowed scientists to predict and manipulate the behavior of physical phenomena with remarkable precision. Nevertheless, the truths which science yields are still *relative* truths, subject to periodic revision as new theories replace old ones. For this reason, when we ask questions about the ultimate or *absolute* nature of reality, science is inherently incapable of giving us ultimate or absolute answers.

This is an important point because science in our time has come to be widely regarded as the sole arbiter of truth. We even hear adherents of some spiritual traditions enthusiastically proclaiming that, at last, science has 'proven' their teachings—as though spiritual truths cannot really be valid unless they have been confirmed by science. But the Absolute Truth revealed by Gnosis is not of the same kind as the relative truths formulated by science. When Jesus said, "Know the Truth and it shall make you free," he wasn't talking about Einstein's theory of relativity. And when the Buddha said, "The gift of truth is the highest gift"[72], he wasn't referring to quantum mechanics.

Another reason for stressing the difference between scientific and mystical truth is that today quite a few seekers think that Enlightenment is simply a matter of "shifting their paradigm," or acquiring a "new worldview." Now, it is true that the paradigms suggested by new developments in science such as quantum mechanics are much more compatible with mystical teachings than was the old materialist paradigm of classical mechanics. It is also true that learning about quantum mechanics may help remove certain intellectual barriers to Enlightenment—especially for people who were brought up to believe science supports a materialist worldview. But no matter how revolutionary a scientific paradigm is, or how compatible a particular worldview may be with mysticism, they are still only conceptual constructs. And while a seeker's paradigm or worldview will almost certainly change during the course of his or her spiritual journey, it is crucial to remember that the Absolute Truth revealed by Gnosis transcends *all* conceptual constructs, *all* paradigms, and *all* worldviews, whatsoever. It's a way of knowing that, as Shankara says,

> is beyond the grasp of the senses. The intellect cannot understand it. It is out of reach of thought. Such is Brahman, and "That art Thou".[73]

Or, as the *Lankavatara Sutra* puts it,

> It [Noble Wisdom] is not comparable to the perceptions attained by the sense-mind, neither is it comparable to the cognition of the discriminating and intellectual-mind. Both of these presuppose a difference between self and not-self.[74]

This brings us to the most fundamental difference between our ordinary ways of knowing and Gnosis or Enlightenment. All our ordinary ways of knowing—whether conceptual, experiential, or scientific—involve, as the *Lankavatara Sutra* says, a duality between subject and object, a knower and what is known, an experiencing self and a world that is experienced. But the Truth which mystics bear witness to is precisely that this dichotomy is *imaginary*—that, in Reality, there is no distinction between 'self' and 'world,' 'subject' and 'object,' 'knower' and 'known,' or 'experiencer' and what is 'experienced.' Here's how Abraham Abulafia describes it:

> You shall then arrive at the intelligible, and you will find all these one—that is, the intellect and the object of intellection and the intelligible are all one.[75]

The fourteenth-century Sufi Mahmud Shabistari agrees:

> When thou gazest long upon thy origin, behold!
> It is the seer and the seer seen.[76]

So does his contemporary, the Kashmiri Shaivite Lalleshwari, who says this of Shiva:

> You are the seer and the seen.
> You are the world and its Lord.[77]

Before going any further, however, we should say that, just because Gnosis cannot be attained through any of our ordinary ways of knowing, this does not mean you have to check your intellect at the door when you embark on a spiritual path. On the contrary, the intellect is very useful—especially in the beginning stages. For one thing, if you don't understand the teachings, you cannot put them into practice. You also have to make practical judgments about such things as whether or not a particular teacher is genuine. Many people have been taken in by charlatans simply because they failed to exercise common sense when a so-called 'guru' started demanding exorbitant fees, or pressuring them to engage in immoral conduct. So by all means use your thinking mind when appropriate. But do not allow it to venture beyond its proper sphere of operation. Here is how Rumi sums up the role of the intellect on a spiritual path:

> Intellect is good and desirable to the extent that it brings you to the King's door. Once you have reached His door, then divorce the intellect! From this time on, the intellect will be to your loss and a brigand.[78]

What Enlightenment Is . . . Sort of

So far, we have been talking about what Gnosis or Enlightenment is *not*. It is not conceptual knowledge, it is not experiential knowledge, and it is not scientific knowledge. But is there anything positive we can say about it—something that might at least point us in the right direction? Actually, there *are* a few terms which suggest something of what we might call the *flavor* of Gnosis.

One of them is *Realization*. This is an especially apt word, because even in our everyday usage, it indicates a kind of sudden shift in awareness which cuts through our normal step-by-step mental processes. The Hindus have a famous analogy which illustrates how this works. They compare it to a man who sees a snake by the side of the road and jumps back in alarm. On second look, however, he *realizes* that the 'snake' is not a snake at all. It is just a piece of old coiled rope. Notice that this "realization" of the true nature of what he is seeing involves a sudden transformation in his actual perception of the situation. Gnosis also entails a sudden transformation of perception, only with Gnosis it is the perception of the entire cosmos that is altered, not just one particular phenomenon within it.

A similar term mystics often use for Gnosis is *Recognition*. Here, for example, is how the twentieth-century Tibetan master Lama Lodo describes what happens when the mind cognizes emptiness:

> There will be a spontaneous recognition that the mind which has been meditating on emptiness and the state of emptiness itself are one and the same. Each will mutually recognize the other.... This is like the encounter between a mother and a long-lost child. When the mother and child meet each other, the mother will naturally and spontaneously recognize her child and be filled with a natural joy.[79]

One advantage of using *recognition* as a synonym for Enlightenment or Gnosis is that not only does it indicate a sudden shift in awareness, but it also implies that what is now being cognized has been cognized before. Likewise, Gnosis doesn't involve apprehending anything new. Rather it's a *re*-cognition of the Reality that has been present all along.

A more technical way of describing Gnosis is to call it *knowledge through identity*. Although this particular phrase was coined by Franklin Merrell-Wolff, the idea is implicit in the teachings of virtually all the great mystics. For instance, we have already heard the *Lankavatara Sutra* say that "Self-realisation is based on identity and oneness." So, too, Shankara writes,

> Until a man wakes to knowledge of his identity with the Atman, liberation can never be obtained; no, not even at the end of many hundreds of ages.[80]

And this is what Meister Eckhart says of his own Gnosis:

> Then I received an impulse that will bring me up above all the angels. Together with this impulse, I receive such riches that God, as he is "God," and as he performs all his divine works, cannot suffice me; for in this breaking-through I receive that God and I are one.[81]

Another common way of characterizing Gnosis is to call it a *Union with the Divine*. Like knowledge through identity, this expression emphasizes the abolition of the sense of separation between oneself and Ultimate Reality. Here is how the Upanishads describe it:

> In the union with him [the Atman] is the supreme proof of his reality. He is the end of evolution and non-duality. He is peace and love.[82]

Christian mystics also often speak of "union with God." Thus, the author of *The Book of Privy Counseling* declares,

> Man's highest perfection is union with God in consummate love, a destiny so high, so pure in itself, and so far beyond human thought that it cannot be known or imagined as it really is.[83]

The tenth-century Sufi Abu Bakr al-Kalabadhi puts it this way:

> The condition of union, which is my passing away from self, does not allow me to witness any but Him [God].[84]

Perhaps the most universal way of describing Gnosis—one found in virtually all mystical traditions—is *Awakening*. For example, the Upanishads say this of Brahman:

> He is known in the ecstasy of an awakening which opens the door of life eternal.[85]

Likewise, Abraham Abulafia writes,

> All is imagination and mockery, like a dream which passes by in the night which, when the sleeper awakes from it, thus shall he find it.[86]

Rumi compares our deluded condition of "heedlessness" with its opposite, "wakefulness":

> The pillar of this world, oh beloved, is heedlessness. Wakefulness is this world's bane.
> Wakefulness comes from that world; when it prevails, this world is laid flat.[87]

And this is precisely what happened to the Buddha. His experience of this world as being samsara was "laid flat" when he woke up to its true nature. This is why from then on he was called the *Buddha*, which literally means the "Awakened One." So "Realization," "Recognition," "Knowledge through Identity," "Union with the Divine," "Awakening"—these are some of the expressions mystics have used to try to convey what Gnosis is like, but really none of them can do it justice. Whenever we "realize" or "recognize" something in an ordinary way—or when we "wake up" from an ordinary dream—we experience these things as happening to some 'self' inhabiting some 'world.' Gnosis, however, is Waking Up from that life-long dream that there is any 'self' or any 'world' to begin with!

Chapter 4

Understanding Delusion

> *Originally, everything was conceived as one great whole, and the life of the Creator pulsated without hindrance or disguise in that of his creatures. Everything stood in direct mystical rapport with everything else, and its unity could have been apprehended directly and without the help of symbols. Only the Fall has caused God to become "transcendent". Its cosmic results have led to loss of the original harmonious union and to the appearance of an isolated existence of things.*
>
> — Gershom Scholem (Jew)

Attaining Enlightenment actually boils down to something very simple. All you really have to do is stop *ignoring* your true nature and start *paying attention* to it. When attention returns to its Source in Consciousness Itself, there is an opportunity to Realize that "Oh, of course, THIS IS IT! THIS IS WHO I AM! THIS IS WHAT EVERYTHING IS!" But if becoming Enlightened is really that simple, why, as a matter of historical fact, have so few managed to do it?

The problem is that ordinarily our attention is distracted by the delusion that we are something else—namely, a separate self. Even though this self has no real existence, as long as the mis-perception persists that it does, our true nature cannot be Realized. To go back to the analogy of someone who mistakes a rope for a snake, as long as that person continues to see the snake, the rope's true nature will remain hidden. In order to see the rope, the illusory 'snake' must be destroyed. The same applies to the illusory 'self', which is why the author of *The Book of Privy Counseling* says,

> You must realize and experience for yourself that unless you lose self you will never reach your goal. For wherever you are, in whatever you do, or however you try, that elemental sense of your own blind being will remain between you and your God.[88]

And you will find the exact same teaching in all the great traditions. Thus, Shankara writes,

> When the ego is completely destroyed, the mind is cleared of the obstacles which obstruct its knowledge of oneness with Brahman.[89]

Likewise, Bokar Rinpoche declares,

> When the mind is totally purified from the duality of subject-object, the fruit is revealed: realization of the non-dual truth of the mind.[90]

Here's how the fourteenth-century Sufi poet Hafiz puts it:

> Between lover and Beloved there is no veil.
> Hafez! Thou thyself art thy own veil.
> Rise from this "between".[91]

From a mystic's point of view, then, the purpose of a spiritual path is not to acquire anything new, because you already *are* that Consciousness which underlies all things. The real purpose of a spiritual path is simply to remove the delusion of self which veils this Reality. This, however, is easier said than done. Why? Because the delusion of self is far more complex than a phantom snake projected onto a rope. So before setting out to dismantle this delusion, it behooves us to try to gain some understanding of how it arises and evolves.

Now describing this process is no easy task for several reasons. For one thing, a complete description would require formulating a full-blown spiritual psychology—something which is way beyond the scope of this work. Furthermore, while such a spiritual psychology might be able to give a fairly detailed account of the development of the delusion of self *after it has arisen*, it could never explain its origin—at least not as an historical event occurring in time. The reason, as we shall see in a future chapter, is that according to the mystics, time itself is part of this delusion. This is why Hindus and Buddhists insist that the delusion has no beginning, while other traditions, like Judaism and Christianity, give mythological explanations for its genesis which are always set in a sacred time-before-time or *in illo tempore* (to borrow an expression from the great religious scholar Mircea Eliade).

Keeping these limitations in mind, then, we shall try to sketch as briefly as possible, and in the most generic terms we can find, how the delusion of self arises and evolves into what Hindus and Buddhists call "maya," Sufis describe as a covering of "seventy thousand veils," and Christians term a "vale of tears" so that the seeker can get at least some idea of what he or she is up against.

How the Delusion of Self Arises

As we have already seen, the delusion of being a separate self starts with a simple error in cognition—the mistaking of an imaginary distinction between 'subject' and 'object' to constitute a real boundary. Prior to this (in a logical rather than temporal sense), there is only nondual Consciousness, enjoying Perfect Happiness, Eternal Bliss, and Selfless Love which informs Itself in and as the whole Cosmic Dance we call the universe. Once this First Distinction has been reified, however, everything changes. The nondual nature of Consciousness is instantly eclipsed, and in its place arises a dualistic experience of ourselves as being a 'subject' entranced by an 'objective' and alien world of forms that we now perceive as *not*-self. But while this initial cognitive error may be the beginning of delusion, it is by no means the end of it, for it triggers a cascade of additional mis-perceptions which distort our entire field of awareness in radical and devastating ways.

First, because under delusion we now feel cut off from our own forms, our original Perfect Happiness is transformed into a profound, existential loneliness. But, because we also "remember" the Bliss of our former condition, out of this loneliness is born an equally profound and existential longing to return once again to our Lost Paradise. The only way to accomplish this, however, would be to wrest our attention away from the world of forms, and allow it to collapse back into that Infinite Ocean of Consciousness from which it sprang. Then, with no more basis for drawing a distinction, the boundary between 'self' and 'world' would vanish, presenting an opportunity to Realize that, all along, it never had more than an imaginary existence. And yet, because this boundary is precisely what defines us as a self, the prospect of its annihilation seems to us tantamount to self-annihilation. As a result, the original selfless Love inherent in Consciousness Itself becomes transformed into a self-centered fear of total extinction. From this point on, then, the interplay between these three primordial seeds of suffering—loneliness, longing, and fear—will determine the future course of our development as individual selves.

How the Delusion of Self Evolves

With the way back blocked by fear, but driven by loneliness and longing to do something, we decide to move in the opposite direction, as it were, out towards the world of forms. Although this 'decision' has, in reality, been dictated by loneliness, longing, and fear, it seems to us to have been generated from within, as an autonomous act of *self-will*. Thus, believing ourselves to be the masters of our fate, we embark on what will become a life-long quest to end our suffering and secure our happiness somewhere outside of ourselves in the world at large. And the main way we go about trying to accomplish this task is to create and reify more boundaries.

To begin with, in order to locate ourselves in the world of forms, we create and reify a boundary around a set of phenomena constituting a particular body-mind. But by identifying with a particular body-mind we also and necessarily identify with that body-mind's desires, aversions, and other emotions. As a result, our own search for happiness gets channeled into an attempt to grasp those things that the body-mind wants, while avoiding those things that it doesn't want. But since all the things the body-mind wants (as well as the body-mind itself) are impermanent, this strategy can yield only temporary happiness which must inevitably be followed by more suffering. Nevertheless, seeing no alternative, we push forward, despite the futility of our efforts.

Next, if we have become identified with a human body-mind, we try to further enhance and protect ourselves by exercising our capacity for thought and language. This we do in concert with other humans by collectively creating and reifying a host of social, political, religious, and/or philosophical boundaries, which serve to solidify our sense of being separate selves. For example, identifying with kinship boundaries establishes and delimits our family, clan, and social identity. Identifying with caste or class boundaries defines and delimits our relationships to others within a specific social structure. Identifying with economic boundaries defines and delimits our ownership (or lack thereof) of different kinds of property, while identifying with political, religious, and/or philosophical boundaries defines and delimits our membership in various communities sharing similar ideas, values, and worldviews.

Yet despite the advantages which come from creating and reifying these collective boundaries, we still cannot escape our suffering, nor find abiding happiness. In fact, for each benefit we gain, there arises some corollary misery we must endure. Thus, while relationships with family and friends may produce feelings of intimacy and joy, they can just as easily excite animosity and grief. And although social and economic relationships may bring an increase in wealth, power, and position, they are also the cause poverty, injustice, and oppression. And although identifying with a particular religious or ideological community may lend our lives purpose and meaning, such affiliations also generate mistrust, conflict, and war.

What's more, the deeper we become enmeshed in these external relationships, the more they act back on us to shape and condition our own internal dynamics. Over time experiences of pleasure and pain, success and failure give rise to predilections and preferences which harden into more or less fixed attachments to people, places and things. These attachments, in turn, come to mold our present and future conduct into conditioned patterns of behavior which simultaneously limit our freedom of action and further strengthen our perception that we are, indeed, separate individuals.

Finally, our capacity for thought and language not only allows us to create and reify an increasingly complex web of shared boundaries, but also to monitor our own progress trying to navigate through them. This we do by translating our *lived*-experience into an interior stream of images, ideas, memories, expectations, and judgments, which our thinking minds weave into an intricate and on-going narrative. This is *The Story of I,* in which each of us ends up starring as a full-blown ego-self. And although, like any good soap-opera, this story has a host of supporting characters and shifting sub-plots, the dramatic tension always boils down to the same question with which the tale began: Will *I* be able to avoid suffering and attain happiness, whether it be in my new house, or on my new job, or with my new lover, or on my next vacation, or simply eating my next meal? Moreover, because all these 'things'—houses, jobs, lovers, vacations, meals—are ephemeral, this story has no end. Hour after hour, day after day, year after year it continues to completely captivate our attention, thereby keeping us perpetually distracted from and ignorant of our true nature.

The Great Path of Return

As spiritual seekers, then, our task is to work our way backward through this whole tangled maze of self-centered conditioning and attachments, desires and aversions, boundaries and distinctions, until we arrive once again at that First Distinction which separates us from the rest of the world. If at this point we can Recognize that this distinction is imaginary—that, in reality, there is no 'self' and no 'world'—the whole house of cards collapses, and our original Identity as Consciousness Itself stands revealed. This is why in many traditions the mystical path is called the Great Path of Return, or as the Hindus say, the *nivritti marga*. Here is how the ninth-century Christian mystic John Scotus Eriugena describes it:

> It is, then, the common end of all created things to return, by a kind of dying, into the Causes which subsist in God; and it is the property of the intelligible and rational substance, by the power of contemplation, to become One with God; and, through Grace, to become God Himself.[92]

Ibn al-`Arabi puts it this way:

> The final end and ultimate return of the gnostics ... is that the Real is identical with them. This station is possessed only by the gnostics.[93]

Gershom Scholem sums up the Kabbalist path by saying,

> The consensus of Kabbalistic opinion regards the mystical way to God as a reversal of the procession by which we have emanated from God. To know the stages of the creative process is also to know the stages of one's own return to the root of all existence.[94]

And the eighteenth-century Taoist Liu I-ming writes,

> The Tao is clear, yet this clarity requires you to sweep away all your clutter. At all times watch out for your own stupidity, be careful of how your mind jumps around. When nothing occurs to involve your mind, you return to true awareness. When unified mindfulness is purely real, you comprehend the great restoration.[95]

So what are the main guidelines for finding our way back along this path to "true awareness"? This is what we will be exploring in the next chapter.

Chapter 5

Love and Truth

> *Love and knowledge can never be totally separated. Each Sufi order only stresses one without ever denying the other. In fact, Sufi love ('ishq) is understood by Sufis as the realized aspect of gnosis.*
>
> — Seyyed Hossein Nasr (Muslim)

There are two main ways to dismantle the delusion of self and attain Enlightenment. One is to seek Truth, the other is to cultivate Love. In India those who seek Truth are called *jnanis* and the path they follow is called *jnana yoga* or the path of knowledge. Those who cultivate Love are called *bhaktas* and the path they follow is called *bhakti yoga* or the path of devotion.

At first, these two paths may seem very different—especially to us Westerners. We tend to think of Truth as something intellectual that relates only to the mind, while love is something emotional that relates to the heart. For mystics, however, Love and Truth represent two aspects of the same underlying Reality. This is because the Truth which Gnosis reveals is the truth of Selflessness, and Love—true Love—*is* selfless. Love, then, is simply the Truth in action. This is why in many traditions Love and Truth are said to be like the two wings of the same bird. If either wing is missing, the bird cannot fly. Both are essential, because, as St. Catherine of Siena writes:

> Love follows upon understanding. The more they know, the more they love, and the more they love, the more they know. Thus each nourishes the other.[96]

Nevertheless, depending on their motivation and temperament, most seekers will be drawn either to seek Truth or cultivate Love as the central theme of their quest. So let's take a closer look at these two different approaches to see how each of them functions to undo the delusion of self.

Jnana: The Path of Knowledge

If you are a jnani, what initially motivates you to embark on a spiritual path is a thirst for answers to those age-old questions which human beings have been asking since the dawn of time. Here is how the *Svetasvatara Upanishad* posed them over two thousand years ago:

> What is the source of this universe? What is Brahman? From where do we come? By what power to do we live? Where do we find rest? Who rules over our joys and sorrows, O seers of Brahman?[97]

Taking such questions seriously gives rise to a relentless *inquiry*, which comes to constitute the primary practice of the jnani's path.

At first, this inquiry usually assumes the form of a philosophical investigation. You read lots of books, attend various lectures, listen to recorded talks, go to conferences and workshops, etc.—all of which will expose you to a host of new ideas, theories, and belief-systems. You may even come to adopt a whole new worldview. But if your inquiry goes no further than this, it won't bear any real spiritual fruit. In the end, all you will have done is to substitute one set of concepts for another. If you want to discover the Truth which Gnosis reveals, your inquiry has to become far more personal and empirical. It has to become a practice of *self*-inquiry in which you start paying close attention to your own experiences and the 'you' who is supposed to be having them.

In order to conduct this kind of self-inquiry, you need to be able to at least temporarily free your attention from all those distracting thoughts and emotions that form the Story of I. And the way to do this to take up a practice of *meditation*. By practicing meditation you can train your attention to become calm, clear, and stable. Once you have developed some mental stability, you will be able to contemplate different aspects of your experience directly—that is, without the intervening filter of thought. This, in turn, will allow you to gain *non-conceptual insights* which by-pass the thinking mind. While such insights fall short of full Gnosis, they do provide genuine glimpses of Reality. To give but one example, the twentieth-century American mystic Suzanne Segal recounts what happened to her during a meditation retreat as follows:

> Nearly three hours after I had begun meditating the first morning of the retreat, I opened my eyes and rose from my cushion as if I were drunk, walking without the sensation of possessing a body. The world no longer looked the same; solid matter had been transformed into the luminous transparency of silence....
>
> My mode of perceiving had been jarred out of its ordinary pattern. It was impossible to focus separately on objects because the boundaries between them had receded into the background, supplanted by a luminosity so powerful that everything in the visual field appeared to melt together into one large radiant mass.[98]

What Segal is describing is sometimes called a *unity experience* and is actually quite common on a spiritual path. The important thing to notice, however, is that it was triggered not by any new thoughts she had about the world, but by an actual shift in perception which permitted her to see things in a new light. For a little while, the veil of duality was partially lifted, and she was able to experience directly the Oneness that lies behind it.

It is even possible to have a direct insight or *gnostic flash* into the nature of Ultimate Reality Itself. This happens in a moment when, for whatever reason, your whole self-centered conditioning gets temporarily suspended. Once the moment has passed, however, and your conditioning returns, you will once again be swallowed up in the Story of I. Here is how St. Augustine describes a gnostic flash he attained while in a state of deep contemplation:

> I entered into the innermost part of myself, and I was able to do this because you [God] were my helper. I entered and I saw with my soul's eye (such as it was) an unchangeable light shining above this eye of my soul and above my mind....
> And then, in the flash of a trembling glance, my mind arrived at That Which Is. Now, indeed, I saw your *invisible things understood by the things which are made*, but I had not the power to keep my eye steadily fixed; in my weakness I felt myself falling back and returning again to my habitual ways, carrying nothing with me except a loving memory of it and a longing for something which may be described as a kind of food of which I had perceived the fragrance but which I was not yet able to eat.[99]

So even though Augustine had a genuine glimpse of "That Which Is," it did not last. He only got a peek before returning to his "habitual ways," which is to say, before his self-centered conditioning again overwhelmed him. So, in order to attain a *full* Gnostic Awakening, you have to be able to do more than just suspend your self-centered conditioning during meditative states. You have to disrupt and destroy it in your everyday life. And the way to do this is to engage in practices of *morality*.

Moral practices include such things as keeping precepts and cultivating love and compassion. Keeping precepts interrupts those patterns of behavior that are motivated by a desire to enhance and protect yourself, while cultivating love and compassion actually transforms your motivation from being self-centered into a selfless concern for others. And the more selfless your life becomes, the more it will conform to the Ultimate Reality of Selflessness which you are trying to Realize. This is why Lao Tzu writes this of the Tao and those who follow it:

> The myriad creatures rise from it yet it claims no authority;
> It gives them life yet claims no possessions;
> It benefits them yet exacts no gratitude;
> It accomplishes its tasks yet lays claim to no merit....

> Therefore the sage benefits them yet extracts no gratitude,
> Accomplishes his task yet lays claim to no merit.[100]

Finally, even though devotion is the primary practice of bhaktas, as a jnani you, too, will have to become fully devoted to your quest. You must be willing to surrender yourself completely to the Truth you seek. Perhaps no one has expressed this more eloquently than Merrell-Wolff, who was about as pure a jnani as you can find. Here is some of what he wrote on the subject:

> In the final state of perfection he [the jnani] possesses no longer opinions of his own nor any private preference. The Truth possesses him, not he, Truth.... He must offer, upon the sacrificial alter, the pride of the knower. He must become one who lays no possessive claim to knowledge or wisdom. This is the state of the mystic ignorance—of the emptied heart.[101]

Bhakti: The Path of Devotion

If you are a bhakta, instead of a thirst for Truth, your main motivation for embarking on a spiritual path will be an intense love and longing for some form of the Divine. This will lead you naturally to adopt devotion as your primary practice. Here is how Narada, the legendary Hindu author of the celebrated *Bhakti-Sutras*, describes it:

> Whole-souled devotion means giving up every other refuge and taking refuge in God.[102]

And, of course, you will find almost identical teachings given by bhaktas of all the great traditions. Thus, when Jesus was asked which is the greatest commandment, he answered,

> You shall love the Lord your God with all your heart, and with all your soul, and with all your mind. This is the greatest and first commandment.[103]

And Abraham Abulafia told his disciples this:

> Cast behind yourself everything that exists apart from the Name in your soul in truth ... and do not place any thought in the world upon anything apart from Him, may He be blessed.[104]

So, too, Abu Bakr al-Kalabadhi gave this advice:

> Thou shouldst be entirely responsive to the call (of God), removing from thy heart all thoughts of departing from God, so that thou art present with all that is God's, and absent from all that is not God's.[105]

But even though devotion forms the center-piece of your path, as is the case with jnanis, you will still need to engage in other kinds of practices, and for many of the same reasons. For example, when you try to focus your attention completely on God, you, too, will find that it is constantly distracted by that Story of I running through your head. This will prompt you to take up a practice of mystical prayer[106] which parallels the jnani's practice of meditation insofar as the immediate purpose of both is to train attention to be calm, clear, and stable. Also, like jnanis, in order to disrupt and destroy the self-centered conditioning which dominates your life, you will need to keep moral precepts and cultivate love and compassion for other beings. And finally, just as in the end jnanis must practice devotion by surrendering themselves to Truth, so you will have to practice inquiry if you are ever to completely Realize the True Nature of the Divine Beloved you have come to love and long for to the exclusion of all else.

The big advantage of being a bhakta, however, is that the love unleashed by your devotional practices will spill over to animate these other practices as well. Because the more you long for the Divine, the more eager you will be to demolish the delusion of self which stands between you. Here is how the great sixteenth-century Hindu bhakta Mira Bai expresses her relationship to the god Krishna (also called Gopal):

> You cannot call this true devotion,
> To bathe one's forehead and apply tilak
> Without cleansing the impurities of the heart.
> That cruel cur desire
> Has bound me with the cord of greed.
> The butcher anger remains within me,
> How can I hope to meet Gopāl?
>
> The greedy senses are like a cat,
> And I keep on giving them food.
> Weakened by my hunger for sense-objects
> I do not take the Name of God.
> I worship not God but myself,
> And glow with ecstasy.
> Now that I have built up
> This towering rock of pride,
> Where can the water of true wisdom collect?[107]

Jnana vs. Bhakti

Although historically the majority of mystics, both East and West, have been bhaktas, today many educated seekers look down on the bhakti path as somehow inferior. The reason is usually because such people have already learned enough to know that, from the mystics' esoteric point of view, Ultimate Reality transcends all distinctions between 'I' and 'other', 'subject' and 'object', 'self' and 'world'. Therefore, the idea of devoting oneself to some form of the Divine strikes them as hopelessly dualistic and naive—the kind of exoteric practice only fundamentalists would find appealing. The fact, however, is that *all* seekers—no matter how intellectually sophisticated—consciously or unconsciously conceive of Ultimate Reality in dualistic terms. Even if they no longer believe in a Big-Daddy-in-the-Sky, they still think there is some sort of Enlightened Mind, or Awakened State which they currently lack. Of course, mystics themselves often talk this way, but that is only a concession to the limitations of language. Truly speaking, Ultimate Reality is not any kind of *objective* condition—even a very subtle one—which you can someday attain. Ultimate Reality is that Consciousness which you already *are*, right here and now! As long as you remain deluded, however, you *cannot help* but think of it dualistically, because duality is the very essence of delusion.

What makes the practice of devotion exoteric, then, is not that Ultimate Reality manifests to seekers in some external form. It is that seekers stop short with this manifestation. They take it to be the end of the path, when actually it is just the beginning. For what Gnosis discloses is that the Divine not only transcends all forms of distinction, but is also and equally immanent in them as their true being. This is why Anandamayi Ma says,

> Just as it is said: "Wherever my glance falls there Krishna appears." If anything is perceived that is not Krishna, one cannot speak of true Vision.[108]

The nineteenth-century Hasidic master Menahem Nahum agrees:

> The Creator's glory fills the whole earth; there is no place devoid of Him. But his glory takes the form of garb; God is "garbed" in all things. This aspect of divinity is called *shekhinah*, "in-dwelling," since it dwells in everything.[109]

And this is precisely why Meister Eckhart insists insists that

> Everything stands for God and you see only God in all the world.[110]

So, if you consider yourself too advanced to practice devotion, think again. The real question is not how can bhaktas see God in a particular form, but how is it that you can not?

Saying this, of course, is not meant to disparage the path of jnana in any way. As we shall see in the chapters ahead, each has its advantages and disadvantages. The point here is only that if you are a seeker with strong bhakta inclinations, you shouldn't try to suppress them out of some misplaced intellectual pride. Otherwise, your journey may end up being far more difficult than necessary. When it comes to spiritual matters, even jnanis must learn to follow the wisdom of their hearts.

The End Is Selflessness

Whether you begin as a jnani or a bhakta there is one thing you must never lose sight of: The end is the same. Here's how the twentieth-century Hindu mystic Ramana Maharshi explains it:

> Whatever the means, the destruction of the sense of 'I' and 'mine' is the goal, and as these are interdependent, the destruction of either of them causes the destruction of the other; therefore, in order to achieve the state of Silence which is beyond thought and word, either the path of knowledge which removes the sense of 'I' or the path of devotion which removes the sense of 'mine' will suffice. So there is no doubt that the end of the paths of devotion and knowledge is one and the same.[111]

One way to understand the relationship between the two paths is to compare the jnani to a detective in a mystery novel who sets out to find her self. After an exhaustive search, she finally "removes" the sense of *I* by failing to find any such entity. A bhakta, on the other hand, is more like a knight in one of those old troubadour romances who is utterly devoted to his lady-love. The way he "removes" the sense of *mine* is by surrendering everything he has to his beloved. Finally, when there is nothing left to give but himself, he surrenders that as well. So no matter how you get there, abolition of self is the goal of all genuine mystical paths. Thus, the Taoist Chuang Tzu writes,

> I say, the Perfect Man has no self; the Holy Man has no merit; the Sage has no fame.[112]

The Buddha agrees:

> Therefore, I say, the Perfect One has won complete deliverance through the extinction, fading away, disappearance, rejection, and getting rid of all opinions and conjectures, of all inclinations to the vainglory of I and mine.[113]

And God tells St. Catherine of Siena,

> Because she has left all, she finds all. Because she has stripped herself of herself she is clothed in me.[114]

Menahem Nahum explains it this way:

> Seek to make yourself into a vessel for God's Presence. God, however, is without limit; "Endless" is His name. How can any finite vessel hope to contain the endless God? Therefore, see yourself as nothing; only one who is nothing can contain the fulness of the Presence.[115]

For this reason, Rumi admonishes his fellow Sufis:

> So behead your selfhood, oh warrior! Become selfless and annihilated like a dervish!.[116]

This is why I say, if all the teachings of all the mystics of all the traditions had to be summed up in a single word, that word would be *selflessness*. Selflessness is the *Truth* to which all mystics bear witness. Selflessness is the *Way* by which this Truth can be Realized. And Selflessness is the *Fruit* of that Realization.

CHAPTER 6

Four Principles of the Path

> *A buried treasure is not uncovered by merely uttering the words "come forth". You must follow the right directions, dig, remove the stones and earth from it, and then make it your own. In the same way, the pure truth of Atman, which is buried under Maya and the effects of Maya, can be reached by meditation, contemplation and other spiritual disciplines such as a knower of Brahman may prescribe.*
>
> — Shankara (Hindu)

Whether you are a jnani or a bhakta, all the spiritual practices you will be undertaking are governed by four fundamental principles: *attention, commitment, detachment,* and *surrender.* These principles apply not only to the practices in a general way, but to each moment of their implementation. Therefore, it's a good idea to have some understanding of what, from a mystic's point of view, they actually entail. So, let's examine them one at a time.

Attention

The twentieth-century Christian mystic Simone Weil sums up the importance of attention in no uncertain terms:

> Attention animated by desire is the whole foundation of religious practices.[117]

As we have already seen, paying attention is key to attaining Enlightenment. Only when our attention is freed from the Story of I does an opportunity to Realize our true nature open up. But what exactly is this thing we call "attention"?

Obviously, attention is closely related to awareness, but the two are not synonymous. As we shall see in later chapters, it is possible to be fully aware and yet not be attending to anything in particular. So perhaps we should think of attention as a *power* of awareness. In fact, let us define attention as *the power of awareness to focus on various objects that arise in the total field of consciousness.* These can be sensory objects like sights, sounds, sensations, etc. Or they can be mental objects—thoughts, images, memories, fantasies. Most of the time, our attention is absorbed by combinations of sensory and mental objects which make up the various events and activities of our everyday lives.

Sometimes, attention seems to be subject to our control. This is true even when we find the object or activity we need to attend to unpleasant. A good example might be filling out your income tax returns. If you are like most people, this is not a task you relish. Nevertheless, with a little effort you can still force yourself to focus on it long enough to get the job done.

Sometimes, however, attention seems *not* to be under our control. For example, you might be trying to concentrate on figuring out your tax returns when, suddenly, you hear a loud crash coming from the street outside your house. If something like this happens, you will have a hard time keeping your attention focused on your taxes. Instead, it will automatically fly towards that sound, like iron to a magnet. In such cases, we often say that something has "captured" our attention.

Situations like this also show that attention is something quite distinct from our other mental faculties, such as thinking, judging, or feeling. If, for instance, you do hear a loud crash, it will be your attention that responds first. Then, once it has fastened onto the sound, your thinking mind might say something like, "What was that? Oh, it must have been a car crash. How terrible!" In other words, only *after* attention has moved to the sound will thoughts, judgments, and feelings *about* what you heard come into play.

This distinction between what we might call *naked* or *bare* attention and the other faculties is quite important for spiritual practices, especially when it comes to meditation and mystical prayer. Many meditation and prayer manuals talk about learning to "control the mind," or "mind training," but the English word *mind* is a pretty vague term. It *can* mean attention, but more commonly it refers to our thought processes. When mystics talk about "training the mind," however, what they usually mean is not so much learning to control our thoughts, but our attention, so that little by little we can begin to liberate it from the Story of I.

Commitment

Buddhists often refer to spiritual practices as "skillful means." Now, learning any kind of skill in life usually requires a commitment. If you want to learn to play the piano, for example, you have to make a commitment to practice on a regular basis. What's more, this practice will not always be enjoyable, especially in the beginning. Usually, you start by playing a prescribed series of notes or scales over and over again. Even though you might find this quite boring at times, you still have to maintain your commitment to practice; otherwise, you will never be able to play with the kind of freedom that comes from real mastery. The same holds true for spiritual practices like meditation, prayer, keeping precepts, etc. If you want to master them you have to make the same kind of commitment to practice.

But beyond committing to engage in specific practices, there is an even deeper kind of commitment you will have to make if you are going to become a serious seeker. Sooner or later, you are going to have to choose what the main goal of your life is to be: Is it to attain worldly success or spiritual Realization? This is crucial because, as Jesus says,

> No one can serve two masters; for a slave will either hate the one and love the other, or be devoted to the one and despise the other. You cannot serve God and wealth.[118]

And you will find the exact same teaching in other traditions as well. Thus, the Buddha told his disciples,

> There is a path that leads to worldly gain.
> Another road leads to nirvana.
> Let the seeker, the disciple of the Buddha,
> Embracing seclusion,
> Take the path to wisdom and enlightenment. [119]

Likewise, the Upanishads declare,

> There is the path of wisdom and the path of ignorance. They are far apart and lead to different ends.[120]

Here's how Rumi puts it:

> Oh friend! Which are you? Are you ripe or raw? Are you dizzy from sweetmeats and wine, or a knight on the field of battle?[121]

The reason for stating this choice so starkly is that, from a mystic's point of view, worldly pursuits represent a kind of "practice" in their own right. The more you act out of your self-centered conditioning, the stronger that conditioning grows. Consequently, even if you engage in formal spiritual practices a few hours a day, but spend the rest of your time conducting business as usual, you won't make much headway. The Tibetans compare this kind of part-time practice to someone involved in a lop-sided game of tug-of-war. For example, if you meditate for only one out of twenty-four hours, they say it's as though you were a single person pulling against a team of twenty-three people at the other end of the rope. The same is true with the path as a whole. It's not something you can do only in your spare time. Ultimately, it's going to require a total commitment on your part.

In psychological terms, this means re-writing your Story of I. Instead of identifying yourself as a worldly seeker whose fundamental commitment is to enhance and protect yourself, you must assume a new role—that of a spiritual seeker dedicated to completely dismantling the delusion that you are any such entity. The fifteenth-century Christian mystic St. Catherine of Genoa gives a glimpse of what true spiritual commitment entails:

> So vehement is the soul's instinct to rid itself of all that impedes its own perfection that it would endure hell itself to reach that end. For that reason the soul tenaciously sets about casting aside all those things that could give the inner self specious comfort.[122]

For some seekers this will mean becoming an *external renunciant*—that is, someone who literally gives up all worldly ties and possessions to live as a monk, nun or wandering mendicant. Many of the world's greatest mystics adopted this life-style, and there are a number of good reasons for doing so. One is that external renunciation provides a kind of crash course in detachment. Money, job, friends, family, material security, and social status are all abandoned with a single stroke, giving you much more time to pursue your formal practices. Here is how the Buddhist *Anguttara-Nikaya Sutra* sums up the advantages of such a life:

> Full of hindrances is household life, a refuse heap; but pilgrim life is like the open air. Not easy is it, when one lives at home, to fulfill point by point the rules of holy life. How, if now I were to cut off hair and beard, put on the yellow robe and go forth from home to the homeless life?[123]

External renunciation, however, is not for everyone—nor is it universally recommended. Judaism discourages such a life-style, while in Islam it is positively forbidden. In these traditions the ideal, even for someone walking a mystical path, is to remain in the world as a householder, fulfilling all one's obligations to one's family and community.

One reason for this negative attitude is that becoming an external renunciant for the wrong reasons can be spiritually disastrous. If, for example, by forsaking your role as a householder you left your family destitute, such a selfish act would certainly undercut any benefits renunciation might confer. And if your motive was to prove your spiritual superiority over other people, then, instead of helping to dismantle the delusion of self, your renunciation would actually end up reinforcing it.

In fact, true renunciants do not really "decide" on such a course of action. They simply obey an irresistible call that wells up from the deepest recesses of their souls. Here is how Lalleshwari describes what happened to her:

> Because of my love for God
> a flood of renunciation
> filled my mind.
> I stopped tying up my hair
> and threw away my sārī.
> I wrapped myself in an old robe

> and went to live in a lonely place,
> occasionally keeping company with *sādhus*.[124]

Moreover, while external renunciation may be appropriate for some seekers, it is neither a necessary nor sufficient condition for completing the path. Many great Gnostics attained full Enlightenment without ever abandoning lay life. This is because the real problem lies not in worldly things, *per se*, but only in our attachments to them. Thus, the great fourteenth-century Tibetan master Longchen-pa writes,

> The appearances themselves do not bind (you to the delusions of *Samsāra*) because if you do not attach by clinging to the appearances, they will not defile you, since there is no connection. The bondage is the attachment, and it is important to abandon that attachment.[125]

This is also why Ramana Maharshi, who was himself a thorough-going external renunciant, used to tell his disciples this:

> Whether you continue in the household or renounce it and go to the forest, your mind haunts you.... It is no help to change the environment. The one obstacle is the mind; it must be got over whether in the home or in the forest. If you can do it in the forest, why not in the home? Therefore, why change the environment? Your efforts can be made even now, whatever be the environment.[126]

In fact, in some ways walking a spiritual path as a householder can be more powerful than taking the road of external renunciation. As a householder you will encounter more situations that trigger your self-centered conditioning, which means you will have more opportunities to interrupt and destroy it.

But although becoming an external renunciant may not be essential for walking a mystical path, it *is* essential that you become an *internal renunciant*—i.e., someone who, while remaining in the world, renounces all hope of attaining happiness from it. Until you can do this, you will always be torn between worldly and spiritual pursuits, and never able to submit yourself completely and whole-heartedly to the path and its demands.

Detachment

Making a commitment to the spiritual path naturally leads to cultivating detachment from worldly things. This is because, as the Hasidic masters say,

> There [in the highest realms] all things are as one; Distinctions between "life" and "death," "land" and "sea," have lost their meaning. But none of this can happen as long as you remain attached to the reality of the material world.[127]

In fact, cultivating detachment is regarded as indispensable in all mystical traditions. Hui-Neng explains why:

> If we never let our mind become attached at any time to any thing, we gain emancipation. For this reason we make "non-attachment" our fundamental principle.[128]

Mira Bai agrees:

> Give up faith in the world.
> Mirā is the slave of courtly *Giridhara* [Krishna],
> She has adopted the path of simple detachment.[129]

And after comparing detachment to the other virtues, Meister Eckhart concludes that

> Detachment is the best of all, for it purifies the soul and cleanses the conscience and enkindles the heart and awakens the spirit and stimulates our longings and shows us where God is and separates us from created things and unites itself with God.[130]

But despite its universality, detachment has been one of the least understood of all spiritual principles. The most common error seekers make is to take detachment to mean the complete eradication of all desires and aversions. Such people imagine that if they were truly detached, the most beautiful objects could be paraded before them and they would experience not a smidgen of pleasure; or that innocent children could be slaughtered at their feet and they would feel not a flicker of pain. But this kind of cold-blooded stoicism is emphatically not what spiritual detachment is about. In fact, what this notion of detachment actually represents is the supreme dream of the ego which would like nothing better than to be completely insulated from the world's sufferings. Such a state of indifference, however, is about as far as you get from genuine Enlightenment, so we had better take a closer look at what mystics mean when they talk about cultivating detachment.

First of all, what is to be detached from are not *all* desires and aversions, but only *personal* or *self-centered* ones—that is, desires and aversions which have as their aim the enhancement or protection of the self. Sometimes this is made clear in the teachings themselves, as when Anandamayi Ma insists that

> It is *personal* desire that is the very cause of suffering.[131]

Much of the time, however, it is not made clear, as when the Buddha says,

> Make headway against the current with your energy.
> Scrupulously avoid desire, O noble one.[132]

One reason for this omission is that the words used in English translations are not as precise as the words in the original languages. For example, the

Buddhist *Dhamapada* (from which the above quote was taken) was written in the Pali language. Now the Pali word for desire is *tanha*. But *tanha* only means desire for self-gratification. It emphatically does *not* mean such things as the "desire" for Liberation or the "desire" to make other beings happy.[133] In fact, a path that isn't animated by a burning desire for either Truth or God can easily degenerate into a set of lifeless rites and rituals, devoid of any real spiritual value. Thus, the nineteenth-century Russian Orthodox mystic Theophan the Recluse warns his students:

> Take care not to fall into the way of those who walk coldly along with correct outward behavior, yet lack the inner feelings which sanctify a man and attract the grace of God.[134]

The same applies to aversion. Self-centered aversion to people, things, or situations is certainly an obstacle on the path. But an aversion to the world of delusion is not only a positive feeling that should be fostered, it is often considered a prerequisite for successfully engaging in spiritual practices. Thus, the contemporary Buddhist master Lama Gendun Rinpoche says,

> If we think carefully about the unsatisfactory nature of ordinary worldly existence, we will recognize that it is characterized by suffering. We should therefore aim directly at Buddhahood and turn our minds away from worldly values. In this case there is a firm foundation for our spiritual path.[135]

Another reason that misunderstanding about detachment arises is because many spiritual texts were originally meant to serve only as notes for oral instructions given by teachers in face-to-face meetings with their students. Consequently, they employ a short-hand style which omits detailed explanations of all the psycho-spiritual subtleties of a particular teaching. In these cases, we have to rely on the context to make clear what sort of desire or aversion is being referred to. For example, when Anandamayi Ma says, "So long as there is desire, the experience of want and sorrow is—from the worldly point of view—but natural,"[136] she is talking about *self-centered* desire. But when she declares that "All desire must be for God only,"[137] she is talking about love and longing for the Divine, which is obviously something positive to be cultivated.

One way to avoid confusion about this is to get into the habit of mentally inserting the phrase, "self-centered," in front of terms like *desire* and *aversion* whenever the context calls for it. So, for instance, consider the following passage from the *Bhagavadgita*:

> Wisdom is clouded by [*self-centered*] desire, the ever present enemy of the wise, [*self-centered*] desire in its innumerable forms, which like a fire cannot find satisfaction.[138]

But even though self-centered desires and aversions are obstacles on the path, still this does not mean that you should try to suppress them. For one thing, such a strategy can never work. Any desire, aversion, or other emotion that you try to repress will only re-emerge later in another form. But more importantly, even if you could get rid of desire and aversion, this is not the goal of a mystical path. Why? Because, like everything else in the cosmos all emotions are, in reality, manifestations of the Divine. It is only when we experience them in distorted form, through the prism of the Story of I, that they cause us suffering. In their natural or liberated form, they are what the Tibetans call the "wisdom energies" of our innate Buddha nature; or, as the Kabbalists put it, "Divine sparks" which have fallen from the World of Love.

In future chapters we will be discussing practices designed to "purify" these sparks and "transform" these energies, by recognizing their true nature. In the meantime, it is important to remember that you can only recognize the true nature of anything by paying attention to it when it is *present* in Consciousness—never when it is *absent*. Therefore, it's a big mistake to try either to push away desires, aversions, and emotions once they have arisen, or try to stop them from arising in the first place. Instead, what you need to do is to cultivate *true* detachment which, spiritually speaking, means that you try to stay present with whatever arises in Consciousness, *without grasping at anything, or pushing anything away*. In other words, instead of reacting to emotional phenomena in your habitual way, you simply allow them to arise and pass, all on their own. By cultivating this kind of detachment, you can begin to interrupt your conditioned patterns of behavior.

This is a little like shifting a moving car into neutral. The engine is still running but it's no longer propelling the car forward in the direction it has been going, and so it gradually rolls to a stop. And the more you can do this with your life—the more you can remain in a detached and unfettered state—the more a space of awareness begins to open up in which there is the possibility of moving in a totally new direction, of acting in a completely unconditioned way—a way which is genuinely spontaneous and free, because it flows not from your deluded ego, but from Consciousness Itself.

Surrender

This brings us to the last and highest principle, *surrender*, which is extolled by mystics of all traditions. But what does it really mean?

At the most rudimentary level, every time you let go of some attachment, you may be said to have surrendered it. And because detachment follows from making a commitment, and making a commitment from trying to pay attention, it would seem that surrender simply grows out of the first three principles. But while this is true in a certain sense, there is a subtle yet important difference between surrender and the other principles. Paying attention, making a commitment, and practicing detachment are all things that, from a relative point of view, you can do by exercising your self-will. Surrender, however, always requires the relinquishment of some portion of will.

This capacity to surrender your self-will is essential for walking a spiritual path because, for most people, the sense of self-will lies at the core of who they think they are. And yet, from an absolute point of view there really is no such thing as self-will—which is why Krishna tells Arjuna in the *Bhagavadgita,*

> A man totally confused in his self-consciousness imagines: *I act.*[139]

In the Hindu and Buddhist traditions, the delusion that there is some self who can will actions is considered to be the primary thing that perpetuates our self-centered conditioning, or *karma,* as it is called in the East. Here is how Walpola Rahula explains it from a Buddhist perspective:

> The Sanskrit word *karma* (from the root *kr* to do) literally means 'action', 'doing'. But in the Buddhist theory of karma it has a specific meaning: it means only 'volitional action', not all action.... "Thirst', volition, karma, whether good or bad, has one force as its effect: force to continue—to continue in a good or a bad direction. Whether good or bad it is relative, and is within this cycle of continuity (*samsāra*).[140]

To be free of the delusion of self, then, means to be free of self-will. Thus, the Upanishads say,

> The man who surrenders his human will leaves sorrows behind and beholds the glory of the Atman by the grace of the Creator.[141]

Mystics of the three Abrahamic traditions express this using different terminology, but the practical result is the same. When you act out of your own volition, you are opposing your will to God's will. This naturally puts you in conflict with Creation and causes you to suffer. The solution, then, is to surrender your own will and defer to God's will in all things, which is why Rumi declares,

> No one has reached maturity except him who has been freed from self-will.[142]

Teresa of Avila agrees:

> What matters is not whether or no we wear a religious habit; it is whether we try to practice the virtues, and make a complete surrender of our wills to God.[143]

Unfortunately, however, that is something you can never actually do. Why? Because as long as you are *willing* yourself to surrender your will, you are exercising the very will that must be surrendered. And yet if you make no effort to surrender your will, nothing will change. Your self-centered conditioning will continue to grow stronger and stronger—which is why mystics seem forever to be urging us to exercise our will to do things like pay attention, make a commitment, practice detachment, and, yes, even surrender our will! So how can we escape this dilemma?

Well, first of all, you may have noticed that this *paradox of practice,* as we might call it, closely resembles the philosophical paradoxes we ran into in chapter 3 that result from trying to describe the nondual nature of Reality. As is the case with those philosophical paradoxes, paradoxes of practice can never be finally resolved by the thinking mind. They can only be *dis*solved by Gnosis. In the meantime, you can take the mystics' exhortations this way: *As long as you believe you have self-will, instead of using it to pursue worldly things which will only serve to deepen your delusion, why not apply it to those disciplines and practices that can destroy that delusion forever?*

Moreover, if you do this, you will start to discover a kind of judo trick that happens at every juncture of the path. It is precisely by making an effort to surrender your will and *failing,* that your will gets stymied and your effort exhausted. And whenever your will gets stymied and your effort gets exhausted surrender happens. This, in turn, opens you to a mysterious guidance that will carry you into the next stage, until finally you come to feel that it is no longer 'you' who are doing the practices at all. Rather, the practices are doing you—or, as the thirteenth-century Zen master Eihei Dogen used to say about the Buddha's *dharma* (teachings and practices),

> You turn dharma, [then] dharma turns you.[144]

In theistic traditions this kind of guidance is attributed to the action of a Divine grace, which is always available as a free gift, given either by God or one's Guru. Even so, you must still make an effort to open yourself to receive it, for as Ramana Maharshi says,

> The Grace of the Guru is like an ocean. If he [the seeker] comes with a cup he will only get a cupful. It is no use complaining of the niggardliness of the ocean; the bigger the vessel the more he will be able to carry. It is entirely up to him.[145]

Likewise, Ibn al-`Arabi writes,

> The gift of God is not withheld. But you want Him to give you something that your preparedness cannot receive. Then you attribute the withholding to Him in that which you seek from Him, and you do not turn your attention toward the preparedness.[146]

And this "preparedness" consists precisely in exhausting your own efforts in order to free up enough space for grace to operate. Here is how Theophan the Recluse explains it:

> Nothing comes without effort. The help of God is always ready and always near, but it is only given to those who seek and work, and

> only to those seekers who, after putting all their own powers to the test, then cry out with all their heart: Lord help us.[147]

Summary of Part I

So, I hope all this has given you an overview of what the mystics teach about delusion, Enlightenment, and the spiritual path, as well as some understanding of the two basic approaches—jnana and bhakti—and the four principles of attention, commitment, detachment, surrender. The rest of this book is for those of you who wish to roll up your sleeves and actually put these teachings into practice. Some sections give instructions more suited to jnanis, others give instructions more suited to bhaktas, while some are for both. But whichever you feel you are at the present time, you should still at least read through all the chapters, even if you don't plan to engage in the practices described. Many seekers begin their journeys as jnanis, but end up bhaktas, and vice versa. Consequently, you should have some idea of what *all* the different practices entail in case you want to go back and undertake one or more of them at a later date.

The Way of Selflessness

PART II: *Making Preparations*

Chapter 7

Finding a Teacher

> *Every person truly in search of God should take refuge in a reliable guide and follow such methods of sadhana as may enable him to rise above all conflicting and distressing situations in the world.*
>
> — Anandamayi Ma (Hindu)

Whether you are a bhakta or a jnani, you can always begin a spiritual path on your own. But to complete it you will eventually need to find a spiritual teacher or *guru*, because as the fourteenth-century Eastern Orthodox monks Callistus and Ignatius of Xanthopoulos write,

> If a man is unlikely to take an unexplored path without a true guide; if no one will risk going to sea without a skillful navigator; if no man will undertake to learn a science or an art without an experienced teacher, who will dare attempt a practical study of the art of arts and the science of sciences, to enter the mysterious path leading to God ... without a guide, a navigator and a true and experienced teacher?[148]

And you will find the same advice given by mystics in all traditions. Here's what Zen master Dogen says:

> The practice of Buddha's teaching is always done by receiving the essential instructions of a master, not by following your own ideas.[149]

Rumi agrees:

> Whoever enters the way without a guide will take a hundred years to travel a two-day journey....
> Whoever undertakes a profession without a master becomes the laughingstock of city and town.[150]

And the Upanishads declare:

> This sacred knowledge is not attained by reasoning; but it can be given by a true Teacher.[151]

The reason all these mystics insist you need a teacher is because without one you have only your ego to rely on. But, as we have already seen, your ego is the main obstacle to Enlightenment. So this is like a prisoner relying on the warden to help him escape. If you engage in spiritual practices without a true teacher to guide you, chances are your ego will co-opt whatever insights you gain or experiences you have, making it that much more invincible.

But then the question is this: Where can you find such a teacher? Actually, from the Ultimate point of view, there is really only One Teacher—Consciousness Itself. However, as Ramana Maharshi explains,

> As long as you think that you are separate or are the body, so long is the outer Master also necessary and he will appear as if with a body. When the wrong identification of oneself with the body ceases the Master is found to be none other than the Self.[152]

In fact, since *all* forms are, in Reality, forms of the "Self"—i.e., Consciousness Itself—the Teacher can manifest in any form, embodied or not. The ancient shamans were often taught by animals seen in visionary or dream states. The teachers of many famous mystics appeared to them in dreams. Ramana Maharshi was guided to Enlightenment through an encounter with death. Even the Buddha, who had no physical teacher, required the appearance of the morning star to attain Full Awakening.[153] For the vast majority of seekers, however, the Teacher first manifests in the form of a flesh-and-blood human being.

Unfortunately, many Westerners today are reluctant to submit to the guidance of a human teacher. The two main reasons for this are egoic pride and the fear of being taken advantage of by a charlatan. In our own time, this fear has been fanned by a number of well-publicized scandals involving people who have claimed to be spiritual teachers. But, as the Sufis say, it would be foolish to throw out all the coins in a purse just because it was found to contain some counterfeits. Indeed, the very fact that anyone takes the trouble to make counterfeit money proves the existence of an authentic currency. So, while it is certainly necessary to exercise discretion in selecting a spiritual teacher, to shun all teachers out of false pride or undue paranoia would be a serious mistake.

How Teachers Function

At the most rudimentary level, spiritual teachers serve many of the same functions as teachers of secular subjects. In particular, they can give you detailed instructions for engaging in various practices, and offer advice on how to overcome specific obstacles. Theophan the Recluse, for instance, describes the vital role a teacher plays for seekers who want to perform the Jesus Prayer, which is the main devotional practice of Eastern Orthodox mystics:

> These directions should be followed under the eye of a teacher who knows the correct way of performing the Prayer.... Since methods of this kind naturally lead to a certain degree of concentrated attention and warmth, whoever does not have by him a reliable judge, capable of explaining to him the nature of the change that has taken place in him, may come to imagine that this limited warmth is indeed what he is seeking and that grace has descended upon him, whereas in fact it is not there as yet. And so he begins to think that he possesses grace, without actually having it. Such is the nature of illusion; and this illusion will thereupon distort all the subsequent course of his inner life.[154]

In the beginning stages of a path your teacher need not be fully Enlightened. The only real requirement is that he or she has had deeper experiences and more penetrating insights than you. Most seekers will study with a number of such teachers during their journey and benefit greatly from their help. Eventually, however, you will want to find a fully Enlightened teacher, or at least one who has had a clear gnostic flash. This is because only someone who has directly apprehended Ultimate Reality knows precisely where the door to it lies, and so can keep you moving in that direction.

Having an Enlightened teacher becomes especially important if and when you start encountering paranormal phenomena, such as synchronistic events, telepathic communications, prophetic dreams, spiritual visions, etc. In the West these are usually referred to as *miracles*. In the East they are known as *siddhis*. Of course, many modern seekers will doubt that such things possess any 'objective' reality, but that is really beside the point. Whether seekers believe in them or not, most will still have 'subjective' experiences of these kinds of phenomena to one degree or another. And while such experiences can be the source of genuine guidance (as we shall see in future chapters), they can also be quite dangerous.

For instance, some seekers who have paranormal experiences may think they are losing their minds, and so be frightened off the path altogether. More often, however, the danger lies in the opposite direction. This happens when seekers become fascinated by these experiences and try to cultivate them for their own egoic ends. The contemporary Sufi scholar Dr. Mir Valiuddin describes where this can lead:

> Many true travelers on the Path to God, when they were gifted with thaumaturgic powers (karāmāt), they felt proud of their occult and mysterious powers, turned away from the path of love of God and fixed their gaze on the flattery of ephemeral creatures and this fleeting world. Thus, they lost the taste for direct observation of God and fell into the deepest depths of degradation.[155]

And you will find similar warnings echoed in virtually all traditions. Thus, Dogen writes,

> [Zen teachings] are not to be understood through the discriminations of thinking; much less can they be known through the practice and verification of supernormal powers.[156]

And Anandamayi Ma gives this advice:

> Having left aside sense objects, do not remain entangled in supernormal powers. Supernormal powers are but a stage. They may be beneficial; they may also be harmful. But through them you will not attain to the Supreme, the Ultimate.[157]

Now, the problem with having a teacher who is not Enlightened at this stage of the game is that he or she may be just as frightened or fascinated by your paranormal experiences as you are. A teacher who has clearly apprehended the Ultimate Nature of Reality, however, will not be swayed by any distorted views, and so can help you correctly interpret the significance of what you are experiencing and advise you on the best way to handle it.

Enlightened teachers can also help you recognize and avoid making certain errors common in the more advanced stages of the path, such as becoming attached to blissful states, objectifying direct insights, and mistaking transcendent experiences for full Realization. We will be discussing these pitfalls more thoroughly in a future chapter. For now the point is simply that even the best teachers, if they are not Enlightened, are themselves prone to falling into these traps, in which case they will be unable to show you how to deal with them.

Another reason for having a fully Enlightened teacher is that he or she provides a living example of Gnosis in action—i.e., a life of Selfless Love, based on the Truth of Selflessness. This is important both for overcoming any doubts you may have about where the path leads, and because it can serve as a powerful inspiration to walk your own path all the way to the end.

Finally and perhaps most profoundly, an Enlightened teacher can be a manifestation of and conduit for that grace we talked about in the last chapter. Sometimes, simply being in the presence of such a person is enough to spark a Gnostic flash, if not complete Realization. More commonly, however, an Enlightened teacher serves to awaken what many traditions call the *Inner Teacher*. This can happen in a number of ways.

The Inner Teacher

First, your human teacher might start appearing to you in dreams to give you teachings custom-tailored to fit your individual needs. Now, many seekers assume that such dreams are being projected into their minds by their human teacher from the 'outside,' as it were. But from a mystic's point of view, the situation is the reverse. Your human teacher has all along been a projection of your

Inner Teacher who, in turn, is actually a projection of your True Self. So, when your human teacher starts showing up in your dreams, it simply means that your True Self is beginning to manifest to you in a more direct and intimate manner. Here is how Ramana Maharshi describes it:

> The Guru is both "external" and "internal." From the "exterior" he gives a push to the mind to turn inward; from the "interior" he pulls the mind towards the Self and helps in quieting the mind. That is *guru-krpa*. There is no difference between God, Guru and the Self.[158]

The Inner Teacher may also appear in an archetypal form appropriate to your tradition. Here, for example, is how Teresa of Avila describes how the image of Christ manifests to Christians in visionary states:

> I speak of an "image," but it must not be supposed that one looks at it as at a painting; it is really alive, and sometimes even speaks to the soul and shows it things both great and secret.[159]

Among Tibetan Buddhists it is common for the Inner Teacher to manifest as an archetypal wisdom deity such as Manjushri. Contemporary Tibetan master Tsoknyi Rinpoche describes the ways in which this can happen:

> Manjushri is the embodiment of knowledge and wisdom, the principle that explains or gives knowledge when there is ignorance.... Sometimes it is possible that Manjushri will literally show his face before you by appearing and giving answers to your questions. At another time you might just be remaining in equanimity, and an answer to your question arises from within yourself. That could also be said to be the blessing or inspiration of Manjushri.[160]

Sometimes the Inner Teacher manifests as a more or less constant presence, giving guidance on a regular basis. Anandamayi Ma received counsel from a Divinely-inspired voice or *kheyala*. In similar fashion, Socrates insisted that

> [A] prophetic voice to which I have become accustomed has always been my constant companion, opposing me even in quite trivial things if I was going to take the wrong course.[161]

If this kind of thing should happen to you, it is still advisable to seek out a human teacher who can confirm that what you are experiencing is, indeed, a genuine manifestation of the Inner Teacher and not some fantasy fabricated by your ego. There are many people who profess to be guided by inner teachers. But the trouble is, these so-called "inner guides" are always telling them how to attain their desire, never how to detach from them; how to love themselves, never how to love others; how to enhance themselves, never how to surrender themselves. Remember, the role of a true spiritual teacher—whether inner or outer—is not to tell you what you *want* to hear, but what you *need* to hear, which is often quite a different matter.

Recognizing an Enlightened Teacher

So, the next question is this: How can you tell whether or not a teacher is truly Enlightened? And the answer is that there is no way you can be *absolutely* certain. This is because there is no single ideal to which all Enlightened teachers conform. In fact, teachers can and do vary greatly in their appearances, personalities, life-styles, and methods. The Buddha, for example, was an external renunciant who emphasized jnana practices of meditation and inquiry. Although Jesus lead the life of a mendicant wanderer, he was by no means an ascetic. While eschewing all personal possessions, he nevertheless enjoyed feasting and drinking—so much so that he was accused by both friends and foes of being a glutton and a drunkard! Unlike either Buddha or Jesus, Muhammad was not only an exceptional spiritual leader, but a social and political one, as well.

Because these great masters ended up founding whole new traditions, future generations of their followers have generally viewed them as exemplars *par excellence* of Enlightened behavior. But even within these traditions not all teachers have adhered to their founder's example. For instance, many Tibetan teachers, following the example of Padmasambhava who brought Buddhism to Tibet, have had consorts or were married householders. Some Christian mystics, like St. Augustine and John Scotus Eriugena, were masters of philosophical inquiry, while the famous eighth-century Sufi saint Rabi'a led what for a Muslim was an uncharacteristically reclusive life. The point is that if you cling to an image of what you think an Enlightened teacher *should* be like, this can prevent you from recognizing a true teacher who happens not to fit your own mental picture.

But despite the lack of any absolute criteria for determining whether a particular teacher is Enlightened, there are still some general guidelines which may be helpful. When sizing up a prospective teacher, you might want to ask the following kinds of questions:

1. *Is the teacher a hypocrite?* In other words, do they practice what they preach? Practicing what one preaches by itself, of course, is no guarantee of Enlightenment, but it does ensure that you will not be set up for some major disappointment which might sour you on teachers altogether. To give but one example, towards the end of the last century one of the most famous Tibetan teachers to come to America was both an alcoholic and sexually promiscuous. However, he never tried to hide these traits from his students. In fact, he would often sip a glass of gin while giving dharma talks. Such a teacher may not be right for you, but at least you know where he stands before you become his pupil.

2. *Is a teacher's behavior merely unorthodox or actually immoral?* This is somewhat related to the question of hypocrisy, but goes deeper. Many teachers use unconventional or "crazy wisdom" methods as a way of exposing their students' attachments. Ramana Maharshi's attitude towards his mother provides a good example. Shortly after his Enlightenment, Ramana, who was still a teenager at the time, left home to become a renunciant. Years later, his mother found him teaching a circle of students at an ashram they had established. Quite naturally, she wanted him to acknowledge her as his long-lost mother. But despite her numerous entreaties and copious tears, he refused to enter into any special relationship with her. Some of Ramana's students found this display of apparent heartlessness shocking. Eventually, however, his mother let go of her attachment to seeing Ramana as her son, and, instead, became one of his most devoted disciples. So, while Ramana's seeming insensitivity towards his mother was highly unconventional, it was actually an act of great compassion, because it helped steer her towards the path to Liberation. Such behavior is very different from that of charlatans who sexually and/or financially exploit their students under the guise of engaging in crazy wisdom practices.

3. *How does the teacher handle money?* Enlightened teachers who have no other financial resources need to be supported by their students if the students want them to be available to give teachings. In such cases, asking for donations or charging reasonable fees is a matter of practical necessity. This is especially true if the teacher is a householder with obligations to maintain a decent standard of living for his or her family. However, if a teacher insists on living in an extravagant manner well beyond the norm for his or her society, this should definitely be cause for concern. Whoever is dependent on material possessions to sustain their happiness is certainly not Enlightened.

4. *How does the teacher handle power?* For better or worse, spiritual teachers are in a position of power, because being a teacher means that people are willing to listen to and act on their advice. The real question, then, is not whether a teacher has power, but how the teacher uses it. Is it for the benefit of the students, or to gratify his or her own ego? One way to tell is by observing how a teacher reacts to students who question his or her instructions. An occasional show of frustration—especially with students who never attempt to actually put the teachings into practice—does not necessarily signal a lack of attainment. Manifesting such emotions can sometimes help motivate a lazy student, as Jesus tried to do when he scolded his disciples: "Why do you call me 'Lord, Lord', and do not do what I tell you?"[162] However, teachers who chronically belittle their students, or automatically take offense whenever their authority is challenged should be viewed with great suspicion.

Besides asking these specific kinds of questions, you should also watch how a teacher behaves when he or she is "off duty"—i.e., not engaged in giving formal teachings. Most of the time, an Enlightened teacher will exhibit traditional virtues in a completely spontaneous and unpretentious way. Most will also have a good sense of humor, especially when it comes to poking fun at themselves. Above all, you should sense an underlying current of Happiness running through their lives, a fundamental contentment with the way the Cosmos is unfolding, which transcends all inner moods and outer circumstances. Any competent actor can mimic these qualities for a time, but a true teacher will manifest them day in and day out, so pay attention.

Finally, there is one other clue you can look for: Truly Enlightened teachers do not *choose* to teach. They are simply submitting to the Law of Love to which they have become surrendered by virtue of their Realization. This does not mean they never experience delight in teaching. Nothing causes more joy than to see a student becoming less attached, freer, happier, and eventually Wake Up. Nevertheless, if we can speak of Enlightened teachers as possessing 'personal' preferences, most would choose a life of anonymity. After his own Enlightenment, for instance, the Buddha at first had no intention of trying to communicate the Truth he had Realized. On the contrary, according to legend he thought to himself, "If I were to teach the Doctrine, and others did not understand it, it would be a weariness to me, a vexation."[163] Only after the god, Brahma Sahampati, appeared and repeatedly begged him to expound the Dharma for the sake of suffering beings, did the Buddha consent. Likewise, it is said that Lao Tzu composed the *Tao Te Ching* at the insistence of a Gate-keeper, stationed at a mountain pass, who refused to let the sage retire from worldly life until he first committed his great wisdom to writing. So, too, when the Angel Gabriel commanded Muhammad to begin reciting the Holy Qur'an, Muhammad tried to beg off saying, "I cannot recite." Again he was commanded, and again he responded in the same way. Only after the command was given a third time did Muhammad ask what he was supposed to say, thus opening himself to the flood of Revelations that would follow. And while there is no record that Jesus specifically balked at his teaching mission, his own words make clear the humility with which he accepted his role:

> Who is greater, the one who is at the table or the one who serves? Is it not the one at the table? But I am among you as one who serves.[164]

So, if a teacher is so important, how do you go about finding one? First, you should remember that not every teacher is suitable for every student. You must find one that is right for you. This is like someone who possesses a master key that fits many locks. But if the key does not fit yours, it won't do you any good. So don't be afraid to shop around. Listen to lots of talks given by different teachers, attend their workshops, and ask as many questions as you need to. And if you do not find a suitable teacher right away, be patient, because the second thing to remember is that it's not entirely up to you. Ultimately, it is a matter of grace. This is why in many traditions it is said that *When the student is ready, the teacher appears*. Here is how Ramana Maharshi describes it:

> First a man prays to God to fulfill his desires, then a time comes when he does not pray for the fulfillment of a desire but for God himself. So God appears to him in some form or other, human or non-human, to guide him as a Guru in answer to his prayer.[165]

Chapter 8

Tracking Dreams

Those who are empowered by the breath of the Holy Spirit sail along even when asleep.

— Brother Lawrence (Christian)

If you read through the biographies of the world's great mystics, you'll find most of them are peppered with accounts of significant dreams which contained various teachings, prophecies, instructions, and advice. For example, here is how the thirteenth-century Kabbalist Isaac of Acre describes a dream in which the angel Metatron appeared to him:

> While I was yet sleeping I, Isaac of Acre, saw Metatron, the Prince of the Face, and I sat before him, and he taught me and promised me many good things that would come to me.[166]

Ibn al-'Arabi's wife Maryam Abdun had a similar visitation:

> I have seen in my sleep someone whom I have never seen in the flesh, but who appears to me in my moments of ecstasy. He asked me whether I was aspiring to the Way [the Sufi Path], to which I replied that I was, but that I didn't know by what means to arrive at it. He then told me that I would come to it through five things, trust, certainty, patience, resolution and veracity.[167]

The anonymous Christian author of the nineteenth-century Eastern Orthodox classic *Way of a Pilgrim* also reports seeing his deceased teacher in dreams:

> Sometimes also, though very rarely, I saw my departed *starets* [teacher] in a dream, and he threw light upon many things, and, most of all, guided my ignorant soul more and more towards humility.[168]

And Swami Sivananda Radha, a Western disciple of the twentieth-century Hindu teacher Swami Sivananda, writes this about the life-altering instruction she received from her guru in a dream:

> A thundering voice called to me, "Radha! That's enough now come out!" I was just in a big swimming pool having fun, being with many people. No sinful action. "This way!" he said.[169]

Radha then explains how she interpreted it:

> It was very typical of my Guru's voice and his way of speaking. Swami Sivananda did not use many words, and they were very short and direct. That was it. I knew the message was from him, and I understood what the message was. I was not supposed to complete the academic program I had entered. I was not supposed to play in that pool, enjoying the fun. My Guru had other work for me to do and I could not be distracted.[170]

Not all mystics have reported receiving guidance in dreams. Nevertheless, given how widespread the phenomenon is, it would be foolish not to start paying close attention to your own dreams to see if they contain anything of spiritual significance. Of course, as the mystics themselves recognized, not all dreams do. St. Augustine divided dreams into two main categories, those that are true and those that are false. Likewise, Tibetan Buddhists distinguish between clarity dreams and dreams that are merely "karmic" or, as we might say, "egoic" in nature. So how can you tell spiritual dreams from non-spiritual or egoic dreams?

Two Kinds of Dreams

The main difference lies in their content. Egoic dreams are woven from the fabric of our personal histories and reflect the self-centered worries and concerns that arise out of our worldly pursuits. Perhaps the clearest example of such dreams are the ones we tend to have when our minds are preoccupied with some crisis occurring in our waking state. For instance, if you are facing some difficult problem at work, your dreaming mind is apt to continue trying to figure out a solution while you sleep. Similarly, if you have an argument with someone during the day, your mind will often replay it in your dreams, hoping to arrive at a more satisfactory outcome. Because the situations we encounter in these kinds of dreams are simply continuations of our waking experiences, they rarely need any special interpretation. As we all know, however, most of our dreams are considerably more jumbled and their meanings are harder to discern.

The reason for this, according to modern psychology, is that normally when we fall asleep our attention shifts from our everyday cares to those long-range subconscious dilemmas which for one reason or another we are afraid to fully acknowledge. This material is *repressed* during our waking life, but resurfaces in our dreams, only in a disguised or symbolic form. Moreover, because the content of these egoic dreams arise out of our personal histories, the symbols in which they are expressed also tend to be highly personal. This is why interpreting them usually requires spending a lot of time sifting through reams of old memories with the aid of a skilled therapist.

Fortunately, this is far less the case with spiritual dreams. In fact, we could say that, in general, the greater the spiritual content a dream has, the easier it is to interpret. Why? Because spiritual contents are not derived from our personal histories, nor do they express purely personal problems. They come from a transpersonal dimension of Consciousness known to all the great traditions. In the Jewish and Christian traditions, for example, spiritual dreams are viewed as coming either directly from God or via angels who occupy an intermediary realm between the human and Divine. Sufis also hold that during sleep we can enter a realm that is spiritually superior to that of waking life. Ibn al-'Arabi explains as follows:

> Sleep is a state in which the servant passes from the witnessing of the world of sense perception to the world of the *barzakh* [World of Imagination], which is the most perfect world. There is no world more perfect, since it is the root of the origin of the cosmos; it possesses true existence and controlling rule (*tahakkum*) in all affairs.[171]

Similarly, according to the Tibetan tradition, certain types of spiritual teachings called "Mind Treasures" can be directly apprehended in clarity dreams. Contemporary master Tenzin Wangyal Rinpoche describes how this occurs:

> Imagine entering a cave and finding a volume of teachings hidden inside. This is finding in physical space. Mind treasures are found in consciousness rather than in the physical world. Masters have been known to find these treasures both in dreams of clarity and when awake. In order to receive these kinds of teaching in a dream, the practitioner must have developed certain capacities, such as being able to stabilize in consciousness without identifying with the conventional self. The practitioner whose clarity is unobscured by karmic traces and samsaric dreams has access to the wisdom inherent in consciousness itself.[172]

The Realm of the Archetypes

Perhaps a better way for modern seekers to understand the transpersonal nature of spiritual dreams is through the work of the twentieth-century psychologist, Carl Jung. That which distinguishes what we are calling spiritual dreams from ordinary dreams, Jung insisted, is that spiritual dreams contain *archetypes*. So what is an archetype? Strictly speaking, an archetype refers to the original form of anything which then serves as a model for the production of similar forms or copies. Jung, however, used the term specifically to refer to those universal psychic principles which manifest as the gods and goddesses, heroes and heroines, whose deeds are recounted in the myths and legends of all the world's cultures. What Jung and later scholars like Mircea Eliade and Joseph Campbell discovered was that despite local variations, the characters in these myths perform the same symbolic functions in stories that deal with the same cosmic themes—life and death, good and evil, love and hate, sin and salvation. In addition (and what is especially relevant for our present discussion), Jung noticed that these archetypes appear spontaneously in the dreams of people from all sorts of backgrounds—*even those who have never been exposed to archetypes in waking life*. Thus, as Campbell put it, "Myths are public dreams, dreams are private myths."

To account for this universality, Jung posited the existence of a *collective unconscious* shared by all human beings. This collective unconscious can be accessed in certain visionary or dream states by any individual irrespective of his or her cultural background. We can glean something of what Jung was talking about by making a brief cross-cultural comparison of our own. For instance, the Eskimo Igjugarjuk gives this account of what happened to him at the end of a vision quest:

> Only towards the end of the thirty days did a helping spirit come to me, a lovely and beautiful helping spirit, whom I had never thought of; it was a white woman; she came to me whilst I had collapsed, exhausted, and was sleeping. But I still saw her lifelike, hovering over me.... She came to me from Pinga [a goddess] and was a sign that Pinga had now noticed me and would give me powers that would make me a shaman.[173]

Similarly, during a dark retreat undertaken when he was still a young man, Longchen-pa had a vision of a beautiful woman riding a horse who gave him a crown of precious jewels and told him,

> From now on, I shall always bestow my blessings upon you and grant you powers.[174]

In the nineteenth century, the Hasidic master Isaac Yehudah Yehiel Safrin dreamed he met the *Shekhinah*–i.e., the feminine aspect of God:

> I fell asleep for a while, and I saw a vision of light, splendor and great brightness, in the image of a young woman adorned with twenty-four ornaments ... And she said: "Be strong, my son," and so on.[175]

And here is the last part of a dream about climbing a mountain that this author had long before he had ever heard of Igjugarjuk, Longchen-pa or Safrin:

> I look out over a breath-taking landscape spread at my feet. The seven continents and seven seas extend before my eyes to a 360 degree horizon. Both the sun and moon are simultaneously visible in the sky, one half of which is night, the other, day, and a sacred hush envelops the world. Suddenly, I become aware of a woman standing at my side, wearing a helmet. She hands me a sword and says, "This sword is as bright as the moon and as sharp as the stars, and with it you can cut through the heart of truth."
>
> I take the sword and hold it in the palm of my hand, and it feels powerful and good. Then I turn to the woman and ask, "Who are you?"
>
> "Don't you know?" she laughs, gently, "I am Athena and I've been with you always."[176]

In the above examples we can see clearly that, just as Jung described, it is the same archetype—*The Feminine Guide*, to give her a generic title—who manifests to empower and encourage seekers from very different times and places. But while Jung's pioneering work has been key to our modern understanding of archetypes, from a mystic's perspective, it nevertheless falls short in one crucial respect. Jung believed that becoming conscious of archetypal influences helps human beings achieve the highest goal of life which, in his view, was to "individuate" from what he thought of as a greater "Self"—i.e., the total Psyche including its unconscious dimensions. According to the mystics, however, the highest goal in life is not any kind of individuation. On the contrary, it is, as we have seen, the attainment of a Gnosis of one's *identity* with that Self or Consciousness which is the ground of all being. In fact, for mystics, the struggle to reach this goal constitutes the Ultimate Archetypal Drama—one which is re-enacted by every seeker who walks a spiritual path. The spiritual interpretation of dreams, then, consists precisely in seeing how the archetypal characters, symbols and motifs that appear in each seeker's dreams fit into and furthers the action of his or her unique version of this universal quest.

Although in rare cases a dream with an exceptionally strong archetypal content can itself precipitate an abrupt shift from worldly to spiritual seeking, for most seekers the process unfolds more gradually. This is usually reflected in their dreams. Because, in the beginning, seekers are still preoccupied with worldly affairs, most of their dreams will be dominated by egoic contents, with archetypal elements appearing only sporadically and in somewhat diluted form. Such "mixed" dreams require a good deal of interpretation in order to fully decipher their meanings. But the more seekers progress on the path, the more archetypal elements will start to emerge, until finally they become quite common. So, don't be discouraged if, in the beginning, your dreams still seem confused and mundane. If you continue to pay attention to them, chances are you will eventually be rewarded with dreams of increasing spiritual significance.

As we said earlier, dreams with predominantly archetypal contents need far less interpretation. Nevertheless, in order to understand them you must still learn the "language" of the archetypes which is the language of symbols.

The best way to do this is to familiarize yourself with the world's great myths, legends, and folk tales. It is also helpful to read comparative studies of Jungian psychologists and scholars. Here we only have space to briefly consider a few kinds of archetypes so as to give you at least some taste of what this symbolic language is like.

Some Common Kinds of Archetypes

First, there are archetypal beings. The loftiest of these beings, and easiest to identify, are those gods and goddesses, prophets and saviors, who are most revered in the tradition to which the dreamer belongs—e.g., Christ for Christians, Buddha for Buddhists, Krishna for Hindus, and Muhammad for Muslims. These exalted figures also tend to be the most important in terms of the messages they convey. This is why, for instance, Sufis insist that if Muhammad speaks to someone in a dream, his words can be relied on as much as if he had spoken them in the flesh.

Just below these supernal beings there is a host of lesser archetypes—angelic spirits, venerable ancestors, mythic animals—most of whom act as emissaries for the higher powers. This is also true of human figures who serve archetypal functions—a high priest or priestess, a pious hermit, a noble knight, a pure virgin, a wise old man or woman. To give one hypothetical example of how this works, you might dream you are speeding along a highway when suddenly you see that the road ahead is blocked by an avalanche. Not knowing what to do, you get out of your car and start milling about with the rest of the travelers. Then you notice an elderly gentleman draped in a cape, beckoning you to approach. When you go over to see what he wants, he points to a little footpath you hadn't noticed before that leads into thick, primeval forest. The message of this dream is that you cannot get to Enlightenment by following the ways of the world. You must travel alone, on foot, and be willing to enter into totally unknown territory.

Of course, not all archetypal beings appear as benevolent. You can also dream of what the Tibetans call "wrathful deities." These manifest in Western culture as devils, witches, warlocks, and vampires who seem intent on doing you harm. But no matter how frightening their outer form, in reality, all archetypes serve to help the seeker in some way. For instance, a demon who pops up in your dreams might represent a "shadow" side of yourself which needs to be acknowledged and accepted, or (depending on the context) some deep-seated fear that you must face and overcome before you can move forward on your journey.

In addition to archetypal beings, certain features of a dream's *terrain* can have archetypal significance—especially if they are unusually awesome, numinous, or pristine. A particularly majestic mountain, for instance, almost certainly symbolizes that Archetypal Mountain known to all spiritual traditions—Mt. Meru in Hindu and Buddhist cosmologies; Mt. Olympus in Greek mythology; Mt. Sinai in Judaism, Golgotha for Christians, Mt. Arafat in Islam, etc. Wherever this sacred mountain is said to be located, it always represents the *axis mundi*, the center of the world, that place where heaven and earth, God and man meet.

If such a mountain appears in a mixed dream, it may indicate that what seems to be a mundane problem actually requires a spiritual solution. For example, suppose you dream you are searching through a city looking for your lost wallet. In the background, looming over the rooftops, there is a huge snow-capped mountain which seems somewhat out of place. Because wallets contain documents that indicate who we are (driver's licenses, credit cards, etc.), they usually symbolize your personal identity. A city—especially a modern one—often represents the arena of worldly affairs. Thus, the dream is saying you will never find your true identity following a worldly path. Instead, you have to become a spiritual seeker and take the path of transcendence.

A desert appearing in a dream can also have archetypal significance, often representing an intermediary region between the sacred and the profane. Thus, it is fairly common for spiritual seekers who are undergoing a "desert experience" in their waking lives (i.e. a period when worldly pleasures no longer satisfy, but spiritual fruits have not yet been tasted) to dream they are wandering around lost in a physical desert. Such dreams often end with the dreamer catching sight of a lake or a stream just ahead, but waking up before he or she has had a chance to reach it. Since water is an archetypal symbol for the regenerating power of the Spirit (think of baptism, bathing in the Ganges, Native American sweats), a dream like this may be taken as a sign of encouragement. Stay on the path, it says, and eventually you will find spiritual refreshment.

Water not only symbolizes the Spirit's capacity to renew us, but also its power to destroy everything that stands between us and our goal. This is why, for example, it is not uncommon for seekers at a certain stage to dream of the coming of a great tidal wave that threatens to sweep everything before it. At first sight, this wave produces nothing but fear. Once it has passed, however, the dreamer is relieved to discover that he or she has survived without a scratch. The purpose of dreams like this is to reassure you that in the future, even though it may feel as if everything you have is being annihilated, this is necessary if you are ever going to reach your goal.

Many dreams tell a story. Archetypal dreams have *archetypal plots* which are variations of the plots of the world's great myths and legends. One of the most universal is the quest for some kind of magical treasure—the Golden Fleece, the Holy Grail, a Wish-Fulfilling Gem—all of which, in the mystics' view, represent Realization, Enlightenment, or Gnosis. But, as in any good story, first there are bound to be barriers to overcome, oceans to cross, mountains to climb, dragons to slay. And these, of course, represent those spiritual obstacles—all our self-centered desires and aversions, attachments and fears—which must in the end either be transformed or surrendered.

It is even possible, especially during more advanced stages of the path, to have dreams whose archetypal contents are so clear that they need little or no interpretation—provided, of course, that you are familiar with the traditional characters and symbols in which the Archetypes are clothed. For instance, anyone familiar with the Christian tradition will recognize how the following dream of the Franciscan monk Brother Leo illustrates the power of unconditional love to cleanse sin and vanquish guilt:

> Leo saw two ladders leading up to heaven, one as red as blood, the other as white as lilies. At the top of the red ladder there appeared Christ, his face full of wrath. St Francis beckoned to his brothers not to fear and to climb the ladder. They try, but fall. Francis prays, but Christ displays his wounds and thunders, "Your brothers have done this to me." So St. Francis runs down and leads his brethren to the white ladder, which they scale effortlessly and without mishap, to find Mary at the top, all smiles, to welcome them.[177]

But the most powerful spiritual dreams are those in which the seeker receives direct instructions or teachings that require no interpretation whatsoever. After leaving Tibet and settling in Italy, for instance, the contemporary Buddhist teacher Namkhai Norbu had the following dream about his own teacher back home:

> My master said to me, "It has been many years that we haven't seen each other. How is your practice going?" I said, "Well like this and like that." And he asked, "What practice have you been doing?" I explained that I had been doing my best to take into daily life the practice of *trechod*. "You haven't been doing any of the practice of *togel*?" he continued. And I said, "Well, no, I haven't been doing the togel." He asked, "Well, why not?" "Well," I answered, "because you told me that I had to perfect the trechod first. I had to get it very stable. So I am working to perfect and make very stable my trechod." He said, "Well, do you have any doubts about your knowledge of togel?" I said, "No, no, I don't have any doubts. I just haven't been doing that practice. He said, "Well you better get to it. Do the practice of togel. That is very important."[178]

Finally, we should mention that dreams with exceptionally strong archetypal contents often have a vivid, numinous quality which egoic dreams lack. In fact, it is not uncommon to wake from an important archetypal dream convinced that it was somehow more 'real' than what we call real life. And, insofar as such dreams serve to lead you on a journey from delusion to reality, that's actually true.

Cultivating Spiritual Dreams

Many mystics have developed practices specifically designed to foster spiritual dreams. The tenth-century Kabbalist Rabbi Hai Gaon gives this description of a Kabbalist dream practice:

> There were several elders and pious men who [lived] with us and knew them [the Names (of God)] and fasted for several days, neither eating meat nor drinking wine, [staying] in a pure place and praying and reciting great and well-known verses and [their] letters by number, and they went to sleep and saw wondrous dreams similar to a prophetic vision.[179]

Abu Sa'd Kharkushi recommended that seekers who want to receive true dreams should maintain physical cleanliness, cut their fingernails short, sleep on their back or right side, and recite certain prayers.[180] And the Tibetans have developed highly advanced practices, not only for encouraging archetypal dreams, but also for fostering a lucidity which allows you to actually engage in spiritual practices while you are in the dream state. In addition to such traditional methods, modern psychologists have developed a number of procedures for encouraging and remembering dreams which can also be adapted by spiritual seekers. In what follows, then, we present brief generic versions of a few of these techniques, organized according to the four principles which govern all spiritual practices—attention, commitment, detachment, surrender.

1. *Pay Attention.* You can think of archetypal dreams as being authored by a Cosmic Dreamer, who is trying to communicate with you. If you are a bhakta, think of this Dreamer as your Divine Beloved. As you fall asleep, direct your attention to your Beloved and request whatever guidance might be appropriate. Here, for example, is one of the prayers Abu Sa'd Kharkushi suggests:

   > God I beseech you to grant dreams that are true rather than false, beneficial rather than harmful, remembered rather than forgotten.[181]

   If you are a jnani, you might want to try the following Tibetan practice for encouraging dreams with more archetypal content. First, make a strong resolve to remember your dreams. Lie on your left side, with your left hand under your cheek and use one of your fingers to close your left nostril. Next, visualize a letter "A" tinged with red in your throat chakra and keep your attention gently focused on that as you fall asleep. If you don't remember any dreams in the morning, try the same thing again the following night, but increase the intensity of redness of the "A." Continue doing this on successive nights until you start remembering your dreams.[182]

2. *Make a Commitment.* Like most practices, to be effective you must make a commitment to do this practice every night for an extended period of time—two or three months at least. You should also commit to keeping a dream journal in which you write down your dreams every morning. The sooner you do this after you wake up the better. Recording your dreams will not only help you remember them, but will also allow you to go back and review sequences of dreams at a later date. If during a

particular night you have too many dreams to write down, choose one or two that seem to be the most significant. Rely on your intuition to make this decision, not your intellect.

3. *Practice Detachment.* When you record your dreams it is essential that you practice detachment. This means not embellishing episodes that please you, nor censoring episodes that you find embarrassing or unpleasant. One of the most valuable things about dreams is that they bring to light obstacles that, for one reason or another, your ego doesn't want to acknowledge. Don't allow your ego to paper things over again in the morning.

4. *Surrender to the Dream.* One of the biggest differences between most psychological approaches to dream work and a spiritual approach is that psychologists tend to ask how a dream serves the ego-self. As a spiritual seeker, however, you should be asking how you can serve the Cosmic Dreamer which represents Consciousness Itself.

One concrete way to do this is, whenever possible, to act out in your waking life some situation that occurs in your dream. For instance, if you dream you are walking down a particular street in the town in which you live, the next day you should try to take a walk down that same street in your waking life. Even if nothing significant happens as a result of doing this, it still provides a concrete sign to the Cosmic Dreamer that you are taking your dreams seriously. This usually results in your having more dreams with more archetypal contents.

Needless to say, you should never act out any malevolent situation you dream about, such as committing violence against another person. It is still important to pay attention to such dreams, however, because they often have a lot to show you about self-centered attachments and conditioned behaviors you need to interrupt and abandon.

Interpreting Your Dreams

Even if we had the space to devote a whole volume to the various ways dreams can be interpreted, it would still not exhaust the subject. This is because dream interpretation is much more of an art than a science. However, here are a few pointers that may help.

1. Give every dream you record a title—preferably the very first one that comes to mind. Titles that you think of spontaneously often contain valuable clues as to the dream's meaning.

2. After you have written a dream down, spend some time alone pondering its archetypal symbols and situations. Then ask yourself how they relate to your own path—the practices you are doing, the obstacles you are encountering, and the attachments you are wrestling with. You should

try to do this the first day after you've had the dream, while it is still fresh in your memory.

3. If there is something in a dream that you suspect is important, but can't figure out what it means, ask for clarification as you fall asleep the next night. Make sure to record all your dreams the following morning, even if at first glance they seem to have nothing to do with the question you posed. Often, while pondering a dream later on, you will see that it actually provides a very precise answer, only expressed with a new set of symbols.

4. Every three to six months you should set aside an afternoon or evening to read over your dream journal. Treat it like some surrealistic novel written by another person. Doing this can reveal recurrent themes and motifs which, when seen in isolation, seem to have little significance, but seen in a larger context fit into patterns that are rich with meaning.

Sharing your dreams with a skilled teacher or members of a dream group can also be helpful. But remember that the way you know when an interpretation is correct is not just because it makes logical sense, but because it elicits an emotional response. This applies whether the interpretation comes from your own mind or someone else's. The only exception to this rule is when an interpretation leaves you positively *numb*. This is different from simply feeling neutral or indifferent. You have a sense of shutting down and perhaps becoming defensive. If this is your reaction, it may mean that the interpretation is correct, but you are not yet ready to hear it. If you are the one offering an interpretation to someone who responds this way, do not badger them about it. It will do no good, and besides, you could still be wrong. In dream work especially, there is no place for dogmatism.

Finally, if you grew up with a materialist worldview, doubts about the validity of your dream experiences are almost certain to arise–especially if you start having truly archetypal dreams directing you to alter the course of your life in fundamental ways. Under these circumstances your mind is bound to give rise to thoughts such as, "How can dreams have anything to do with reality? Taking dreams so seriously is stupid. After all, they are just imaginary creations."

There are two answers to these kinds of doubts. The first is to remember that, from a mystic's perspective, dreams are, indeed, imaginary. But so is all of your experience, including your waking life. The second and more profound answer is simply to acknowledge that you don't know what, if anything, is ultimately Real. That's what you are on a spiritual path to find out! In the meantime, instead of asking whether a particular dream is real, try to discover the value of its message. Is it leading you deeper into selfishness and delusion or towards Love and Truth? Whether awake or dreaming, if you are a true spiritual seeker, this is the only question that really matters.

Chapter 9

Going on Retreat

> *Nothing benefits the heart more than a spiritual retreat wherein it enters the domain of meditation.*
>
> — Ibn 'Ata'llah (Muslim)

Going on retreat is one of the oldest and most universal of mystical disciplines. It originated in shamanic times when men and women seeking guidance would leave the relative comfort and safety of their villages and venture out alone into the wilderness, crying for a vision. Igjugarjuk, an Eskimo shaman, explains why this was necessary:

> True wisdom is only to be found far away from people, out in the great solitude, and it is not found in play but only through suffering. Solitude and suffering open the human mind, and therefore a shaman must seek his wisdom there.[183]

Not only shamans, but after them the founders of virtually all the world's great religious traditions continued to seek their wisdom in solitude. Thus, the original Hindu seers, or *rishis,* used to retire to the forests in order to Realize their Oneness with Brahman. Moses climbed Mt. Sinai in search of a direct encounter with God. Buddha attained his Enlightenment, meditating alone under the Bodhi Tree. Jesus fasted for forty days and nights in the desert in preparation for his ministry, and Muhammad received the first verses of the Qur'an while sequestered in a cave on Mt. Hira. It should come as no surprise then that the mystics of these traditions have been following in their founders' footsteps ever since. Listen, for instance, to what Krishna tells Arjuna in the *Bhagavadgita*:

> The man of discipline will train himself,
> continually in a secret place,
> Alone, restraining himself and his thoughts completely.[184]

Likewise, Longchen-pa used to give this advice to his students:

> One should take the examples of holy persons and do practice....
> Steadfastly tolerate (harsh conditions) alone in remote mountain places.
> With determination get the real essence.[185]

This has been true even in Judaism and Islam which, as we have seen, shun external renunciation as a permanent life-style. Still, the mystics of these traditions have insisted on the necessity of making temporary retreats every so often in order to get away from worldly affairs. Thus, Abraham Abulafia instructed his Kabbalist students as follows:

> Cleanse the body and choose a lonely house where none shall hear thy voice....In the hour when thou preparest thyself to speak with the Creator, and thou wishest Him to reveal His might to thee, then be careful to abstract all thy thought from the vanities of this world.[186]

And here's how Ibn al-'Arabi puts it:

> Every seeker of the Lord must be alone within himself with his Lord in his inmost consciousness.... Otherwise, he will never recognize Him.[187]

Using a modern metaphor, we could say that for mystics solitude is the laboratory of the soul. Just as scientists construct laboratories in order to eliminate all those factors that are extraneous to their experiments, spiritual seekers go on retreat to eliminate, or at least minimize, all those external stimuli that distract them from their practices. With no phones to answer, no friends to talk to, no emails to read, no bills to pay, no jobs to perform, there is much less to trigger those thoughts and emotions that make up the Story of I. Like a fire deprived of its fuel, then, the story begins to weaken. This, in turn, allows a seeker to concentrate on whatever practices he or she has chosen with a power and intensity not normally attainable amid the hustle and bustle of everyday life. This is why, as a general rule, the more often you can go on retreat, the more rapidly you will progress on the path.

Specific Reasons for Going on Retreat

There can be any number of specific reasons for a seeker to go on retreat. For instance, you may want to immerse yourself in the study of some sacred text, seek inner guidance on how to overcome a particularly tough obstacle, or concentrate on encouraging spiritual dreams. Perhaps the most common reason for going on retreat, however, is to learn formal meditation or prayer practices, like the ones we shall be introducing in future chapters of this book. Ideally, every time you are ready to take up a new practice, you should try to do so in a retreat setting, where you will have as few distractions as possible. This is not an absolute requirement. It is certainly possible to begin a new practice at home. But if you can do it on retreat, it will help you absorb the essentials of the practice more quickly.

Another reason for going on retreat is to deepen and refine whatever meditation or prayer practice you are already doing as part of your daily life. Practicing on retreat once or twice a year will reveal subtleties that are almost impossible to notice without the mental stability and clarity a retreat makes possible. Moreover, even though you won't be able to maintain the same degree of stability and clarity after you return, you will still find that the overall quality of your practice has permanently improved.

Finally, as we shall see later in this book, there are some advanced practices which require, if not making a full-blown retreat, at least spending extended periods of time in seclusion. This is because these practices need to be performed in states of very deep contemplation which most seekers find very difficult if not impossible to attain under normal circumstances.

How to Go on Retreat

One of the first questions people ask about going on retreat is this: How long should it be? Actually, there is no set rule. You can make a retreat for a day, a week, a month, or a year or more. The standard length in many Sufi orders is forty days. In the Tibetan Buddhist tradition serious seekers go on retreats that last three years, three months, and three days. In general, the longer the retreat is, the more effective it will be. But even if you can only go for a day or two, it will still be worth the effort. In most Western countries today, it is not hard to find spiritual organizations which offer retreats open to the public that last anywhere from a weekend to ten days or longer.

There are two basic ways to go on retreat: solo or with a group. Going on retreat with a group has several advantages—especially for beginners. A good group retreat comes with a built-in regimen. There are set times for prayer, meditation, teachings, eating, sleeping, and so on. If the retreat is held at a retreat center established specifically for this purpose, you also get the benefit of a trained staff who can take care of most of your basic needs. That way you will have fewer distractions and more opportunity to concentrate on whatever practices you are doing.

In addition, group retreats are usually conducted under the auspice of an experienced teacher who can help you with any problems that may arise in your practice, as well as with understanding any spiritual experiences your practice generates. This latter type of guidance is particularly important for seekers who have not yet gained some detachment from their own thought process. When spiritual practices produce novel or extraordinary experiences, the ego-mind is very prone to misinterpret their significance in ways that end up reinforcing, rather than weakening, the Story of I. This is why Ibn al-'Arabi's warns us:

> For God's sake, do not enter retreat until you know what your station is, and know your strength in respect to the power of imagination. For if your imagination rules you, then there is no road to retreat except by the hand of the shaykh [teacher] who is discriminating and aware. If your imagination is under control, then enter the retreat without fear.[188]

Once you have been on a few group retreats you should try going solo. Many seekers find that their practice becomes more intimate and penetrating when they are completely alone. Although it is possible to do a solo retreat in your own home, generally it's better to go somewhere else. That way you won't be tempted to call a friend, read the newspaper, or turn on the TV when you get bored. Some retreat centers offer hermitage facilities for people wanting to do solo retreats, but renting a room in a quiet hotel or motel will do almost as well.

When you go on a solo retreat it's very important to establish and maintain a strict schedule. If you don't, you're likely to end up whiling away your time reading, napping, going for walks, or just plain goofing-off. Here is a sample schedule which you can adjust to suit your own needs.

5:30 AM	—	Wake up
6:00 AM	—	Hatha yoga (or stretching exercises)
6:30 AM	—	Formal meditation or prayer session
7:30 AM	—	Breakfast (prepare, eat, clean-up)
8:30 AM	—	Free time
9:30 AM	—	Formal meditation or prayer session
11:30 AM	—	Read spiritual texts
12 Noon	—	Lunch (prepare, eat, clean-up)
1:00 PM	—	Free time
2:00 PM	—	Formal meditation or prayer session
5:00 PM	—	Free time
6:00 PM	—	Supper (prepare, eat, clean-up)
7:00 PM	—	Read spiritual texts
8:00 PM	—	Formal meditation or prayer session
9:30 PM	—	Go to Sleep

Many people find it physically painful to sit for prolonged periods of time in a single posture. To relieve this problem, the formal meditation or prayer sessions in this schedule can be broken up into *rounds* of twenty-five or fifty-five minutes each, with five minutes of slow walking or stretching in between.

Some traditions encourage fasting while on retreat, but most recommend eating lightly. The Tibetans give this advice: *two-thirds full, one third empty.* Intoxicants should be strictly avoided, as should any activities not related to your practice, such as writing letters to relatives, catching up on office work, making plans to remodel your house, etc. Notice, however, that this schedule does include periods of free time during which you can go for walks, read spiritual texts, take a nap, or practice informally. For most types of retreats, it is counter-productive to push yourself too hard. Here's what the twentieth-century Tibetan master Gen Lamrimpa suggests:

> Both during and between meditation sessions, it is extremely important to maintain an appropriate balance between tension and the softness of relaxation. Try not to be too lax or too tight. Forcing, either to maintain too severe a discipline between sessions or holding the object of meditation too tightly, will obstruct any kind of realization or attainment. At the same time, too much relaxation will be a waste of time.[189]

There are a few exceptions to this rule. One is if your purpose for making a retreat is to seek Divine guidance. In Native American cultures this kind of retreat is called a *vision quest,* and it requires making the utmost effort to clear your mind of its usual egoic chatter. George Sword, a Lakota medicine-man of the last century, explains how it's done in his tradition:

> The usual way to seek a vision is to purify the body in an *Initi* [sweat] by pouring water on hot stones and then go naked, only wrapped in a robe, to the top of a hill, and stay there without speaking to anyone of mankind or eating, or drinking, and thinking continually about the vision he wishes....
>
> He should remain on the place he prepares until he receives either a vision or has a communication. He should stay there awaiting this as long as he is able and can live, if it need be for him to do so.[190]

Obviously, inexperienced seekers should never attempt this kind of extremely rigorous retreat without the supervision of a qualified teacher.

Re-entering the World After Retreat

Depending on how long and/or intense a retreat has been, seekers can encounter difficulties when they return home and have to resume their daily lives. This is perfectly natural, especially for beginners, so if it happens to you don't be alarmed. It's the spiritual equivalent of the culture shock that Western travelers often feel when they return from foreign lands where the pace of life is slower and more relaxed than in their own countries.

One of the things that can make this transition seem harder than necessary is a tendency for returnees to try to hang onto their "retreat minds"—those mental states characterized by exceptional stability and clarity which, as we said earlier, retreats facilitate. Not only is it unrealistic to think you can maintain such states in the midst of a busy work-a-day schedule, it also indicates you have formed an attachment to them, or rather to your memory of them. If this happens, try to practice detachment by letting go of that memory and becoming more aware of your immediate surroundings. Chances are this in itself will bring a little more stability and clarity to whatever mental state you happen to be in at that moment.

Once you have returned home, it is also important to continue with whatever formal meditation or prayer practices you were doing on retreat. For reasons we shall see later, meditation and prayer practices are of little benefit unless you engage in them on a daily basis. If you are lax about this and think retreats can substitute for a regular practice, you are in danger of becoming a retreat junkie—i.e., someone who bounces from one retreat to another solely to experience the spiritual "highs" retreats can produce. In the end, all this will accomplish is to create a new kind of conditioning. Instead of enhancing yourself by pursuing worldly pleasure, you will be doing it by pursuing spiritual ones, but the dynamic is the same. Far from dismantling your delusion of self, you will actually cause it to grow stronger, so take heed.

The Way of Selflessness

Part III: *Entering the Path of Knowledge (Jnana)*

Chapter 10

The Chain of Conditioning

> *It is by descending into the depths of his own self that man wanders through all the dimensions of the world; in his own self he lifts the barriers which separate one sphere from the other; in his own self, finally, he transcends the limits of natural existence and at the end of his way, without, as it were, a single step beyond himself, he discovers that God is "all in all" and there is "nothing but Him".*
>
> — Gershom Scholem (Jew)

In chapter 4 we saw how the delusion of self begins with a simple cognitive error and eventually evolves into a complex pattern of self-centered conditioning that culminates in the Story of I. This is what distracts our attention and keeps us ignorant of our true nature. Much of the path for both jnanis and bhaktas, then, consists of interrupting and dismantling these patterns and this story. The Buddha likened this to a metal-worker purifying silver:

> The wise man, carefully, moment by moment,
> One by one,
> Eliminates the stains of his mind,
> As a silversmith separates the dross from the silver.[191]

Here's how Rumi describes it:

> Purify yourself from the attributes of self, so that you may see your own pure essence![192]

And St. Catherine of Genoa writes,

> Once stripped of all its imperfection, the soul rests in God with no characteristics of its own, since its purification is the stripping away of the lower self in us. Our being is then God.[193]

Now this whole process may seem quite daunting—especially when we consider that, from a relative point of view, our self-centered conditioning has been building up for an entire lifetime, if not (depending on your worldview) many previous lifetimes as well. It might seem, then, that it would take an equally long time to undo. Fortunately, this is not the case. Because the self is, in fact, imaginary, it must be constantly maintained by the activity of the imagination. In other words, we repeatedly create and reify our selves and the world from scratch in every moment of experience. It is only because this recurs with such rapidity that we get the impression the self is some solid entity persisting through time. In the Eastern traditions, they compare this to whirling a torch around in a circle at night. If you whirl it fast enough, it appears that there is a stationary ring of fire hovering in space, when no such 'ring' actually exists. It's simply an optical illusion created by the circular movement of your arm. So, too, with the illusion of self. It arises based on a chain of conditioning which gets triggered every time something appears in consciousness.

If you are a jnani taking the path of knowledge, the first thing you want to do is to try to gain some awareness of the way this chain of conditioning works. Only when you can see in detail how the links are formed in your own experience will you be able to interrupt them and, by so doing, start to dismantle the delusion of self. And the way to accomplish this is to begin practicing self-inquiry by focusing your attention on your own reactions to the various phenomena you perceive.

Starting Self-Inquiry

As an aid to this kind of inquiry, different traditions have provided different descriptions of just how this conditioning operates. Perhaps, the most detailed is the Buddhist teaching known as the *twelve-linked chain of co-dependent arising*. Because this teaching employs technical terms unfamiliar to most non-Buddhists, I have simplified and reduced it to the following more generic nine-link version which hopefully you'll find helpful.

THE NINE-LINK CHAIN OF CONDITIONING

1. Reification of the Self
2. Chronic Restlessness
3. Mental Identification
4. Judging Good, Bad, or Indifferent
5. Desire and Aversion
6. Grasping, Avoiding, Willing
7. Deliberation
8. Deciding
9. Rumination

So, let's go through this chain one link at a time to see how it functions. After we discuss each of the links, take a moment to sit quietly and conduct a little inquiry. See if you can observe what is being talked about in your own immediate experience. If you need to use your imagination to generate some of the phenomena described—a judgment, a desire, a plan, or a memory—feel free to do so.

1. Reification of the Self

The first link in the chain of conditioning is the creation and reification of that First Distinction or Boundary which constitutes our initial experience of being a separate self. Because this distinction is created by the imagination operating at such a primitive level, it is almost impossible to detect in ordinary states of consciousness. Some people, however, can get glimpses of this primordial sense of self during certain extraordinary states.

If, for example, you have ever become lucid just before fully waking up in the morning and found you had no idea of *who* or *where* you were, only *that* you were, then you have tasted the pure I-am-ness which immediately follows the reification of the First Distinction. But even if you have experienced such a state, chances are you can't enter it at will, or make it last for more than a few fleeting seconds.

In future chapters we will be discussing several meditative techniques to help you do just that, but for now don't worry about it. We only mention it here as a reminder that the creation and reification of self does, in fact, occur in every moment of experience, whether you are aware of it or not.

2. Chronic Restlessness

For most seekers self-inquiry really begins here in the second link of the chain. One of the things you may notice when you try to sit still is that your attention becomes quite restless. Now, this restlessness is actually a manifestation of that primordial search for happiness which is born of existential loneliness, longing, and fear. Under normal circumstances our only respite from this search comes when our attention is so fully absorbed in some activity that we actually start to lose our sense of being a separate self. Most of the time, however, our attention remains stuck in this chronically restless mode, always on the lookout for whatever phenomena might appear next in consciousness.

Because we hardly ever try to resist this chronic restlessness of attention, most of the time we experience it only as a vague background current of uneasiness flowing through our lives. When we attempt to make our attention stand still, however, this restlessness comes to the fore and grows in intensity. If this happens to you now, allow yourself to experience it fully. Observe that this restlessness is precisely what keeps your attention moving *away* from the Happiness inherent in your true nature and drives you to seek, instead, some other kind of happiness 'out there' in the external world.

3. Mental Identification

The next thing you might notice is that whenever some phenomenon arises in consciousness, your thinking mind immediately tries to identify and label it: "What sort of object is this? Does it have a name?... Ah, yes, it's a dog barking in the distance." Now this happens very fast and at a sub-conscious level, so we usually don't actually hear our minds asking and answering such questions. Sometimes, however, we do. Going back to an example we used in a previous chapter, if you were to hear a loud crashing sound, and didn't immediately know what it was, you might, indeed, catch your mind trying to label and identify it: "What was that? It sounded like a car crash. Yes, that's what it was! I hope no one was hurt."

The reason it's important to become aware of this process is that in the very act of identifying and labeling phenomena our minds are actually creating the boundaries and distinctions which separate one set of phenomena from another and grouping them together into imaginary 'objects' that seem to exist outside of us. As with the creation of the First Distinction, however, this is an extremely subtle and difficult process to detect. In future chapters we will analyze it more closely, but for now it will suffice if you can simply observe how your mind identifies and labels various phenomena that appear in consciousness.

4. Judging Good, Bad, or Indifferent

Immediately after the thinking mind has identified a particular object, you might notice that another subliminal series of questions arises: "Does this object pose a threat to me? Or is it something that might bring me benefit? Or is it something which won't affect me at all?" In other words, does it fall into one of three categories—*good, bad,* or *indifferent*?

As with identifying and labeling objects, sometimes you can hear this evaluation actually being articulated in your head. Listening to a waiter in a restaurant recite the specials of the day, for instance, you might find your mind commenting on each dish: "Eggplant, Yuk!... Chicken is boring.... Oh! Lamb curry, that sounds good!" Most of the time, however, such judgments are made with little or no verbalization. But whether verbalized or not, it is important to become aware that your mind is, in fact, constantly evaluating everything in terms of these categories, because most of the time whenever you judge anything to be 'good', 'bad', or 'indifferent', you are doing so from a self-centered perspective. In other words, what you're really trying to determine is whether the object in question is good, bad, or indifferent for *me*? Consequently, whenever you act on such judgments in an habitual manner, you are perpetuating your self-centered conditioning.

Recognizing how much such judgments govern our lives is particularly important on a spiritual path, because if we are ever going to free ourselves from the Story of I, we must start to relate to our environment in a radically different way. Instead of thinking only in terms of what is 'good' or 'bad' for *me,* we must start to open our hearts and minds to what is 'good' or 'bad' for everyone concerned. Eventually, we will even come to see that Ultimate Reality transcends such categories altogether.

5. Desire and Aversion

Next, you might notice that, depending on how the mind judges an object, different feelings about it will arise. If the mind finds it to be 'indifferent,' chances are you will experience apathy or boredom, and your attention will move on to the next thing appearing in consciousness. If, however, the mind judges the object to be 'good' or 'bad,' a feeling of desire or aversion will arise, in which case your attention will focus more intensely upon it.

Bear in mind that the 'object' which arouses desire or aversion need not be something material, like a fancy wristwatch you see advertised on the Internet. It may be something quite subtle—the memory of a pleasant experience you once had, or the thought of something unpleasant which you fear might happen in the future. Also, desires and aversions themselves can be gross or subtle. That is, they may be purely biological in nature—like hunger, thirst, and sexual attraction. Or, they may be more psychological—as say, a desire for approval or the fear of being criticized. In any case, what you want to pay particular attention to is how the mind automatically identifies whatever desires and aversions arise as belonging to your self. As we have already seen, this false identification of self with the body-mind's desires and aversions is what gives rise to our attachments and causes our most immediate forms of suffering. For this reason, this fifth link is one of the most pivotal in the whole chain.

6. Grasping, Avoiding, and Willing

Next, you may notice that, whenever a feeling of desire or aversion for any object arises, this will usually be followed by an impulse to either grasp or avoid it. So, for example, if you *do* see a watch on the Internet, you might feel a strong urge to order it on the spot. But, again, the object which arouses such a grasping impulse might be something more subtle. If a pleasant memory arises, you might try to hang onto it by recalling other similar memories. Or, if an unpleasant one arises, you might try to avoid it by thinking of something else instead.

Now the distinction between desire/aversion, on the one hand, and grasping/avoiding, on the other, is not always obvious or clear cut. The essential difference is that, while desires and aversions arise involuntarily, grasping and avoiding always involve some element of volition. Walking down a street, for example, you may smell the aroma of pastry coming from a nearby bakery. If you are a pastry-lover, desire will automatically arise. This is not something you can control through an act of will. Grasping, however, enters with the thought, "I've just got to have a piece of that pastry!" If you decide to obey this impulse, you will head straight for the bakery. But if you are on a diet, you might decide to resist your desire and just keep on walking. So, although the distinction between desire/aversion and grasping/avoiding is subtle, it is nevertheless a crucial one for spiritual practitioners to make, because it is precisely at this juncture that you can, in a relative sense, exercise your self-will. Instead of compulsively grasping after things you desire, or pushing away things you dislike, you can let your desires and aversions arise and pass without acting on them.

This, as we have already said, is what spiritual detachment is all about, and your best opportunities to start practicing it come right here, in the sixth link of the chain of conditioning. The more you sever this link by practicing detachment, the weaker your conditioning will become, and the less suffering you will experience.

7. Deliberation

The next thing you might notice is that whenever a strong impulse arises to grasp or avoid some object that is not within immediate reach, your thinking mind starts planning how best to acquire or evade it. This is where the whole process can get very complicated. Your mind may recall similar situations from the past in order to remember what actions you took then and how they turned out. It may also spin imaginary scenarios about the future in which it tries to envision the best way to proceed. Although logic plays a role in this kind of deliberation, the process is rarely a purely rational one. Feelings of anticipation, impatience, envy, anxiety, and doubt, as well as biases based on your cultural background, will all have an impact on shaping your plans. Eventually, you will want to become aware of as many of these factors as possible. For now, however, the important thing to notice is just how self-centered most of your deliberations are. Even when you do consider the interests of other people, they usually take second place to your own. Coming to realize the extent of your own self-centeredness may be painful, but it is necessary if you are ever going to free yourself from it.

On the more positive side, you should also notice that, whenever you do put the interests of others above your own, it is almost always motivated by a strong feeling of love and compassion. In the future we shall be discussing specific ways to cultivate more love and compassion in your life. In the meantime, however, try to observe, not only what a powerful force love and compassion is for cutting through self-centered conditioning, but also how joyful you feel when you actually do act on behalf of others and not just yourself.

8. Deciding

After a period of deliberation about how to get what you want and avoid what you don't want, your mind will eventually come to a decision about the best way to proceed. As in the sixth link, this decision will seem to involve an act of self-will. The main difference between them is that, having spent some time consciously weighing alternatives, your decision here in the eighth link will appear to be less impulsive and more focused. This puts you in a better position to catch the actual moment in which the decision is made. Why this is important will become clear later when you conduct an inquiry into the true nature of self-will. For now, simply try to observe how the mind seems to suddenly shift gears once it decides on a particular course of action.

9. Rumination

In the ninth link you may notice that your attention often continues to be captivated by thoughts about some event long after it has passed. This can happen regardless of whether the event was pleasant or unpleasant. For example, you may be called upon to give a presentation at work. If the presentation goes well, your mind is apt to keep ruminating about it for days to come in order to savor your success. But even if you botched the presentation, your mind will continue to fixate on the suffering and humiliation you experienced.

Ruminating on memories of the past not only keeps us wrapped up in the Story of I, it also plays a key role in the building up of attachments. Dwelling on pleasurable experiences generates a desire to repeat them in the future, while dwelling on painful ones strengthens our aversion to having them again. In either case, we become attached to habitual ways of behaving, based on our self-centered desires and aversions. This, in turn, serves to re-enforce our conditioned responses to whatever new phenomena appear in consciousness, not only causing the chain to repeat itself, but to grow ever stronger in the process.

Continuing Inquiry

You will almost certainly not be able to observe all nine links in this chain of conditioning—let alone their countless sub-links—the first time you look. If you're like most seekers, you will need to practice quite a bit, both formally and informally, before you even begin to become aware of what is going on. Practicing formally means you set aside some time every day—say, ten or fifteen minutes—just to sit still and observe how you respond mentally and emotionally to whatever arises in your awareness. Don't worry about trying to observe these links in the order we presented them here. All you need to do, especially in the beginning, is identify what is occurring during the time you set aside for practice. Usually, what you will find is either the kind of ruminating that forms the ninth link, or the deliberating that makes up the seventh link, since these are the activities which occupy our minds most of the time.

Practicing informally means that you continue to make this same inquiry every so often during the course of your day, whether you are at work, at home, visiting friends, or having a meal. Get in the habit of occasionally checking in to see what you are thinking about, or if your mind is judging things, or whether desire or aversion has arisen, or an impulse to grasp or avoid something is present. The more frequently you can do this, the more the activities of these links will begin to reveal themselves. This in turn will provide you with increasing opportunities to start interrupting your own self-centered conditioning and, by so doing, weaken the chain.

Chapter 11

Concentration Meditation

> *As if by compulsion the mind runs after the gratification of desires that bring suffering. The mind has become uncontrollable. By the repetition of a divine Name or mantra and by meditation, this illness can be cured.*
>
> — Anandamayi Ma (Hindu)

If you are like most people, the biggest obstacle you encountered trying to conduct the kind of inquiry we described in the last chapter is that your attention kept getting distracted. This is due to the chronic restlessness found in the second link of the chain of conditioning. In the East, they call it having a "monkey mind." Thubten Chodron, a contemporary Buddhist nun, explains in this way:

> Just as monkeys play with an object for a few moments and then leave it in boredom and dissatisfaction to look for another thing to amuse them, so too do we run from thought to thought, emotion to emotion, place to place, trying to find some lasting happiness. Always searching for happiness outside ourselves, we overlook the real cause of happiness: our minds.[194]

But, of course, this is not just a problem for Buddhists. From the very beginning it has afflicted seekers of all traditions. Thus, over two thousand years ago the Svetasvatara Upanishad declared,

> The chariot of the mind is drawn by wild horses, and those wild horses have to be tamed.[195]

And here is what St. Augustine wrote about this problem in the fourth century:

> They strive to comprehend things eternal, whilst their heart fluttereth between the motions of things past and to come, and is still

> unstable. Who shall hold it, and fix it, that it be settled awhile, and awhile catch the glory of that ever-fixed eternity.[196]

If you are a jnani, the way to train your attention to stop this constant running from one thing to another and be "settled awhile," is to take up a formal practice of meditation.

Three Stages of Meditation

Over the centuries, mystics of all traditions have developed a great variety of meditative techniques. But just as a tree with many branches grows from a single trunk, virtually all of these different types of meditation take as their starting point some form of *concentration*. Learning to concentrate your attention constitutes the first stage of practice. So how does this work?

In chapter 6 we defined attention as the power of awareness to focus on various objects. This focus can be broad or narrow, much like a theater light which can be opened up into a floodlight that illuminates an entire stage, or can be closed down into a spotlight directed on just one thing—say, the face of a singer sitting on a stool. When you practice concentration it's like turning your attention into a spotlight which you focus single-pointedly on one object, regardless of whatever else is going on in the background. Here is how the Buddha described it:

> What now is Right Concentration?
> Fixation of the mind to a single object, (lit. One-pointedness);—this is concentration.... Develop your concentration; for he who has concentration understands things according to their reality.[197]

Krishna gives Arjuna virtually the same instruction:

> On this seat, restraining the function
> of his thought and senses,
> he fixes his mind on one point. He will practice
> discipline to purify himself.[198]

Likewise, the seventeenth-century Christian mystic Jacob Boehme writes,

> Cease but from thine own activity, steadfastly fixing thine Eye upon *one Point*.... For this end, gather in all thy thoughts, and by faith press into the Centre.[199]

Overcoming chronic restlessness through the practice of concentration leads to the second stage of meditation, *stabilization*. Here, attention becomes very stable and very clear. Different traditions have different names for this state—"serenity," "sobriety," "collectedness," etc. The Sanskrit term is *shamatha*, which is usually translated as "tranquility" or "calm-abiding." When calm-abiding is attained, the mind rests in a space of undistracted awareness.

Phenomena still arise in Consciousness, but attention no longer tries to follow after them or give them names. As a result, the third link in the chain of conditioning—identifying and labeling—is temporarily broken.

The last stage of meditation is *contemplation*. Once attention has been stabilized, it can be used to contemplate all sorts of phenomena—inner or outer, subtle or gross—unmediated by thought. As we saw in chapter 5, the ability to experience phenomena nakedly, without mental elaboration is what allows a seeker to gain direct, non-conceptual insights into their true nature. Because there are so many kinds of phenomena, and so many ways to contemplate them, at this juncture meditation starts to branch out into that vast array of practices and sub-practices that we find in the various traditions.

Some of these practices, like the Hindu *raja-yoga*, involve concentrating on increasingly subtle objects which leads the meditator into deeper and deeper states of absorption or *samadhi*. Other meditation practices, such as the Buddhist *vipassana*, bring naked attention or "mindfulness" to bear on the phenomena of everyday life. Still others combine contemplation with analytic inquiry to help deconstruct the imaginary worlds our thinking minds create. There are also practices for cultivating compassion, liberating emotions, and fostering lucidity during sleep—all of which we will be discussing in the chapters ahead. None of these practices, however, can be properly performed unless you have first developed a stable, undistracted mind through concentration.

Choosing a Meditation Object

In the Hindu and Buddhist traditions a common object to begin concentrating on is a *mantra*—-i.e., a short phrase such as "Om Namah Shivaya"—or even more simply, a Divine Name, like "Hare Krishna" or "Amitabha Buddha." In fact, the use of a short prayer or name as an object for developing concentration is found in virtually all traditions and is perhaps the most universal. Other objects, however, have also been employed. Some traditions recommend concentrating on specific points of the body, such as the tip of one's nose. Others use subtle energy centers located along the spine called *chakras*. Eastern Orthodox Christians often meditate on icons, while Kabbalists have used the letters of the Hebrew alphabet. Candles, crystals, and even ordinary rocks can also serve as meditation objects. So, the question arises, which one is best?

From an objective point of view, no one object is better than another. The only important thing is that you are able to concentrate on it. However, subjective factors can certainly play a significant role in determining what object is right for you. If you are a Christian, for instance, the name "Jesus" would be an appropriate choice, whereas "Krishna" would probably not be. Sometimes, it boils down to a completely personal idiosyncrasy. It is said of the great Buddhist master, Shantideva, that he had a hard time finding something he could get his mind to focus on, until finally he started meditating on the horn of a yak.

An object that seems to work best for many modern seekers is the breath. One reason for this is that the breath doesn't carry any theological baggage.

This can be especially important for people who have had negative experiences of religion while growing up. If that is true of you, trying to focus on a mantra or a Divine Name might raise a lot of doubts. You might think, "I don't really believe in Jesus or Krishna, so why am I repeating this name over and over?" Most people, however, have no doubt that they breathe. Consequently, using the breath as an object for concentration does not present this kind of problem for them.

Another reason to use the breath is convenience. Because your breath is always with you, you can meditate on it anytime, anywhere. But if you are using something like a candle, you are likely to run into situations where trying to meditate will be awkward. For example, you might show up at your dentist's office and be told by the receptionist, "Oh, I'm sorry, Dr. Harris is running a little late this morning. Please have a seat and we'll call you." Now to a dedicated meditator this represents a wonderful opportunity for practice. But if you have to dig a candle out of your pocket, set it up on a table, and stare at it, the rest of the people in the waiting room might think you are a little weird. If, however, you use your breath to concentrate on, you will be a lot less conspicuous. You can just sit there, watching your inhalations and exhalations, and no one will know the difference.

Establishing a Disciplined Practice

After you have chosen your meditation object, the next thing you need to do is establish and maintain a regimen of practice. This means making a commitment to doing formal meditation at least once a day. If you can meditate two or even three times a day, all the better! If you want to take one day a week off, that's okay. Some meditators find this keeps their practice fresh. But be consistent. Try to take the same day off every week, so that the discipline of your practice doesn't fall prey to momentary whims which can lead to its complete breakdown.

The importance of maintaining a disciplined practice cannot be over emphasized. This is like working out at a gym in order to get your body in shape. It won't do much good to just run down there every once in while and do a few push-ups. To really tone up your muscles, and keep them that way, you need to exercise on a regular basis. Exactly the same thing applies when it comes to training your attention to concentrate on a single object.

One way to maintain a disciplined practice is to choose a specific time for your sessions—either in the morning or evening—and stick to it. Another technique is to fit your meditation sessions into your regular schedule. For example, if your morning routine is to wake up, use the bathroom, eat breakfast, and then shower, you might fit a meditation session in between using the bathroom and eating breakfast. The advantage of this way of scheduling your practice is that it won't be tied to the clock, so even if you sleep in on the weekends, you still won't miss your morning session.

It's a good idea to use an alarm clock or timer to let you know when a particular session is over. This will help prevent your attention from being distracted by thoughts about how long you have to go. If you do use an alarm clock or timer, place it somewhere out of sight so that you won't be tempted to glance at it while you are meditating.

Eventually, you will want to meditate from twenty to thirty or more minutes per session, but you can start with five or ten minutes and work up to this. It is much better to begin with a length of time you feel comfortable with than to bite off more than you can chew and become discouraged. Most people find the more they practice, the easier meditation becomes.

What follows are some step-by-step instructions to get you started in a meditation practice. Although they are based on the assumption that you are using the breath as your object of concentration, most will apply no matter what object you have chosen.

Instructions for Concentration Meditation

STEP ONE: *Finding the Right Posture*

The first thing to do is to get into a comfortable posture. In most Eastern traditions the *full-lotus* position is considered the best. To get into the full-lotus, sit on a firm cushion placed on the floor or on a mat. Cross your legs, pulling your left foot up onto your right thigh and your right foot up onto your left thigh.

If this is too difficult you can try sitting in the *semi-lotus* position. This is the same as the full-lotus except that you only pull one foot up onto your thigh. At first, these positions may feel awkward or even painful. But if you take the time to get used to them, in the long run they turn out to be very comfortable and stable postures. If, however, you are older, or have leg or back problems, sitting in a lotus position may not be possible for you. Don't worry about it. For the vast majority of meditation practices sitting on a chair will do just fine.

Whether you use a cushion or chair, it is important to sit upright. Keep your back and shoulders straight, but then let your whole body relax, like a coat draped on a coat-hanger. Also make sure the muscles in your diaphragm are relaxed so that your breath can flow naturally and easily all the way down into your lower abdomen. Next, either fold your hands in your lap or place them on your knees where they won't fidget. You should also rest your tongue lightly against the roof of your mouth. This will help prevent the accumulation of excess saliva.

It's good to experiment a little in order to find what works best for you, but once you have settled on a particular posture, *always sit in exactly the same position*. The idea is to keep your body as still as possible so that it doesn't distract your attention. A restless body reflects a restless mind, and vice versa.

STEP TWO: *Keep Your Eyes Open*

For this kind of meditation it is important to keep your eyes open. The reason for this is that later on you will want to bring the undistracted awareness you cultivate in your formal practice to bear on all the other activities of your life—walking, eating, cleaning, working, etc. It is much easier to learn to meditate with your eyes open than to learn to do all these things with your eyes closed.

Relax your eyelids and let your gaze fall somewhere on the ground a yard or two in front of you, but don't stare at anything in particular. Once your gaze is set, don't let your eyes wander around looking at various objects. As with the rest of your body, the point is to keep them as still as possible.

STEP THREE: *Set Your Intention*

Before you actually start meditating, it's a good idea to set your intention, not only to engage in the practice itself but also to use whatever insights you gain for the service of others. At the Center for Sacred Sciences many practitioners recite the following dedication:

> *Letting go of all worldly sorrow and joy,*
> *I gladly undertake this practice for*
> *the benefit of all beings.*

STEP FOUR: *Watching Your Breath*

The basic instructions for a concentration practice are very simple. First, find your meditation object—in this case your breath—then concentrate your attention on it. Closely observe how the breath enters the body with each inhalation, how it turns around when the lungs are full, how it leaves the body with each exhalation, and how it turns around again for the next inhalation when the lungs are empty.

Do not try to control the rhythm of your breath. Let it flow naturally, speeding up or slowing down of its own accord. If pauses develop between your inhalations and exhalations, that's fine. Simply keep your attention in the space of the pause until the next inhalation or exhalation occurs.

For the first couple of weeks, you may want to count each exhalation. When you get to ten, stop and start over. Counting your exhalations can help you become aware whenever your attention wanders, because, if you become absorbed in thinking about something, you will lose track of the count. When you notice that this has happened, don't try to remember where you left off. Just start counting over again at one. You might also find yourself counting, "thirteen, fourteen, fifteen." This also happens because your attention has been distracted. Simply place your attention back on your breath and, again, start counting from one.

Counting is a technique to help you get the feel of what it means to focus attention on your breath without being distracted, but don't get attached to it. Once you have learned what counting has to teach you, drop it and just watch your breath with naked awareness.

STEP FIVE: *Dealing with Distractions*

When you find you have been distracted—whether by sights, sounds, smells, but especially by your own thoughts—first, notice that this has happened. Second, gently but firmly return your attention to your breath. No matter how many times you get distracted, keep repeating this process of noticing you have been distracted and then gently but firmly bringing your attention back to your breath.

STEP SIX: *Following Instructions*

One of the biggest problems beginning meditators have is that they read more into the instructions than is actually there. For example, there is nothing in these instructions about getting rid of thoughts, so don't be upset when they continue to arise. The guiding rule here is to practice detachment—i.e., neither to grasp at thoughts, nor try to push them away. Zen master Hui-Neng explains it like this:

> People under delusion… define [meditation] as, "sitting quietly and continuously without letting any idea arise in the mind." Such an interpretation would class us with inanimate objects; it is a stumbling-block to the right Path and the Path should be kept open. How can we block the Path? By attachment to any definite thought; if we free our minds from attachments, the Path will be clear, otherwise we are in bondage.[200]

This includes thoughts about your practice, which can be particularly seductive. You may be sitting there thinking, "Oh, this a wonderful meditation. Yes, the mind is really getting calm. Any minute now I am going to get Enlightened." If this is what is going on, your attention is still wrapped up in thought. So don't be fooled! As one thought follows another, just ignore them and keep watching your breath.

There is also nothing in these instructions that says meditation should produce altered states of consciousness, or any other extraordinary phenomena—at least not at this early stage. Some beginners start to see bright colors, or hear ethereal sounds, or have beautiful visions right off the bat. If this happens to you, take Gen Lamrimpa's advice:

> It is virtually certain that as the śamatha practice develops, certain types of visions or images will appear to the mind. When they do arise, whether they appear to be helpful or harmful, do not identify with them. Do not become engrossed with them. Do not elaborate on them. If they appear to be good visions, don't think, "Oh! This is tremendously auspicious." If they appear to be negative images, do not be depressed. Simply let them be, and maintain the object of your awareness.[201]

Last but not least, there is nothing in these instructions that says, if you can't keep your attention concentrated on your breath for the entire session, you are not meditating properly. On the contrary, you are *supposed* to get distracted from time to time. Half the purpose of this meditation is to become familiar with the way your deluded mind works. This includes becoming aware of how easily it gets distracted by thoughts and how powerful those thoughts can be. So whenever you recognize that you have been distracted, don't get frustrated. Instead, be grateful, because the more distractions you notice, the more awareness you are developing.

Later, as you gain some mental stability through continued practice, your thoughts will naturally begin to settle down on their own. But you cannot force this to happen by an act of will. It's like trying to get a glass of muddy water to clear up. If you try to do this by stirring the water, it will just get muddier. However, if you put the glass down on a table, and leave it alone for a while, the mud will settle to the bottom and the water will clear by itself. It is the same with meditation. If you don't grasp at thoughts, or try to push them away, they will eventually subside by themselves.

STEP SEVEN: *Avoiding Gross Laxity and Excitement*

In the beginning, your meditation will tend towards one of two defective states, *gross excitement* or *gross laxity*. Gross excitement occurs when your attention gets so absorbed in a train of thought that you completely forget your meditation object. When you fall into gross laxity you also lose track of your meditation object, but the cause is different. Instead of being captivated by obsessive thoughts, you drift into a trance-like stupor.

In order to detect states of gross excitement and gross laxity, you need to use *introspection*. That is, every so often you direct a part of your attention to check in and see how your meditation is going. (Be careful not to do this too often or introspection itself will become a distraction.) If you discover you have fallen into gross laxity, it means you need to make a greater effort to keep your attention focused on your meditation object. If you have fallen into gross excitement, your tendency will probably be to do the same, but this would be a mistake. Gross excitement actually comes from making *too much* effort. What you need to do, then, is just the opposite—relax your effort to focus your attention on your meditation object. Don't surrender it completely, however, or you will fall into laxity.

In the Eastern traditions, they compare this balancing of the effort you need for meditation to tuning a guitar string. If you tighten the string too much, the note will be sharp. If you loosen the string too much, the note will be flat. Likewise, in meditation the goal is to find the optimum point between making too much effort and too little effort. This is something you have to discover for yourself through trial and error.

STEP EIGHT: *Bowing*

After your formal session is over, you should make a small bow in gratitude to all those meditators who have come before you and who developed these practices—sometimes at great cost to themselves—from which you are now benefitting. Then, arise slowly and, without clinging to any particular state, try to carry some minimal level of undistracted awareness into the other activities of your day.

Overcoming Obstacles

Aside from monkey mind, which concentration practice is specifically designed to remedy, there are a number of other obstacles beginning meditators frequently encounter. Here are a few of the most common, along with some pointers on how to overcome them.

1. *Sleepiness*

   This is a very common obstacle, especially when starting a practice. When you intentionally ignore the thinking mind, it often interprets this to mean it is time to go to sleep. Most of the things you can do to address this problem are pretty obvious.

   First, make sure you are getting enough actual sleep at night. If the room you meditate in is stuffy, turn down the heat, or open a window. It even helps to splash cold water on your face just before beginning your session. If you start feeling drowsy in the middle of a session, lift your gaze slightly, so that you are looking straight ahead instead of at a downward angle. Raising your eyes this way often helps to perk up your mind. Most meditators, however, find that the real solution to sleepiness is simply to keep on practicing. As the mind begins to learn that sitting down to meditate is not an invitation to fall asleep, drowsiness tends to dissolve of its own accord.

2. *Kriyas*

   This is a technical term for those involuntary bodily movements, muscles spasms, and uncontrollable trembling or jerking that sometimes manifest as a meditation practice deepens.

   Although *kriya* is a Sanskrit word, the phenomena it describes are known to meditators worldwide. Different traditions have different explanations for *why* these phenomena occur. Christians, for instance, attribute it to the operation of the Holy Spirit. Kabbalists take it to herald an influx of divine power. Hindus consider the manifestation of kriyas to be a sign of inward purification. Whatever the merits of these traditional explanations, unless you have an unusual medical condition (such as epilepsy), the appearance of kriyas is rarely anything to worry about. If you have any doubts, by all means check with a doctor. The advice given in most traditions for dealing with kriyas is simply to ignore them and continue with your meditation. Like sleepiness, kriyas generally constitute a phase of practice which passes on its own.

3. *Lack of motivation*

   Some people are enthusiastic about the idea of meditation, but when it comes to actually sitting down to practice, their motivation seems to evaporate. This is a tricky problem, because, ultimately, the motivation to take up any spiritual practice must come from your own heart. Teachers may inspire you, books may intrigue you, and your own mind may concoct a host of reasons for why you should be meditating: It will make me a better person, reduce my suffering, or please my spouse. But no matter what your mind says, if your heart does not consent, none of this will help. In fact, if you push yourself to engage in any practice before your heart is ready, you run the risk of generating an aversion to it that may be hard to overcome in the future. So, if your heart says "no" to meditation, it is better to skip it and go on to other practices, like keeping precepts. Later, you may have a change of heart and be moved to try again.

On the other hand, if your heart really does yearn to practice, but your mind keeps thinking up reasons not to, that's a different story. Many seekers go through such periods of inner conflict or *spiritual warfare*, as it is often called. We shall take up this problem in more detail in a future chapter, but, in the meantime, here are a couple of immediate things you can do which might help.

First, before you begin to meditate, spend a few minutes reading a spiritual book—not necessarily something intellectually challenging, like a work of mystical philosophy (unless, of course, you find that inspiring), but something that speaks to your heart—perhaps a collection of spiritual poems, aphorisms or short teaching stories. Next, reflect on why you decided to walk this path in the first place. This might include asking yourself some questions: How am I spending my life? Am I wasting it in meaningless pursuits? Or am I taking full advantage of this precious opportunity I have as a human being to discover my true nature?

4. *Lack of confidence*

Some seekers have the necessary motivation but become discouraged when they discover just how difficult it is to keep their attention focused on their breath even for a few seconds. Usually, such people believe they are the only ones who have this problem and so feel they are especially unsuited for practice. The truth, of course, is that the vast majority of meditators experience exactly the same thing. The difference is that successful meditators persist, and so build up confidence, while those who are easily discouraged quit before this has a chance to happen.

If you fall into the latter category, then, instead of forcing yourself to engage in formal meditation right away, begin by seeing if you can concentrate without distraction on just three consecutive breaths. Do this informally every so often during the day. Then, when you are able to concentrate on three breaths without distraction, try four, and when you can concentrate on four, try five, then six, seven, and so on. If you keep going like this, your confidence will gradually increase until the time comes when you are ready to begin practicing in a more formal way.

Refining Your Practice

After you have become somewhat adept at meditating on the inhalations and exhalations of your breath, you can begin to sharpen your concentration even more. The way to do this is to focus on one specific point where the breath passes through your body. Many meditators find the easiest place to do this is their nostrils.

Start your session by concentration on your full breath. When your mind has begun to settle down, gently focus your attention on the sensations you experience inside your nostrils as your inhalations and exhalations pass through them. Continue concentrating on these sensations until the end of your session.

If you find it difficult to focus on the sensations in your nostrils, you can try concentrating either on the rising and falling of your abdomen, or on the sensations in the area of your heart where the breath passes by it. Again, it is good to experiment for a while to see which works best for you, but once you decide on a particular spot, stay with that.

You should also continue using introspection (though less frequently as your practice progresses) in order to detect *subtle excitement* and *subtle laxity*. The difference between gross and subtle excitement is that, whereas with gross excitement, all of your attention is absorbed in chains of thought, with subtle excitement your attention is divided. Part of it remains focused on your breath, while the other part is attending to those stories that thoughts produce. When you notice you have fallen into subtle excitement, the antidote is to focus the *whole* of your attention back on your breath, and then relax your effort slightly. When your whole attention rides easily on your breath, despite the presence of thoughts in the background, then you are well on your way to calm-abiding.

Similarly, the difference between gross and subtle laxity is that with gross laxity your attention is completely diffused in a state of stupor, while with subtle laxity part of it stays with your breath. This kind of subtle laxity is particularly dangerous, because it can fool you into thinking you have attained calm-abiding when you have not. In a state of subtle laxity thoughts no longer distract you, and everything feels vaguely pleasant and peaceful. But, unlike a state of true calm-abiding, there is no clarity. And while a state of subtle laxity may help reduce stress or lower your blood pressure, spiritually speaking it is worthless. This is because without clarity there is no opportunity to gain direct insights. So be on guard! When you find you have fallen into subtle laxity, increase your effort to concentrate on your breath by observing it more closely and in greater detail. Seekers who fail to correct subtle laxity may spend years wallowing in this defective state and never make any real progress.

Signs of Approaching Calm-Abiding

As your practice matures, and your concentration deepens, you may start to experience a series of signs that indicate you are approaching a state of calm-abiding. First, you may experience a kind of heaviness or fatigue in your body, similar to the sensation you have when you are just about to fall asleep. This is often accompanied by a feeling that you are entering a dark tunnel. In fact, your visual field may actually contract and go momentarily blank.

Second, you may become extremely sensitive to any changes in the environment, especially sounds. Even little ones, like the creak of a floor board or a refrigerator turning on, will startle you and cause you to jump.

Next, your breathing may get shallower with extended pauses opening up between your inhalations and exhalations. This may be accompanied by a sensation of weightlessness, almost as if you were levitating.

You may also start to lose awareness of time, so that a half-hour session seems to fly by in five minutes.

As your practice progresses further, you will also begin to experience moments of exceptional mental brightness. It will be as though you had been walking through a forest under a thick canopy of leaves, when suddenly you come to an area where the branches are thinner, and the sun starts to flash through in bursts of illumination.

Finally, you will begin to experience a very specific kind of bliss. It begins with a feeling of joy, followed by a physical sensation at the crown of the head—as if someone were pouring warm oil over your skull—and then continues to spread throughout your entire body, permeating every cell.

As this experience of bodily bliss deepens, it will naturally give rise to more waves of mental and emotional bliss. Be careful, however, not to let such feelings distract you. True calm-abiding is attained only *after* this bliss has subsided, somewhat the way the flames of a charcoal fire eventually settle down to be replaced by an intense but steady radiance.

Not everyone will experience all these signs of approaching calm-abiding, but most meditators will experience at least some of them. The important thing to remember is that, if and when they do manifest, they indicate your meditation is going *just right*. So, don't let these experiences distract your attention, or seduce you into altering your practice. Any effort to speed things up at this point will only serve to throw you off course. "Steady as she goes," should be your motto. Just keep your attention focused on your breath, without trying to grasp or push anything away. Surrender to your practice and let *it* carry you forward at its own pace.

Attaining Calm-Abiding

The way to tell when calm-abiding has been fully attained is this: There's no excitement in the mind. All effort is spontaneously surrendered and attention rests calmly on its object in a space of undistracted awareness. As with laxity, this feels very peaceful and pleasant. But, unlike laxity, in calm-abiding there is also great clarity—a kind of super-awareness. Here's how contemporary Tibetan master Lati Rinbochay describes it:

> The mind is like a mountain, able to abide firmly and steadily on the object.... The meditator has great clarity and feels as though he or she could count the particles in a wall.[202]

Being able to attain a state of calm-abiding quickly and easily in a single session is the goal of concentration meditation. How long this takes will vary greatly from one practitioner to another. Most meditators find that their practice unfolds unevenly in a two-steps-forward, one-step-backward pattern. This is particularly true if you are a householder, shouldering all the responsibilities that come with living in the world. Whenever there is unusual tension or turmoil in your outer life, you are bound to experience more mental distraction. This is perfectly normal, so don't abandon your practice because of it. In fact, as you will learn in a later chapter, there is no such thing as a 'bad' meditation. This is because even distracting thoughts themselves can be used to enrich your meditation. In the meantime, maintain your discipline. Whether your individual sessions seem good or bad, the long-range effect of daily practice is to create greater and greater awareness, which you will begin to experience even in your everyday life. This is why, for really advanced meditators it is said there is no difference between life and meditation, or meditation and life. The two become one.

CHAPTER 12

Choiceless Awareness Meditation

People are tied down by a sense-object when they cover it with unreal imaginations; likewise they are liberated from it when they see it as it really is.... Hence the sense object itself is not the decisive cause of either bondage or emancipation. It is the presence or absence of imaginations which determine whether attachment takes place or not.

— Ashvaghosa (Buddhist)

Once you have been able to at least temporarily subdue your chronic restlessness through practicing concentration, you can begin to use your newly stabilized attention to contemplate the true nature of various phenomena. First, however, you must learn to distinguish your naked experiences from the thoughts which your imagination superimposes upon them. In other words, you must interrupt that mental identification which takes place in the third link of the chain of conditioning.

One way to do this is to engage in a kind of meditation called *choiceless awareness* (or *vipassana,* to use the Sanskrit term). So what is choiceless awareness? Even though we talk about concentration and choiceless awareness as though they were two different kinds of meditation, choiceless awareness actually grows out of concentration quite naturally. Through the practice of concentration you learned to enter a state of calm-abiding by choosing to focus on a single object. In choiceless awareness you maintain this state of clear undistracted awareness, but without choosing to focus on any particular object.

Going back to our theater light analogy, this is like turning a spotlight into a floodlight. Just as a floodlight widens out to illuminate an entire stage and all the actors moving around on it, without itself moving, so in choiceless awareness attention opens up to take in all the phenomena arising and passing in consciousness, without itself moving towards any particular one.

A common way to describe choiceless awareness is to compare it to a mirror. A mirror reflects whatever is placed before it without trying to name it, grasp it, or push it away. So, too, if you train in choiceless awareness, you can perceive all the phenomena arising in consciousness without having to name them, grasp them, or push them away. Buddhists call this ability to see things nakedly *mindfulness*. Here's how contemporary Buddhist teacher Joseph Goldstein explains it:

> Mindfulness is the quality and power of mind that is aware of what's happening—without judgment and without interference. It is like a mirror that simply reflects whatever comes before it.[203]

And you will find this same mirror analogy used by mystics of other traditions as well. Listen, for instance, to Lalleshwari:

> Just as a face is perfectly reflected
> only in a clean mirror,
> so the light of Shiva is reflected
> only in a taintless mind.[204]

Similarly, Chuang Tzu says it this way:

> The Perfect Man uses his mind like a mirror—going after nothing, welcoming nothing, responding but not storing.[205]

The Six Categories of Phenomena

So how do you actually arrive at this kind of mental purity? Because the mind has been so thoroughly conditioned to label phenomena, most meditators find it easier to start with an intermediate step. This is to train the mind to identify phenomena according to a much simpler set of categories than the highly complex ones built into our everyday languages.

To do this, we divide the total field of consciousness-awareness into six subfields, corresponding to our five sense faculties, plus our mental faculty. We can then label and identify each phenomenon according to the field in which it appears, while refraining from making any further conceptual elaborations. Thus, any phenomenon appearing in the visual field, we label "sight"; any phenomenon appearing in the auditory field, we label "sound"; any phenomenon appearing in the field of bodily sensations, we label "bodily sensation"; any phenomenon appearing in the taste field, we label "taste"; any phenomenon appearing in the smell field, we label "smell"; and any phenomenon appearing in the mental field—such as thoughts, ideas, images, memories, fantasies, etc.—we label "thought."

By identifying phenomena in this manner, we can let the thinking mind perform its normal labeling function, while at the same time we interrupt its linguistic habit of grouping phenomena together into seemingly permanent objects. So, for example, if you were doing choiceless awareness right now, instead of taking for granted that you are holding a *book* in your hands, you would carefully note and label all the individual phenomena which constitute your experience of 'book'—i.e., the sights appearing in the visual field, the tactile sensations appearing in the bodily sensation field, the sound of rustling pages appearing in the auditory field, and so on. If, then, your mind produced the thought 'book,' you would note that *that*, too, was just another phenomenon—i.e., a thought phenomenon appearing in the mental field. So now that you have a general idea of what the practice of choiceless awareness entails, here are some specific instructions to get you started.

Instructions for Choiceless Awareness Meditation

STEP ONE: *Start with Concentration*

Sit in your normal meditation posture. Set your intention. Keep your eyes open. Concentrate your attention on your breath and, whenever you are distracted by any other phenomenon, gently but firmly return your attention to your breath. Practice concentrating in this way until your mind has become calm, clear, and stable.

STEP TWO: *Letting Go of Your Object*

After your mind has become calm, clear, and stable, let your attention expand out until it fills the entire field of bodily sensations—what you would normally call your 'body'.

STEP THREE: *Contemplating Bodily Sensation Phenomena*

Once your attention has filled the field of bodily sensations, begin to label whatever phenomena you experience there as "bodily sensation." If your thinking mind insists on identifying a particular sensation with a word like "itch," "tension," or "pain," recognize that these words are just mental phenomena, appearing in the mental field, and label them "thought."

If you get distracted by phenomena appearing in other fields of awareness—especially trains of thought—return your attention to your breath. Practice concentration until your mind again becomes calm, clear, and stable, then allow your attention to expand back into the bodily sensation field.

STEP FOUR: *Contemplating Sound Phenomena*

After you have contemplated phenomena arising in the bodily sensation field for a while, let your attention expand further to include the auditory field. Begin labeling whatever phenomena appear there as "sound." Do not try to identify what kind of sounds they are—i.e., a car horn, a dog barking, a bird call, etc. If your thinking mind insists on naming a particular sound, label that as "thought," and keep your attention in the auditory field. If it seems that no sounds are arising, do not allow your attention to roam around looking for one. Keep it still and steady, like an open microphone. Eventually sounds will appear.

If phenomena in other fields distract you, bring your attention back to the auditory field. If you become totally distracted, focus on your breath until your mind becomes calm, clear, and stable once more. Then, drop the breath and allow your attention to expand back into the auditory field.

STEP FIVE: *Contemplating Visual Phenomena*

After you have contemplated phenomena in the auditory field, let your attention expand to include the visual field and label whatever phenomena appear there as "sight." If you are sitting on a rug or other kind of textured surface, you may start to see faces appearing and disappearing in the rug's pattern. Observing this, your thinking mind is apt to try to convince you that you are not *really* seeing these things—that they are mere apparitions or hallucinations. But such judgments themselves are just thoughts arising in the mental field. Label them "thought" and continue labeling whatever appears in the visual field as "sight."

STEP SIX: *Contemplating Smell and Taste Phenomena*

Ordinarily, tastes and smells arise so infrequently during sitting meditation that it is not worth making a special effort to contemplate the fields in which they appear. If, however, a taste or smell does arise any time during your session, simply label it "taste" or "smell," accordingly.

STEP SEVEN: *Contemplating Mental Phenomena*

After you have contemplated phenomena in the five sensory fields, let your attention expand to include the mental field and label whatever thoughts, images, memories, or fantasies arise there as "thought."

Most meditators find mental phenomena the hardest of all to contemplate, because attention keeps getting caught up in the stories they create. This is why it is important to attain proficiency in concentration meditation before you begin practicing choiceless awareness. Once you do take up choiceless awareness, however, you need to change your attitude towards thoughts. In concentration practice the idea is to ignore your thoughts and so gain some detachment from them. But now, in steps seven and eight of choiceless awareness, the goal is not to *ignore* thoughts, but to actually *observe* them while still maintaining your detachment—something which is a bit more difficult.

One way to prevent your attention from becoming absorbed in trains of thoughts is to pick some word like "cut!" and use it to chop off any thoughts that start to carry you away. Another technique is to purposely generate very vivid thoughts and look directly at them. This usually makes each thought dissolve before it can give birth to a sequence of similar thoughts. The real trick, however, is simply to recognize that, regardless of their content, thoughts are always just thoughts created by the mind.

This is a little like walking through an art gallery. Normally, you would let yourself become engrossed in the subject matter of each of the paintings on display. You might marvel at how life-like a Renaissance portrait seems, or be awed by the colors of an impressionist landscape. You might find a surrealist's dream-scene haunting, or be fascinated by a purely abstract composition. But now suppose you walk through that same gallery, paying attention, not to what the paintings depict, but to the bare fact that all of them are actually just pieces of canvas coated with different colored pigments. Well, this is what you are trying to do when you contemplate phenomena arising in the mental field of awareness. Regardless of whether your thoughts are positive or negative, true or false, silly or profound, what you want to notice is that fundamentally they are all just thoughts and nothing more.

By observing thoughts in this detached way, you can start to gain direct insights into their true nature. This is crucial because, as we have already said, it is the reification of our thoughts which forms the basis for the delusion that we live in a world of multiple objects. So despite the difficulties, it is well worth making an extra effort to become aware of the fact that all the phenomena arising and passing in the mental field are literally imaginary.

STEP EIGHT: *Contemplating Phenomena in the Total Field of Consciousness-Awareness*

Last but not least, allow your attention to expand evenly and steadily throughout the total field of consciousness-awareness. Continue to label whatever phenomena arise according to their designated fields, but do not try to focus on any one field in particular. Do, however, stay mindful of what you are about. You are trying to distinguish between your naked experience of phenomena and the names and labels your thinking mind slaps on them.

In the beginning it is a good idea to spend a week or so contemplating phenomena that arise in each of the fields before trying to observe them altogether in one session. So, for example, in the first week you might focus your attention on the bodily sensation field; in the second on the auditory field; in the third week on the visual; and in the fourth week on the mental field. Then, only in the fifth week would you combine all these contemplations into a single session, letting your attention expand into and incorporate each of the fields in succession until, finally, it fills the total field of consciousness-awareness.

Refining Your Practice

One of the biggest problems meditators practicing choiceless awareness face is that so many phenomena arise and pass in consciousness at the same time, it is easy to feel overwhelmed. There just seems to be too much to keep track of. The key is to keep your attention relaxed, yet alert. Do not try to label every phenomenon that comes and goes, only the ones that present themselves most prominently in awareness. Remember that it is better to observe a few phenomena in each field clearly and vividly than to try to observe them all in a vague or hurried manner. As with concentration practice, it's a question of finding just the right balance between making too much effort and not enough.

You will also find that, as your choiceless awareness practice progresses, it will no longer be necessary to mentally label each phenomenon according to its field. You will be able to observe all phenomena nakedly, just as they are, without having to identify or name them in any way. When you reach this point in your meditation, you may start to glimpse what the Buddhists call the *suchness* of things. Here is how the *Lankavatara Sutra* describes it:

> When appearances and names are put away and all discrimination ceases, that which remains is the true and essential nature of things and, as nothing can be predicated as to the nature of essence, it is called the "Suchness" of Reality.[206]

Finally, when you are able to engage in choiceless awareness for long periods without any distraction, you may become aware that holding your attention steady requires a subtle but distinct mental effort. If you notice you are making this effort, it means you are ready to surrender it. Doing so will bring you into a state of *spacious-awareness*. In spacious-awareness your attention is allowed to spontaneously move toward phenomena, but still without any attempt to name, grasp, or push them away.

One result of letting attention roam freely is that you might begin to perceive not just the nakedness of phenomena arising and passing, but also the space of awareness in which all this happens. Becoming aware of this dimension of experience is important and valuable, but do not fixate on it and start to "space out"—i.e., fall into a trance and lose your clarity. As we shall see in coming chapters, there is much more work to be done and many more insights to be attained, so stay alert!

Combining Concentration and Choiceless Awareness

As we said in the beginning of this chapter, choiceless awareness grows out of concentration, but it should not replace it. By maintaining a concentration practice along with your choiceless awareness practice, you will continue to strengthen your powers of stability and clarity. This, in turn, will heighten your ability to contemplate phenomena nakedly when you engage in choiceless awareness. So, if you are doing two meditation sessions a day, you might want to practice choiceless awareness in the morning and concentration in the evening. If you can only meditate once a day, try alternating between these practices on successive days. If neither of these approaches works for you, make sure you spend at least the first half of every meditative session practicing concentration before you allow your attention to start expanding into choiceless awareness.

Chapter 13

Contemplating Impermanence

> *The world's forms are foam upon the Sea. If you are a man of purity, pass beyond the foam!*
>
> — Rumi (Muslim)

As we said in chapter 6, becoming an external renunciant is not essential for walking a spiritual path. What is essential, however, is to become an *internal* renunciant—i.e., someone who has renounced all hope of finding happiness in worldly pursuits. Here is how Anandamayi Ma describes it:

> Everything in this world is transitory. So also worldly happiness: it comes and the next moment it is gone. If permanent, abiding happiness is to be found, That which is eternal will have to be realized.[207]

For jnanis the most effective way to attain this inner renunciation is by cultivating insights into impermanence. When you can see for yourself that trying to grasp impermanent things leads to suffering, detachment from them naturally follows. This is why mystics of all traditions are constantly drawing our attention to the impermanent nature of everything in this world. Thus, the eleventh-century Tibetan nun Nangsa Obum writes,

> Life is like the setting sun,
> It looks strong and beautiful,
> But before you know it, it is gone....
> Life is like people walking in the streets,
> For a moment we see them and then in a moment they are gone....
> Life is like a beautiful face,
> It is with us when we are young,
> But when we get old it will become ugly....
> If I can find a good guru to teach me about impermanence,
> Even if you friends do not want to practice Dharma,
> I am going.[208]

Chuang Tzu agrees:

> Things have their life and death—you cannot rely upon their fulfillment. One moment empty, the next moment full—you cannot depend upon their form. The years cannot be held off; time cannot be stopped. Decay, growth, fullness, and emptiness end and then begin again.... The life of things is a gallop, a headlong dash—with every moment they alter, with every moment they shift.[209]

This is why Jesus told his disciples,

> Do not store up for yourselves treasures on earth, where moth and rust consume and where thieves break in and steal.[210]

Now all this may sound pretty obvious, but the reality of impermanence is actually very hard for most of us to face. Intellectually we may understand that everything is transitory, that nothing lasts forever, but rarely do we acknowledge this truth in our everyday lives. Our conditioning is so strong that we continue to act as if happiness could be attained by acquiring all kinds of material and emotional goodies. If we want to interrupt this habitual behavior, then we have to start taking the mystics' teachings seriously. And when we do, we discover that these teachings are far more profound than most people realize.

Moment-to-Moment Impermanence

For one thing, when mystics talk about impermanence, they are not simply referring to the fact that even such seemingly immutable objects as mountains and stars will someday be destroyed. As we just said, such knowledge has almost no impact on the way we conduct our daily affairs. The "impermanence" that mystics talk about, however, is something much more immediate and personal. It's the *moment-to-moment* impermanence of our present experience: the fact that all the phenomena which actually appear in the six fields of consciousness—sights, sounds, bodily sensations, smells, tastes, and thoughts—are constantly coming and going.

Listen, for instance, to whatever sounds you are hearing right now. How long do any of them last? If there is a particular sound that seems to persist—like a police siren, or an airplane drone—listen more closely. Isn't the sound itself constantly fluctuating? In fact, if you pay very close attention, you will discover it is made up of lots of little sounds, all vibrating in such rapid succession that they create the impression of being one continuous sound. The same is true of bodily sensations. Again, take a moment to become aware of the feel of this book in your hands. Ask yourself this: Is it a single sensation? Or is it really a mass of mini-sensations—tiny tinglings that vibrate much the way sounds do? Now blink your eyes several times and watch how the entire visual field appears and disappears with each blink. If there are any tastes or smells present, notice that they, too, are all transitory: They come and they go. Finally, turn your attention to the phenomena appearing in your mental field. Thoughts, memories, ideas, images—all arise and pass away with incredible speed. Virtually nothing in your immediate experience ever stands still. Everything is always changing, always in flux.

Now, the reason we normally don't notice this kind of moment-to-moment impermanence is that we are deceived by our own thought processes. As already mentioned, during the third link of the chain of conditioning our thinking mind groups phenomena arising in different fields together into 'things' which it then identifies with such names as *book, car, rock, tree,* etc. This is what gives us the impression that we live in a world of more or less fixed 'objects' that we can grasp onto and hold. But if we could gain some direct insight into the true, transitory nature of all phenomena, we might begin to see just how futile our attempts to cling to anything really are. Here is how the Buddha describes a seeker who has realized this in his own experience:

> He dwells in contemplation of the phenomena, either with regard to his own person, or to other persons, or to both. He beholds how the phenomena arise; beholds how they pass away; beholds the arising and passing away of the phenomena. Phenomena are there: this clear consciousness is present in him, because of his knowledge and mindfulness, and he lives independent, unattached to anything in the world.[211]

One of the best ways to attain this kind of direct insight is to use choiceless awareness meditation to contemplate the moment-to-moment impermanence of the phenomena arising in the six fields of awareness *before* the thinking mind has a chance to invest them with a solidity they don't actually possess. What follows are some step-by-step instructions for doing just this.

Instructions for Contemplating Impermanence

STEP ONE: *Start with Concentration*

Sit in your normal meditation posture. Set your intention. Keep your eyes open. Concentrate your attention on your breath, and, whenever you are distracted by any other phenomena, gently but firmly return your attention to your breath. Practice concentrating in this way until your mind has become calm, clear, and stable. At the same time, become aware that what you call your "breath" is itself impermanent, being made up of myriad bodily sensations which are constantly coming and going.

STEP TWO: *Contemplating Sensation Phenomena*

Once your mind has become calm, clear, and stable, focus your attention on the crown of your head and begin to scan your body, slowly moving your attention down to your face, neck, shoulders, arms, hands, chest, back, stomach, pelvis, buttocks, thighs, calves, feet. Notice that each of the sensations you encounter along the way is impermanent and eventually passes away.

After you have finished scanning your body, allow your attention to expand evenly into the entire field of bodily sensations and continue to observe how all arise and pass away. If any sensation—such as a pain in your knee, or tension in your shoulders—seems to persist, focus on it a little more closely. Ask yourself whether it is really one continuous sensation or constantly changing sensations. Continue practicing this way until you get some direct, experiential insight into the impermanence of all bodily sensations.

STEP THREE: *Contemplating Sound Phenomena*

After you have contemplated the impermanence of phenomena in the bodily sensation field for a while, let your attention expand to include the auditory field. If it seems that no sounds are arising, be patient. Eventually sounds will appear. When they do, notice their impermanence—how each one arises and passes away in consciousness. Continue practicing this way until you get some direct, experiential insight into the impermanence of all sound phenomena.

STEP FOUR: *Contemplating Visual Phenomena*

After you have contemplated the impermanence of phenomena in the auditory field, let your attention expand to the visual field of awareness. Most people at first find it difficult to observe the impermanence of phenomena in the visual field. This is especially true when you are sitting very still. If you are outdoors, however, you will soon become aware of subtle and sometimes not-so-subtle movements in the phenomena you are observing—leaves shimmering, trees swaying, clouds passing overhead, etc. If you are indoors, slowly shift your eyes from left to right, and then from right to left. Notice how everything in the visual field shifts as well. Continue practicing this way until you get some direct, experiential insight into the impermanence of all visual phenomena.

STEP FIVE: *Contemplating Mental Phenomena*

After you have contemplated the impermanence of phenomena in the visual field, focus your attention inwardly on the mental field of awareness. Notice that all thoughts, memories, images are impermanent. Notice how quickly they arise and pass away. Sometimes, when thoughts link up into on-going stories, or a coherent sequence of ideas, they can seem to last for quite awhile. But if you look closely at each individual thought, you will see that it actually dissolves almost as soon as it is formed. Continue practicing this way until you get some direct, experiential insight into the true impermanence of all mental phenomena.

STEP SIX: *Contemplating Phenomena in the Total Field of Consciousness-Awareness*

Finally, allow your attention to expand so that it fills the total field of consciousness-awareness. Relax all effort to hold it still, and enter a state of spacious-awareness. Then, without grasping or pushing away any of the phenomena in any of the fields, simply notice how ephemeral they all actually are. Rest for a while in this spacious-awareness, watching the stream of phenomena flowing by, as you might watch a swiftly moving river while sitting on one of its banks.

You should continue contemplating the impermanence of phenomena in your formal practice until you have gained enough insights to produce an actual shift in your perception. Instead of an environment filled with solid, separate objects, you should begin to feel yourself living in a fluid world where everything is constantly in motion. Some meditators find this direct experience of impermanence quite delightful. For others, however, it can arouse fear. If this happens to you, don't be alarmed. As the twentieth-century Buddhist master Mahasi Sayadaw explains, it is really a sign that your meditation is working:

> When engaged in noticing continuously both the dissolution of the objects and the act of knowing it, he [the meditator] reflects: "Even for the wink of an eye or a flash of lightening nothing lasts. One did not realize this before. As it ceased and vanished in the past so will it cease and vanish in the future....One enjoys life, not knowing the truth. Now that one knows the truth of continuous dissolution it is

> truly fearful....Fearful it is to feel that in the absence of real features and forms the arisings appear to be real. So are the efforts to arrest the changing phenomena for the sake of well-being and happiness. ... Fearful indeed it is to be old, to die, to experience sorrow, lamentation, pain, grief and despair."...
>
> But he should not despair. This condition of his is a sign of insight.[212]

Methods for Maintaining Mindfulness in Everyday Life

Once you have begun to experience moment-to-moment impermanence in your formal practice, the next step is to try to maintain mindfulness of impermanence in your everyday life. For most people, the biggest obstacle to doing this is simple forgetfulness. Normally, we get so caught up in worldly activities and the stories they generate that we just don't remember to pay attention to the impermanent nature of what we are really experiencing.

A good way to overcome this problem is to begin each day with a resolve to be as continuously mindful as possible. Ideally this should be your first thought upon waking up. If you meditate in the morning, you can also reaffirm this resolution at the end of your session, just before you rise from your cushion or chair. Then whatever your next activity is—showering, eating breakfast, going to the bathroom, etc.—do it with as much mindfulness as you can muster.

Some practitioners find it helpful to post little notes saying "impermanence" in strategic locations—say, on your bathroom mirror, or your car's dashboard, or on top of your desk at work. Another technique is to buy a watch with a chime which you can set to sound every hour. Hearing that beep can serve as a regular reminder to become mindful of impermanence in whatever situation you happen to find yourself.

You can also practice a short, three-breath meditation periodically throughout the day. On the first breath, focus attention on your inhalation; then as you breathe out, say silently to yourself, "Concentrate the mind." Again focus attention on the second inhalation and as you breathe out, say silently to yourself, "Relax the body." Then focus attention on your third inhalation and as you breath out, say silently to yourself, "Remember impermanence."

Finally, you should try to stay mindful of impermanence as you fall asleep at night. Notice how not just individual phenomena come and go, but entire fields of phenomena—sights, sounds, bodily sensations—drop out of consciousness. In fact, every night the whole waking world vanishes completely away.

After you have cultivated mindfulness of the impermanence of the various objects in your environment, turn your attention to the impermanence of the desires you have for them and the grasping this generates. By watching what actually happens when you get something you want, you can see how fleeting the resulting gratification really is. For example, if you have a craving for ice cream, you might make it a special practice to become mindful every time you sit down to eat a bowl. Begin by carefully observing the pleasure that arises each time you take a bite. Ask yourself, "How long does this pleasure last? Twenty seconds? Thirty seconds? A full minute?"

You might also notice that, before the pleasure of the first bite fades away, you feel compelled to take a second one, in order to prevent the taste from disappearing entirely. Next, try to resist the impulse to take a second bite until the pleasure of the first one *has* disappeared. Now, ask yourself, "Was losing the pleasure of the first bite really as awful as I had imagined?"

After you finish eating the ice cream, pay attention to what kind of satisfaction you actually feel. Ask yourself, "Was the pleasure really as great as I had anticipated? How long does it last? Ten minutes? Half an hour? A whole hour? Will eating ice cream ever bring me real, abiding happiness?"

If you are not satisfied with just one bowl, by all means have another. In fact, you might want to keep eating ice cream until you are thoroughly sick of it. Then, notice that what is true of over-indulging in ice cream is true of almost all worldly desires. If you try to prolong the pleasures they bring past a certain point, the desires turn into aversions!

You might also want to experiment with abstaining from ice cream altogether for, say, six months. Then whenever a desire for some arises, see how long it actually lasts—a few minutes? half an hour? Whatever the length of time, if you refrain from acting on such desires most of them will fade away on their own.

Along with watching your desires, you should also try to maintain mindfulness of your thoughts in order to see exactly how your thinking mind generates all those little dramas that make up the Story of I. For example, when a desire for some ice cream arises, you might notice that your mind tends to invest this simple urge with all sorts of psychological significance. If things have gone badly at work, you might hear your mind say, "You've had such a rough day, why not go out and get yourself some ice cream. It'll cheer you up." Or, when you do well at work, your mind might tell you, "Why not celebrate with a little ice cream. You certainly have earned it!"

Practicing mindfulness of something as trivial as eating ice cream may seem silly, but doing so is precisely what allows you to gain direct insight into exactly how the chain of conditioning works—especially the grasping and avoiding that arise in the sixth link. Mindfulness is also what lets you break the chain, because when you see for yourself the actual impermanence of all the things you desire, the impulse to grasp or avoid them naturally weakens and your attachments start to fall away. This is how you become a true renunciant, not by forcing yourself to give anything up, but simply by seeing things as they really are. Thus, the contemporary Tibetan master Dilgo Khyentse writes,

> Renunciation is born when you know that there is ultimately no satisfaction in samsāric life.[213]

The Dark Night of the Jnani

The road to renunciation, however, often runs through periods of aridity, or what St. John of the Cross called a "dark night of the senses." This is what he says about it:

> We are using the expression "night" to signify a deprival of the gratification of the soul's appetites in all things.... When the appetites are extinguished—or mortified—one no longer feeds on the pleasure of these things, but lives in a void and a darkness with respect to the appetites.[214]

The reason many jnanis experience these dark nights is because, in the beginning, practicing mindfulness of impermanence tends to show us only its negative aspects—such as the futility of worldly seeking. If you have not yet tasted any of its positive fruits, this can make life look pretty bleak, indeed. Here, for example, is how Merrell-Wolff describes what happened to him:

> I had realized enough to render forever barren the old pastures, and yet not enough to know either peace or satisfaction.[215]

If you go through such a "dark night" or "desert experience" (as it is also sometimes called), you may think you are suffering from some kind of psychological disorder like depression. But if it occurs within the context of a spiritual practice, a genuine dark night is not pathological.[216] In fact, it can mark a crucial turning point on your path. Why? Because if you fully recognize the truth that absolutely every object of experience is impermanent, then for you there can be no turning back, for as Simone Weil explains,

> Everything that appears to be good in this world is finite, limited, wears out ... Men feel that there is a mortal danger in facing this truth squarely for any length of time. That is true. Such knowledge strikes more surely than a sword; it inflicts a death more frightening than that of the body. After a time it kills everything within us that constitutes our ego. In order to bear it we have to love truth more than life itself. Those who do this turn away from the fleeting things of time with all their souls, to use the expression of Plato.[217]

This does not mean that from now on you will have no more worldly desires or attachments. But it does mean you will have crossed a kind of a divide. Such things as money and power, possessions and prestige, will no longer have quite the same allure for you as they once did. Why? Because now you will no longer be looking to them to bring you ultimate happiness. Now you will be looking for ultimate happiness elsewhere—namely, in a Gnosis of your own true Identity.

The Way of Selflessness

Part IV: *Entering the Path of Devotion (Bhakti)*

CHAPTER 14

Verbal Prayer

Do not think that the words of prayer as you say them go up to God. It is not the words themselves that ascend; it is rather the burning desire of your heart that rises like smoke towards heaven.

— Rabbi Zev Wolf of Zotamir (Jew)

As we mentioned in chapter 6, most seekers throughout history have been bhaktas. In the *Bhagavadgita,* Krishna explains why:

> Greater is the toil of those whose minds are set on the Transcendent, for the path of the Transcendent is hard for mortals to attain.
>
> But they for whom I [Krishna] am the End Supreme, who surrender all their works to me and who with pure love meditate on me and adore me — these I very soon deliver from the ocean of death and life-in-death, because they have set their hearts on me.[218]

As Krishna suggests, a bhakta quite literally falls in love with God, and this is what gives the bhakti path its special power. As we all know from our experience with human love affairs, few passions can animate us as much as that burning desire to be united with our beloved. This makes it a lot easier for bhaktas to practice things like the four principles—attention, commitment, detachment, and surrender. So, for example, if you are madly in love with someone, you have no problem paying attention to them when the two of you are together. And even when you are apart, your mind keeps flying back to memories of moments you shared, or zooming ahead in expectation of future meetings. Well, the same thing happens with God. Once you are smitten, you can't stop thinking about your Beloved—a fact celebrated (and sometimes bemoaned) in so much of the bhakti literature. Listen, for example, to the author of the Hebrew psalms:

> As a deer longs for flowing streams,
> so my soul longs for you, O God.

My soul thirsts for God,
for the living God.
When shall I come and behold
the face of God?
My tears have been my food
day and night,
while people say to me continually,
"Where is your God?"[219]

Nor, if you are a true lover, do you have any trouble keeping commitments you've made. Have you ever forgotten to show up for a date with someone you were head-over-heals in love with? So, too, with keeping commitments to your Divine Beloved to engage in various devotional practices. As long as you are motivated by love, undertaking these disciplines will be a joy instead of a burden. Here, for example, is how Rabi'a describes her time spent in evening prayer:

O God, the stars are shining;
All eyes have closed in sleep;
The kings have locked their doors,
Each lover is alone, in secret, with the one he loves.
And I am here too: alone, hidden from all of them –
With You.[220]

As for practicing detachment, if you are really in love, you won't even be tempted to pursue other lovers. The only person you want to be with in all the world is your true love. And again, it's the same if you are a lover of the Divine. Just listen to what the twelfth-century Hindu bhakta Mahadevi says about her Shiva:

I have fallen in love with the Beautiful
One, who is without any family,
without any country and without any peer;
Chenna Mallikārjuna [Shiva], the Beautiful, is my husband.
Fling into the fire the husbands who are
subject to death and decay.[221]

Most important, if you are a true lover, when it comes to surrender you will be more than willing to give up all you possess—even your very life—for the sake of your beloved. How much more so if the One you love is God? Thus, the author of *The Book of Privy Counseling* writes,

> This is the way of all real love. The lover will utterly and completely despoil himself of everything, even his very self, because of the one he loves.[222]

There is, however, a catch to being a bhakta. Virtually anyone with sufficient curiosity about the true nature of things can choose to become a jnani. But to be a bhakta taking the path of devotion you must first have an initiation. Now *initiation* here does not mean undergoing some kind of secret ceremony or becoming a member of a particular religious sect. What it does mean is that you have a personal encounter with the Divine in some form. Until you have had such an encounter, you cannot practice true devotion for the simple reason that you cannot, as Jesus said, love something "with all your heart, and with all your soul, and with all your mind" if you have never experienced it.

How Initiation Happens

Exactly how and when such an initiation occurs, and what form it takes, can vary greatly from individual to individual and culture to culture. In the Hindu tradition seekers often encounter the Divine in the guise of a human guru. Here is an account by an Indian college professor, M.M. Thakore, of the first time he and his wife met Anandamayi Ma. After a long journey, which culminated in a boat ride to an island, they found the famous saint had already retired for a nap. In Professor Thakore's own words,

> We waited in the temple nearby longing for Mother's *darśana* [blessing]. Hours passed and the doors did not open. To our surprise the boatman had followed us and requested us to leave the place immediately as it was necessary for us to cross from the island of Vyasji before dark. He also demanded the fare for the return journey as originally fixed, in case we did not like to come away with him forthwith. We decided not to leave the place without Mother's *darśana* and paid the boatman his fare. After he had gone away, the doors of the room opened and we were graced with Mother's *darśana*. We were so thrilled that we sat near Mother with tears of joy in our eyes. Mother cast Her glance at us full of overwhelming love and said: "So you have come. Do you know why I kept you waiting? You came with a return ticket. This habit of taking a return ticket must be given up."... We felt positive that Mother was not different from the Mother of the World who is all-knowing.[223]

For some seekers, a first encounter with the Divine may come as an interior voice calling them to walk a spiritual path. According to one of his biographers, this is what happened to Ibn al-'Arabi (also known as Muhyi l-Din Muhammed) when he was still just a teenager:

> A prince who was one of his father's friends invited him to dinner along with other sons of princes. When the shaikh Muhyī l-Dīn and the others were all present they ate to repletion, and then the goblets of wine began circulating. When it came to the turn of the shaikh Muhyī l-Dīn, he grabbed the goblet and was just about to drink

> when he heard a voice call out to him: "Muhammad, it was not for this that you were created." He threw down the goblet and left in a daze.[224]

For others, it may take the form of an overpowering *presence* suddenly and unexpectedly breaking through the veil of ordinary appearances. Simone Weil, for instance, grew up in a secular Jewish family in France, without any religious training. As a young woman, her main interest had been in leftist politics. Then one day, while she was recuperating from injuries received fighting the Fascists in Spain, she had the following epiphany:

> In a moment of intense physical suffering…when I was forcing myself to love, but without desiring to give a name to that love, I felt, without being in any way prepared for it (for I had never read the mystical writers) a presence more personal, more certain, more real, than that of a human being, though inaccessible to the senses and the imagination.[225]

For still others, an encounter with the Divine unfolds in a more gradual fashion, as a kind of deepening awareness of some transcendent Wisdom or Force at work in the Universe. This was the case with the great Russian writer Leo Tolstoy. As a young man, Tolstoy had become convinced that God did not exist and religion was a sham. Later, however, when all his worldly success failed to make him happy, he started to envy the simple faith of the peasants on his estate to whom religion seemed to bring such contentment and joy. "Could there really be a God after all?" he began to wonder. Whenever he asked himself this question, his heart would respond with a "yes!"—but his mind continued to say "no!" For more than a year he see-sawed back and forth between affirmation and negation. Finally, one afternoon his inner conflict was resolved in the following manner:

> "What, then, do I seek?" a voice cried out within me. "He is there, the one without whom there would be no life." To know God and to live come to one and the same thing. God is life.
> "Live seeking God, for there can be no life without God." And more powerfully than ever a light shone within me and all around me, and this light has not abandoned me since.[226]

But no matter how or when this kind of initiation occurs, it is not something which you can bring about by an act of your own will alone. It comes spontaneously, as a gift of grace. Still, this does not mean that you are completely powerless, that there is nothing you can do but sit around and wait for the divine lightning to strike.

To begin with, even though you cannot *choose* to fall in love with God, it helps if you are actively seeking such an experience. Again, this is similar to what happens when we fall in love with a human being. Although love can overtake us at the most unexpected moments, our chances of finding someone to love will be greatly increased if we make some effort. For starters, instead of moping around the house all day watching TV, you might begin frequenting places where you are likely to meet a suitable mate. The same is true of the Divine Beloved. If you want to meet God, you have to go where God is. But then the question arises, where is that? Where can God be found? Here is what Allah tells Muhammad, according to a famous *hadith* (saying of the Prophet):

> Neither My earth nor My heaven can encompass Me, yet the heart of My adorer contains Me.[227]

And you will find the same answer given by mystics of all the great traditions. Listen, for instance, to Lalleshwari:

> He lives in your heart.
> Recognize Him.
> Don't look for Him
> here and there,
> wondering, "Where is God?"[228]

Similarly, the fourth-century Christian mystic St. Ephraim of Syria says,

> Here within you are the riches of heaven, if you desire them. ...Enter within yourself and remain in your heart, for there is God.[229]

Before we go any further, however, it is important to understand what mystics mean when they use this term *heart*. In fact, depending on the context, *heart* can have a number of different meanings. So let's take a look at some of the most common.

Four Meanings of "Heart"

For our purposes, we can identify at least four meanings of *heart*, each of which pertains to a different level of spiritual experience. First, and most obviously, it can refer to the *physical* heart. This is usually the case when mystics talk about using the heart as a focal point for some kind of formal practice. Here, for example, is an instruction given by Tibetan master Dilgo Khyentse on how to pray to your teacher as an embodiment of the deity Chenrezi:

> When going to sleep, visualize him in your heart, seated upon a four-petaled red lotus, radiating light which fills the whole universe.[230]

The second level of meaning is the *emotional* heart. This refers to that psychological 'place' where we experience various emotions. These can be negative feelings of the kind Jesus warned against:

> Out of the heart come evil intentions, murder, adultery, fornication, theft, false witness, slander. These are what defile a person.[231]

Or they can be spiritually positive feelings, such as compassion for others, or that all-consuming yearning for God of which mystical poets like Hafiz have sung so much about:

> I have cried a hundred streams across my breast
> hoping to water the seed of kindness in your heart.
>
> My spilled blood freed me from the pain of love.
> I am grateful to the dagger of your glance.
>
> Be kind, grant me an audience, so that with burning heart
> my eyes can constantly rain pearls at your feet.[232]

As we shall see in a future chapter, if you are walking a bhakti path, one of your primary tasks is to purify your emotional heart by transforming all your negative emotions into love and longing for the Divine. The more you can do this, the more you can enter into the *spiritual* heart. This refers to a deep space of awareness, which has been emptied of all content except for a sense of the Divine Presence. Hafiz's contemporary, the Christian mystic Johannes Tauler, describes it this way:

> He [God] is far above every outward thing and every thought, and is found only where thou hidest thyself in the secret place of thy heart, in the quiet solitude where no word is spoken, where is neither creature, nor image, nor fancy.[233]

Finally, when the spiritual heart has been completely purified of all forms whatsoever—even forms of the Divine—then there is an opportunity to Realize what Ramana Maharshi calls the *Radiant* Heart or *Heart-Center.* This, as Ramana explains, is simply another term for the Ultimate Reality, or Consciousness Itself:

> Call it by any name, God, Self, the Heart or the Seat of Consciousness, it is all the same. The point to be grasped is this, that Heart means the very core of one's being, the center, without which there is nothing whatever.[234]

To sum up, then, this "hierarchy of hearts" is really a bhakti version of the same idea we have already come across—namely, that the spiritual journey is a journey which takes place within yourself. By entering into and purifying each of these heart-levels, you can eventually reach that Radiant Heart or Pure Consciousness which constitutes your true Identity.

The Hardened Heart

The first obstacle most bhaktas run up against when they try to enter within is that to one degree or another their hearts have become hardened. This happens as a response to the inevitable disappointments everyone experiences in the process of growing up. Although we're all born with a primordial longing for happiness, when we try to attain it by pursuing worldly things, we usually end up frustrated and disillusioned. As a result, most of us learn a subtle (or sometimes not so subtle) lesson: The more we give free-reign to our longing for happiness, the more suffering we're liable to experience. Not realizing that our mistake isn't that we long for happiness, but that we are looking for it in the wrong places, we conclude the problem lies with the longing itself—that this longing is based on a childish fantasy which we must suppress. Outwardly, then, we abandon the search for true happiness, and settle, instead, for transitory pleasures; while inwardly we bury our real feelings under a facade of cynicism about life and its possibility. This, however, is extremely unfortunate, because, understood rightly, our longing for happiness is actually a call from our True Self to rise from our slumber and begin the long journey Home. Here's how Rumi expresses it:

> In whatever state you may be, seek! Seek water constantly,
> oh man of dry lips!
> For your dry lips give witness that in the end you will find
> a fountain.
> The lips' dryness is a message from the water: "If you keep
> on moving about, without doubt you will find me."[235]

So if you want to be a bhakta, the first thing you have to do is to open your heart to that longing once again. But then the question arises, how can you actually accomplish this—especially if you are one of those people who no longer feels any longing at all?

Well, one way to begin is to pay attention to your physical heart, because the physical heart is where we tend to experience our emotions most concretely. This is reflected in many idioms of our language. For instance, when we feel glad we say, "My heart leapt for joy." When something makes us sad we say, "It broke my heart." Hatred "turns our hearts to stone," while compassion "softens" or "melts" our hearts. In other words, the physical heart serves as a kind of barometer for our emotional states. This is even true of repressed emotions. If your longing for happiness has been completely stifled, you can still experience this as a chronic constriction of the muscles in your heart area—which, of course, is what gave rise to the term "hardened heart" in the first place.

Once you have identified your hardened heart, the next step is to open your heart and liberate the love and longing locked within it. And the way mystics of virtually all traditions recommend doing this is to take up a practice of mystical prayer. Like meditation, mystical prayer unfolds in successive stages: first there is *verbal prayer*; next *prayer-in-the-heart*; then *unceasing prayer*; and, finally, *silent prayer*. So let's start with verbal prayer and see what exactly this entails.

Verbal Prayer

Most people think of verbal prayer as a way of petitioning God for some special favor. From a mystic's point of view, however, this is not its real purpose. The real purpose of verbal prayer is to give voice to that love and longing for the Divine which is buried deep in your heart. Here is how the eighteenth-century founder of the Hasidic movement, the Baal Shem Tov, expressed it:

> The purpose of Creation is only that we pray for God. Material things, this world—such nonsense is not worthy of prayer.[236]

But supposing you have never prayed before and don't know how to go about it. Or perhaps you once knew, but you have become so alienated from God that now you have forgotten. If either is true of you, you might want to take the advice of another Hasidic master of the nineteenth-century, Nahman of Bratslav:

> Even if it happens to be the case that he finds himself incapable of opening his mouth to speak to God at all, yet this is good in itself, namely, the very preparation in which he makes himself ready to speak to God although he cannot actually do so, yet since he wishes to do so, this in itself is very good. And he can make up a prayer and carry on a conversation with himself regarding this very thing. Regarding this very thing he should cry out in prayer that he has become so remote from God that he finds himself unable even to speak to Him. And he should entreat God and beg for Him to open his mouth so that he can converse with Him. Know that very many of the great and famous zaddikim [spiritual masters] related that they only attained to the stage they did as a result of this habit.[237]

Do not be surprised if your first attempts at verbal prayer make you feel self-conscious and uncomfortable. This will be doubly true if you are someone who has taken pride in being a totally independent and self-reliant person. The thought of asking anyone for help—let alone a 'God' you may not even believe in—will almost certainly cause your ego to rebel. You may hear it say, "This is stupid. There is no God, you're just wasting your time." Don't get sucked into an argument with such thoughts, or try to logically convince yourself that God does, indeed, exist. Like Tolstoy, what you are seeking for in prayer is not an intellectual proof of the Divine, but a direct, personal experience. So just ignore whatever doubts your thinking mind raises. Keep your attention focused on your heart and continue to pray, giving vent to whatever emotions arise with as much sincerity as you can muster.

If you persist in this practice, over time chances are your heart will begin to crack a little. The first sign of this is often a sensation of being "pierced" or "wounded" in the chest. Some seekers find this experience to be very sweet. For others, it can be quite excruciating. You may even be inundated by a flood of tears, as though a dam somewhere deep inside had burst. But however painful this may be, the important thing is not to hold back. Before a festering wound can be healed, it must be lanced. Although we may dread having to undergo such an operation, once it is over we feel cleansed and relieved. In the same way, verbal prayer can open our hearts and cleanse them of mistrust and false pride, so that our primordial longing for happiness can flow freely once again.

Sometimes, verbal prayer alone will suffice to provoke a full-blown encounter with the Divine. More often, however, all you will be granted is a brief glimpse of your Beloved. It is as though you were walking down a street when suddenly out of the corner of your eye you spied an extraordinarily beautiful woman or man standing in a window. By the time you wheel around to get a better look, however, they're gone. Still, you have seen enough to make you want to go knock on their door and meet them face-to-face. For most seekers it is the same with their first glimpse of the Divine Beloved. And the way to knock on the Divine Beloved's door is to take up the practice of prayer-in-the-heart.

CHAPTER 15

Prayer-in-the-Heart

Prayer of the mind changes into prayer of the heart, or rather into prayer of the mind in the heart. ... From now on in the usual course of spiritual life there is no other prayer.

— Theophan the Recluse (Christian)

Verbal prayer is a preliminary practice designed to prime the pump of primordial longing. Once the waters have begun to flow, it is time to move on to the next stage of mystical prayer which is prayer-in-the-heart. In prayer-in-the-heart, using many words becomes superfluous and even a distraction. What you want to do now is focus on the love and longing itself. Here is how the author of *The Cloud of Unknowing* describes it:

> Forget everything but God and fix on him your naked desire, your longing stripped of all self-interest.[238]

If you're like most people, however, you'll find this is easier said than done. For one thing, in the beginning the longing which your practice arouses is apt to be quite fragile and fleeting. When you try to find it in your heart, it's not always there. And even when you do, after a few moments you get distracted by other things—especially those thoughts and emotions that make up the Story of I. In other words, you run up against the very same kinds of self-centered conditioning that jnanis face when they start practicing meditation.

Begin with Japa

As with meditation, then, the first step in prayer-in-the-heart is to train attention to be stable and calm by focusing it single-pointedly on one object. By far and away the most common object used by bhaktas of all traditions is the repetition of a short prayer or mantra. In India, this practice is called *japa,* and may be done with a wide variety of mantras, many of which are made up of words with no conventional meanings. For example, this is how Lalleshwari's guru recommended she start doing japa with the six syllable mantra "Om Namah Shivāya":

> O Lallī,
> there are only six syllables
> for you to contemplate:
> *Om Namah Shivāya....*
>
> With one-point mind
> repeat *Om Namah Shivāya....*
>
> O Lallī,
> Lose yourself
> in the repetition
> of *Om Namah Shivāya*.[239]

Mystics of the Eastern Orthodox Church usually repeat what they call the *Jesus Prayer*: "Jesus Christ, Son of God, have mercy upon me a sinner." Theophan the Recluse explains the way it works:

> Thoughts jostle one another like swarming gnats, and emotions follow on the thoughts. In order to make their thought hold to one thing, the Fathers used to accustom themselves to the continual repetition of a short prayer.[240]

Among Sufis the practice of concentrating attention on a short prayer is called *dhikr* (literally "remembrance"). Ibn al-'Arabi gives this brief instruction on how to practice it:

> Occupy yourself with *dhikr*, remembrance of God, with whatever *dhikr* you choose. The highest of them is the Greatest Name; it is your saying 'Allah, Allah,' and nothing beyond 'Allah.'[241]

There is, however, an important difference between the way a prayer or mantra is used by jnanis in a purely meditative practice and the way it is used by bhaktas in a devotional practice. In meditation, the words you say need not generate any particular emotion. In fact, if emotions do arise, you are directed to practice detachment, allowing them to come and go without any grasping or pushing away. For a bhakta engaged in prayer-in-the-heart, however, cultivating love and longing for your Beloved is essential. This does not mean you should try to work yourself up into some artificial emotional state. It simply means that both your mind *and* your heart must be focused on the prayer or mantra as much as possible. Here's Theophan again:

> What you must seek in prayer is to establish in the heart a quiet but warm and constant feeling towards God, not expecting ecstasy or any extraordinary state. But when God does send such special feel-

> ings in prayer, you must be grateful for them and not imagine that they are due to yourself, nor regret their disappearance as if it were a great loss; but always descend from these heights to humility and quietness of feeling towards the Lord.[242]

For this reason, too, it is important not to fall into the habit of saying your prayer or mantra in a mechanical fashion. The mere repetition of words will do nothing to kindle genuine yearning. This is why the Hasidic masters advise:

> Speak the words simply, and devote all your attention to the holy letters and to the meaning of your prayer. It is this true devotion that will bring you to the love and fear of God—and will really set your heart aflame.[243]

Actually, to practice prayer-in-the-heart you do not even need to say a complete prayer or mantra. As we just heard Ibn al-'Arabi say, a single word will suffice. The author of *The Cloud of Unknowing* agrees:

> If you want to gather all your desire into one simple word that the mind can easily retain, choose a short word rather than a long one. A one-syllable word such as "God" or "love" is best. But choose one that is meaningful to you. Then fix it in your mind so that it will remain there come what may. . . . Should some thought go on annoying you demanding to know what you are doing, answer with this one word alone. . . . Do this and I assure you these thoughts will vanish. Why? Because you have refused to develop them with arguing.[244]

To attain greater concentration, many traditions recommend synchronizing your word or prayer with your breath. If you are using a single word, you can say it to yourself on the out-breath and remain silent on the in-breath. If you are using a mantra or prayer with several words, you may want to break it up into two parts, saying the first part as you breathe out and the second as you breathe in.

Many traditions also recommend using prayer beads or a rosary. This is particularly useful for keeping count if your practice calls for performing a certain number of repetitions during a given session. But even if the length of your sessions is determined instead by a specified time (say, half an hour), the use of prayer beads can still be helpful. Manipulating them in conjunction with your repetitions serves to concentrate not only your mind and your heart on the practice, but also your body.

Bringing Attention Into the Heart

When you can stay focused on your prayer or sacred word for fairly long periods without distraction, you are ready to take the next step, which is to actually bring your attention down *into* your heart. Here's the way Theophan describes it:

> Turn to the Lord, drawing down the attention of the mind into the heart, and calling upon Him there. With the mind firmly established in the heart, stand before the Lord with awe, reverence and devotion.[245]

The Upanishads give similar instructions using the mantra *Om*:

> With upright body, head, and neck lead the mind and its powers into the heart; and the OM of Brahman will then be thy boat with which to cross the rivers of fear.[246]

But what exactly does it mean to "lead" attention into the heart? This is rather difficult to put into words. The main point is that, instead of looking down at your heart from inside your head, you should feel that your attention has actually descended into the space inside your heart. If you are not already doing so, one way to accomplish this is to synchronize your word or prayer with your breath. Then, as your inhalations and exhalations pass through your heart area, try to "hear" your word or prayer being silently spoken there. Finally, let your attention sink down after it, as though you were following an anchor line down to the bottom of the sea.

Once attention has descended into your heart, you will feel you have entered a deeper and more spacious dimension of your being. This happens because, even though you are concentrating on your physical heart, what your attention actually comes to rest on is that longing for the Beloved which is located in your emotional heart. Sufi scholar Dr. Mir Valiuddin sums it up this way:

> In this *dhikr* the thought is directed towards the heart, and the heart towards God.[247]

Like meditation, prayer-in-the-heart is a formal practice requiring a long-term commitment. It is important to set aside at least twenty to thirty minutes a day in which to descend as far as possible into that space of your heart where the Beloved resides. If you can do this two or even three times a day, all the better. What follows is a set of detailed instructions for putting this into actual practice.

Instructions for Prayer-in-the-heart

STEP ONE: *Choosing a Sacred Word or Prayer*

The prayer or word you pick for a prayer-in-the-heart practice should be one which expresses your deepest love and longing for the Divine. If you already belong to an established religion, you might want to pick one of the names of God recognized by your tradition, such as "Allah," "Krishna," "Kali," "Lord," "Jesus," etc. If you don't belong to any established religion, you can use a more generic expression, like "God," "Beloved," "Great Spirit," or "Divine Mother." In any case, the most important thing is to find some word or phrase that truly resonates with your own heart.

STEP TWO: *Getting into Position*

As in meditation, you should find a comfortable and stable posture to sit in—either cross-legged on a pillow, or upright in a chair—which you can maintain without moving for the duration of your session (see chapter 11). Once you have found a posture that is right for you, stick with it whenever you engage in formal practice.

Most traditions recommend closing your eyes when practicing prayer-in-the-heart. This certainly cuts out a lot of distractions and will help you to descend into your heart more easily and quickly. If you have the patience, however, you can learn to do this equally well with your eyes open. The advantage of doing it with your eyes open is that later it will be easier for you to practice unceasing prayer, which is performed in the midst of everyday activities. My own advice would be to try keeping your eyes open, but you must decide which is best for you.

STEP THREE: *Set Your Intention*

Before beginning your actual practice, set your intention by reciting an appropriate dedication. Remember that the purpose of your practice is to open your heart to the Beloved, so choose or compose something that reflects this. The following words of the sixth-century Sufi master Imam Zeinol-'abedin are a good example:

> O Lord, busy our hearts with remembrance of You above all other remembrances and occupy our tongues with thanks to You above all other thankfulness. O Lord, open my heart to Your Loving-kindness and fill me with Your Remembrance.[248]

STEP FOUR: *Use your Word or Prayer to Focus your Attention*

Now focus your attention on the inhalations and exhalations of your breath. After a few moments, silently begin to repeat your sacred word or prayer, synchronizing it with each breath. If you have prayer beads, begin to co-ordinate your repetitions with your fingering of the beads. Perform your repetitions in a slow, deliberate manner, paying close attention to what the word or prayer means and the feelings it arouses.

STEP FIVE: *Practice Detachment*

At first, thoughts will continue to flow in what may seem to be a never-ending stream. This is perfectly normal, so don't become discouraged. Whenever your attention gets distracted by these thoughts, simply notice that you have been distracted. Then, with gentle reverence, return your attention to your word or prayer and the longing it expresses. Continue practicing your repetitions in this way until your attention becomes calm and stable.

STEP SIX: *Say your Word or Prayer in your Heart*

When you are able to concentrate on your word or prayer with some stability, begin to focus your attention more closely on the area of your chest where your breath passes near your heart. Then, try to say your word or prayer in the space of your heart.

STEP SEVEN: *Sinking Attention into the Heart*

Once you can stay focused *on* your heart more or less without distractions, you are ready to try drawing your attention down *into* your heart. Continue repeating your sacred word or prayer in the space of your heart and gradually let your attention sink down after it. You can think of it as though you were moving closer to the words in order to hear them more clearly.

When your attention has descended all the way into your heart, relax your effort somewhat, but continue saying your word or prayer with as much longing and devotion as you genuinely feel.

STEP EIGHT: *Bowing*

After your formal session is over, you should bow to your Beloved in gratitude for this opportunity to give expression to your love and longing. Then, arise slowly and, without clinging to any particular emotion or state, try to carry some minimal feeling of devotion with you into the other activities of your day.

Overcoming Obstacles

Practitioners of prayer-in-the-heart encounter many of the same obstacles as do beginning meditators: sleepiness, kriyas, lack of motivation, and lack of confidence. The advice for dealing with them is also similar (see chapter 11). But as a bhakta there is one pitfall which you must be especially vigilant to avoid. As you begin to descend into your heart and leave your mundane worldly thoughts behind, your imagination is apt to start producing vivid spiritual thoughts and images which can seem quite profound. Do not allow your attention to be captivated by them, for as Theophan warns,

> To arrive successfully at our inward objective, we must travel safely past the imagination. If we are careless about this, we may stick fast in the imagination and remain there, under the impression that we have entered within, whereas in fact we are merely outside the entrance ... Images, however sacred they may be, retain the attention outside, whereas at the time of prayer attention must be within—in the heart.[249]

Spontaneous Prayer

If your commitment is strong and you persist in your practice, eventually something quite remarkable will happen. Instead of requiring a conscious effort, your prayer will assume a life of its own. Theophan explains how this works with the Jesus Prayer:

> At first this saving prayer is usually a matter of strenuous effort and hard work. But if one concentrates on it with zeal, it will begin to flow of its own accord, like a brook that murmurs in the heart. This is a great blessing, and it is worth working hard to obtain it.[250]

Now this transition from willed to spontaneous prayer is a phenomenon known in all the great traditions. For example, Javad Nurbakhsh writes of dhikr,

> When the light of zekr [variation of dhikr] clears the heart of the darkness of agitation, the heart becomes aroused and gradually steals the zekr from the tongue, making it its preoccupation.[251]

Likewise, Anandamayi Ma insists,

> There is all the difference between doing *japa* and *japa* occurring of itself.[252]

The reason she says this is that the occurrence of spontaneous japa or prayer gives many seekers their first real taste of what it means to surrender oneself to the Beloved. When this happens, you no longer feel it is *you* who is speaking, but it is the Beloved speaking *through* you. This is why the Hasidic masters declare,

> As long as you can still say the words "Blessed art Thou" by your own will, know that you have not reached the deeper levels of prayer. Be so stripped of selfhood that you have neither the awareness nor the power to say a single word of your own.[253]

Touching the Spiritual Heart

As with all concentration practices, prayer-in-the-heart requires time to bear fruit, so don't expect immediate results. With continued practice your attention will eventually be able to descend all the way down through your emotional heart to stand at the entrance of your spiritual heart. Here you will experience a state of clarity and bliss equivalent to a meditator's calm-abiding. Theophan describes it like this:

> When attention descends into the heart, it attracts all the powers of the soul and body into one point there. This concentration of all human life in one place is immediately reflected in the heart by a special sensation that is the beginning of future warmth. This sensation, faint at the beginning, becomes gradually stronger, firmer, deeper. At first only tepid, it grows into warm feeling and concentrates the attention upon itself. And so it comes about that, whereas in the initial stages the attention is kept in the heart by an effort of will, in due course this attention, by its own vigor, gives birth to warmth in the heart. This warmth then holds the attention without special effort. From this, the two go on supporting one another, and must remain inseparable; because dispersion of attention cools the warmth, and diminishing warmth weakens attention.[254]

Then, once you have actually crossed the threshold into the spiritual heart, you can look back, as it were, at what goes on in the emotional heart without being in the least distracted by it. Eastern Orthodox mystics call this state "sobriety," but, again, it is very close to the kind of spacious awareness which meditators attain. Thus, Theophan writes,

> With sobriety we observe movements that come out of the heart itself; with discernment we foresee movements which are about to be roused in it under the impulse of external influences. The rule for sobriety is: after every thought has been banished from the soul by the memory of God's presence, stand at the door of the heart and watch carefully everything that enters or goes out from there.[255]

As we said in the last chapter, an encounter with God is not something you can force through will-power alone. There is always an element of grace that is beyond anyone's power to command. But if you have been cultivating love and longing through devotional practices like verbal prayer and prayer-in-the-heart, chances are you have already received some kind of response. This is especially true if you have managed to enter your spiritual heart, because here there is very little to distract your attention from that Divine Presence which lies at the core of your being. But whenever or however it happens, once you do encounter your Beloved in some form, it means you will have received your bhakti initiation, and the way will be open to continue with devotion as the primary practice of your path.

Chapter 16

Remembrance Through Unceasing Prayer

> *Whoever turns to God by remembering Him frequently will eventually turn to Him in all his affairs.*
>
> — Ibn Ata'llah (Muslim)

If you practice prayer-in-the-heart in a disciplined manner, then eventually you should be able to enter into the Presence of the Divine on a fairly regular basis. But, as is the case with human love affairs, after awhile you will no longer be satisfied by these periodic rendezvous. Instead, you will want to enjoy the company of your Beloved all the time. This leads to the next stage of devotion which is the constant remembrance of the Divine, even in the midst of your daily activities. When this happens, your practice really starts to mature, for as Theophan the Recluse says,

> The essence of the whole thing is *to be established in the remembrance of God, and to walk in His presence.*[256]

Anandamayi Ma agrees:

> His presence and the remembrance of Him must be sustained unceasingly.[257]

This is why Menahem Nahum advises,

> Attach your thought always to the Creator; do not turn it away even for a moment to think of the vanities of this world. As soon as you turn your thought elsewhere you are considered as an idolater.[258]

Maintaining Constant Remembrance of the Beloved

The constant remembrance of the Divine is to bhaktas what maintaining continuous mindfulness is to jnanis. And, as with jnanis, the main obstacle is forgetfulness. Ordinarily, during the course of a normal day our attention gets so caught up in the Story of I, and the self-centered conditioning on which it's based, that we completely forget about the Beloved residing deep in our hearts. So how can we interrupt this conditioning and remember to keep at least a portion of our attention centered on the Divine?

Most sacred societies have built-in ritual reminders—the ringing of church bells, temple gongs, calls to prayer, recitation of blessings, etc.—which occur throughout the day. If you are living in a secular society that lacks such public prompts, you may want to adapt some of the personalized techniques we suggested for jnanis trying to maintain mindfulness, such as posting notes to "remember the Beloved" at home and at work, or setting a wristwatch to chime on the hour.

Another method for attaining the constant remembrance of God is to carry on a continuous internal conversation with Him. This is what the seventeenth-century Christian mystic Brother Lawrence recommended:

> We need only to recognize him present within us, to speak with him at every moment, and to ask for his help, so that we will know his will in perplexing events, and will be able to carry out those things we clearly see he asks of us, offering them to him before doing them, and thanking him afterward for completing them. During this continual conversation we are thus taken up in praising, adoring, and ceaselessly loving God for his infinite goodness and perfection.[259]

But the method most widely employed by bhaktas of all traditions has been to engage in what Christians call *unceasing prayer*. As its name implies, this entails repeating your sacred word or prayer, not just in your formal sessions, but during all your daily activities. Here's how the sixth-century Christian mystic Abba Philemon describes it using the Jesus Prayer:

> Whether you eat or drink, or talk to someone outside your cell or on the way somewhere, do not forget to recite this prayer with a sober and attentive mind.[260]

Anandamayi Ma gives the exact same instructions for japa:

> While attending to your work with your hands, keep yourself bound to Him by sustaining *japa*, the constant remembrance of Him in your heart and mind.[261]

Indeed, many bhaktas consider their tradition's ritual prayers to be but a prelude to practicing unceasing prayer, for as Rumi says,

> After all, the purpose of this ritual prayer is not that you should stand and bow and prostrate yourself all day long. Its purpose is that you should possess continuously that spiritual state which appears to you in prayer: Whether asleep or awake, writing or reading, in all

> your states you should never be empty of the remembrance of God; rather you should be one of *those who are constantly at their prayers* [Koran LXX 23].[262]

How to Practice Unceasing Prayer

Now saying a sacred word or prayer over and over continuously may sound like a lot of hard work, and for most seekers in the beginning it certainly will be. The anonymous author of *The Way of a Pilgrim* tells of the difficulties he faced trying to repeat the Jesus Prayer, which he had learned from his *starets* (spiritual master) while working as a gardener one summer:

> For a week, alone in my garden, I steadily set myself to learn to pray without ceasing exactly as the *starets* had explained. At first things seemed to go very well. But then it tired me very much. I felt lazy and bored and overwhelmingly sleepy, and a cloud of all sorts of other thoughts closed around me. I went in distress to my *starets* and told him the state I was in.[263]

Some traditions recommend that practitioners start with a limited number of repetitions, which can then be gradually increased. This is just what the starets counseled our anonymous pilgrim to do. He was to confine himself to 3,000 repetitions per day for a while before attempting more. As our pilgrim reports, this worked well for him:

> For two days I found it rather difficult, but after that it became so easy and likeable, that as soon as I stopped, I felt a sort of need to go on saying the Prayer of Jesus, and I did it freely and willingly, not forcing myself to it as before.[264]

Islam enjoins ritual prayers five times a day for all believers. Taking advantage of this requirement, Sufi shaykhs often instruct their students to end these ritual prayers with a dhikr which they are then to continue repeating silently a certain number of times as they go about their normal business. By gradually increasing the number of these repetitions, the students are eventually able to fill the gaps between the ritual prayers with a continuous flow of dhikr. Here, for example, is how Dr. Mir Valiuddin describes the way members of the Chishtiyya Order learn to increase their repetitions of a dhikr called *dhikr Pas-i-anfas* (dhikr of the guarding of the respirations):

> In the beginning, this *dhikr* is performed a thousand times after the *Ishā* (night) prayer, and five hundred times after the *Fajr* (dawn) prayer. The number is gradually increased until it issues forth involuntarily.[265]

Perhaps the simplest way to begin practicing unceasing prayer is to keep repeating your sacred word or prayer after your formal prayer-in-the-heart sessions are over for as long as you remember to do so. You can then make a point of resuming your repetitions whenever you find yourself between activities, such as commuting to and from work, or during your lunch breaks, or even while you are sitting on the toilet. Over time, each of these relatively short periods of repetition can be extended until, like the Sufi's dhikr, they all run together into one single stream.

Finally, as your practice of unceasing prayer deepens, you may even come to experience your own bodily functions as being themselves forms of prayer. If, for instance, you have been coordinating your word or prayer with your breath, you may find the two get so thoroughly fused that your breath literally *becomes* the prayer. This, as Dr. Mir Valiuddin explains, is where the practice *dhikr Pas-i-anfas* ultimately leads:

> The *dhākir* should try his utmost to attain perfection in this *dhikr*, and perfection is attained when respiration itself become the *dhākir*, without the volition and consciousness of the *dhākir*.[266]

Or, if you have been focusing on your heart, the prayer may become completely integrated with the rhythm of its beating, which is what happened to our Eastern Orthodox pilgrim:

> After no great lapse of time I had the feeling that the Prayer had, so to speak, by its own action passed from my lips to my heart. That is to say, it seemed as though my heart in its ordinary beating began to say the words of the Prayer within at each beat. Thus for example, *one*, "Lord," *two*, "Jesus," *three*, "Christ," and so on. I gave up saying the Prayer with my lips. I simply listened carefully to what my heart was saying....
>
> In this blissful state I passed more than two months of the summer.[267]

However you get there, once unceasing prayer becomes firmly established in your life, you will almost certainly come to feel as Lalleshwari did:

> Eating without the name of Shiva,
> drinking without the name of Shiva,
> sleeping without the name of Shiva,
> walking without the name of Shiva,
> living without the name of Shiva,
> are all just a waste of prāna [energy].[268]

The Benefits of Unceasing Prayer

Unceasing prayer brings about the same kind of inner renunciation for bhaktas as mindfulness of impermanence does for jnanis, only by a more circuitous route. First, it weakens your chain of conditioning by shifting more and more of your attention away from the Story of I and focusing it, instead, on the Beloved.

As a result, your heart becomes increasingly purified of worldly desires and aversions, while your thinking mind grows calmer and more detached. Here's how the nineteenth-century Eastern Orthodox Christian Ignatii Brianchaninov describes it:

> Unceasing prayer . . . leads a man into holy simplicity, weaning his mind from its habit of diversity in thought, and from devising plans about himself and his neighbors, keeping him always in scantiness and humility of thoughts. This composes his training. He who prays ceaselessly gradually loses the habit of wandering thoughts, of distraction, of being filled with vain worries, and the more deeply this training in holiness and humility enters the soul and takes root in it, the more he loses these habits of mind.[269]

This, in turn, allows you to pay even more attention to the Divine, which now begins to disclose Itself in all sorts of spontaneous and unexpected ways. For some, these glimpses may come as a series of "tastings" which, as Ibn al-'Arabi explains, over time increase in length and intensity:

> In the view of the Tribe [Sufis] tasting is "the first beginnings of self-disclosure." It is a state which comes upon the servant suddenly in his heart. If it should stay for two instants or more, it is "drinking."[270]

Others may have feelings of being pulled toward the Divine by an irresistible current. Here's how St. Catherine of Genoa expresses it:

> As it is being drawn upwards, the soul feels itself melting in the fire of that love of its sweet God.[271]

Still others may find themselves suddenly overwhelmed and completely transported outside of themselves, as this Hasidic master describes:

> When a person says the words of prayer so that they become a throne for God an awesome silent fire takes hold of him. Then he knows not where he is; he cannot see, he cannot hear. All this happens in the flash of an instant—as he ascends beyond the world of time.[272]

But no matter what sorts of favors you receive from your Beloved, all of them serve to increase your inner renunciation—or what Sufis call *spiritual poverty*—because, as Rumi writes,

> When you enter the world of poverty and practice it, God bestows upon you kingdoms and worlds that you never imagined. You become ashamed of what you longed for and desired at first. You say, "Oh! Given the existence of something like this, how could I have sought after such trifles?"[273]

In other words, inner renunciation occurs, not so much because you become aware of the impermanence of worldly pleasures, but because these pleasures pale in comparison to the bliss of the Beloved's Presence. And the more you experience this bliss, the less attached you are going to be to material things. Anandamayi Ma sums it up this way:

> In the measure as one loves God, detachment from sense objects ensues. To concentrate on God means to become drawn towards Him. And *vairāgya* (detachment) means becoming disentangled from sense objects. Feeling pulled towards the Divine and indifferent to sense objects occurs simultaneously. Renunciation happens of itself. There is no need to give up anything. This is real, genuine renunciation.[274]

The Dark Night of the Bhakta

It must be noted, however, that this process of Divine self-disclosure is not always a smooth one. Most bhaktas find that periods of spiritual consolation and bliss alternate with periods of aridity and dark nights, which if anything, are even more agonizing than those endured by jnanis. Why? Because the main reason jnanis experience dark nights is that, although they have achieved some degree of detachment from worldly pursuits, they have not yet tasted any of the path's spiritual fruits. If you are a bhakta, however, your detachment from worldly things will have been brought about precisely because you *have* experienced such spiritual favors. But this means that when the favors are no longer forthcoming, you will be doubly deprived—that is, unable to savor *either* worldly *or* spiritual delights. Here, for example, is what St. Catherine of Genoa says about one of her own dark nights:

> Incapable of feeling any joy, the Soul seemed to be stifled in melancholy, completely at a loss as to what to do. Neither heaven nor earth offered it a place of rest, and it avoided the company of men and the remembrance of past joys or sadness.[275]

Some bhaktas even feel betrayed by their Beloved. They blame God for withholding His love and so their anguish is mixed with anger. Listen to Mira Bai who actually berates Krishna for denying her His company:

> Why do You torment me?
> For Your sake I abandoned the world
> And my family.
> Why do you now forget me?
> You lit the fire of the pain of absence,
> But You have not returned to put it out....
> Thou has promised to save Thy devotees,
> Redeem Thy pledge![276]

Still others blame themselves and become overwhelmed with feelings of self-loathing and guilt. This was the case with Brother Lawrence who gives the following account of his trials:

> During the first ten years I suffered a great deal.... It seemed to me that all creatures, reason and God himself were against me, and that faith alone was on my side. I was sometimes troubled by thoughts that this was the result of my presumption, in that I pretended to be all at once where others were able to arrive only with difficulty. Other times I thought I was willingly damning myself, that there was no salvation for me.[277]

The truth, however, as all these mystics ultimately discovered, is that dark nights and periods of aridity do not come about because God has ceased to love you and is withholding His grace. On the contrary, these dark nights are themselves expressions of God's love and gifts of His grace. How so? Well, we can compare this to what used to happen in an old-fashioned courtship when a woman didn't just hop into bed with the first sweet-talking man to come along. She made him wait until he had proved that his love was genuine. And it is the same with Divine Love. There will be times when you, too, will feel as though your Beloved were testing you to see whether you are someone who is just looking for a one-night stand, or is ready to make a life-long commitment. A bit of Sufi lore, shared by Shaykh Muhammad Hisham Kabbani, wonderfully captures the essence of this kind of trial:

> God has given Gabriel the responsibility to look after the needs of His servants on earth. He says to him, "O Gabriel! take care of the heart of My believer. Remove from the heart of my believing servant the sweetness that he experienced in My love. Let me see how he will long for Me and whether his love is true."[278]

So the agony you experience in these dark nights is really a blessing in disguise, because this is what will motivate you to undertake any task, bear any hardship, make any sacrifice in order to be permanently united with your Beloved. For as Anandamayi Ma says,

> By the keen sense of want of the divine presence, a desperate yearning ensues and this will open the way to Self-realization.[279]

The Way of Selflessness

Part V: *Cultivating Love and Compassion*

Chapter 17

The Mystics' View of Morality

The reason the Buddha made keeping the Precepts so important was not so much for ethical reasons as for its bearing on mind development and its goal of the attainment of highest cognition and enlightenment. One cannot progress towards this goal if he is living a wicked or self-indulgent life.

— Dwight Goddard (Buddhist)

One of the reasons both jnanis and bhaktas experience dark nights when they start practicing detachment has to do with motivation. We are so conditioned to base our behavior on getting what we want and avoiding what we don't want that it's hard to imagine any other way of functioning in the world. Without the incentive of self-interest, why do anything at all? The problem is we have not yet discovered another, spiritually more mature motive for acting—one that transcends self-interest. So what is this more mature motive?

Actually, we all already know what it is, because it occurs naturally in our lives. We are talking, of course, about love and compassion. Whenever we are moved by love or compassion for another being, we are quite capable of setting aside our own interests in order to serve theirs. And the more we act out of this selfless impulse, the more we manifest that Love and Compassion inherent in Consciousness Itself. This is why all traditions regard cultivating love and compassion as indispensable to walking a spiritual path. Indeed, as Bokar Rinpoche says,

> Without love and compassion, every other practice, no matter how deep it may appear, is not a path to awakening.[280]

Now, the way to actively cultivate more love and compassion in your life is to start by interrupting your self-centered conditioning. And the way to do this is to begin keeping moral precepts. Unfortunately, this is a discipline many modern seekers neglect. No doubt this is due in part to a misunderstanding of what moral precepts are really all about—at least, from a mystic's perspective.

So before we delve into the specifics of how to practice keeping precepts, let us look at some of the most common misconceptions people have.

Three Views of Morality

In Western society today there are two dominant views of morality—1) the traditional, exoteric religious view, and 2) the more modern secular humanist view. Neither of these, however, represents the mystics' view.

The secular humanists' view of morality is based on a materialist paradigm that does not recognize any spiritual dimension to reality at all. Everything that exists is reducible to and can be explained by the interaction of matter and energy, including us human beings. For secular humanists, then, moral laws are not objective laws built into the structure of the cosmos. Rather, they are purely subjective inventions of our own brains. Similarly, judgments of right and wrong, good and bad are not absolute. All are relative, determined solely by cultural conventions, religious biases, and/or personal preference. As a result, the arguments which secular humanists make for adhering to moral precepts or ethical standards (as they prefer to call them) are not cosmological but sociological. If, they contend, everyone lived according to mutually agreed upon ethical standards, then as members of an ethical society we would all experience more happiness and less suffering.

Of course, when secular humanists make this argument they are not referring to any kind of *spiritual* happiness. Being materialists, in their view we *are* our bodies and nothing more. Consequently, the only real meaning happiness can have is to achieve the maximum satisfaction of bodily desires for material things like food, clothing, shelter, etc. Even the satisfaction of our "higher" needs for things like love, respect, creativity, and self-fulfillment ultimately depends on material conditions such as physical health and an affluent environment. This is why secular humanists usually present their ethics as part and parcel of a larger social and political program whose goal is the creation of a utopian society (or at least an approximation thereof) in which everyone's material requirements will be met to the fullest extent possible.

Now the problem mystics have with this humanist view of morality is that it does not address the *fundamental* causes of suffering and happiness, which, as we have seen, are only secondarily linked to the material conditions of our existence. The real source of our suffering is ignorance of our true nature caused by the delusion that we are separate selves, doomed to sickness, death and decay. This does not mean, however, that mystics are not interested in social and political problems, or concerned about issues such as poverty, peace, and justice. On the contrary, some of the world's greatest mystics have also been its greatest activists and reformers. What's more, this continues to be the case in our own time as exemplified by people like Gandhi, Simone Weil, and Thich Nhat Hanh—all of whom were and are *socially engaged* (to use a modern Buddhist term.) Still, mystics do not have any illusions that society can be perfected in a materialist sense or that, even if it could, this would make us all happy. Suffering, they insist, is not ultimately a material problem, but a spiritual one. For mystics, then, the improvement of society is not the main reason to practice morality. Mystics would practice morality even if there was no chance of improving society—in fact, even if there was no society at all! Even if they were stuck on a desert island with nothing but insects and reptiles, mystics would still keep precepts, practice virtues, and cultivate selfless love and compassion in order to interrupt their self-centered conditioning, dismantle the delusion of I, and attain Gnosis.

Unlike secular humanists, exoteric religionists do consider moral laws to be absolute, because, in their worldview, these laws reflect an Absolute Spiritual Reality. In this sense, moral laws are every bit as objective as any of the laws of physics. True, we are free to obey or disobey moral laws, but, in the end, we cannot escape the consequences of our actions. Good actions lead to happiness, bad ones to suffering. Of course, these consequences may not manifest within our limited life-spans here on earth. Like everyone else, exoteric religionists recognize that wicked people can survive to a ripe old age surrounded by their ill-gotten gains, while virtuous people often die young and in pitiful circumstances. But for exoteric religionists, physical death is by no means the end. In their view, we are in essence spiritual beings, rooted in a Spiritual Dimension of the Cosmos. So, even though our physical bodies may perish, something of us survives to experience the results of our actions—for better or worse.

Exactly how these results manifest is, of course, explained differently in different traditions. Generally speaking, Judaism, Christianity, and Islam maintain that, depending on the kind of life you have lived here on earth, you will go either to heaven or to hell when you die. According to Hindu and Buddhist cosmologies, on the other hand, you will continue to reincarnate in this realm of samsara until complete liberation is attained. In the meantime, whether you will be reborn into more or less favorable circumstances in your next life depends on how you behave in this one. And yet, despite these differences in the particulars of their belief systems, all exoteric religionists agree that *As you sow, so shall you reap*. Consequently, the exoteric religionists' motives for practicing morality are more personal than social. They hope to avoid future suffering and attain future happiness, whether this be in some postmortem state or a future incarnation.

In many respects, the mystics' view of morality is closer to the exoteric religionists' than to the secular humanists' view. Mystics certainly agree that moral laws are not just human inventions, but reflect "objective" or "absolute" cosmic principles. Exoteric religionists, however, tend to regard the precepts of their own moral codes as being absolute in themselves. When confronted with contradictions between their code and those of other traditions, they usually respond by declaring that those whose codes differ from theirs are either woefully misguided or downright demonic. Now, it must be admitted that some mystics, isolated in their own traditions, have held such views as well. But other mystics—especially ones who have lived in close proximity to people of different traditions—have seen things quite differently.

To give but one example, Ibn al-'Arabi was a faithful Muslim, who followed the moral laws revealed to the prophet Muhammad in the Qur'an. But growing up in the multi-cultural milieu of fourteenth-century Spain, he also learned to respect Christians and Jews, even though they followed different laws given by different prophets. For Ibn al-'Arabi, however, such discrepancies posed no problem:

> The knowledge with which they [the prophets] have been sent is according to the needs of their communities, no more nor less, since communities vary, some needing more than others.
> ...Thus, what is forbidden in one Law is permitted in another, from the formal standpoint. This does not mean that it is always permitted, since the divine Command [i.e., God's continuing self-disclosure] is [always] a new creation that is never repeated: so be alert.[281]

In other words, moral codes are to a certain extent relative. They can change over time with new revelations fashioned to meet new circumstances. But this does not mean that mystics like Ibn al-'Arabi hold that moral codes are *completely* relative. Whatever differences exist in their formulations, all derive from and reflect an Absolute Truth which, as we have already seen, is the Truth of Selflessness.

Selflessness, then, constitutes a universal moral Meta-Principle according to which actions *can* be judged right or wrong, good or bad. Self-ish actions are bad and wrong because they perpetuate the delusion of self that causes suffering. Self-less actions are good and right because they breakdown this delusion, making possible a Realization of our true nature and the Abiding Happiness that comes with it.

Notice that this is *not* a matter of individual, subjective opinion, as secular humanists claim. Obeying or disobeying the Law of Selflessness has definite consequences, whether an individual is aware of this fact or not. Thus, mystics concur with exoteric religionists, that in this sense the moral law is every bit as objective as the laws of physics. And yet at the same time, the actual moral codes which embody and articulate this Moral Meta-Principle are, as Ibn al-'Arabi recognized, relative and flexible. Why? Because an action that is selfless for one person, in one culture, at one time, may be selfish for another person, in another culture, at another time. So despite the fact that specific precepts do, indeed, vary from tradition to tradition, the Law of Selflessness is the common thread on which they all are strung.

For mystics, then, the essence of morality does not lie in outward conformity to all the details of a given code. The essence of morality is to be found in the purity of our inner intentions. From a mystic's point of view, moral precepts are designed to guide us toward selfless actions, and most of the time they do. But when we encounter situations where they do not, we must allow the Meta-Principle of Selflessness to override the particular precept and, as Jesus said, obey the *spirit* of the law rather than its *letter.*

Mystics also agree with exoteric religionists that there is some aspect of our being which does not perish with the body and will suffer the moral consequences of our deeds in this life and beyond. Unlike exoteric religionists, however, mystics do not practice morality because they aspire to a better rebirth or the pleasures of some celestial paradise. This kind of motivation might get you started on a spiritual path, but in the long run it will prove ineffective, for as St. Catherine of Siena writes,

> Fleeing sin for fear of punishment is not enough to give eternal life, nor is it enough to embrace virtue for one's own profit.[282]

In fact, if you continue practicing morality just so you can get into heaven and avoid hell, this self-centered grasping will itself become an obstacle. Thus, Rabi'a declares,

> I carry a torch in one hand
> And a bucket of water in the other:
> With these things I am going to set fire to Heaven
> And put out the flames of Hell
> So that the voyagers to God can rip the veils
> And see the real goal.[283]

Now, as we just said, the "real goal" for mystics is to attain Realization, and the reason they practice morality is to undo the self-centered conditioning which prevents this Realization from occurring. This is why the eleventh-century Sufi sage Al-Ghazzali writes,

> The aim of moral discipline is to purify the heart from the rust of passion and resentment, till, like a clear mirror, it reflects the light of God.[284]

Similarly, Longchen-pa says that training in morality

> purifies the habits of *samsāra* and dispels the stains from the essential nature, and causes enlightenment to be fully attained.[285]

So, too, Theophan the Recluse insists,

> The heart alone, despite all purification—if purification is possible without grace—will not give us wisdom; but the spirit of wisdom will not come to us unless we have prepared a pure heart to be its dwelling-place.[286]

How Precepts Function

So, how exactly do precepts purify our hearts? The first thing a precept does is to focus attention on everyday situations in which we are most likely to be acting out of self-interest. For instance, if you undertake to keep the precept *not to deceive others* and really try to practice it, you will start to become more mindful of those situations in which you *do* in fact deceive others. Just becoming aware that you are acting deceptively, however, does not mean you will able to stop—at least not immediately. In most cases, your self-centered conditioning is much too strong to be interrupted by a simple act of will. Like all spiritual practices, then, keeping precepts requires a real commitment.

This is an important point to emphasize, because it is easy for practitioners to get discouraged when they find they cannot alter their behavior overnight. Often they become very self-judgmental. They think there must be something wrong with them—that they are weak-willed or just plain no good. Not only is this kind of attitude counter-productive, it misses the whole point of the practice. Precepts are teaching tools designed to teach you about yourself—or rather about your delusion of self. In order to learn their lessons you must apply the virtues of courage, patience, and humility to your practice.

If you are able to do this, then as times goes by, you'll find you can view your own behavior with increasing impartiality, much like a zoologist watching animals in the wild. This, in turn, allows you to begin to see precisely what motivates your actions in the very moment they are unfolding. For example, when you catch yourself telling a lie, you might notice it is being prompted by some kind of grasping or attachment. If you are lying to someone you love, perhaps it's because you have become attached to them and want to retain their affection. If you are at work, you might be lying because you are attached to your job and are afraid of being fired for some mistake that you're covering up.

In any case, the more you can see that your behavior is based on an attachment, the more you have an opportunity to let that attachment go. This happens not because you have formed some psychological theory about what is causing your behavior, but because you directly see how grasping and attachment condition it. Suddenly, you realize, "It's this grasping and attachment that is causing my fear and my suffering!"—and so you drop it right there in the very moment it arises.

Keeping precepts purifies your heart and mind, because they allow you to have just these kinds of direct insight into exactly how your grasping and attachments create your conditioning. And the more insights you have, the more freedom you gain. Real freedom means to be free where it counts, in all the ordinary activities of your life—on the job, in relationships, doing the dishes, shopping—because that is where real suffering is generated.

Chapter 18

Keeping Precepts

Check all the activities of the ego, and the selfishness they involve.

— Shankara (Hindu)

If you already belong to an established religion, you should, of course, adhere to its precepts. If not, you may want to practice the following Ten Selfless Precepts used by our Practitioners Group at the Center for Sacred Sciences. They are as follows:

I vow to practice these *Ten Selfless Precepts.*

1. **RESPONSIBILITY:** To take responsibility for my life. Not to blame others for my own unhappiness, nor make excuses for my own mistakes.
2. **SELF-DISCIPLINE:** To regard each moment as a precious opportunity for spiritual practice. Not to waste time in frivolous pursuits, nor overindulge in drugs, alcohol, or escapist entertainments.
3. **HARMLESSNESS:** Not to injure or kill any being heedlessly or needlessly.
4. **STEWARDSHIP:** Not to waste the resources upon which other beings depend.
5. **HONESTY:** Not to deceive myself or others by word or deed.
6. **INTEGRITY:** Not to take what does not belong to me.
7. **HONOR:** To regard my word as sacred; not to give it lightly but, once given, strive to honor it under all circumstances.
8. **SEXUAL RESTRAINT:** To make of sex a sacrament, not to profane it in the pursuit of selfish ends.

9. **CHARITY**: Not to be possessive of people or things, but to give unsparingly of my assets, both material and spiritual, for the alleviation of suffering.

10. **REMEMBRANCE**: To recite these precepts once a day, renewing my vows and remembering this path which I have freely chosen.

Notice that the practice begins with a dedication: I vow to practice these *Ten Selfless Precepts.* This is important because it expresses your resolve to actually put these precepts into practice, rather than just pay lip-service to them. Now let us examine these precepts in more detail.

1. RESPONSIBILITY

To take responsibility for my life. Not to blame others for my own unhappiness, nor make excuses for my own mistakes.

This precept embodies a crucial spiritual insight—namely, that *suffering is always self-generated.* If this were not so—if suffering depended on anything outside yourself—then there would be no possibility of ending it and finding true, abiding Happiness. This is why the precept of taking responsibility for your life is so important. As long as you are blaming anyone or anything outside yourself for your own unhappiness, or making excuses for mistakes you've made, you will not be able to see that the real cause of suffering always lies within you.

Now, the way to begin practicing this precept is simply to start paying attention to your thoughts and speech. If you become attentive to what you think and say throughout the day, you will start to notice how often you try to excuse your behavior. This may involve nothing more than concocting a little white lie to explain why you were late for an appointment: "Sorry, there was a traffic accident on the highway." Or you may find yourself trying to rationalize away something more serious, like an extra-marital affair: "I only did it because you've been so distant lately and I was lonely." But whether major or minor, the net effect of making excuses is to deflect attention from your own actions and the selfish motives that govern them. And if you're unwilling to face your behavior, there's no way to change it.

Likewise, if you begin to watch what you think and say more closely, you'll see how many times a day you try to place the blame on someone else whenever you feel unhappy. For example, you might go to a restaurant where the food is terrible, so you blame the cook for making you suffer. The cook is certainly responsible for the taste of the food, but not for your suffering: Your suffering is your responsibility. Or on the job, you might blame your unhappiness on a rude co-worker, and think, "If only that person weren't here, I'd be happy." But, again, it doesn't matter how rude someone is, your suffering comes not from them, but from your response to them.

Sometimes it is not any particular person we blame for our unhappiness, but something more impersonal, like fate, or bad luck, or even God. This kind of blaming is harder to notice, because we don't always express it in concrete words or thoughts. Often, it manifests as a mood of self-pity. You find yourself sitting around feeling sorry for yourself, because you are not richer, or more beautiful, or more intelligent, or because you have gotten sick, or lost a lover, or been laid-off from work. You feel unhappy and depressed and so you blame the circumstances of your life, rather than look inside to see the suffering's true source.

Once you become mindful of this tendency to blame others and make excuses, you can begin to check it. Whenever you catch yourself complaining to a friend that someone or something else is causing your unhappiness, simply discontinue that train of thought. This does not mean you should never express your feelings, or talk about the circumstances which triggered them. It's one thing to say, "I'm having a difficult time getting along with my co-worker," but quite another to say "My co-worker is making me miserable." The important point is to realize you have a *choice* in how you are going to respond mentally and emotionally to any situation. This is what "taking responsibility" actually means.

2. SELF-DISCIPLINE

To regard each moment as a precious opportunity for spiritual practice. Not to waste time in frivolous pursuits, nor overindulge in drugs, alcohol, or escapist entertainments.

Notice that this precept has two parts. The first part serves as a reminder that every moment of your life is valuable. Why? Because in every moment you have an opportunity to gain insight into delusion and, ultimately, to become free of it. The second part of the precept is *not to waste time in frivolous pursuits.* This is important for several reasons. For one thing, the spiritual path itself requires time for doing things like studying teachings and engaging in practices of meditation or prayer. Obviously, the more time you spend in frivolous pursuits the less time you have for these activities.

But aside from such practical considerations, curtailing frivolous pursuits is valuable in its own right. This is because, whenever you do so, the second link in your chain of conditioning—chronic restlessness—comes to the fore. Now if you look into this restlessness, you might discover something very interesting. Not only is it a manifestation of your search for happiness 'out there' in the world, it is at the same time an attempt to escape something 'in here'—namely, your sense of being a separate self. What this shows is that, despite the fact you spend so much of your life trying to enhance and protect yourself, ironically, when you are alone with this self you actually experience it as something painful. Thus, your compulsion to engage in frivolous pursuits is really motivated by a desire to get away from yourself. This is why, if you ask most people what they like about watching movies, attending a football game, going dancing, or getting drunk they will tell you, "because when I do these things I feel like I can lose myself."

Now the trouble with this strategy is that, although losing yourself in some frivolous pursuit may temporarily alleviate your suffering, it also totally absorbs your attention. Consequently, there's no possibility of attaining any insights into the self's true nature and, by doing so, liberating yourself from suffering altogether. So when the movie is finished, the game is over, or the state of intoxication wears off, your old sense of self returns and you're right back where you started from. If, on the other hand, you resist the impulse to escape from your sense of self by engaging in frivolous pursuits, and, instead, you're willing to look into it with undistracted mind, then your chances of discovering the self's true nature increase dramatically.

Having said all this, however, it is important to notice that this precept does not require that you *never* indulge in drugs, alcohol, or escapist entertainments—only that you don't *over*-indulge. Some traditions insist on total abstinence from one or more of these things. But our precepts are lay precepts, designed for householders who have chosen to take everyday life as their spiritual path. Therefore, the aim of the precept of self-discipline is not to completely abandon ordinary recreational activities, only to stop indulging in them compulsively as a means of escaping from yourself.

So, then the following question arises: What constitutes *over*-indulgence? Since this will be different for different people, each practitioner must decide for him or herself. A good place to begin is to pay attention to exactly what motivates your behavior. If, for example, you sit down in front of the television and start flipping through the channels for something to watch simply because you're lonely or bored, that's a pretty good indication you're over-indulging. This is quite different from watching a program you had planned to see in advance. Or, if every time you feel stressed, you gulp down three or four martinis and pass out on the couch oblivious to the world, that is almost certainly a sign of over-indulgence. This is different from enjoying a little wine with dinner, or having a few drinks at a party. Again the point is, whenever you engage in any activity as a way of distracting yourself from your suffering, you're missing an opportunity to discover its true cause, and so free yourself from it forever.

3. HARMLESSNESS

Not to injure or kill any being heedlessly or needlessly.

There have always been some seekers who take a vow not to kill any beings, period. In our own day, this usually entails becoming a vegetarian. Dietary practices like this can be very productive. But, at the same time, it's important not to imagine that by forswearing all meat you can escape one of the most fundamental laws of this world—the *law of sacrifice*. Up and down the food chain, every life form ends up sacrificing itself so that some other life form can live. Most vegetarians make a distinction between "sentient" and "non-sentient" beings—which is useful for the purposes of their practice. But it must also be recognized that such distinctions are ultimately imaginary. In reality, there is no hard and fast line between a cow and a carrot. In fact, there is no hard and fast line between life and non-life. On the relative plane, the whole Cosmos is nothing but one continuous cycle of creation and destruction—a great sacrificial feast in which we all participate, whether we like it or not.

The same holds true if you become a strict pacifist—that is, someone who vows not to commit violence against another human being under any circumstances. If you ever find yourself in a position where your vow is actually put to the test, this will present a powerful opportunity for spiritual practice. In the meantime, however, you must guard against developing spiritual pride, which, in this case, is to believe that you are somehow morally superior to those who are not pacifists. You must recognize that whatever social peace and justice you presently enjoy depends on people who *are* willing to engage in violence—those soldiers, police, judges, and jailers, who enforce the laws and defend us against criminals and aggressors. This is simply the way human societies function—at least, in their present stage of development—and there is no reason to suppose things will change radically in the foreseeable future.

So if you feel personally called upon to become a vegetarian or a pacifist, by all means do so. But if you think that these practices will somehow allow you to rise above the "sordid realities" of this world, you are mistaken. Worse, you are in danger of missing what the practice of harmlessness is really about. The real question is not *whether* to participate in the world as we find it; the real question is how to do it *skillfully*. Are you going to participate in an ignorant, grasping, and self-centered way? Or, are you going to do it selflessly, with awareness, compassion, and gratitude? This is what the precept to refrain from killing any being "heedlessly" or "needlessly" helps us to attain.

To vow not to kill any being *needlessly* means you recognize that there are some situations in which killing may be not only necessary, but actually the most selfless thing to do. Someone who kills a mass murderer about to slaughter innocent people is an obvious example. It may sometimes be necessary to kill predators in order to protect an endangered species on which they prey; or to cull animal herds to prevent them from being devastated by starvation and disease. So, too, a good deal of modern medicine involves the wholesale destruction of micro-organisms, such as viruses, bacteria, and parasites, in order to alleviate human suffering and prolong human life. The difference here has to do with motivation. In situations like the ones above you can ask yourself this question: Am I killing some being to satisfy my own pleasure or convenience? Or am I killing because that is what is required for the good of the whole?

The more subtle part of this precept is not to kill any being *heedlessly*. In other words, if you must kill, do it with mindfulness. If a mosquito lands on your cheek, don't just swat it in an unthinking way. Be aware that you are actually taking a life and what that means. Make a conscious decision as to whether or not it is really necessary. Similarly, whenever you sit down to eat, don't just take your food for granted. Realize that whatever is on your plate was once a living being. Be grateful to those plants and animals who have given their own lives so that you can live. There is no life without death. Do not try to blot this reality out of your mind through heedlessness. The spiritual path is not about *escaping* suffering and death, but *transcending* them by seeing their true nature.

4. STEWARDSHIP

Not to waste the resources upon which other beings depend.

This precept is especially appropriate for our modern, industrial society, which is inundating our whole environment with tons of waste materials whose cumulative effects may well prove to be catastrophic. Still, from a strictly spiritual point of view, the main reason to practice stewardship is not to save the planet. If more people practiced it, this would certainly be a welcome result. But, spiritually speaking, it does not really get to the heart of the problem. The main reason to practice stewardship is to cure ourselves of the delusion that happiness can be achieved through the consumption of material goods. This is why, as a spiritual seeker, you would practice stewardship even if there was no hope of saving the planet. Even if the world's leading scientists announced it was already too late, the damage had been done, the green-house effect was irreversible, and in ten years all life would be wiped out—you would still want to be careful not to waste the resources upon which other beings depend.

So how do you practice this precept? And how will it transform you spiritually? Most of us already know the answer to the first question. Not wasting resources means doing simple things, like recycling cans, bottles, and paper products. It means not buying things you do not need in the first place. It means not wasting food, heat, gas, electricity, etc. It means not throwing away things other people can use, but taking the time to find out what charitable organizations you can donate them to. Today, there are any number of books full of practical tips on how to implement stewardship in your daily life.

The answer to the second question is that the way practicing stewardship transforms you is to increase your mindfulness of your own consumer mentality and the self-centered grasping it generates. Once you have identified this grasping, you can then check it, thereby opening a space of awareness in which to cultivate a genuine respect and appreciation for the things you *do* use.

To give but one example, suppose the car you own is getting old, its paint is fading and the fenders have lot of dents in them. Now, if you have a consumer mentality, one day while you are out driving you might notice a sports car which you recently saw in a TV commercial whiz by. In the commercial the car was being driven by a handsome guy with a glamorous blonde leaning against his shoulder. Remembering this image, you feel a combination of distaste for the car you now own, and a wish to have the kind of sports car that just passed you by. In other words, the fifth link in the chain of conditioning—desire and aversion—kicks in. This will immediately be followed by the grasping that arises in the sixth link, which prompts you to think, "Damn it, I deserve a car like that, too!" Then, in the next moment, you'll find you have fallen into the seventh link, deliberation, in which your mind furiously starts trying to figure a way to finance a sports car of your own. And if you, in fact, do manage to get one, what's going to happen? At first you will feel quite thrilled. But after a few months the thrill will wear off. And in a year or two the paint will start to fade, and the fenders will get dented, and so where will all this have gotten you?

If, on the other hand, you have cultivated a sense of stewardship, then every time you climb into your old car, you'll be mindful of how much work went into its manufacture. You'll think of the engineers who designed it, the miners who extracted the metals, the glass-makers who made the windshields, the assembly-line workers who bolted it all together, the painters who painted it, the truckers who hauled it to the lot where you bought it. It's really quite amazing—all that coordinated human energy—and here you are reaping the benefit! Because of all these people's work, you are now able to drive comfortably along on a road instead of riding on the back of a burro. Pondering this, you will start to appreciate how incredibly fortunate you are. After all, how many people in the world actually drive their own cars? Nor did you really do anything to deserve this bit of luck. You just happened to be born in a particularly prosperous country. If you had been born in many other countries, you would be lucky to own even a burro! So, instead of dissatisfaction and envy, you'll be filled with gratitude and delight.

This is what practicing stewardship is really all about. It breaks you out of that isolation which comes from always focusing on yourself, and begins to reconnect you to the whole human family. Through simple mindfulness, you start to realize that all the material things you depend on—your house, your clothes, your food, your car—were shaped by other people's hands, and bear the stains of other people's sweat. And beyond that, stewardship is also about reconnecting you to the materials, themselves—the ground your house stands on, the wood in its walls, the metals in your appliances, the fabrics in your furniture, the electricity in your wires—all of which are miraculous manifestations of Consciousness Itself, dancing that wondrous Cosmic Dance we call the Universe.

5. HONESTY

Not to deceive myself or others by word or deed.

One of the most common ways seekers deceive themselves concerns their own need (or lack thereof) for practicing this precept. Most of us like to believe we are basically honest people who rarely tell lies. But if we pay close attention to what we actually say, we usually find this is not really the case. In fact, most of us lie in lots of little ways, but then mask our dishonesty with all sorts of rationalizations.

For instance, someone might ask you out on a date. You don't want to go, so you tell them, "Oh, I've already got plans for Friday night. Maybe some other time." If another person were to point out to you that you had just told a lie, you might say, "Well, yes, but I only did it because I didn't want to hurt their feelings." Now, maybe that's true. Maybe you told that lie out of a completely selfless concern for the other person. But maybe you were lying because you didn't want to take the time to try to communicate your true feelings in a compassionate and tactful way. If that's the case, you are deceiving yourself with a rationalization.

People who are normally honest can even deceive themselves about major forms of misconduct without being fully aware of it. A few years ago there was a news story about victims of a hurricane who filed insurance claims after their homes had been destroyed. What the reporter discovered was that many people exaggerated the value of their losses in order to take advantage of windfall insurance payments. These people were not professional crooks or con-artists, but supposedly decent folks. One school teacher who was interviewed confessed to feeling some guilt about what she had done, but said, "Everyone else was getting extra money, so I felt I deserved some, too." In her heart of hearts she knew she was being dishonest, but her grasping mind came up with a way to justify her actions anyway.

It's even possible to use this very precept as a rationalization for harming others. Suppose, for example, someone criticizes you, and you respond by cataloging all of their own shortcomings. If you then defend your outburst by saying something like, "I just had to tell the truth, because I have taken a vow not to lie," you are using the precept not to foster selflessness, but as an excuse for exacting revenge.

Misusing precepts like this is something we always have to be on guard against. There may, indeed, be times when you want to draw attention to another person's faults out of a genuine desire to help them improve. But if this is truly your intention, you will try to do it as constructively as possible, and certainly not as a way of retaliating for reproaches leveled against yourself.

6. INTEGRITY

Not to take what does not belong to me.

There is a lot more to this precept than first meets the eye. It doesn't just mean to refrain from stealing in the grossest sense of the term—i.e., committing crimes such as shop-lifting, theft, or burglary. It also means not pocketing little items like pens and pencils from your work place and taking them home for your own personal use. It means that if a store clerk gives you too much change, you return the excess amount. When tax time comes around, it means not trying to hide income which you have an obligation to report, or to claim deductions for expenses you did not in fact incur.[287] And if you continue practicing this precept with diligence, you will find there are even more subtle things you can "steal." If you hog a conversation at a dinner party, you are robbing other people of a chance to participate. If you choose your sister's wedding day to announce that you need to have open-heart surgery, you are stealing the attention that rightfully belongs to her on that occasion. If you are over-protective of family and friends—especially youngsters—you may be stealing opportunities for them to make their own decisions and learn from their own mistakes.

Ultimately, practicing the precept of integrity will lead you to discover that nothing truly belongs to you—not your house, your car, your family, your friends—not even your own body! In reality, they all "belong" to Consciousness, because it is Consciousness which manifests them. So, if you want to practice this precept to the fullest extent, you will give everything you possess back to Consciousness and never claim anything for yourself again.

7. HONOR

To regard my word as sacred; not to give it lightly but, once given, strive to honor it under all circumstances.

As with other precepts, the first step is to become aware of those situations in which you break your word—even in seemingly insignificant ways. For instance, while talking to a co-worker you might offer to get some information for them, and end by saying, "I'll give you a ring tomorrow." But, when tomorrow rolls around you find you are very busy, and so you catch yourself thinking, "Oh, well, my colleague doesn't really need that information right away—I'll call him later in the week." For the purposes of this precept, however, it doesn't matter whether your colleague really needs the information right away or not. What matters is that *you gave your word* that you would call the *next* day. So, no matter how busy you are, you should try to honor it—even if you have to sacrifice a coffee break or part of a lunch hour to do so.

The second step is to become mindful about what comes out of your mouth in the first place, so that you don't end up giving your word *lightly*. This means not casually saying, "I'll call you tomorrow," without really considering whether you will actually be able to follow through. It's much better to say, "I'll try to get the information you want, but it may take me a week or more to get back to you, because I'm pretty busy these days."

Sometimes, this can put you in an uncomfortable position—especially when people pressure you to make promises you are not really prepared to keep. In such cases you must have the courage to say "no" and mean it. Learning to say "no" is very important for spiritual seekers, because there are a lot of "no's" on the path: "No, I can't go to your party Friday, because that's the night I go to my meditation class." "No, I can't tell your aunt Tilly you're not home, because I've taken a precept not to lie." "No, I can't have sex with you even though we're on a business trip alone in a strange city where no one will ever find out, because I promised my spouse I'd be faithful."

Once you have given your word, the next step in practicing this precept is to *strive* to honor it. Sometimes we cannot help breaking a promise. Physical conditions simply make it impossible to fulfill. You may have promised your family you would be home for dinner, but you get a flat tire on the way. There is nothing you can do about that, except call to say you will be late. Sometimes it is not just physical circumstances which prevent us from keeping a promise. Situations can arise unexpectedly which have a higher moral priority. If you promised to be home for dinner, and you see an accident on the highway in which people have been injured, obviously your first duty is to stop and help them, even though this means breaking your promise to your family. Sometimes it will be difficult to decide which is more important. Suppose, for example, you are rushing home because it is your twenty-fifth wedding anniversary, and you see a car pulled over with the hood-up. A couple of young men are standing around talking nonchalantly. If no one appears to be hurt, and there are plenty of other cars on the road, you might pass them by, assuming someone with a less pressing engagement will stop to help. In such cases, you just have to make the best decision you can. That is all that is ever required—that we do the best we can. But we do have to *strive* to really make it the "best."

Finally, it is important to keep promises you make to yourself. Let's say you decide to go on a ten-day meditation retreat. Having never been on such a long retreat, you may get nervous as the date of the retreat approaches and start having doubts. If you listen to your mind, you will hear it making up all sorts of excuses for why you shouldn't go: "I really can't afford to take so much time off from work." "I've just begun a new relationship with someone and right now it's more important to spend the time with that person." Or, "It's really selfish to go away because my cat will miss me so." In short, you must be just as vigilant about not breaking promises made to yourself as you are about not breaking promises made to others—particularly when it involves a commitment to engage in some form of spiritual practice.

8. SEXUAL RESTRAINT

To make of sex a sacrament, not to profane it in the pursuit of selfish ends.

The second part of this precept is easier to understand than the first, so let's start with that. What does it mean *not to profane sex in the pursuit of selfish ends*? First of all, it means that we must learn to control our sexual behavior, so that we don't end up hurting others in attempts to gratify our own desires. For a number of historical reasons, it was necessary for societies in the past to formulate very strict guidelines as to when and where sexual restraint had to be exercised. Before the advent of reliable birth control, for example, sexual intercourse usually led to childbirth. As a result, most traditions had a prohibition against pre-marital sex—especially for women. This helped to insure that children would be born into a viable family capable of caring for them. In pre-industrial societies this was particularly important because it was almost impossible for a single woman to financially support herself, let alone a house full of children. But, as we all know, things have changed. Not only have modern methods of birth control allowed us to separate sex from procreation, but in giving women an opportunity to work, the industrial revolution has rendered obsolete most of the economic and social reasons for adhering to traditional sexual prohibitions. Yet, despite these momentous changes, there are still many situations in which we can profane sex by causing suffering if we fail to practice restraint.

Starting with the most obvious, we must refrain from rape or in any way physically forcing someone to have sex against their will. We must not commit adultery or try to seduce a person who is already in a committed relationship. Unless we are prepared to take full responsibility for raising a child, we must also refrain from engaging in sexual intercourse without proper birth-control. This is something men have to assume responsibility for just as much as women. Even though it may now be economically feasible for a woman to raise a child on her own, this is not necessarily best for the child. Usually, children fare better when they have the emotional and spiritual support of two parents instead of only one.

Rape, adultery, and reckless procreation—these actions are clearly profane, because they cause direct suffering to others. But we also profane sex more subtly when we try to use it to manipulate people for our own selfish ends. Withholding sex to pressure your spouse into giving you something you want is a good example. So is demanding sex from an employee in exchange for a raise; or, in the opposite case, sleeping with your boss in order to further your career.

At an even subtler level, we can manipulate people sexually without ever engaging in any overt activity. Some men and women relish making themselves as attractive as possible in the hopes of arousing sexual desire in others. If they succeed, they feel no need to physically consummate their conquest. Simply knowing that they *could* have seduced their victims constitutes enough of a psychological triumph to give their egos a temporary boost.

In general, keeping the precept of sexual restraint makes us more mindful of all aspects of our sex lives, both internal and external. Many practitioners are surprised to discover just how much of their time and energy is consumed in pursuit of sexual gratification, whether in fact or in fantasy. This is not to say there is anything wrong with sex *per se*. The problem lies in our deluded attitude towards it. We falsely believe that if only we could find the right partner, or the right technique, sex would satisfy our quest for happiness. But whatever kind of sex we have—whether it's a one-night-stand or part of a long-term relationship—the pleasure we gain will always be ephemeral. Only Enlightenment can bring us abiding happiness, and so the ultimate way we profane sex is by pursuing it as if it had the same value.

Of course, we do this with other things as well—money, power, fame—but for most people sex holds a special allure. This is because, on those rare occasions when we can fully surrender ourselves, sex is, indeed, capable of catapulting us into states of ecstasy in which we are transported beyond our limited egos and, for a fleeting moment, can taste the Bliss of Consciousness Itself. And yet the very fact that sexual surrender on the physical plane can so closely mimic surrender on the spiritual plane is precisely why all mystical traditions have regarded it as a particularly dangerous distraction. Instead of struggling to discover that limitless Ocean of Happiness which Gnosis discloses, we end up chasing mere flecks of its foam.

For this reason, many traditions have recommended complete celibacy as the easiest and most effective way to deal with sexual desire and the social entanglements it so often entails. If we exercise restraint, however, it is possible to walk a spiritual path without vowing total abstinence. In fact, it is even possible to transform sex itself into a precious opportunity for spiritual practice—which brings us back to the first part of our precept, *to make of sex a sacrament*. So, what exactly does this mean?

St. Augustine defined a *sacrament* as "the visible sign of an invisible grace." Now the invisible grace of which sex is a sign is love. In other words, sex becomes sacramental when it is engaged in not for the sake of satisfying your own desires, but in order to express genuine love. This does not mean you have to be madly in love with someone in order for sex to be sacred. In fact, being "in love" often involves feelings of possessiveness and jealousy that really are signs not of love but of self-centered grasping. Nor does sacramental sex necessitate making a life-long commitment to your partner. What it does mean is that you truly care for that person and are concerned about his or her welfare.

Of course, there are many people who love their partners but do not consider themselves to be the least bit spiritual. In such cases, sex is still a sacrament, only the participants are unaware of it. The task of the spiritual seeker is to make sex a *conscious* sacrament. How can this be done? Very briefly, there are three ways.

The first is to recognize that true, selfless love is, indeed, a grace—i.e., a "gift" which comes from the Divine. This recognition makes the person who arouses love in us an "ambassador of God." When you engage in sex with this in mind, then, in addition to being an expression of love for that person in his or her own right, it also becomes an expression of gratitude for the Divine gift which you have received.

The second and more advanced way to make sex a sacrament only becomes possible when you gain a deeper insight, which is to realize that your lover is an actual manifestation of Consciousness. By sexually surrendering yourself to this Divine Manifestation, then, you transform what was once a purely personal activity into an embodiment of the Archetypal Union between the human lover and the Divine Beloved. If there is also present the conscious intention to conceive a child, sex becomes an embodiment of the Archetypal Act of Creation as well.

The third and most difficult way to sacralize sex is to engage in those formal sexual practices which have been developed by certain Hindu and Buddhist schools of *tantra*. What makes these practices so difficult is that they require not only the guidance of a qualified teacher, but also a regimen of yogic training to control the subtle energies which is every bit as rigorous as the physical training of an athlete headed for the Olympics. Without a teacher and this kind of discipline, tantra is definitely not something to dabble in. In fact, practicing it improperly can have disastrous consequences for a seeker's mental and spiritual health. This is why the Tibetan masters say that a tantric practitioner is like a snake in a hollow piece of bamboo. It has only two ways to go—straight up, or straight down.

9. CHARITY

Not to be possessive of people or things, but to give unsparingly of my assets, both material and spiritual, for the alleviation of suffering.

For most people in our society charity means writing a check for some worthy cause, participating in various fund-raising events, or if you are exceptionally wealthy, giving a million-dollar endowment to some university or hospital. Now while such activities may be of great social benefit, from a spiritual point of view, they have a number of problems.

One of them has to do with motivation. People who practice charity in this way usually do so, at least in part, out of a desire to receive something in return, whether this be a tax write-off, the admiration of their peers, or a building named after them. In other words, although outwardly altruistic, their acts are still inwardly dictated by self-centered conditioning. The main reason to engage in charity as a spiritual practice, however, is to create concrete opportunities for us to interrupt this conditioning and act selflessly, without any expectation of a reward. As with practicing the other precepts, of course, most seekers find this is easier said than done.

The first step in practicing charity is to become aware of exactly what sort of attachments you have. And the way to do this is to pay close attention to your thoughts whenever you are faced with an opportunity to give something, no matter how small. In this country, for example, many grocery stores have a little can on the counter where you can deposit spare change to help cure some disease or fund some philanthropic enterprise. Now, the average person in our society can afford to give something—say, twenty-five cents—but do you? If not, then next time you see one of those cans, ask yourself, "Why not?" and notice the answers your mind generates. You might, for instance, find yourself thinking this: "I'm not going to give to one of those organized charities, because so much of the money goes to big salaries for their executives." Then, on your way out of the store you might pass a transient with a sign saying, "Hungry—Please Help." Again, watch how your mind comes up with reasons to pass him by: "That guy's probably an alcoholic. If I give him money, he'll just blow it on a bottle of cheap wine." Finally, when you get home, a couple of young college students might knock on your door soliciting money for orphans in Africa. Again, you might find yourself thinking this: "How do I know these kids aren't con-artists?"—so you end up muttering something about having given at the office and send them on their way. Watching your thought processes in these situations can make you acutely aware of how reluctant you are to part with even a single quarter—especially when doing so promises no benefit for yourself.

The next step is to pay attention to your emotional and physical reactions whenever anyone approaches you for money. For example, if you think that they are trying to take advantage of you, you'll grow anxious and defensive. The muscles in your chest will constrict slightly, your breathing will get shallow and you will feel your heart close down. In short, what you will experience is suffering—not major suffering to be sure—but suffering nonetheless. This is important to notice, because right then you have an opportunity to ask yourself, "Is my suffering coming from something *outside* of myself—from the person asking me for money? Or, is it something that arises *inside* me, based on my own attachments?" Then you can try a simple experiment. The next time someone approaches you for a hand-out, ignore whatever grasping thoughts your mind produces, and give them some change. Watch how your muscles relax, how your heart begins to open, and your thoughts starts to clear. Once you have this kind of insight into the connection between an attachment and the suffering it causes, letting go of the attachment becomes easy.

This brings us to another thing wrong with the way charity is usually practiced. Most people only give every so often—usually on holidays or at the end of the tax year. But this means their opportunities to engage in charity are quite limited. Rather than donating a lump sum once a year, it would be more beneficial for spiritual purposes to spread your donation out, giving away a few dollars every week. Or you might take a vow that every time you see one of those little cans in a grocery store you will donate some amount—even if it's only a few pennies. If you are particularly zealous, you might make it a point to give something to someone at least once every day. Whatever you decide, the important thing is to find concrete ways to practice the precept of charity as often as you can.

A big problem many people have with practicing charity is determining how much of their assets they should give away. Obviously, there is no set figure. It all depends on your personal circumstances. If you are a householder, you have responsibilities to your family. You can't give away money you've been saving for your children's education just to satisfy your own aspiration to practice charity. However, you should give at least enough to cause a little internal resistance. Why? Because if there's no resistance, chances are you haven't touched into an attachment, and uncovering attachments so you can surrender them is the whole point of this practice.

You should also be aware that the attachments which practicing charity exposes are not necessarily material. For instance, in our culture people are very possessive of their time. You might be coming out of a supermarket and see some elderly woman struggling with an armload of packages. Obviously, she could use some help, but you pass her by because you are in a hurry to get home to watch your favorite TV show. Charity in this situation does not mean giving something material but something more intangible. It means giving of your time and energy.

Finally, the precept of charity includes giving of your spiritual as well as your material assets. This means sharing the experiences and insights you gain on the path so that others can learn from them. Here, however, you must be especially careful about your motivation. If you treat your experiences and insights as something to brag about, you are just feeding the Story of I. On the other hand, if, out of a false sense of modesty, you keep silent about your experiences and insights when others would genuinely benefit, you are withholding the greatest gift anyone can bestow. So be mindful. A good rule of thumb is to speak of spiritual experiences only to someone who seems sincerely interested, and then only divulge those things which directly relate to that person's situation.

Of all the precepts, practicing charity is in many ways the most powerful. Nothing brings our self-centered conditioning into the light of awareness more quickly or vividly than trying to give unsparingly of our assets. Moreover, if you continue to practice with diligence, you will discover a great secret. It is quite literally *better to give than to receive,* because everything we receive with a grasping mind ultimately increases our sufferings. But whatever we give away with love and compassion increases our joy, and ultimately carries us to Enlightenment Itself. Thus, when we practice charity we begin by giving away quarters and end by giving away our very selves.

10. REMEMBRANCE

To recite these precepts once a day, renewing my vows and remembering this path which I have freely chosen.

You cannot practice these precepts unless you know precisely what they are. Reciting them once a day accomplishes this. It plants them deep in your psyche, so you don't have to muddle about trying to remember which precept applies in which situation. They will be internalized, waiting to be triggered by specific events that arise during the course of a normal day. You might, for example, find yourself rushing out of that supermarket and, when you see that little old lady struggling with her packages, your vow of charity will automatically kick in. A space of awareness will open up and you will suddenly become very mindful. You will clearly see your attachment to your TV show but, at the same time, you will also see a way to break it, because right then and there you'll have an opportunity to drop your attachment and help the old woman, instead.

That is how all these precepts work. They make us mindful of those situations where we can actually do something to break through our conditioned behavior. Some seekers have even experienced precepts popping up in their dreams. But whether dreaming or awake, if you continue to practice these precepts, you will experience for yourself their profound transformative power. When you look back after six months or a year, you will see that you are a different person, because you will be *living* a different life. This is what true spiritual transformation is all about—which is why you cannot restrict your spiritual practice to just those times set aside for formal meditation or prayer. You can have lots of insights in meditation and wonderful experiences while praying; and you can listen to spiritual music and hang spiritual pictures on your wall: but if you are not practicing selflessness day-by-day, none of this will have any deep effect. This is why Teresa of Avila says,

> You must not build upon foundations of prayer and contemplation alone, for, unless you strive after the virtues and practice them, you will never grow to be more than dwarfs.[288]

Chapter 19

Sending and Taking

Even as a mother protects with her life
Her child, her only child,
So with a boundless heart
Should one cherish all living beings,
Radiating kindness over the entire world.

— Metta Sutta (Buddhist)

As we saw in the last chapter, practicing moral precepts allows you to identify and interrupt actions based on self-centered desires and aversions. The next step is to begin to actively cultivate selfless love and compassion as a basis for your actions. The importance of this practice for both jnanis and bhaktas cannot be over-emphasized. Jesus, for example, calls *loving your neighbor as yourself* the second greatest commandment, while Krishna tells Arjuna,

> I love my devotee—
> the man of discipline always happy,
> Controlling himself, firm of will,
> accepting all creatures
> With solidarity and compassion,
> not selfish, not self-centered.[289]

The Qur'an spells out in detail what it means to act compassionately:

> Show kindness to parents, and to near kindred, and orphans, and the needy, and to the neighbour who is your kin and the neighbour who is not your kin, and the fellow-traveller and the wayfarer and those whom you have power over.[290]

And in Tibetan Buddhism, cultivating love and compassion is considered a foundation for all other spiritual disciplines, for as the nineteenth-century Tibetan master Jamgon Kongtrul declares:

> The whole basis of mind training is contained in the two principles of throwing out concern for your own welfare and taking complete hold of the welfare of others.[291]

Notice, however, that there is something interesting about *how* these mystics describe the cultivation of love and compassion. Jesus refers to it as a "commandment," Krishna links it to "discipline," and Jamgon Kongtrul says it requires "training." But if, as we said in chapter 17, love and compassion occur naturally in our lives, why all this insistence on making them into what sounds like some sort of austere practice?

Overcoming the Fear of Love

The reason we need to *practice* love and compassion is that, although they do, indeed, occur naturally, under delusion we are afraid to completely surrender ourselves to them. This is rooted in our existential fear that surrendering our identity as a separate self will result in annihilation. In our everyday human relationships this existential fear manifests as the specific fear that if we really threw out "concern for our own welfare" and took "complete hold of the welfare of others," people would take advantage of us. Thus, when feelings of love or compassion do arise they are usually countered by feelings of anxiety and apprehension. We crave the happiness that love promises but, at the same time, we cling to the very thing that stands in the way of fully experiencing that happiness—concern for ourselves.

In order to overcome our fear of love and compassion, we need to exercise the virtue of courage. There is simply no other way to truly dispel our fear than to face it squarely and convince ourselves, through our own experience, that it's unfounded. We can compare this situation to that of a child who is afraid of the water because she hasn't yet learned to swim. Now, there are a number of things you can say to try to reassure her. You can explain that if she just relaxes, the water itself will hold her up. You can show her how to move her hands and feet in a certain manner. But the only real way the child is going to overcome her fear and learn to swim is to actually get in the water and try it. Moreover, once the child does this everything changes. The very same medium which originally filled her with terror becomes transformed into a source of wonder and delight. So we might say the rule for swimming is *you have to act before you can know* and it is the same with cultivating selfless love and compassion. In the beginning you have to make an effort to practice despite your fear of what might happen. This is why St. Teresa of Avila insists:

> You must do violence to your own will, so that your sister's will is done in everything, even though this may cause you to forgo your own rights and forget your own good in your concern for theirs, and however much your physical powers may rebel. If the opportunity presents itself, too, try to shoulder some trial in order to relieve your neighbour of it.[292]

Like the child learning to swim, however, this doesn't mean you have to dive into the middle of the ocean the first time out. You can begin in the shallows and then, as you gain confidence, work your way into deeper waters. Similarly, most seekers find it is easier to cultivate selfless love and compassion gradually, taking it one step at a time.

Start with Sending and Taking

A good way to begin cultivating selfless love and compassion is to engage in what the Tibetans call "sending and taking" or *tong-len*. This is a practice in which you visualize yourself taking on the suffering of other beings while sending out love and compassion to them. Of course, this same practice is found in other traditions as well. For example, the ninth-century Sufi Shaykh Sari Saqati expresses its essence beautifully:

> I would that all the sorrow and grief which burdens the hearts of others descend on my heart, that they be delivered from grief.[293]

And in Christianity, Christ's bodily incarnation provides a Cosmic Archetype of sending and taking, insofar as God takes on Himself the suffering and death of an ordinary human being in order to demonstrate the redemptive power of His limitless love. But only the Buddhists (as far as I know) have developed sending and taking into a precise, formal practice which allows you to begin confronting and dispelling your fears of love and compassion in the safety of a meditative environment.

Traditionally, the Buddhist practice of sending and taking is divided into four phases, based on four categories of suffering beings. These are 1) your *self;* 2) your *friends;* 3) *strangers;* 4) and your *enemies.*

One reason for doing sending and taking in this order is that most practitioners find it easiest to cultivate love and compassion for themselves, and hardest for their enemies. But there is another more profound reason. If you cannot fully experience your own suffering, you cannot develop genuine compassion for others. Why? Because *compassion* means literally to "suffer with" (*co* = "together"; *passion* = "suffering"). This is what distinguishes compassion from pity. When we feel pity for someone, we are looking down on them from some place of imagined invulnerability, as though whatever is happening to them could never happen to us. So even though we may be moved to help such a person in some way, the psycho-spiritual effect of pity is actually to distance us from their suffering. When real compassion is present we feel we are right down in the trenches with the person who is suffering, because we know what they are going through based on our own experience. This is why it is so important to cultivate love and compassion for yourself before trying to cultivate it for others.

Phase 1: *Instructions for Sending and Taking with Yourself*

The ability to enter that space of undistracted awareness or sobriety, which you have already discovered practicing choiceless awareness or prayer-in-the-heart, is a prerequisite for the successful practice of sending and taking. If you try to do sending and taking without this kind of spaciousness, you will very likely be overwhelmed by the intensity of the feelings that the practice arouses. In spacious awareness, however, there's plenty of room for even the most explosive emotions to reveal themselves without resistance, like thunderstorms passing through an empty sky.

STEP ONE: *Begin by Stabilizing Attention*

If you have been practicing meditation, begin by concentrating your attention on your breath or other object. Once you have attained some stability, allow your attention to expand into the total field of consciousness-awareness. Spend a few minutes just resting in this spacious awareness, without trying to grasp or push away any phenomena that arises within it.

If you have been practicing prayer-in-the-heart, concentrate your attention on your sacred word or prayer, then use it to bring your attention into the space of your heart. Once you feel you are in the Presence of your Beloved, stop saying your word or prayer and spend a few minutes relaxing in the vastness of that Presence.

STEP TWO: *Take Yourself as the Focus of Compassion*

Now, if you are currently experiencing any major suffering in your life, bring to mind what has caused it. If not, try to recall as vividly as possible some situation from the past in which you experienced intense suffering. For example, you might try to remember a period of serious illness, the break-up of a relationship, or the death of a loved one. Allow the memory of this event to arouse whatever feelings of anguish, pain, anger, or sorrow you experienced at that time.

STEP THREE: *Focus on the Feeling of Suffering*

Once you can actually *feel* the suffering which the situation you are recalling has aroused, stop *thinking* about it. Do not try to analyze what happened, or get sucked into any mental dramas of justification and blame. Recognize all such thoughts as being part of the Story of I which your thinking mind is creating in order to make the suffering go away. In this practice you want to do just the opposite. Instead of rejecting your suffering, you want to embrace it, to experience it *completely*. So, if thoughts continue to arise, just allow them to come and go without getting distracted, and stay focused on the *sensation* of suffering itself. Where do you feel it—in your stomach, your heart, throat, or head? What sort of qualities does it have? Is it heavy, hot, burning, aching? The point here is not to wallow in your suffering, but to get to know it as intimately as you would the body of a long-time lover.

STEP FOUR: *Breathe your Suffering into your Heart*

Next, as you inhale, gather whatever anger, sorrow, or pain you are feeling and breathe it into your heart. If you are good at visualization, you can imagine these feelings as having the form of hot, black smoke. Either way, breathe in deeply and allow the whole dark mass of suffering to dissolve in the space in your heart. It does not matter how much suffering you feel or how intense it becomes, because truly speaking that space in your heart is as infinite as Consciousness Itself. So, there is no need to be afraid. The more suffering you can breathe in, the wider your heart will open to accommodate it.

STEP FIVE: *Breathe out Love and Compassion*

Now, as you exhale, breathe out love and compassion for yourself. Again, if you are good at visualization, you can imagine this takes the form of radiant, white light, which you exhale through all the cells of your body so that it envelops you like a warm, luminous cloud. Because love and compassion are inherent in Consciousness Itself, you do not need to make any special effort to generate them. To the extent that you were able to open your heart to suffering when you inhaled, selfless love and compassion will flow out as you exhale. Accompany these feelings with a heart-felt wish or prayer that you might be relieved of all your suffering and, instead, be filled with boundless joy, peace, and happiness.

STEP SIX: *Synchronize Your Feelings with your Breath*

Repeat this process of inhaling suffering and exhaling love and compassion until your emotions become effortlessly synchronized with each of your breaths. The idea is to get to the point where you no longer have to *think* about what you are doing. You can simply and nakedly *feel* your suffering entering your heart, dissolving there, and then flowing out as selfless love and compassion.

STEP SEVEN: *Do Sending and Taking for All Beings*

Finally, bring your formal session to a close by taking in the suffering of all beings as you inhale, and sending out selfless love and compassion to all beings as you exhale. End with a heart-felt wish or prayer that, like you, every being in the universe may be relieved of whatever anguish, pain, or sorrow they are experiencing and instead be filled with boundless joy, peace, and happiness.

After ending your formal session, spend a few minutes making an inquiry into what you have just experienced. Here are some specific things to reflect on:

1. If at first you find that it is difficult to arouse any strong feelings doing this practice, it's probably because you are afraid to really experience them fully. Remember, however, that unless you can plumb the depths of your own suffering, you will not be able to relate to the suffering of others, so stick with the practice. Just as a child playing in the shallow waters begins to lose her fear of the ocean, the more familiar you become with your feelings, the more your fear of them will dissipate.
2. If the opposite happens, and you find yourself drowning in a torrent of emotion, it means you are still getting sucked into the Story of I which your thinking mind weaves. The solution is to spend more time developing spaciousness by practicing choiceless awareness or prayer-in-the-heart before you start doing the actual sending and taking. Once you have generated sufficient spacious awareness, you will be able to view the 'I' in the story not as your self, but as another suffering being in just as much need of love and compassion as any other.
3. You may also find it difficult to imagine yourself being happy. For a variety of reasons, many people come to feel that they don't deserve happiness, especially if they haven't done anything to earn it. But from a mystical point of view, happiness is not something you "deserve" or have to "earn." Happiness is your birthright—the very essence of your being. All you have to do is Realize it! In the meantime, even if you can't envision yourself actually *being* happy, at least try to feel that existential *longing* for happiness buried in the deepest recesses of your heart.
4. Finally, if you have been able to experience your own suffering, and to feel your own longing for happiness, then consider that this is basically how all people feel—not only all people, but all sentient beings. Every living creature suffers and every living creature longs to be happy. In this sense, then, both suffering and the

longing for happiness are *im*personal. They don't *belong* to you or anyone else. They are universal experiences shared by every being on the planet.

Phase 2: *Instructions for Sending and Taking with Friends*

The next phase of sending and taking involves practicing with people you feel kindly towards. Tibetan teachers suggest starting with your mother because they assume generating selfless love and compassion for your mother will be easiest. Sadly, as many Tibetans themselves have discovered, this is not always the case for Westerners in our time. So if you are someone who has difficulty generating love and compassion for your mother, you might want to start with some other family member or a close friend instead.

STEP ONE: *Entering Spacious-Awareness*

Again, if you have been practicing meditation, begin by concentrating your attention on your breath or other object. Once you have attained some stability, allow your attention to expand into the total field of consciousness-awareness. Spend a few minutes just resting in this spacious awareness, without trying to grasp or push away any phenomenon that arises within it.

If you have been practicing prayer-in-the-heart, concentrate your attention on your sacred word or prayer, then use it to bring your attention into the space of your heart. Once you feel you are in the Presence of your Beloved, stop saying your word or prayer and spend a few minutes relaxing in that Silent Presence.

STEP TWO: *Take a Friend as the Focus of Compassion*

Choose a friend who is currently having some problems to be the focus of your practice. Bring that person vividly to mind and try to recall as clearly as possible some of the kind things they have done for you, or some of the good times you have shared together.

STEP THREE: *Focus on their Suffering*

Next, focus on any specific type of suffering your friend may be experiencing, whether physical, mental, or emotional. Are they sick, depressed, having financial difficulties, or involved in a troubled relationship? As you feel your heart begin to open, make a strong resolve to take their suffering on yourself, thinking, "May this person be relieved of all their anguish and pain."

STEP FOUR: *Breathe their Suffering into Your Heart*

Now, as you inhale, breathe your friend's suffering into your own heart. Imagine, if you can, that it takes the form of hot black smoke. Breathe in deeply and try to experience your friend's anguish and pain as your own. Then, allow these feelings to completely dissolve into the vastness of your heart.

STEP FIVE: *Breathe out Love and Compassion*

Next, generate the wish—"May I do everything possible to make my friend happy." Make this wish concrete by imagining that you give them whatever you have that would make them happy—money, emotional support, spiritual insights—even your own healthy body if need be. If you can, visualize that whatever you are giving them takes the form of radiant white light which you breathe out through your heart towards your friend in luminous waves of love. Accompany this with a heart-felt wish or prayer that your friend be relieved of all his or her suffering and, instead, be filled with boundless joy, peace, and happiness.

STEP SIX: *Synchronize Your Feelings with Your Breath*

Synchronize taking in your friend's suffering with your in-breaths, and sending out selfless love and compassion with your out-breaths. Ignore whatever thoughts arise *about* you and your friend and keep your attention focused on the naked quality of the feelings, themselves. Continue inhaling your friend's suffering and exhaling your own selfless love and compassion for the rest of your session.

STEP SEVEN: *Do Sending and Taking for All Beings*

Finally, bring your formal practice to a close by expanding the waves of love and compassion you have generated to include all beings everywhere. Breathe in their suffering as you inhale, and breathe out selfless love and compassion as you exhale. End your session with a heart-felt wish or prayer that every being in the universe may be relieved of whatever anguish, pain, or sorrow they are experiencing and, instead, be filled with boundless, joy, peace, and happiness.

Phase 3: *Instructions for Sending and Taking with Strangers*

After you have practiced with a friend for a while, you should try to do sending and taking with a stranger—that is, someone you interact with, but don't know personally. For example, you might choose a clerk at the store where you regularly shop, or a teller at your bank, or your neighborhood gas station attendant. Before you begin your formal practice consider that, even though you may not even know this person's name, he or she is a human being like you, and so experiences the same kinds of suffering you do.

Take this person as the focus of your sending and taking meditation. Imagine some specific form of suffering—divorce, illness, bereavement—he or she might be enduring, and *follow steps one through seven as you did above with your friend.*

Phase 4: *Instructions for Sending and Taking with Enemies*

Last but not least, you should try to practice sending and taking with an enemy—that is, someone whom you feel has harmed you in some way and so aroused your anger, animosity or fear. Before beginning, go over in your mind exactly what the person has done to cause you such anguish. Next, try to remember times when you have behaved in a similar fashion. Ask yourself, "What motivated me to act the way I did?" Was it not because you were experiencing some form of suffering? In fact, whenever anyone behaves cruelly towards others, it is a sure sign that they themselves are suffering. So consider that if you respond to your enemy's cruelty with cruelty, this will not only increase your own suffering, it will eventually transform you into the very sort of person you presently despise. Make a strong revolve to break this cycle by practicing sending and taking instead.

Now, bring your enemy to mind and try to recall as vividly as possible some specific things they did that caused you to suffer. Allow yourself to fully feel both your pain and your anger. Next, try to imagine what it might be like to walk in their shoes. Try to recognize what kinds of suffering they were experiencing which motivated them to act the way they did. Then, *follow steps one through seven as you did above, using your enemy as the focus of your practice.*

Dealing with Resistance

If you are practicing sending and taking with enough intensity, you will almost certainly encounter some resistance. For instance, you might find yourself balking at the idea of giving away your own healthy body to a friend whose body is being ravaged by cancer. This does not mean you have failed in your practice. On the contrary, it means the practice is working as it should. How so? By making you acutely aware of an attachment you have—in this case to your body. As with most practices, this is a large part of what sending and taking is designed to do, because you can only release attachments in those moments when you become aware of them. So, instead of reacting to resistance with discouragement, greet it with gratitude. Try to see that behind whatever resistance you feel lies an attachment and that this attachment is the real cause of your suffering!

Incorporating Sending and Taking into Your Life

As we said earlier, formal sending and taking is a kind of meditative rehearsal for cultivating selfless love and compassion with living beings. As such, you should incorporate it into your schedule of regular practices, doing it once a day for an extended period of time—say, several months. But even after you have stopped practicing formally, sending and taking will always remain an important tool for dealing with suffering. This is because you are bound to encounter many situations where there will be nothing else you can do for someone except to engage in this practice.

For example, you may see people on the television news who are victims of war, famine, or natural disasters; or you may pass a homeless person sleeping in a doorway; or you may hear the wail of an ambulance siren as it carries some total stranger to the hospital. In such cases, you can simply pause for a few moments to breathe in their suffering and breathe out your heart-felt wish that they be happy. Although this gesture may appear to be insignificant, consider that even one complete breath of sending and taking creates a ripple of love and compassion that will reverberate throughout the entire cosmos until the end of time.

You may also find yourself dealing with family members or friends who suffer from seemingly intractable problems, such as alcoholism, drug addiction, or other self-destructive behaviors. When all ordinary efforts to help have failed, doing sending and taking may be the only way left to continue manifesting your love and compassion for them. Be careful, however, not to expect that your practice will bring about some miraculous cure. Whenever you do sending and taking for someone it is really as much for your own benefit as it is for theirs. This is because the more you allow the current of selfless love and compassion to flow through your life, the more it will dissolve the links in your chain of conditioning, for as God tells St. Catherine of Siena,

> Where the fire of my sweet charity is, the water of selfishness cannot enter to put out this sweet fire in the soul.[294]

Chapter 20

Serving Others

> *Once for all this short command is given to you: "Love and do what you will." If you keep silent, keep silent by love, if you speak, speak by love; if you correct, correct by love; if you pardon, pardon by love: let love be rooted in you, and from this root nothing but good can grow.*
>
> — St. Augustine (Christian)

Sending and taking is a good way to begin opening your heart to selfless love and compassion, but to take the next step you have to apply what you learn in your formal practice to your everyday life. This is usually easier for bhaktas than jnanis, because if you are a bhakta, you have already fallen in love with some form of the Divine. And just as worldly lovers naturally want to share the joy they feel with other people, so you, too, will naturally want to share with others the joy you feel in your relationship with your Beloved.

Jnanis, on the other hand, often assume that cultivating love and compassion is an auxiliary practice, and that inquiry and meditation are all they need to carry them to Enlightenment. But this is not true. In fact, if you are a jnani, it is even more important for you to cultivate selfless love and compassion. The reason is that almost everyone who starts on a spiritual path does so out of self-interest: They want to end their own suffering. Now the way bhaktas overcome this selfish motivation is to begin surrendering themselves to God. But because jnanis lack such a Divine focal point for self-surrender, it's much harder for them to overcome their initial self-centeredness. But if they don't take steps to overcome it, this will become a tremendous obstacle, as Tibetan master Lama Lodö explains,

> If anyone says "I" am going to achieve enlightenment, this grasping prevents him from reaching a non-dual state. Complete enlightenment is for the sake of other beings.[295]

In other words, if you are a jnani, the way out of this trap is to change your attitude. Instead of practicing to attain Enlightenment for yourself, you should practice so that you can help others attain it. In Buddhism this is called taking the *bodhisattva vow,* one version of which goes like this:

> However innumerable sentient beings are, I vow to save them.
> However inexhaustible the defilements are, I vow to extinguish them.
> However immeasurable the dharmas are, I vow to master them.
> However incomparable enlightenment is, I vow to attain it.

But whether you take a formal vow or not, the real question is this: How can you actually implement this intention in a practical way? And the answer is very simple: by performing as many concrete acts of service to others as possible.

Serving Others as a Spiritual Practice

In the Hindu Tradition, serving others is called *karma yoga,* or the yoga of action. Anandamayi Ma describes it this way:

> By doing service heart and mind are purified—be convinced of this! To engage in service is a very powerful *sādhanā;* do not become impatient. Rather serve your people with the utmost calm and have a kind word for everyone.[296]

Now, if you are an external renunciant, practicing karma-yoga is a pretty straightforward matter. Here, for example, is what a twentieth-century Buddhist monk Nyogen Senzaki says about such a life:

> A Buddhist monk is celibate and leads the simplest life possible. He never charges for any kind of work he does, being only too grateful to do something for his fellow men. He accepts used clothes or old shoes and wears them. Any excess food or money he gives away. He sleeps quietly without worries, having none in his possession.[297]

If you are a householder, the situation is a bit more complicated. As we said earlier about the precept of charity, you can't just give away money you've saved for your children's education to the first beggar who comes to your door. To practice karma-yoga as a householder you need to exercise the virtue of justice.

Nowadays, we tend to think of justice only in social or political terms. From a spiritual point of view, however, justice is rooted in something much more organic. This goes back to an insight which the ancient Greeks had—namely, that social and political justice grows out of each person's ability to order his or her private life based on the principles of reason, harmony, and good judgment. In other words, justice begins at home. It's what determines how we allocate our time, energy, and material resources in accordance with the responsibilities we have to our families, friends, and the community at large. So, if you practice karma yoga within the bounds dictated by justice, it won't conflict with your duties as a householder.

In fact, you can actually transform these duties themselves into acts of karma yoga. This is because, whether you are a renunciant or a householder, the essence of the practice is the same. It's to cultivate selfless love and compassion by doing whatever you do, not for yourself, but for the benefit of others and the good of the whole. So, let's look again at the four categories of beings we used in the practice of sending and taking and see how we might go about cultivating love and compassion for them in our daily lives.

Cultivating Love and Compassion for Your Self

The biggest mistake most people make when it comes to cultivating love and compassion for themselves is to think it means gratifying their self-centered desires. For instance, if you have just gotten over a serious illness, you might hear your mind say something like, "Oh, poor me, I have endured so much suffering lately. Now I need to be compassionate to myself and buy some new clothes." If you pay attention, however, you will see that both your suffering, and the desire to buy new clothes, stem from the delusion that you *are* your body-mind. Consequently, when your body gets sick, you think *you* are sick. Likewise, when your mind tells you that buying clothes for your body will make *you* happy, you believe it. So how can you cultivate love and compassion for yourself in this kind of situation without succumbing to self-indulgence?

Here we might take a clue from St. Francis of Assisi who referred to his body as "brother donkey." Now this may sound rather disparaging to our modern ears, but that's not at all the way he meant it. In agrarian societies, like the one Francis grew up in, donkeys were hard-working animals and highly valued by the peasants who owned them. So too, our bodies are of great value to us. Indeed, most traditions insist that only beings inhabiting human bodies have the capacity for Enlightenment. So, when Francis addressed his body as "brother donkey," he was actually expressing his gratitude for having one. But, at the same time, it provided a constant reminder that his body was not his *true* Self.

If you, too, get into the habit of viewing your body as "brother donkey," then whenever it makes any of its needs known, instead of automatically indulging them, you can respond with sympathy and compassion. For example, if your body gets hungry in the middle of a meditation session, you might say, "Poor donkey, I know you are hungry and I promise I won't let you starve. In a little while I'll give you something tasty and nutritious to munch on, but for now you must exercise a little patience." Or if your body gets sick, you can comfort it by saying, "Don't worry donkey, I've made an appointment for you to see the doctor tomorrow morning. In the meantime, why don't you get some rest while I catch up on my spiritual reading."

The same thing applies to your thinking mind. Whenever it gets stressed out worrying about what will make you happy, you can say, "Poor donkey mind, I know you are only trying to be helpful, but now that we're on a spiritual path, you don't have to be concerned about my happiness anymore. All I ask is that you take care of those everyday tasks—balancing the checkbook, making shopping lists, paying the rent, etc.—which you do so well."

Carrying on this kind of conversation with your body-mind will naturally generate some measure of detachment from it. Then, just as peasants can appreciate their donkeys without losing track of their own human identities, so you can appreciate your body-mind without confusing it with your True Identity—Consciousness Itself.

Cultivating Love and Compassion for Family and Friends

Most of us have somebody in our lives for whom we feel a deep and genuine love. Even so, we are usually afraid of what might happen if we surrendered ourselves to this love completely. Instead, we take the attitude, "I'll love you *if* you love me back." This makes us place all sorts of conditions on our love, treating it as a kind of bargaining chip to be doled out in bits and pieces, depending on what we hope to get in return. Consequently, even in our closest relationships, we often feel like we are driving with the brakes on—which, in a way, we are. Practicing selfless love and compassion means taking the brakes off and learning how to love *un*conditionally, without worrying about what will happen to *me*, or what *I* will get back.

The way to start doing this is to pick someone you especially cherish—a family member, a lover, a friend—and ask yourself, "What prevents me from loving this person without any conditions, whatsoever?" Then try to become aware of specific situations in which you find yourself withholding your love from them. For instance, maybe your spouse has left you a pile of dirty breakfast dishes to wash. As you scrub away, you might hear your mind say, "Damn it, I'm not going to put up with this anymore. What does he (she) think I am, some sort of housemaid!" Notice that right in that very moment you are placing a condition on your love—namely, that your spouse does his or her fair share of the housework. Moreover, you can actually feel this manifesting as a painful contraction in the area of your heart. So, whenever you catch yourself imposing conditions like this on your love, try an experiment. Let go of whatever story your mind has created, and instead think, "What a wonderful opportunity this is to perform some little service for the one I hold so dear." Then, focus your attention on your heart and feel it begin to open up, releasing little ripples of sweetness which spread through your whole body.

Cultivating Love and Compassion for Strangers

Up until a hundred years or so ago most human beings lived in small, close-knit rural communities where encountering a stranger was a relatively rare event. Today it is just the opposite. Most of us now live in dense urban centers, or sprawling suburbs where we are confronted with strangers at almost every turn—pedestrians we bump into on busy city streets; passengers we sit next to on packed buses, trains, or airplanes; drivers we zoom by on crowded freeways; gas station attendants who pump our gas; waiters and waitresses who bring us food; store clerks, salesmen, and cashiers from whom we purchase our goods; even the disembodied voices of receptionists and secretaries who answer our phone calls. So how can we cultivate unconditional love and compassion for all these countless people whose lives continually intersect with ours, if ever so briefly, throughout the day?

Well, again, the first thing we have to do is become aware of the conditions we place on our love whenever we are in the company of these strangers. Because most of us feel overwhelmed by their sheer numbers, our usual response is to turn our attention inward, to withdraw into an imaginary world of memories, plans, and daydreams. We don't want to be bothered by all these nameless people *unless* (and here comes the first condition) they can serve us in some way—fix our car, cash our check, bring us a meal, etc. Moreover, if the quality of their service fails to live up to our expectations (which is the second condition), we get irritated and upset. In other words, even when we do interact with strangers, our attention is focused not on them, but on ourselves—on *our* interests, *our* needs, *our* expectations.

One of the best ways to interrupt this particular pattern of conditioning is to use a variation of the three-breath meditation described in chapter 13. Whenever you catch yourself retreating into a world of inner thoughts, immediately focus on your breath. Then, as you exhale, concentrate your attention in the present moment. On your second exhalation, relax your body. Finally, as you exhale for the third time, let your attention flow out to all the people around you and, instead of asking, "What can they do for me?" ask "What can I do for them?" If you can stay in this space of open, undistracted awareness, you will be surprised at how many opportunities to serve others present themselves.

For example, if you are riding the bus to work, you may notice an elderly person standing nearby to whom you can offer your seat. Or, as you are preparing to get off, you may become aware that some guy behind you seems to be in an exceptional hurry, and so you step aside to let him through. Later, on your job, you may get a chance to gladden the heart of a grumpy elevator operator by sharing a joke, or to flash a smile at a harried receptionist, or reassure a waitress who bungles your order that everyone makes mistakes. Simply by staying mindful of the needs of others, and responding with little acts of kindness, you can transform your encounters with almost everyone you meet into opportunities for cultivating unconditional love and compassion.

What's more, if you practice this diligently, over time you will find something else begins to happen. The more your attention focuses on concern for others, the less it will fixate on concern for your self. As a result, you will be able to perform your own work in a far more relaxed and carefree manner, which will naturally make those around you feel more relaxed and carefree, as well. In this way, even your own joy can be converted into service for the good of the whole!

Cultivating Love and Compassion for Enemies

When it comes to enemies the problem is not just that we place conditions on our love and compassion. We actually react to them with opposite emotions of resentment, anger, and hatred. What's more, even though these reactions cause us considerable suffering, we cling to the belief that such feelings are justified. Thus, our ego minds are apt to greet any suggestion that there might be another way to respond by insisting, "I have a *right* to feel this way!"

Now, in a sense, this is true. Everyone has a right to suffer. No one can take that away from you. But, from a mystic's point of view, it's not a question of whether your feelings are justified. It's a question of whether they lead to happiness or not. And while acting on feelings of resentment, anger, or hatred may give you a few moments of perverse pleasure, in the long run they will bring more suffering to both you and others—which is why the Buddha said,

> Animosity does not eradicate animosity.
> Only by loving kindness is animosity dissolved.
> This law is ancient and eternal.[298]

So if you want to break this cycle of suffering, you have to drop all your self-justification and try a radically different approach. Here is what Jesus recommended:

> I say to you that listen, Love your enemies, do good to those who hate you, bless those who curse you, pray for those who abuse you.[299]

Jesus, of course, was famous for advising seekers to love their enemies, but he was by no means the only mystic to do so. Listen, for instance, to Anandamayi Ma:

> If someone does something bad, you should feel nothing but affection and benevolence towards him or her. Think: "Lord, this is also one of Thy manifestations!" The more kindly and friendly you can feel and behave towards everybody, the more will the way to the One who is goodness itself open out.[300]

Now as anyone who has ever done it knows, loving an enemy can be a real challenge. The reason is that nothing brings to light our deepest attachments to things more clearly than being confronted by someone who threatens to deprive us of them. And, of course, that is precisely what our enemies do. Thus, before we can cultivate genuine love and compassion for our enemies, we must first identify and surrender those attachments which stand in the way. So, while loving your enemies is a difficult practice, it is also an extremely powerful one, because our enemies are our best teachers. This is why Jamgon Kongtrul writes,

> All those who hurt me are worthy of gratitude since they are my companions and helpers for gathering the accumulations of merit and pristine wisdom and for clearing away the obscurations of disturbing emotions and conceptual knowledge.[301]

The way to begin this practice is to pick someone you presently consider to be an enemy and resolve to regard that person as your teacher. Then, whenever you find yourself in his or her presence, become especially mindful of your own mental and emotional responses. Watch how your thinking-mind starts recounting all the ways he or she has harmed you, and how these thoughts give rise to feelings of resentment, animosity, or hatred. When you can see this clearly, remember the following teaching given by the Buddha:

> "He abused me, mistreated me, defeated me, robbed me,"
> Harboring such thoughts keeps hatred alive.
> "He abused me, mistreated me, defeated me, robbed me,"
> Releasing such thoughts banishes hatred for all time.[302]

Notice the Buddha does not say you should suppress your thoughts, only *release* them. Simply let them pass without getting sucked into the stories they weave. Next, allow yourself to fully experience whatever negative emotions come up and try to identify the specific attachment upon which each is based. For example, your enemy/teacher may be a co-worker who has been badmouthing you to your boss behind your back. If so, chances are the animosity you feel towards this person is based on an attachment to your job and a fear of losing it. But as we've said before, our attachments are not always to things as obvious or as concrete as a job. Perhaps your enemy/teacher is an in-law who arouses your anger by constantly criticizing the way you are raising your children. In a case like this, your in-law is probably calling into question an image you have of yourself as being a good parent.

Other attachments are built so firmly into our deluded sense of self that we have trouble recognizing them as attachments in the first place. For example, your enemy/teacher may be a deranged neighbor who likes to play loud music at all hours of the night. When you complain he whips out a gun and threatens to shoot you. No doubt this will cause a flood of adrenalin to rush through your veins, which is perfectly natural. But if you feel actual hatred for your neighbor, this is because he has exposed one of the most deep-seated attachments a person can have—i.e., to maintaining biological life.

Whatever attachment you uncover, the point is to try to see it's the attachment and not your enemy that is the real cause of your suffering. In this regard, your enemy is like an archer and your attachments a target. As long as you hold onto your attachments, there is something for your enemy's arrows to hit. But if you surrender your attachments, the arrows have nowhere to lodge and so fly harmlessly by.

Finally, once you have identified the specific attachment that is causing your resentment, animosity, or hatred, turn your attention to your enemy. Remember to be grateful to him or her for bringing it to light. Next, try to see that he or she is suffering from exactly the same kind of negative emotions that you are experiencing right in that moment. Then, instead of reacting with animosity generated by your own suffering, ask yourself, "What can I can do to help alleviate my enemy's suffering?"

Amazing as it may sound, once you start to get direct insights into how this works, you will actually look forward to encountering your enemy again, because you will realize what a wonderful teacher he or she really is! This is what the twentieth-century Zen student Satomi Myodo discovered while serving in her master's kitchen under the direction of his overbearing wife, Mrs. Ro, and their spiteful daughter. Looking back on this trying time, Satomi writes,

> That I can now travel down the path of gratitude is entirely thanks to the gift of four years of Mrs. Rō's severe discipline and molding. When I think of her from time to time, I feel a swelling of gratitude in my heart, together with such a longing for Mrs. Ro and a fondness for her daughter that my eyelids soon grow hot. Truly, Mrs. Rō was a flesh-and-blood Kannon [bodhisattva of compassion] to me, and her daughter was Seishi Bodhisattva [teacher of wisdom].[303]

It is important to note that Satomi *voluntarily* submitted to Mrs. Ro's despotism as part of her spiritual training. When it is only your own welfare that is at stake, this can be an extremely fruitful practice. In general, however, cultivating unconditional love and compassion does not mean you should acquiesce to injustice, tyranny, or other misuses of power. Of course, you still want to try to cultivate love and compassion, but at the same time, as a member of society, you also have a responsibility to take appropriate action. So what makes an action appropriate?

Taking Appropriate Action

Spiritually speaking, *appropriate action* is action which is based on a union of compassion *and* wisdom. Now, the wisdom aspect of appropriate actions comes from insights—especially insights into the nature of social boundaries. As we saw in chapter 4, our capacity for thought and language allows us to create all sorts of boundaries which define and determine our social relationships. As such, they are useful and necessary to the conduct of our lives. The problem is that, under delusion, we tend to reify these boundaries. This makes it difficult to change them even when circumstances change and they cease to serve their original purposes. As a result, we become trapped in our own imaginary constructs. If, however, we gain some insight into the true nature of these boundaries, then we are free to take appropriate action by altering or redrawing them in more compassionate ways. So let's look again at some of our prior examples to see when and where appropriate action might be called for.

In the case of a spouse who leaves dirty dishes for you to wash, if this happens only occasionally, you can simply treat it as an opportunity for cultivating unconditional love and compassion. If, however, this is part of a larger pattern of behavior which saddles you with so much housework you don't have time to do any spiritual practices, then you need to take appropriate action. You need to sit down with your spouse and talk about re-drawing the boundaries which determine who does what chores. What makes this action *appropriate* is that, if you can't do your spiritual practices, you won't be able to cultivate those qualities which will better enable you to serve all beings—including your spouse.

The same applies to your disparaging in-law. If his or her remarks are directed to you alone, there is no need to do anything except continue practicing love and compassion. If, however, they are made in front of your children and undermine your parental authority, then appropriate action is required for the sake of your whole family. Re-drawing boundaries in this case might mean trying to establish a closer relationship with your in-law in the hopes that he or she will come to understand how harmful such behavior is. If this fails, you may have to do the opposite and draw even tighter boundaries which limit your in-law's contact with your children. Remember, re-drawing boundaries is a creative act, so you may have to experiment with several approaches. The important thing is that whatever happens, you must try to maintain in your heart a compassionate intention to serve the interests of everyone involved.

Sometimes, as in dealing with a deranged neighbor, you will find yourself in a situation where all normal boundaries have been violated. In cases like this, you may have to take decisive, unilateral action to reimpose them—either by reporting your neighbor to the police, or, if there's no time for that, trying to forcibly restrain him yourself. But you must still try to act for the good of the whole. This means your intention should be not only to protect yourself and others in your community, but also to protect your neighbor from harming himself by actually shooting an innocent person.

The Benefits of Cultivating Love and Compassion

Many seekers get discouraged when they realize how difficult it is to cultivate true, unconditional love and compassion. Instead of transforming them into saints, they find their practice keeps revealing deeper and more subtle layers of self-centered conditioning. Along the way there will be occasional breakthroughs, little gems of insight. But most of the time the practice proceeds in a two-step-forward, one step-backward fashion, so it is important to exercise patience. If you do, you'll discover the real purpose of this practice is not to turn you into a saint who has risen above the common herd. On the contrary, the real purpose of practicing compassion is to teach you just the opposite—that you are *no different* from other people; that you, too, are a poor suffering being, just like everyone else. Here's how St. John of the Cross describes it:

> Softened and humbled by aridities and hardships and by other temptations and trials in which God exercises the soul in the course of this night, individuals become meek toward God and themselves and also toward their neighbor. As a result, they will no longer

> become impatiently angry with themselves and their faults or with their neighbor's faults. Neither are they displeased or disrespectfully querulous with God for not making them perfect quickly.[304]

In other words, what trying to cultivate selfless love and compassion teaches is humility. This is essential, because it is only after you've learned humility that you can begin to understand the true nature of compassion, which, as we've already said, means "to suffer with." And the more you actually suffer *with* people, the more you come to understand suffering doesn't belong to anybody. It's universal. Then, as this understanding deepens, the very distinctions you have been making between 'friends', 'strangers', and 'enemies' starts to seem less substantial. Friends turn into enemies, enemies into friends, and strangers into both. What then is the real difference between them? Or between them and you, for that matter? Like you, they are all sentient beings. Like you, they all experience suffering. Like you, they all long for happiness.

When this truth begins to take root in your heart—not just as a philosophical idea, but as a *lived* experience—practicing compassion becomes easy. It doesn't have to be generated, and it doesn't necessarily involve any gushy emotions. It's simply a matter of looking at someone who is in pain and recognizing that that person's suffering is the *same* as your suffering, just like seeing yourself in a mirror. Having exhausted the *effort* to love, you find that true love flows of its own accord, quietly and without any fuss, because, as Longchen-pa says:

> With the compassion which does not arise, does not cease,
> and is selfless,
> Being-for-others is always available. It does not need to
> be brought about.[305]

So while practices of inquiry and meditation can free your mind from attachments, only love can cleanse your heart and, in the process, reveal one of the sublimest secrets of the path: Love is not a *means* to happiness, love *is* happiness! And if you are a jnani, getting even a taste of this can bring about a profound shift in your motivation. The intellectual thirst for Truth, which originally prompted your quest, will become increasingly fused with that far more personal longing for Love which animates your bhakta cousins. And the more you surrender yourself to this Love, the closer you will come to Truth, because ultimately they are identical.

Chapter 21

Serving God

Even the living sight of my eyes
Is service at Your court.

— Rabi'a (Muslim)

Serving others with unconditional love and compassion is, of course, just as important for bhaktas as it is for jnanis, but if you are a bhakta your motive will be slightly different. It will be part and parcel of a larger aspiration to serve God in *everything* you do, for as Rumi writes,

> When you seek the Beloved's desire and pleasure, seeking your own desire is forbidden.[306]

Why? Because, as God tells St. Catherine of Siena,

> Consider, then, dearest daughter how it goes with the soul. Either she must serve and hope in me, or she will serve and hope in the world and herself.[307]

In other words, if you are ever going to prove yourself worthy of a permanent Union with your Beloved, you must give up your own agenda, and commit yourself completely to God's. This is why Anandamayi Ma recommends this:

> In the morning, as soon as you wake up, pray: "Lord, accept as thy service everything I shall do today." At night again, before falling asleep, pray: "In self-surrender I bow to Thee placing my head at Thy holy feet." Try to spend the whole day in this spirit.[308]

So let's take a closer look and see how you can put this aspiration to serve God in everything you do into actual practice.

Serving God in your Relationships with other People

The first and foremost way you can serve your Beloved is by serving your fellow human beings with unconditional love and compassion, because, as the Christian Apostle John writes,

> Let us love one another, because love is from God; everyone who loves is born of God and knows God. Whoever does not love does not know God, for God is love.[309]

Similarly, in the Jewish *Midrash* we read this:

> As the All-present is called compassionate and gracious, so be you also compassionate and gracious and offer they gifts freely to all.[310]

And the thirteenth-century Sufi poet Sa'di says simply,

> Worshiping God is serving people.[311]

As we said before, serving others usually comes easier to bhaktas than jnanis because if you are a bhakta, love is already your primary motivation for walking the path. Nevertheless, when you try to translate this love into everyday action, you'll almost certainly run up against the same kind of self-centered conditioning as jnanis do. Therefore, everything we said in the last chapter about serving other people applies to you. As a bhakta, however, you still have one big advantage over jnanis. Because you have glimpsed God within your own heart, you know that He dwells in the hearts of everyone, whether they realize it or not. Consequently, you can see other people as carriers of the Divine and act accordingly. Here's how Theophan the Recluse describes it:

> Every visitor or every person we meet should be welcomed as a messenger from God. The first question we should always ask is this: what does the Lord wish me to do with or for this person? We should receive everyone as though they were the image of God, reverencing them and ready to help them all we can.[312]

Now "reverencing" other people does not mean treating them in a socially inappropriate manner, like kissing the feet of the mailman who brings a package to your door. Such behavior will only embarrass people and make them feel uncomfortable. All you really need to do is pay attention to *who* they truly are. Just take a moment to look directly into the eyes of whomever you happen to be with and you will see that the same light of Consciousness which shines in you is shining in them. If you make it a habit of doing this, then, even though you continue to play whatever social role destiny has assigned to you—father, mother, lover, spouse, worker, boss, etc.—at a deeper level, you will come to realize that it's all a giant Cosmic Masquerade in which your Beloved keeps appearing to you in a myriad different disguises. Listen, for example, to the way Anandamayi Ma talks about the roles she played in her life:

> This body has served the husband, so you may call it a wife. It has prepared dishes for all, so you may call it a cook. It has done all sorts of scrubbing and menial work, so you may call it a servant. But if you look at the thing from another standpoint you will realize that this body has served none but God. For when I served my father, mother, husband and others, I simply considered them as different manifestations of the Almighty and served them as such.[313]

Serving God at your Work Place

The second way you can serve your Beloved is through whatever work you do. Again, Anandamayi Ma explains it to us:

> All work must be done as a service to God. The longer you can remain stirred inwardly by the feeling of His presence, the more will your body, your mind and your actions progress towards the Divine.[314]

Theophan agrees:

> Consecrate all your activities inwardly to God; and then all your life will be dedicated to Him. What more is necessary? Nothing.[315]

Now many seekers, when they first hear teachings like this, start wondering whether they should change jobs or professions. Perhaps it's better to be a nurse, or a school teacher, or a social worker, or to join some charitable organization helping poor people in a far off corner of the globe. Some householders may even be tempted to give up their worldly life and become external renunciants. And, of course, if you feel a genuine call to pursue another career, or live a renunciant life, then by all means do so. But unless what you are presently doing is actually harmful, there is really no need to change anything.

This is true even if your current job seems quite mundane, like driving a truck, selling real estate, or working as a secretary. Although these occupations may not appear to be as spiritually glamorous as nursing or social work, they are just as necessary to the functioning of modern societies, and so just as valuable. The real trick to dedicating your work to your Beloved is not to alter the things you are already doing, only your reasons for doing them, for as Brother Lawrence says,

> Our sanctification depends not on changing our works, but on doing for God what we would normally do for ourselves.[316]

So, for example, ordinarily, when you take a job you enter into a contract with your employer in which you agree to spend a certain amount of time performing certain tasks in exchange for a certain amount of money. In a relative sense, then, you are working for your boss. If you are a bhakta, however, you also recognize that this relationship between you and your employer is really only a convenient social fiction. From a higher point of view, you are not working for a human being at all: You are working for God.

To see more clearly how this is true, consider that whatever natural talents you possess were conferred on you at birth by grace. It was also due to grace that you were born into circumstances where those talents could be developed through education and training into the skills your present job requires. And, finally, it was because of grace that a job requiring just those skills became available at the very time you were looking for one. So, while at the relative level it is perfectly appropriate to say, "I work for my boss," from a spiritual perspective your true boss is your Beloved—which is why Theophan gives this advice:

> Whatever your occupation, great or small, reflect that it is the omnipresent Lord Himself who orders you to perform it and who watches to see how you are carrying it out. If you keep this thought constantly in mind you will fulfil attentively all the duties assigned to you and at the same time you will remember the Lord.[317]

If you really take this teaching to heart, it will transform your whole attitude toward your job. For instance, suppose before entering the spiritual path, you were one of those people who was always on guard against being cheated. As a result, whenever your employer asked you do something extra—something for which you felt you were not being properly paid—you reacted with indignation and resentment. However, as a bhakta whose primary motive is not to earn money, but to please God, you will actually be grateful for an opportunity to do more. In fact, even if you weren't getting paid at all, you would still be eager to perform whatever tasks were at hand, simply for the joy of serving your Beloved.[318]

Or, suppose you were a very ambitious person, who was more than willing to take on extra work in the hopes of getting a promotion. Then, if you were rewarded for your efforts, you would probably feel your job was very exciting and enjoyable, at least for awhile. If, on the other hand, someone else got your promotion, chances are you would experience major suffering. The reason for this is you had been working not for the joy of the work itself, but for the goodies you hoped it would bring. When you work solely for your Beloved, however, you find that doing your work well is all the reward you need. Here is how Krishna describes such a devotee:

> He is glad with whatever God gives him, and he has risen beyond the two contraries here below; he is without jealousy, and in success or in failure he is one: his works bind him not.[319]

Serving God in your Daily Routines

Changing your motivation from serving yourself to serving God can not only transform your attitude toward your paying job, but also all those ordinary little household tasks which most people find tedious and unpleasant. How so? Well to begin with, whenever you are doing something like washing the dishes, just ask yourself, "Why am I doing this?" In the past, you might have answered, "Because I have to keep my house clean so when people come to visit they won't think I'm a complete slob." But if you have devoted your life solely to God, then what other people think of you is irrelevant. All that matters is acceptance by your Beloved. So, now your answer will be, "I have to wash these dishes for my Beloved." And you can adopt this same attitude towards all your other household chores, such as taking out the garbage, washing the laundry, sweeping the floors, etc. Instead of doing them for yourself, you can do them for God.

At first, articulating your intentions this way may seem a little contrived. But, if you stop to think about it, doing these chores for God instead of yourself is actually a far more realistic way to live. Why? Because, like the relationship between worker and boss, the whole idea of 'ownership' is a social fiction, based on imaginary boundaries. In Reality, nothing truly belongs to you—not your dishes, your house, your clothes, your car, or anything else. In Reality, all these 'things' are actually Divine manifestation and, hence, 'belong' to the Divine. So if you are a true lover of God, you will naturally want to take care of God's things.

This even applies to taking care of your body, which, again from a spiritual point of view, was given to you not for your own use, but to serve as a vehicle for Enlightenment. So whenever you eat a meal, brush your teeth, wash your face, or comb your hair, you should consecrate these activities to this end, for as Menahem Nahum says:

> Corporeal things—eating, drinking, and the rest of human needs—if you do them just for the sake of fulfilling your desires—have no life. But if you eat to sate your *soul*, and raise up the eating, drinking, and other needs to God by your good intentions, then you fulfill "Know Him in all your ways" (Prov. 3:6) and all your deeds are for the sake of heaven.[320]

Serving God and Self-Inquiry

Just as it is necessary for jnanis to cultivate unconditional love and compassion, if you are a bhakta aspiring to serve God, it will be necessary for you to practice self-inquiry. The reason, as we said earlier, is that, like a jnani, when you try to act on your aspiration, your own self-centered conditioning will block you at almost every step of the way. So, in order to expose and surrender all the subtle graspings and attachments upon which this conditioning is based, you too will have to pay attention to everything that arises in your heart and mind throughout the day. Sufis call this kind of mindfulness *Mohasebeh*. Here's how the twelfth-century master Mohammad ibn-e Mahumd Amoli describes it:

> Mohasebeh means to be constantly searching into and examining the states and actions of the self. Day by day and hour by hour, one should take account of whatever arises in one's being, whether positive or negative, so as to become aware of the qualities of one's states.[321]

As a bhakta, you must be especially watchful for any attempt by your ego-mind to impose conditions on your service to your Beloved. For instance, you might hear yourself promising to give up meat if God cures you of some illness. Or, you might find yourself offering to donate extra money to charity if you are granted the raise you asked for at work. But Ramana Maharshi reminds us that

> To be complete, surrender must be unquestioning; the devotee cannot bargain with the Lord or demand favours at His hands.[322]

So, whenever you realize you are serving yourself rather than your Beloved—whether in relationships with other people, on the job, or working around the house—conduct a little self-inquiry. Try to identify whatever personal desires or aversions are prompting you to act this way, and practice detachment from them. Then turn your attention back to your Beloved with as much love and devotion as you genuinely feel, and try to follow Brother Lawrence's advice:

> We must serve God in holy freedom. We must work faithfully, without turmoil or anxiety, gently and peacefully bringing our minds back to God as often as we find ourselves distracted.[323]

CHAPTER 22

Be Grateful for Everything

You thank God for the good things that come to you but you don't thank Him for the things that seem to you bad; that is where you go wrong.

— Ramana Maharshi (Hindu)

Most of us begin a spiritual path in order to escape from suffering, but as Theophan the Recluse says:

> The true sign of spiritual endeavour and the price of success in it is suffering.... Those who work feebly and carelessly may go through the movements of making great efforts, but they harvest no fruit, because they undergo no suffering.[324]

This idea that facing suffering is an essential component of the spiritual path is found in the teachings of all mystical traditions. For example, contemporary Tibetan Buddhist teacher Alan Wallace writes,

> Those who have truly entered the door of Dharma will begin to respond actively to unfavorable circumstances in a way that transforms them. How? By cultivating the attitude that whatever misfortune may arise is a blessing.[325]

And Menahem Nahum gives us this advice:

> Accept whatever portion the Lord gives you in love, whether it be for good or for ill and suffering.... Compare this to those bitter medicines that are needed to heal the body. The same are needed for healing the soul.[326]

Such teachings, of course, go completely against one of our most deeply ingrained tendencies—that is, to avoid suffering at all costs. And yet, at a certain point, this is precisely what we must stop doing. Instead of always trying to run away from suffering, we must turn around and confront it head-on. Why? Because, as we have already seen, the only way we can really free ourselves from suffering is to gain direct insights into the mechanisms which cause it. And the only way to gain these insights is to observe suffering *as it is unfolding in the present moment*. Here's how contemporary Buddhist scholar Walpola Rahula explains this principle:

> We must therefore clearly and carefully mark and remember that the cause, the germ, of the arising of *dukkha* [suffering] is within *dukkha* itself, and not outside; and we must equally well remember that the cause, the germ, of the cessation of *dukkha*, of the destruction of *dukkha*, is also within *dukkha* itself, and not outside.[327]

This is why some seekers have taken up various austere practices, like wearing coarse clothing, sleeping on stone floors, or undertaking frequent fasts. Such disciplines can be valuable for bringing to light hidden attachments we aren't ordinarily aware we have. If you wonder whether you're attached to watching TV, for example, try giving it up for a month. But engaging in excessive austerities can also be dangerous, not only to your physical health, but also to your spiritual welfare. Instead of providing opportunities to dispel the delusion of self, such practices can actually strengthen it by making you proud of your capacity to endure increasing degrees of pain. This is why most mystical traditions warn against extreme forms of asceticism. Thus, Krishna tells Arjuna,

> Deceitfulness and ego impel some men.
> Desires and passions fortify them.
> They practice dire austerities
> not enjoined by the Scriptures.
>
> These fools starve the elements
> that stay together in the body,
> And they starve me who am in the body.
> People like this are of demonic resolve.[328]

The Buddha, too, taught a "middle way," which he described this way:

> To give oneself up to indulgence in *Sensual Pleasure*, the base, the common, vulgar, unholy, unprofitable, and also to give oneself up to *Self-mortification*, the painful, unholy, unprofitable; both of these two extremes the Perfect One has avoided and found out the *Middle Path* which makes one both to see and to know, which leads to peace, to discernment, to enlightenment, to Nibbana.[329]

Similarly, Muhammad declared,

> He who has guided you toward the world played a traitor to you,
> and he who insisted that you should practice unnecessary austerities

> and self-mortification caused you grief and trouble, and he who showed you the path of God was your real well-wisher and adviser.[330]

Besides, life itself usually serves up enough suffering without our having to artificially create it. All we really need to do is change our attitude. Instead of looking at the suffering we do experience as something to be avoided, we should try to see it as a precious opportunity for spiritual practice.

Actually, if you have been cultivating mindfulness and compassion, or have been trying to serve God in everything you do, chances are you've already discovered how this works. Usually the more suffering you experience, the more clearly you can identify and surrender whatever attachments have caused it. As a result, you may have come to feel grateful for some of the hardships you've encountered. If so, the trick is simply to expand your sense of gratitude to encompass *all* of life's sufferings—including the big ones, such as pain, sickness, old age, and death.

Being Grateful for Sickness and Pain

Virtually everyone experiences physical pain sometime in their life. When this happens our first impulse is to get rid of it as soon as possible. Rarely do we stop to consider what a blessing pain really is. Without pain we wouldn't know something had gone wrong with our bodies. There are cases of people who, due to a malfunction of the nervous system, don't feel any pain at all. If they happen to lean against a hot stove, the only way they can tell that their flesh is burning is by the smell. So, even at this purely biological level, we should be grateful for our capacity to feel pain.

But physical pain can serve us in spiritual ways as well. For example, you may have noticed that when you are experiencing intense pain, your attention focuses so strongly on that sensation that it is very hard to concentrate on anything else. This, of course, makes it difficult to perform practical, everyday tasks. If you are a meditator, however, or have been practicing contemplative prayer, pain can work to your advantage. Instead of being in a hurry to get rid of it, try taking the pain as an object of concentration, or think of it as a manifestation of your Beloved. Precisely because the pain holds your attention so firmly, you may find you can reach states of clarity and bliss greater than you have ever attained before.

Likewise, sickness can also be a boon for someone trying to walk a spiritual path. For one thing, it often forces us to change our self-centered patterns of behavior in ways we could never do through our own volition. This was the case with the Muslim sage Al-Ghazzali. At the height of a successful academic career at a renowned university in Baghdad, Al-Ghazzali had a crisis of faith in which, as he put it, "the glass of my naive belief in God was broken." After examining and rejecting various philosophical and theological proofs of God's existence, he realized that the only way to escape his doubts would be to attain Gnosis. He also realized that, in order to do this, he would have to leave his comfortable worldly life and follow the path of the Sufis, who alone could teach him the requisite practices. Yet, despite all this, he still could not bring himself to actually take such a drastic step. Here is how he described his predicament:

> One day I would form the resolution to quit Baghdad and get rid of these adverse circumstances; the next day I would abandon my resolution.... Worldly desires were striving to keep me by their chains just where I was, while the voice of faith was calling, "To the road! To the road!"[331]

This went on for six months until one day,

> The matter ceased to be one of choice and became one of compulsion. God caused my tongue to dry up so that I was prevented from lecturing....
>
> Thereupon, perceiving my impotence and having altogether lost my power of choice, I sought refuge with God most high as one who is driven to Him, because he is without resources of his own.... He made it easy for my heart to turn away from my position and wealth.[332]

Now being struck dumb provides a fairly dramatic example of how sickness can mark a turning point in a person's life. But any illness that makes you reflect on what is truly important is a great blessing. This is why Jamgon Kongtrul says that if you get sick you should think along these lines:

> If this [illness] hadn't happened, I would have been distracted by materialistic involvements and would not have maintained mindfulness of dharma. Since this has brought dharma to my attention again, it is the guru's or the Jewels' activity, and I am very grateful.[333]

Of course, none of what we have said should be interpreted as an admonition not to take appropriate medication if you are in pain, or go to a doctor if you get sick. But there is always a lag between the time when you first seek a remedy and when the remedy takes effect. So, instead of allowing your mind to fill this gap with a lot of worries about what may or may not happen, you can turn whatever pain or illness you are experiencing into an opportunity for practice.

Being Grateful for Old Age

Many people in our modern, materialist society have an almost pathological horror of growing old. One reason, of course, is that old age brings with it an increase in aches and pains, illnesses and infirmities. But there is also another, psycho-spiritual reason. Growing old reduces our capacity to enjoy worldly things, like rich food, robust sex, strenuous sports, and rugged travel. And because we equate the enjoyment of these activities with success in life, growing old seems to be an indication of personal failure and a cause for shame. Consequently, we do everything we can to hide its signs for as long as possible. To this end we spend literally billions of dollars on cosmetics, hair-pieces, herbs, vitamins, drugs, and surgeries simply to disguise the perfectly natural fact that we are all growing old.

In the past, traditional cultures have had a far more balanced view of old age. Of course, they, too, were aware of the physical deterioration it entails. But, at the same time, they appreciated the kind of wisdom only age can bestow. When we are young, every new event in our lives seems fraught with cosmic significance. The first time we fall in love, we're convinced no one has ever loved as much. And when we lose that love, we're equally convinced no one has ever despaired as much. If we adopt new philosophies, it's because we're certain they alone hold the keys to truth. If we take up some social or political cause, we think the future of civilization itself is at stake. If we have to fight a war, it's to end all wars. If we make a revolution, it's because we believe the world can be saved at a single stroke. But time tempers our passions. Lovers come and go, philosophies get discredited, causes become obsolete. Revolutions of the present ossify into the orthodoxies of the future, and there are always new wars to fight. In short, all the burning issues that animate our youth fade into flickering memories as insubstantial as dreams. And yet, what we lose in fervor we gain in perspective—*if* we can open ourselves to it.

Having been chastened in our own views, we grow more tolerant of the views of others. Problems that once seemed so urgent now appear less pressing, and our once boundless optimism gets circumscribed by prudence and discretion—which is why in former times the counsel of the elders was so highly valued as a check against the zeal of the young.

But if old age can confer such wisdom on us concerning worldly affairs, how much more so when it comes to spiritual matters. In particular, growing old drives home the lesson of impermanence in a way no words ever can. Not only is impermanence confirmed by the transitoriness of our experiences, it's etched into the very wrinkles of our skin, and the creaking of our bones. For some people, there is no more powerful incentive to get serious about spiritual practice than the appearance of their first grey hairs. Only then are they really ready to heed teachings like this from Anandamayi Ma:

> The day that is gone never returns. Invaluable time is slipping away. Devote your days to the endeavour to draw close to the Lord of the Humble. When extreme old age supervenes, you will be too sluggish, too feeble to concentrate on God's name. How will you then make up for what you failed to do in good time?[334]

In addition to furnishing an incentive for spiritual practices, old age can also provide us with the time needed to pursue them in earnest. This is one reason many spiritual societies have viewed growing old as a blessing rather than a curse. According to the classic Hindu model, for instance, an ideal life should unfold in four stages. The first two—that of a student and a householder—are devoted primarily to worldly affairs. It is only in the third stage, when a person enters middle age and begins turning over their social responsibilities to the next generation, that spiritual life really begins. Finally, in the fourth and last stage, one becomes an external renunciant or *sannyasin* whose time is now totally dedicated to attaining Gnosis. And there is no reason why most of us today cannot follow this pattern. Instead of frittering away our so-called "golden years" playing golf, taking pleasure cruises, or going on shopping sprees, we can engage in our formal practices with an intensity and dedication not possible in the life of a busy householder.

Being Grateful for Death

The only thing that most of us fear more than old age is death. But since there seems no escaping it, the way we deal with death is to try to think about it as little as possible. Mystics of all traditions, however, recommend we do just the opposite. Rather than remain in a state of perpetual denial, they urge us to look death squarely in the eye. Buddhism, for instance, has many manuals which contain detailed instructions for how to meditate on corpses in various stages of decay. Here are some brief excerpts from the *Visuddhimagga Sutta*:

> Realizing the nature of the swollen corpse that has gradually become puffed up like a goldsmith's bellows with air, and considering that the same lot will befall his own body and those of others, the disciple should develop his meditation....
>
> This [festering corpse] is a corpse discharging matter from lacerated parts, or it is a corpse that is loathsome on account of its abominable state of suppuration. The meditation of the foulness of the festering corpse should be practiced by thinking upon it and repeating the words "Vipubbaka-patikkulam," "festering and putrid thing."...
>
> [Worm-infestation] is to be found in a corpse several days old, when masses of worms issue forth from the nine doors. This state may be found alike in the dead body of a man, dog, jackal, buffalo, horse, elephant, python, and so on. The disciple should meditate upon it in any of these forms.[335]

Al-Ghazzali gives similar advice:

> Let man in every hour look to his limbs and his extremities. Let his thoughts dwell upon how the worms must needs devour them, and upon the fashion in which his bones shall rot away. Let him wonder whether the worms are to begin with the pupil of his right eye or of his left; for there is no part of his body that shall not be food for the worms.[336]

And Abraham Abulafia suggests a visualization practice in which you imagine meeting the Angel of Death face to face:

> In its left hand is burning fire, and in its right hand a two-edged sword, performing the vengeance of the covenant, and in its mouth is a consuming fire, and he comes to you and asks you to give him his share of your self; and he is half of your existence, for example, and he seeks to cut off your limbs, one by one, and you see it all with your eyes.[337]

Although these practices may seem morbid to our modern sensibilities, the real point is that, of all the various forms of suffering, as a spiritual seeker you have the most to learn from death.

First of all, contemplating death teaches you the value of human life. In the Abrahamic traditions, of course, human life is considered a unique opportunity for spiritual salvation, never again to be repeated—which is why St. Catherine of Siena says this:

> While you are alive you have a season of mercy, but once you are dead it is your season of justice.[338]

Hindus and Buddhists, on the other hand, believe life is cyclical, composed of a beginningless round of births and deaths. Moreover, according to these traditions there are many realms besides the human in which you can be reborn—hell realms, hungry ghost realms, animal realms, god realms, etc. Only during a human birth, however, do you possess both the intelligence and motivation to engage in those spiritual practices which lead to complete liberation from this whole wretched existence. The trouble is, such human births are exceedingly hard to attain, and, therefore, exceedingly precious. Thus, Shankara writes:

> What greater fool can there be than the man who has obtained this rare human birth together with bodily and mental strength and yet fails, through delusion, to realize his own highest good?[339]

So even though the Abrahamic and Eastern traditions differ in their postmortem views, their fundamental message is the same: Human life is extremely valuable, and pondering this fact can provide one of the most powerful motivations for walking a spiritual path. Simply ask yourself this: "Do I really want to waste my time here piling up useless possessions and pursuing transitory pleasures when it is possible to attain permanent, abiding happiness?"

Contemplating the inevitability of death can also help free you from attachments to worldly possessions and pursuits. Whenever you find yourself lusting after earthly goodies, you might want to take this advice from St. Augustine:

> Thou seest him [a rich man] living, consider him dying. Thou markest what he hath here, mark what he taketh with him. What doth he

> take with him? He hath store of gold, he hath store of silver, numerous estates, slaves; he dieth, these remain, he knoweth not for whom. For though he leaveth them for whom he will, he keepeth them not for whom he will.[340]

If you contemplate death deeply enough, it can even lead you directly to Enlightenment. This is precisely what happened to Ramana Maharshi. While still a teenager he was suddenly overwhelmed by the certainty that he was going to die. But, instead of turning away from this terrifying knowledge as most people would, he decided to make it the subject of an inquiry. Here is how he describes it:

> The shock of the fear of death drove my mind inwards and I said to myself mentally, without actually framing the words: 'Now death has come; what does it mean? What is it that is dying? This body dies.' And I at once dramatized the occurrence of death. I lay with my limbs stretched out stiff as though *rigor mortis* had set in and imitated a corpse so as to give greater reality to the enquiry.... 'Well then,' I said to myself, 'this body is dead. It will be carried stiff to the burning ground and there burnt and reduced to ashes. But with the death of this body am I dead? Is the body I? It is silent and inert but I feel the full force of my personality and even the voice of the 'I' within me, apart from it. So I am Spirit transcending the body. The body dies but the Spirit that transcends it cannot be touched by death. That means I am the deathless Spirit.' All this was not dull thought; it flashed through me vividly as living truth which I perceived directly, almost without thought-process.... Fear of death had vanished once and for all.[341]

The Benefits of Being Grateful for Everything

Learning to be grateful for everything can transform your experience of the world in fundamental ways, because you will cease to perceive everything in accordance with dualistic judgments of 'good' and 'bad.' Of course, you will still recognize a relative difference between such things as pleasure and pain, sickness and health, life and death. But, at the same time, you will also come to see that, from a higher perspective, whatever happens is *spiritually good* insofar as it has something to teach you, for as Rumi declares,

> Each and every part of the world is a snare for the fool and a means of deliverance for the wise.[342]

Beyond this it is even possible to begin getting glimpses of that Non-dual Reality which transcends dualities altogether. Then, instead of automatically grasping at whatever your mind judges to be pleasant and rejecting whatever it judges to be unpleasant, you can start to accept *all* of life as part of that "Great

Perfection" (as Tibetans call it), or the "Play of God" (as the Hindus say) or as a "Divine Self-disclosure" (as the Sufis put it). St. Catherine of Siena describes a person who has reached such an exalted stage like this:

> She holds all things in reverence, the left hand as well as the right, trouble as well as consolation, hunger and thirst as well as eating and drinking, cold and heat and nakedness as well as clothing, life as well as death, honor as well as disgrace, distress as well as comfort. In all things she remains solid, firm, and stable because her foundation is the living rock.[343]

This does not mean that the road ahead will now be completely free of obstacles. There will still be battles to fight, beasts to tame, and treasures to win. But as we shall see in the next chapter, you won't have to endure all these trials alone. Help is always available, *if* you know how to access it.

Chapter 23

Effort and Grace

> *It is necessary that we should labor and exercise ourselves, since divine grace does not give life nor render pleasing unto God except that which the soul has worked; and without work on our part grace refuses to save.*
>
> — Catherine of Genoa (Christian)

Whether you're a bhakta or a jnani, if you're like most seekers, after awhile you're going to make an unexpected and frustrating discovery. Here's how contemporary Tibetan master Lama Gendun Rinpoche describes it:

> When we first become interested in spiritual things, we discover to our disappointment that although we feel attracted to certain ideals, we have great difficulty in remaining faithful to them. This is due to the overwhelming influence that our 'natural' tendencies have on us. We find ourselves behaving badly despite our good intentions. It is only as the habit of doing good grows as strong as and even stronger than the habit of doing evil, that our new-found spiritual force starts to make itself felt.[344]

By "habit of doing evil" he means, of course, our self-centered conditioning, which, as the Rinpoche indicates, most seekers find is much more difficult to undo than they had first imagined. As the months and years drag on, attempts to maintain a meditation or prayer practice, keep precepts, cultivate love and compassion, or serve God seem to provoke increased internal resistance. If anything, worldly desires appear to grow stronger, attachments more intractable, and the poor student is assailed by vacillation and doubts. In fact, many traditions liken what happens during this stage of the path to a war waged against oneself. For example, Rumi writes,

> The prophets and saints do not avoid spiritual combat. The first spiritual combat they undertake in their quest is the killing of the ego and the abandonment of personal wishes and sensual desires. This is the Greater Holy War.[345]

Lalleshwari gives this account of her spiritual battles:

> With great effort
> I rooted out the enemies
> lust, anger, and ego.[346]

The Buddha, too, uses martial metaphors when he declares:

> One may conquer a million men in a single battle;
> However, the greatest and best warrior
> Conquers himself.[347]

Now, the underlying psychological cause of this conflict is that the seeker's mind is starting to forge a new, *spiritual* Story of I to replace the old, worldly one. And because these two stories overlap for a time, the seeker experiences a kind of schizophrenia in which it seems he or she is also being split into two warring selves—one spiritual, the other worldly.

Faced with this inner polarization, the spiritual self assumes that the only thing standing between it and Enlightenment is the continued existence of the worldly self. In order to eliminate this worldly self, then, the spiritual self employs all its powers of self-will and control in an effort to subdue and finally destroy its supposed foe. But what the spiritual self still does not fully get is that it's not just the worldly self which needs to be destroyed, it's *any* experience of self—including a spiritual one—because *all* experiences of self are based on the same fundamental subject/object delusion. Ironically, however, the worldly self *does* get it—at least on an intuitive level. So the reason it resists the spiritual self's efforts to engage in practice is not just because it wants to hang onto its old self-centered ways of behaving. It resists, because it knows that if the spiritual self were to actually succeed in its quest for Enlightenment, it would spell doom for them both.

Seen from this perspective, then, the seeker's internal struggle is not really a battle between the forces of Good and Evil, God and Satan (although it's sometimes depicted this way.) Rather it is a manifestation of that primordial tension between the self's existential longing for happiness and fear of annihilation, which has been buried under all the petty dramas that comprise the Story of I , but which the seeker's spiritual practices are starting to bring to the forefront of awareness once again.

Spiritual Warfare

This kind of spiritual warfare may last longer and be more intense for some seekers than for others. But, whether long or short, for most it constitutes a necessary phase of the path. Why? Because, while in the beginning we certainly need to exercise our powers of will and control in order to counter our conditioning, in the end this approach cannot bring us to Enlightenment. What is ultimately required is not self-conquest, but self-surrender. But, as we said in chapter 6, this is something we usually learn only after we've made a great effort. It is through trying and *failing* that we eventually get to the point where we're ready to surrender our own will to something greater. Here's how Rumi describes it:

> A person assumes that he will drive out blameworthy characteristics by his own labor and struggle. When he fights very hard and has exhausted all his forces and means and is in despair, then God says to him: "Did you think this would happen through your power and activity and intelligence? ... Seek forgiveness for these thoughts and imaginings. For you flattered yourself that the thing would be achieved through the use of your own hands and feet and not that it would be achieved through Us. Now that you see that it has come to pass through Us, seek forgiveness, for He is forgiving.[348]

And as we also said, whenever we "seek forgiveness," and cease to rely solely on our own efforts, we open ourselves to the guidance of a Divine grace which comes to us from beyond the ego. This is why Theophan the Recluse advises us that

> The soul should realize how powerless it is alone; therefore, expecting nothing of itself, let it fall down in humility before God, and in its own heart recognize itself to be nothing. Then grace—which is all powerful—will, out of this nothing, create in it everything.[349]

And Ibn al-'Arabi agrees:

> When man renounces his own individual desire, shrinks from his own ego, and prefers his Lord over all else, then God sets up before him ... a divine guidance ... [which] casts to him from his Lord that within which lies his felicity.[350]

Now surrendering one's self-will usually comes easier to bhaktas, because they already have a form of the Divine to whom they can surrender it. But eventually jnanis must let go of their own wills, as well. And when they do, they, too, will be able to receive this same kind of guidance—even if they don't ascribe it to God. So, for example, although Buddhism recognizes no Supreme Being, the Buddha of the *Lankavatara Sutra* describes a "sustaining power of the Tathagatas [Archetypal Buddhas]" and explains its importance to his disciple, Mahamati:

> By the bestowal of this sustaining power, the Bodhisattvas are enabled to avoid the evils of passion, hatred and enslaving karma; they are enabled to transcend the dhyana [meditation] of the beginners and to advance beyond the experience and truth already attained; they are enabled to demonstrate the Paramitas [virtues]; and finally to attain the stage of Tathagata [Buddhahood]. Mahamati, if it were not for this sustaining power, they would lapse into the

> ways and thoughts of the philosophers, easy-going disciples and the evil-minded, and would thus fall short of the highest attainment.[351]

How Guidance Manifests

For most seekers this mysterious guidance or grace begins to operate in little ways. In concentration meditation, for instance, you may have been making a great effort to attain a state of calm-abiding. Then, one day, you just give up and—bingo—you find you are suddenly there. The same thing can happen if you have been trying to practice unceasing prayer. In a moment when you no longer have the energy to repeat your word or phrase even one more time, something takes over and it begins to repeat itself automatically. Something similar can happen with cultivating love and compassion. Say you have been trying and failing for months to generate unconditional love for a belligerent co-worker. Then one day, when you are just about to return one of his insults with an insult of your own, suddenly, words of sympathy and support pop out of your mouth instead, leaving you with no idea where they came from.

You might also get a spontaneous inspiration to customize your practice in order to fit your own individual forms of conditioning. When one of my students noticed how impatient she became every time she drove her car, it suddenly occurred to her to take a vow of strict obedience to all speed laws for the next six months. By adopting this simple discipline she was able to transform her daily driving routine into a spiritual practice that allowed her to identify and surrender those attachments which had been causing her distress.

Guidance can also come through what Carl Jung called *synchronicity*—the conjunction of two or more events, which have no apparent causal connection, but which nonetheless hold some meaning for the person who experiences them. One example of this, which happened to St. Augustine, proved to be a major turning point on his path. While sitting in his garden one afternoon, crying over his inability to forsake his worldly life and surrender himself completely to God, he heard the voice of a child saying, "Take up and read; Take up and read." Then, as he writes:

> Checking the torrent of tears, I arose; interpreting it to be no other than a commandment from God to open the book, and read the first chapter I should find.… Eagerly then I returned to the place where …I had laid the volume of the Apostle [Paul] when I arose thence. I seized, opened, and in silence read that section on which my eyes first fell: *Not in rioting and drunkenness, not in chambering and wantonness, not in strife and envying; but put ye on the Lord Jesus Christ, and make not provision for the flesh in concupiscence.* No further would I read; nor needed I: for instantly at the end of this sentence, by a light as it were of serenity infused into my heart, all the darkness of doubt vanished away.[352]

And, of course, as we've already seen, dreams can be a very powerful conduit for this kind of guidance. Namkhai Norbu recounts how an entire ceremony for a spiritual practice came to him over several nights of dreams, which culminated in the following scene:

> In the dream it seemed as if the dream of the previous night had been recreated exactly. At my left there was the figure that was reddish-brown with one eye. Once again she was holding many objects in her hand; this time she gave me a bead of crystal.
> It was now clear that this being was assisting me as I gave instructions. I took the crystal into my hand, and looked at it. At the center of the crystal I saw a word. As soon as I saw that special word, I knew that this being was indeed Ekajati. I also had a very clear dream vision of the guardian Ekajati who advised me, saying: "This is the time to open your mind treasure of life's circle of Vajra, the dakini practice for obtaining long life."[353]

Norbu then goes on to describe how upon waking up he spontaneously wrote out the entire ceremony in a notebook, not once but twice. Except for some grammatical errors, a comparison of the two notebooks showed them to be identical, thereby confirming in his own mind the authenticity of the text.

At first, it is easy to treat such occurrences as being products of pure serendipity. But if you pay attention, you will notice that this kind of grace or guidance usually comes at the end of a pattern in which making an effort leads to exhaustion and exhaustion forces a surrender. And the more you learn to trust this process, the more quickly you can abandon your own efforts and let grace take over. Eventually, it is even possible to reach a stage where grace guides you in virtually all your activities. Here's how the author of *The Cloud of Unknowing* describes it:

> Then that same spiritual love which you feel will tell you when you should speak and when you should be still. And it shall guide you discreetly in all your activities without any error, and teach you mystically how you should begin and cease in all such doings of nature with a great and sovereign discretion. For if, by grace, you accustom yourself to this love, and let it continually work within you, then if it is necessary for you to speak with others, or to eat with them, or abide in their company, or to do anything else that accords with common Christian customs and with nature, this love shall first stir you softly to speak or do these other things, whatever they be. And if then you do not do them, this love will pain your heart sorely and let you have no peace until you do whatever it guides you to. And in the same manner, when you are speaking or in engaged in any such other mundane activity, if it be necessary for you to be still, and engage in contrary works which are holy—as fasting is to eating, or being alone is to being in company—this love will guide you to these things as well.[354]

In the meantime, during the darkest periods of spiritual combat, when it seems there is no help to be had from any quarter, don't lose faith. No matter how difficult the practices seem, or how big the obstacles appear, or how strong the resistance grows, it is imperative that you do not give up prematurely. Otherwise, you will never actually exhaust your effort and so make room for grace to operate. This is why Hafiz writes,

> Although Union with the Beloved
> Is never given as a reward for one's efforts,
> Strive, O heart, as much as you are able.[355]

The Way of Selflessness

Part VI: *Dismantling the Delusion of Self*

Chapter 24

Liberating Thoughts

> *The seeker after liberation must work carefully to purify the mind. When the mind has been made pure, liberation is as easy to grasp as the fruit which lies in the palm of your hand.*
>
> — Shankara (Hindu)

In the middle stages of a spiritual path your primary task is to transform the story of yourself as a worldly seeker, pursuing worldly goals, into that of a spiritual seeker, pursuing Gnosis or Union with the Divine. But once this psycho-spiritual conversion is complete, it's time to go deeper, and begin to dismantle the delusion that you are any kind of self—worldly *or* spiritual.

Now, as we have already seen, the delusion of self has two main components—thought and emotion. This is true whether you are a jnani or a bhakta. Here's how contemporary Buddhist teacher John Myrdhin Reynolds describes it in jnana terms:

> It is often said that all sentient beings are in reality Buddhas. But how did they become ordinary deluded sentient beings? It is due to the two obscurations: that resulting from the passions and that resulting from wrong knowledge. When these two layers of obscuration are thoroughly purified and eliminated, one becomes a Buddha.[356]

Similarly, Theophan the Recluse puts it in terms of seekers following a bhakti path:

> Those who truly strive to serve God do not aim at gaining merit. All they care about is to purify themselves from the passions, from all passionate thoughts and feelings.[357]

It is important to remember, however, that thoughts and emotions by themselves do not constitute obscurations. Seen from the point of view of the Absolute, they, too, are manifestations of Consciousness's Divine Play. Obscurations are caused only by *reified* thoughts which constitute the Story of I, and by *self-centered* emotions which drive that story forward. Keeping this caveat in mind, then, let's take a closer look at each of these two components. In this chapter we will discuss how to purify thoughts, and in the next chapter we will see how to purify emotions.

So what do you have to do to purify and eliminate thoughts? Surprisingly the answer is, nothing. Why? Because thoughts, like all phenomena, are impermanent. Consequently, if you leave them alone, they will simply dissolve, or, as the Tibetans say, *self-liberate*. Dilgo Khyentse explains it this way:

> It is completely natural that thoughts keep on arising. The point is not to try to stop them, which would be impossible anyway, but to liberate them. This is done by remaining in a state of simplicity, which lets thoughts arise and vanish again without stringing onto them any further thoughts.[358]

So then how exactly can you learn to do this?

Liberating Thoughts for Jnanis

If you are a jnani, the way to train yourself to let thoughts self-liberate is to continue your basic choiceless awareness meditation, but with a few small yet crucial refinements.

First, if you are like most meditators, in trying to maintain detachment from your thoughts you've developed a subtle aversion to them. This will be especially true if you've experienced deep states of clarity, where all thoughts temporarily cease. Because such states are usually very blissful, when your thoughts start up again there is a tendency to regard them as hindrances to your meditation. If this negative attitude towards thoughts has crept into your practice, you must identify and surrender it. The way you will know you have succeeded is that, not only will you be able to maintain detachment from thoughts, but you will also feel totally *relaxed* when they are present.

Second, you must allow thoughts to self-liberate *as soon as they arise*. This, to use a Buddhists image, is like drawing pictures on water. Even before the picture is finished, it's already in the process of dissolving away.

Third, you must not let your thinking mind *elaborate* on the thoughts you are allowing to self-liberate. This includes thoughts about the practice itself: "Look, there is a thought. Now, I will allow it to self-liberate!" In the beginning, of course, you won't be able to prevent your mind from engaging in this kind of commentary. What you can do, however, is to let even *those* thoughts self-liberate. Eventually, with continued practice, the naked observation of how a thought both arises and self-liberates will occur simultaneously. Then, as Dilgo goes on to say,

> When you no longer perpetuate the movement of thoughts, they dissolve by themselves without leaving any trace. When you no longer spoil the state of stillness with mental fabrications, you can maintain the natural serenity of mind without any effort.[359]

What follows, then, are some specific instructions for choiceless awareness meditation which incorporates these refinements on liberating thoughts.

Instructions for Liberating Thoughts in Choiceless Awareness

STEP ONE: *Begin by Entering the Mental Field*

Start by concentrating on your breath (or other object) until you have attained some measure of calmness and stability. Then, allow your attention to expand through the five sensory fields until it comes to rest in the mental field of consciousness. Without trying to grasp anything or push anything away, notice that "thoughts are just thoughts"—i.e., they are all imaginary.

STEP TWO: *Try Holding Onto Thoughts*

Now purposely generate a thought such as "the sky is blue." Try to hold it in awareness for one whole minute. Note that "holding" a thought is not the same as repeating it over and over. Holding a thought means not letting the original thought self-liberate for the full sixty seconds.

Continue trying to do this with a variety of thoughts until you are experientially convinced that it cannot be done.[360]

STEP THREE: *Allow Generated Thoughts to Self-liberate*

Next, try doing the opposite. Purposely generate a thought, but make no attempt to hold it. Watch as it self-liberates—i.e., dissolves completely away without your having to do anything.

Try this with other thoughts which you purposely generate until, again, you are experientially convinced that all thoughts naturally self-liberate in the same manner.

STEP FOUR: *Allow Spontaneous Thoughts to Self-liberate*

Now relax and let your thoughts flow spontaneously. Notice how they all self-liberate, as soon as they arise. If you become aware that your attention has been captivated by a train of thought, look directly at whatever thought is currently present in your mind and watch that one self-liberate.

STEP FIVE: *Allow All Phenomena to Self-liberate*

Finally, allow your attention to expand into the total field of consciousness-awareness. Spend a few minutes just resting in this space of undistracted awareness, without trying to grasp or push anything away. Now notice that *all* the phenomena, not just thoughts, arise and self-liberate on their own. Consequently, there is no need to do anything except observe them. Here is how Dudjom Rinpoche describes it:

> Whatever perceptions arise, you should be like a little child going into a beautifully decorated temple; he looks, but grasping does not enter into his perception at all. So you leave everything fresh, natural, vivid, and unspoiled.[361]

Liberating Thoughts for Bhaktas

If you are a bhakta, it is just as important to learn how to let thoughts self-liberate as it is for jnanis. However, you will probably want to take a somewhat different approach. This is exemplified by the great Baal Shem Tov. Here is what scholars Arthur Green and Barry Holtz say about his teachings:

> He spoke against the attempts of his contemporaries to either do battle with distracting thoughts or to see them as vanities that should simply be ignored. Just as he taught that each moment in life may be an opening to the Presence of God, he taught that each distraction in prayer may become a ladder by which to ascend to a new level of devotion. For one who truly believes that all things are from God and bear the Creator's mark can make no exception for the fantasies of his or her own mind![362]

So how exactly do you turn distracting thoughts into a "ladder" for devotion? Well, again, it is not a matter of taking up some new practice. All you need to do is to refine the practice of prayer-in-the-heart which you have already learned.

First, whenever distracting thoughts arise you must recognize that, as the Bal Shem Tov said, they don't belong to you. Like everything else in the universe, they come from God and go back to God. So, instead of trying to push them away as though they were something distasteful, you should treat them as something precious, like the notes of a little melody which your Beloved is playing just for you. Then, as the thoughts self-liberate and return to their Divine Source, they will carry your own feelings of gratitude and love along with them.

In this practice it is important to remember that the content of the thought—good or bad, right or wrong, spiritual or worldly—is irrelevant. They all come from God and should be returned to God without any judgment or grasping on your part. This attitude of complete devotion is beautifully expressed in a prayer by the nineteenth-century Hindu saint Ramakrishna to the Divine Mother:

> O Mother, here is sin and here is virtue; take them both and grant me pure love for thee. Here is knowledge and here is ignorance; I lay them at thy feet. Grant me pure love for thee. Here is purity and here is impurity; take them both and grant me pure love for thee. Here are good works and here are evil works; I lay them at thy feet. Grant me pure love for thee.[363]

What follows, then, are some specific instructions for incorporating this approach to liberating thoughts into your regular practice of prayer-in-the-heart.

Instructions for Liberating Thoughts in Prayer-in-the-Heart

STEP ONE: *Begin by Stabilizing Attention*

Focus attention on your sacred word or prayer, then use it to bring your attention into the space of your heart. When your attention has descended into the depths of your heart, relax your effort, but continue saying your word or prayer with as much longing and devotion as you genuinely feel.

STEP TWO: *Offer All Distracting Thoughts to the Beloved*

When other thoughts arise, remember that they do not really belong to you, but, like all things, are gifts from God. Instead of trying to push them away, allow them to return to your Beloved, accompanied by your reverence and gratitude.

STEP THREE: *Spontaneous Prayer*

If you have been practicing prayer-in-the-heart on a regular basis, after a while your word or prayer will start repeating itself spontaneously. Again, if other thoughts arise, immediately offer them back to your Beloved. When you reach this stage of practice, no thought can be a distraction, because all thoughts direct your attention back to the Divine. At this point, there is nothing more for you to do. Just remain humble and attentive to your Beloved. Here is how the author of *The Book of Privy Counseling* describes it:

> Leave your thought quite naked, your affection uninvolved, and your self simply as you are, so that grace may touch and nourish you with the experimental knowledge of God as he really is.[364]

Liberating the Energy of Thought

One important side effect of letting thoughts self-liberate is that it will enhance the clarity of your awareness. This happens because all thoughts carry some emotional charge. In the case of those run-of-the-mill thoughts that make up our normal mental chatter, the energy of this charge is so weak as to be hardly noticed. But when it comes to thoughts about people or things that arouse intense emotions—whether positive or negative—the energy will be stronger. In either case, when your thoughts form into a story, the energies they contain serve to heighten the drama. If, however, you allow your thoughts to self-liberate, their energies will also be liberated. This is something you can actually feel in your body. It's as though when a thought disintegrates it emits a tiny electrical impulse. Then, if you pay close attention, you will notice that each of these little bursts of liberated energy "brightens" your field of awareness. And, of course, the more powerful the energy of any particular thought, the more pronounced this brightening will be. Reynolds explains it this way:

> When a thought arises bearing a strong charge of energy, such as a thought of desire or a thought of anger, then the Awareness (rig-pa) present at the thought's liberation will be that much stronger and clearer. Thus, the passion (Skt. kleśa) becomes the friend and helper of Rigpa, instead of its enemy and opponent.[365]

Liberating Thoughts in Everyday Life

After you have practiced liberating thoughts during your formal meditation or prayer session, you should start trying it in everyday situations. This is particularly valuable for interrupting conditioned trains of thought that lead to conflicts with other people. For example, you might find yourself getting drawn into one of those recurring arguments with your spouse in which accusations are followed by counter-accusations, all building to a bitter climax that never really resolves anything. If you have been practicing liberating thoughts, then the instant you realize what's going on, you can halt the argument simply by allowing whatever thought next arises in your mind to self-liberate unspoken. With the chain broken, and all obscurations temporarily removed, a window of stillness will open through which the spontaneous action of grace can shine.

Of course, you don't have to wait for an argument to practice liberating thoughts. Whenever you find yourself getting caught up in old memory loops, running commentaries, or idle fantasies, you can let all these imaginings self-liberate. By practicing this repeatedly, you will begin to dismantle the Story of I, because you will develop an on-going, experiential insight into just how insubstantial the thoughts which comprise it really are. This is why Huang Po says,

> If you would spend all your time—walking, standing, sitting or lying down—learning to halt the concept-forming activities of your own mind, you could be sure of ultimately attaining your goal.[366]

Chapter 25

Purifying Emotions

Blessed are the pure in heart, for they shall see God.

— Jesus of Nazareth

The simplest way to purify a self-centered emotion is to liberate whatever thought evoked it. So, for example, when you notice you're getting upset thinking about an old injury someone once caused you, if you let the memory of that injury dissolve, in a few moments the feelings will usually dissolve as well. There is, however, another way to purify emotions which is more difficult, but also more profound. This involves not just letting emotions dissipate, but actually freeing them from the Story of I. When this happens even so-called negative emotions can be experienced as expressions of the Love and Wisdom inherent in Consciousness Itself.

In order to understand how this works, we first need to get rid of some preconception about emotions which are imbedded in our very language. Words like *fear, anger, envy,* etc. almost automatically connote emotions that are 'bad' and should be avoided. But, as we mentioned in chapter 6, mystics view emotions as being a kind of neutral *energy* whose value depends on its use. For instance, electricity in itself is neither good nor bad. It all depends on what we do with it. Using electricity to torture people is bad, but using it to light your house is good. In the same way, when we use emotional energy in the service of self, it leads us deeper into delusion and, therefore, is 'bad.' On the other hand, when we use it in the service of other beings or God, it leads us towards Enlightenment and so is 'good.' Here's the way Lama Gendun Rinpoche puts it:

> The emotion itself is not a problem. It is simply mental activity, energy on the move, which becomes either positive or negative according to our reaction to it. If this energy of the mind occurs in a state of confusion, a state of clinging or resistance, we have what we call ordinary 'emotions' which give rise to different forms of suffering. If however this same energy manifests without confusion,

> it completely avoids becoming emotional and operates as wisdom activity which benefits living beings.[367]

As Lama Gendun suggests, emotions cannot be *completely* purified until confusion has been *completely* eliminated, which only happens with Enlightenment. Nevertheless, it is important to start practicing now, and this for two reasons. First, if you don't know how to purify negative emotions, their re-emergence following a Gnostic flash can abort full Awakening and plunge you back into the realm of delusion. Second, even before Enlightenment, whatever fragments of emotional energy you do manage to purify can be channeled into enriching your spiritual practice, instead of fueling the Story of I.

So then how, exactly, do you go about purifying your emotions? And what exactly can you do with them once you have accomplished this? In fact, there are two approaches you can take. One, which is most suitable for bhaktas, is to transform all emotional energies into love and longing for the Divine. The other, which both bhaktas and jnanis can practice, is to transform emotions into what the Tibetans call "wisdom energies" that can then be used in the service of other beings.

Transforming Emotions into Love and Longing for The Divine

The reason negative emotions can be transformed into love and longing for the Divine is because all emotions are rooted in love. You can see this by considering that whenever you get angry, it is because you have been deprived of something you love; whenever you feel fear it is because something you love is being threatened; whenever greed arises, it's because you want to acquire something you love and whenever you experience envy, it is because someone else has acquired something you would love to have. So even those feelings that end up causing us suffering actually spring from a kernel of love. This is why the Kabbalists insist that all emotions contain in their core a "divine spark" which has fallen from the "World of Love." Thus the way to transform emotions back into love is simple: Whenever an emotion arises, you must identify the feeling of love that lies at its root. Then, redirect the energy of that feeling towards your Beloved residing in your heart. Here, for example, is what the Bal Shem Tov (as paraphrased by Green and Holtz) used to say about transforming lust:

> A person who is distracted by sexual desire during worship should not seek to drive that desire from the mind, but rather should come to know that such desire itself is but a fallen spark from the World of Love, which seeks to be uplifted in the ascent of prayer. The thought needs to be "purified in its root," so that the energy animating it can be redeemed and brought back to God.[368]

In fact, the more intensely you feel an emotion like lust, the more potential it has to enhance your practice. This is illustrated by a story about Ramakrishna and one of his disciples, Turiyananda:

> Once, when Swami Turiyananda was a young boy, he approached his Master, Sri Ramakrishna, and appealed to him to help him become free of lust. Sri Ramakrishna replied, "Why do you want to be free of lust? Rather increase your lust." Then the disciple fully understood that to increase lust meant to increase lust for God and give one's whole heart to Him.[369]

For most seekers, however, learning to transform emotions into love and longing for the Divine is not as easy as it sounds—especially amidst all the dramas of a householder's life. Usually, when some negative emotion arises, we are so quickly caught up in the story it generates, we don't even remember there is a spiritual way to handle it. For this reason, it's a good idea to begin learning how to transform emotions during your formal prayer-in-the-heart practice. What follows are some specific instructions for doing just that.

Instructions for Transforming Emotions into Devotion

STEP ONE: *Begin by Stabilizing Attention*

Focus attention on your sacred word or prayer, then use it to bring your attention into the space of your heart. When your attention has descended into the depths of your heart, relax your effort, but continue saying your word or prayer with as much longing and devotion as you genuinely feel.

STEP TWO: *Transform Other Emotions into Love*

If some other feeling arises, don't push it away. Instead, try to identify the person or thing you love which lies at the root of your emotion, and focus your attention on that. For example, if you find yourself lusting after someone whom you find sexually attractive, concentrate your attention directly on the sensation of the desire. If you are angry at your spouse for breaking a favorite coffee mug, concentrate on the love you had for that object. Or if you feel envious of a friend who is going on vacation, concentrate on your own yearning to get away from it all. In other words, dig into whatever you are feeling until you uncover the love that lies at its root. Then remember, only God can ever truly satisfy you, and so refocus your love and direct it toward the Presence of your Beloved in your heart.

Transforming Emotions Into Wisdom Energies

Transforming emotions into wisdom energies is a little more complicated. It's based on the insight that, while all emotions have love as their root, each emotion represents a unique way of manifesting that love. Consequently, you don't even have to transform a particular emotion such as fear or anger into some other emotion like love or longing in order to purify it. All that is really required is to recognize the true nature of the emotion's energy. This is done by liberating the emotion from those thoughts that weave it into the Story of I. Then, the very same emotion which, in the context of the Story of I, appeared to be something negative, is now experienced as something beneficial. This is what John Scotus Eriugena means when he says that

> No vice is found which is not the shadow of some virtue.[370]

And you will find similar teachings in all the great traditions. Nevertheless, the Tibetans seem to have the most precise methods for actually performing this emotional alchemy. Consequently, we'll use the instructions they give as the basis for our own practice.

The Five Emotional Energies

Tibetans distinguish five fundamental types of emotional energy which under delusion manifest as *desire, aversion, envy, pride,* and *ignorance* or *bewilderment.* Of course, in our culture we distinguish a lot more emotions than just these. Still, they can all be subsumed under these five basic categories:

1. *Desire* includes lust, avarice, and greed, as well as sorrow, sadness, and grief, which arise when what is desired has been lost, stolen or is otherwise out of reach.

2. *Aversion* includes aggravation, anger, and hatred, as well as anxiety, fear, and dread. In other words, it is the energy which animates the entire spectrum of "fight or flight" responses.

3. *Pride* includes conceit, vanity, arrogance, and all forms of narcissism.

4. *Envy* includes jealousy, suspicion, and mistrust, as well as that chronic trepidation which comes from always feeling left behind in life.

5. *Ignorance* or *bewilderment* includes feelings of confusion, stupidity, dullness, torpor, exhaustion, and sloth.

Whenever these emotional energies appear in the context of the Story of I, they are experienced as what the Tibetans call *afflicted emotions* because they bring suffering to ourselves and others. If we recognize their true nature, however, these same five afflicted emotions instantly transform into the five wisdom energies which, in reality, they are. Thus:

1. Desire transforms into the *discriminating wisdom of love and compassion.*
2. Aversion transforms into the *mirror-like wisdom of perfect clarity.*
3. Pride transforms into the *wisdom of equanimity or sameness.*
4. Envy transforms into *all-accomplishing wisdom.*
5. Ignorance or bewilderment transforms into the *wisdom of all-encompassing space* which is a Tibetan metaphor for Gnosis or Enlightenment.

It is because of this great potential possessed by even the most afflicted emotions that Lama Gendun Rinpoche declares,

> On this path we do not seek to abandon the five emotions, only to look directly at their essence or reality, upon which they are automatically transformed right then and there into the five wisdoms.[371]

In order to get some inkling of how the five afflicted emotions actually transform into wisdom energies, let's take a closer look at each of them in turn.

Desire and Discriminating Wisdom

To see how desire, when liberated, transforms into the discriminating wisdom of love and compassion, consider what happens when we first fall madly in love with someone. In order to better please our lover, we become very discriminating. We take note of his or her smallest likes and dislikes: What is our lover's favorite color? Does he or she take their coffee with cream, sugar, both, or neither? Does he or she like to go dancing, read books, or walk barefoot on the beach? What makes this kind of energy afflicted is that, under delusion, its discriminatory power is pressed into the service of our own self-interest. At the very least, we want the person we love to love us back. If our emotion is severely afflicted, we want to dominate and control that person in every aspect of their lives.

When the energy of desire is liberated from the Story of I, the qualities of love and discrimination remain, but we no longer demand anything in return. Because our love is truly self-less, and we are able to give it without any strings attached, no suffering can arise. Tibet's most famous yogini, the legendary Lady Tsogyel, explains it this way:

> Know that desire and covetousness are Discriminating Awareness—
> You will find sensory distinction in no other place
> Than a mind hungering for beautiful things, wanting the whole world.
> Look into the intrinsic freshness of your desire
> And there is Boundless Light, Amitābha [the Buddha of Compassion]!
> Detached from radiance, your pleasure is purified.[372]

Aversion and Mirror-like Wisdom

When the Tibetans say that aversion once liberated transforms into mirror-like wisdom, what they mean is that the energy of emotions like anger and fear can produce states of exceptional clarity in which the mind becomes like a polished mirror that reflects everything placed in front of it without any distortion. If you have ever been confronted by someone who threatened you with violence, you may have had some inkling of how this is possible. Normally, when we are faced with this kind of danger, our attention fixates on ourselves and what might happen to *me*. This causes us to react out of either afflicted fear or afflicted anger. If afflicted fear arises we can become disorientated and immobilized or "frozen with fear." If afflicted anger arises, we usually feel an urge to strike out in a "blind rage" in order to annihilate whoever is causing our suffering.

But when fear or anger is liberated from this concern for ourselves, instead of clouding our mind, the energy of the emotion purifies it. Suddenly our awareness seems to expand to all horizons, and our thoughts become clear and precise. If action is required, we have the strength to take it, but now it is aimed at resolving the situation with as little harm to anyone as possible. What's more, we don't even feel that we are the ones doing anything. Rather, we seem to be impartial witnesses, watching everything that unfolds from a place of extraordinary peace and calm. Here is Lady Tsogyel again:

> Know that aggression and malice are Mirror-like Awareness itself—
> Radiance and clarity have no other source
> Than a hostile mind filled with anger and enmity.
> Look into your anger
> And there is the strength of Diamond Being, Vajrasattva [Buddha of Insight]!
> Detached from appearances, you are purified in Emptiness.[373]

Pride and the Wisdom of Equanimity or Sameness

To understand how pride, once liberated, transforms into the wisdom of equanimity, consider what happens when people praise us for achieving something important. For a little while, at least, we feel we are "on top of the world," utterly secure, magnanimous, and at ease. What makes this feeling afflicted is that it depends on those around us confirming an image we have of ourselves as being in some way superior to others. Sooner or later, however, new challenges are bound to arise, and so we will have to seek confirmation of our supposed preeminence all over again. If others now disconfirm our self-image, we will experience embarrassment, shame, and humiliation.

When the energy of pride is liberated from our self-image, the feeling of ease remains, but it no longer depends on having our superiority confirmed by others. Why? Because we realize that, in reality, all these self-images are the same in being imaginary and without foundation. Consequently, there is no longer any reason to claim credit for 'my' successes, nor be upset by 'my' failures. Whatever life brings, we respond from a place of deep, unshakable equanimity. Lady Tsogyel puts it this way:

> Know that pride and vain complacency are Awareness of Sameness—
> Primal purity in meditative composure cannot be found
> Except in an ambitious mind that believes itself supreme.
> Look into natural purity
> And there is a fountain of jewels, Ratnasambhava [Buddha of Spiritual Wealth and Equanimity]!
> Detached from the state of Emptiness, light-form is pure.[374]

Envy and All-Accomplishing Wisdom

To get some idea of how liberated envy transforms into all-accomplishing wisdom, consider what can happen when a colleague at work gets promoted. If we respond by measuring our own meager accomplishments against their seemingly greater ones, afflicted envy will arise. We feel inadequate and depressed because someone has outperformed us in some way. Or we might become resentful and blame our boss for failing to recognize our own hidden talents. Either way, we feel victimized, cheated, and passed over. We are full of restless energy, but don't know quite what to do with it. Often, we end up channeling it into some form of destructive behavior aimed at punishing ourselves or those around us.

But when the energy of envy is liberated from our obsession with self, we no longer feel we have to compete with others. If a colleague gets a promotion, we genuinely share in their joy. In fact, instead of resenting their success, we are inspired to emulate it. We feel that we, too, can accomplish wonderful things—which is why the energy of envy is called "all-accomplishing wisdom." Here is Lady Tsogyel again:

> Know that envy and alienation are All-Accomplishing Awareness—
> Efficiency and success have no other source
> Than a bigoted mind that is quick to judge and holds a grudge.
> Look behind jealous thoughts
> And there is immediate success, Amoghasiddhi [Buddha of Unobstructed Action]!
> Detached from crass envy and subtle resentments, whatever occurs is pure.[375]

Ignorance and Gnosis

Before we can discuss how ignorance transforms into Gnosis, we must distinguish between two meanings of the term. When mystics talk about *ignorance,* they are usually referring to that *fundamental* ignorance of our true nature which is the root cause of our delusion. And while all kinds of emotional sufferings flow out of it, strictly speaking, this fundamental ignorance is not itself an emotion. However, the word *ignorance* can also refer to a specific state of *mental* ignorance or bewilderment which does generate afflicted emotions such as apathy, doubt, confusion dullness, and exhaustion.

But while fundamental ignorance and mental ignorance are different, they are actually related in an inverse fashion. Mental ignorance manifests only when our fundamental ignorance—i.e., our delusion—begins to break-down. This is because the more firmly we believe in the reality of self and world, the clearer our course of action appears. We think we know what we want, and we're highly motivated to go out and get it. Our only problem seems to be a strategic one of finding the right means to achieve our goals. Along the way, we may experience some setbacks and defeats, but we still continue to forge ahead, confident that in the end we will attain the happiness we seek. For people lost in this kind of delusion, bewilderment rarely arises.

Real bewilderment usually manifests only when we begin to question this whole approach to life. Perhaps, our defeats start to out-number our triumphs and we despair of ever finding the right strategy. Or perhaps, even though we continue to pile up 'successes', true happiness continues to elude us. As a result, we begin to doubt the value of our accomplishments and become confused about what to do next. All our efforts start to seem futile, our motivation dries up, and we sink into apathy. Finally, we can reach a condition of total mental ignorance in which we no longer know what to think or do, or even what we want. But, as we shall see in a later chapter, it is precisely in this kind of state of extreme mental ignorance that Gnosis becomes possible. This is why the Tibetans insist that ignorance, when liberated, transforms into Enlightenment, or "Dynamic Space," as Lady Tsogyel calls it:

> Know that ignorance and stupidity are Awareness of Dynamic Space—
> There is no other way to hold fast to the path
> Than through ignorance and a dense understanding.
> Look into ignorance
> And there is Dynamic Visionary Panorama, Vairocana [Buddha of Complete Enlightenment]!
> Detached from hypnotic states, whatever arises is pure.[376]

How to Transform Afflicted Emotions

As we already said, the way to actually transform afflicted emotions into wisdom energies is to free them from the Story of I and then look directly at their true nature. But, as with transforming emotions into love and devotion, this practice is not easy to do in the midst of a busy householder's life. Therefore, it's a good idea to first train within the context of your formal meditation or prayer practice.

It is also a good idea to start your training with one particular afflicted emotion. Most people find that different emotions dominate different periods of their lives, depending on what's going on at the time. For instance, if you are in the process of breaking up with a spouse or lover, you may be experiencing a lot of sadness or jealousy. If you have been the victim of a crime, you may be filled with anger, or haunted by fear. If you have recently won a promotion, you may experience recurring bursts of pride; or, if a colleague has won the promotion, you may be consumed with envy. So first try to identify which afflicted emotion is currently most prominent in your life and start there. Continue practicing with that one emotion until you have some experiential knowledge of how to transform it. This may take anywhere from several weeks to several months. Then try transforming the same emotion whenever it arises during the course of your daily life.

Once you know how to transform your afflicted emotion in everyday situations, you can stop doing it in your formal practice. If, in the future, another afflicted emotion becomes dominant in your life, you can go back to practicing formally with that emotion, then repeat the whole process. Below are some specific instructions for how to transform emotions in your formal practice.

Instructions for Transforming Emotions into Wisdom Energies

PRELIMINARIES

Choose one of the four afflicted emotions—desire, aversion, envy, or pride—to practice with, and stick with that for the duration of your session. (If you are trying to transform mental ignorance or bewilderment, see the special instructions at the end of this chapter.)

In order to remind yourself that the practice of transforming afflicted emotions must always be undertaken within prescribed moral boundaries, recite a precept appropriate to the emotion you have chosen. For instance, if your are going to transform sexual desire, you can recite the precept of sexual restraint; or if you are going to work with anger, you can recite the precept of harmlessness.

STEP ONE: *Entering Spacious-Awareness*

As when you do sending and taking, it is important to enter a space of undistracted awareness before trying to transform an afflicted emotion. If you don't, you are likely to be overwhelmed by the intensity of the feelings your practice arouses. In spacious awareness, however, there is plenty of room for even the most volatile emotions to fully manifest.

If you have been practicing choiceless awareness, begin by focusing attention on your breath (or other object). Once you have attained some stability, allow your attention to expand into the total field of consciousness-awareness. Spend a few minutes just resting in this space of undistracted awareness, without trying to grasp or push away any of the phenomena that arise within it.

If you have been practicing prayer-in-the-heart, focus attention on your sacred word or prayer, then use it to bring your attention down into the space of your heart. Once you feel you are in the Presence of your Beloved, stop saying your word or prayer and spend a few minutes abiding in the vastness of that Presence.

STEP TWO: *Arouse the Emotion to Be Transformed*

Now, try to remember as vividly as possible some recent situation in which you experienced the afflicted emotion you have chosen to transform. For example, if it is sexual desire, recall the circumstances in which you were strongly attracted to someone. If it is anger, recall the circumstances in which you last felt very angry; if it is pride, recall some accomplishment of which you feel intensely proud; or if the emotion is envy, recall the person who last aroused your envy.

STEP THREE: *Focus on the Naked Feeling*

Once you can actually *feel* the afflicted emotion, pay close attention to the specific effects it produces. For instance, if you are focusing on sexual desire, notice how aware you have become of even the smallest details of the way the person you desire looks, moves, and acts. If you are focusing on anger, notice how it wipes away all other distracting thoughts and keeps your attention clearly concentrated on the object of your anger. If you are focusing on pride, notice that the feeling of equanimity which it generates is also mixed with a subtle undercurrent of anxiety. And if you are focusing on envy, notice how it fills you with a restless energy that seems to have nowhere to go.

STEP FOUR: *Liberate the Emotion from the Story of I*

Once you can feel the emotion and its effects, stop generating any more thoughts about it. Recognize that all such thoughts are part of the Story of I and allow them to self-liberate. Then, without any grasping or rejecting, focus your attention directly on the naked sensation of the emotion. If thoughts continue to arise, just let them dissolve and keep focusing on the sensation itself.

STEP FIVE: *Feel the Emotion as Pure Energy*

Try to locate where in the body you actually feel the sensation of this emotion—in your head? throat? stomach? groin? Once you have located the sensation, try to experience it as pure energy without any judgments as to whether it is 'good' or 'bad,' 'pleasant' or 'unpleasant.'

STEP SIX: *Release the Energy into Your Entire Body-Mind*

If the energy of your emotion seems to be trapped in a particular place in your body, relax the muscles in that area and allow the energy to flow throughout your entire body-mind. Gently breathing into a blocked area can help relax the muscles and release the energy there.

STEP SEVEN: *Recognize the Wisdom Quality of the Energy*

While continuing to focus on the energy itself, try to recognize how its true nature manifests when the thoughts that make up the Story of I are no longer present to distort it. For example, if you have been focusing on sexual desire, notice that the warm, discriminating alertness of desire is still present, even though you have stopped thinking about the person who aroused it. Likewise, the cool clarity of anger remains even though you have dropped all thoughts about whoever you were mad at. So, too, the equanimity of pride lingers, but now you no longer feel anxious about having to prove anything through your achievements. And, once its been liberated from the Story of I, the restless energy of envy can be experienced as the potential for creatively responding to any kind of situation that might arise.

STEP EIGHT: *Ending your Session*

If you have been able to transform your afflicted emotion into a wisdom energy, rise from your meditation and carry this energy with you until it naturally dissipates.

If you have not been able to transform your afflicted emotion, relax your attention into the total field of consciousness-awareness, or the presence of the Beloved, and allow all your thoughts and feelings to self-liberate into that space until you are once again calm and relaxed.

Instructions for Transforming Ignorance into Gnosis

As with the four other afflicted emotions, to transform mental ignorance into Gnosis all you have to do is recognize its true nature. In order to do this, however, you need to be in an extremely deep state of bewilderment—one in which you have lost all your bearings and arrived at a complete cul-de-sac. While it is possible for some seekers to generate such a state by exhausting all their mental and emotional energies trying to solve some intractable problem or paradox, this requires an intensity of effort which few of us are capable of generating by will power alone.[377] Consequently, you probably won't be able to practice transforming mental ignorance unless or until your spiritual path or life circumstances bring you to a place where it arises on its own. If you do find yourself in such a situation, skip ahead and read chapter 33, "Kenosis." Otherwise, stick with trying to transform the other four afflicted emotions, both in your formal practice and in your everyday life.

CHAPTER 26

Deconstructing the Delusion of Time

Time has no meaning in the sight of God.

— Meshullam Feibush (Jewish)

One reason why the Story of I is so compelling is that it seems to unfold in time. This does two things. First, it solidifies our experience of being a separate self by creating the impression we have a personal history stretching back at least to our birth, if not beyond (depending on your worldview.) Second, questions about what is going to happen to this self in the future generate the dramatic tension that keeps the story interesting: "Will I get the present I want for my birthday? Will I get the girl or boy I've fallen in love with? Will I get the job I applied for? Will I get the new house I bid on? Will I win the lottery?" How these questions get answered in time constitutes the story's plot. Without time there would be no suspense, no excitement, nothing to hold our attention. But what if time doesn't really exist? What if time is just an imaginary construct which we have reified along with all the other reified boundaries and distinctions that constitute our delusion?

This is, in fact, precisely what the mystics claim. Shankara, for example, distinguishes two kinds of time that are roughly equivalent to our notions of subjective and objective time. But then he declares,

> All are equally imagined. The special distinction that external phenomena (appear to) have of belonging to two times itself has no other cause but being imagined.[378]

Likewise, K. Venkata Ramanan writes that, according to the great Buddhist philosopher Nagarjuna,

> Space and time are not substances. There is nothing like an absolute time which remains as a reality apart from successive events. Time and space are derived notions, modes of reference.[379]

Ibn al-'Arabi agrees:

> Time is an imaginary entity having no existence. It is denoted by the movements of the spheres [heavenly bodies] or those of objects occupying a place when the question "When?" is asked.[380]

Given how crucial time is to the Story of I, the question of its true nature is not just an academic one. It is extremely personal, because if time is, indeed, imaginary as the mystics insist, then dismantling the delusion that it is real will go a long way towards dismantling the delusion of self, as well. So, let's take a closer look and try to see for ourselves why the mystics say time doesn't really exist.

What is Time?

Most of us probably understand that the units we use to measure time with—*seconds, minutes,* and *hours*—are, like the units we use to measure lengths with—*inches, feet,* and *yards*—all imaginary. They are human inventions which could just as well be replaced by different units, defined on different scales. In fact, when it comes to measuring lengths, almost everyone living outside of the United States uses the metric system, which uses *millimeters, meters,* and *kilometers.*

Still, the kinds of objects we measure, either with yards or meters, appear to be real enough. For instance, you can stretch out a tape measure along a piece of lumber and determine that its length is 22 inches. But what is the 'object' we are measuring with seconds, minutes, and hours? When you hold up a clock and see that the digital display indicates that 22 seconds have elapsed, what is it that you are actually measuring? At least with the piece of lumber, you can pick it up, nail it to another piece of lumber, and start to build a house. When it comes to 'time', however, there seems to be, literally, nothing to grab hold of.

Actually, time has been something of a mystery to us humans since we first started thinking about it. Some peoples, like the Native American Algonquin, had no word for 'time' before the Europeans arrived. The way they tracked the changes in their environment was by making reference to concrete events. Thus, autumn was called the "leaf turning moon," while the way to find out someone's age was to ask, "How many moons like this have you seen with your own eyes, grandfather?"

In the pre-industrial civilizations of Europe and Asia time was viewed as a series of circles turning within circles—days turning within months, and months within years—all periodically returning to their points of origin within one Great Circle or "Wheel of Time." But then, in the seventeenth century, the physicist Isaac Newton devised a new linear concept of time based on his calculus. Here is how he described it:

> Absolute, true and mathematical time, of itself and from its own nature, flows equably without relation to anything external.[381]

In the twentieth century, the concept of time changed again when Albert Einstein suggested that it's simply the fourth dimension in a space-time continuum in which all objects and events can be located. Accordingly, as Einstein himself wrote,

> The distinction between past, present, and future has only the significance of a stubborn illusion.[382]

Einstein notwithstanding, most people experience their lives as unfolding within a framework consisting of at least three basic temporal divisions—the *past*, the *present*, and the *future*. One reason for this is the tensed structure of our language which makes it almost impossible to even think about an event without automatically placing it in one of these categories. But is this really the way the world is divided? Or are we simply being fooled by our own linguistic constructs?

To find out, we will conduct a little inquiry into our actual experience of time. And, for reasons which will become clear later, we will do this in two parts. First, we'll investigate the *past* and the *future*. Then, once we have determined the true nature of these temporal divisions, we will investigate the *present*.

Part One: *Inquiring into the Past and Future*

If the past, present, and future really exist, there must be boundaries which separate each of them from the others. So let's begin by looking at the future and ask, is there a boundary which separates it from the present? To answer this question, just sit quietly and see if you can observe exactly when a future moment becomes this present moment. Is there some kind of 'line' that is crossed?

Now try the same thing with the past. Can you detect some boundary which divides it from the present—some 'line' across which a present moment slips into the past?

If you are like most people, you won't find any boundaries separating either the future from the present, or the past from the present, so it seems there is only the present. This, of course, is not to say that things don't change. But when do you actually experience this change?

For instance, the sound of a finger snapping is ephemeral. It comes and goes. As an experiment, try putting your fingers together as though you were about to snap them. Pause and notice that, although you might think to yourself that the snap is still in the future, in fact, no snap at all is being experienced. What *is* being experienced is a thought about a still non-existent snap. Now a thought, as we have seen, is a mental phenomenon appearing in the mental field of Consciousness, which means it is imaginary. Therefore, *all* thoughts about the future are imaginary.

Next, ask yourself this: In what time dimension does this thought appear? Even though it is a thought *about* the future, doesn't it appear in the present? Check this out by generating the following thoughts about the future:

1. What do you expect to have for dinner tonight?
2. Where do you think you will be at this time tomorrow?
3. What will you do on your next day off?
4. Where will you be next New Year's eve?

Even though these thoughts refer to the future, don't they all always appear in the present?

Now go ahead and snap your fingers. Notice that what occurs is a sound phenomenon appearing in the auditory field of awareness. Notice also the division of time in which you actually experience this sound. Don't you experience it in the present? And isn't this also true of all the phenomena appearing in the other sensory fields of awareness—sights, sounds, bodily sensations, tastes, and smells? Don't they all always appear in the present?

What we can conclude from these little experiments is that we never experience anything in the future. Everything we experience is always experienced in the present. The only future we ever experience is an imaginary one composed of certain kinds of thoughts, such as plans, predictions, expectations, apprehensions, anticipations, etc. So even though we can spend many hours lost in thoughts *about* the future, the future itself never comes into existence.

Now, what about the past? Like the future, what we call the past is actually made of thought phenomena appearing in the mental field of awareness—memories, reflections, images, and recollections—which are also always experienced in the present. For instance, all that exists of the finger-snapping sound you made a few moments ago is a memory of it in your mind. There is no actual sound. The trouble is, we assume that memories like these represent events which have actually occurred and, therefore, possess some sort of objective reality. But how could we verify this assumption?

The most common way to try to verify what has happened in the recent past is to compare our own memories and recollections with those of others who were also there. Much of the time we find ourselves agreeing, at least in general, on what transpired. Sometimes, however, we do not. For instance, have you ever had an argument with a family member about who-said-what-when? Or have you ever attended a trial in which several witnesses gave contradictory testimony concerning some incident they were all supposed to have observed firsthand? Whatever consensus we reach about what happened in as short a time ago as yesterday is always tentative and subject to change.

When it comes to trying to ascertain what happened in the more distant past, we find that even accounts on which professional historians have reached wide agreement can never be finally fixed. In 1947, for example, a team of archaeologists, excavating the ruins of a place called Qumran near the Dead Sea, discovered a series of ancient scrolls. Piecing all the evidence together, they announced that the scrolls had been written by members of a Jewish monastic community called the Essenes who had lived at Qumran around the time of Jesus. This interpretation was accepted as an historical fact for more than fifty years. On August 15, 2006, however, the *New York Times* reported that a couple of Israeli archaeologists had recently concluded that Qumran had no connection with the Essenes or the scrolls at all. Instead of housing some exotic religious cult, it had been the site of nothing more glamorous than a pottery factory.

The reason the past can never be fixed once and for all is that, like the future, it is comprised of thoughts which are inherently imaginary. Nevertheless, most of us still feel that the past is somehow more real than the future. This is because we can introduce physical evidence to support our memories of yesterday, but not our speculations about tomorrow. Such support may involve pointing to an old snapshot of Aunt Ginny to prove she was at cousin Harry's wedding, playing a police surveillance tape for a jury in order to verify what a defendant said, or publishing the results of carbon dating from an archeological site to prove a theory about how long ago it was occupied by humans. But no matter what sort of evidence is presented, it is always presented in the *present*. This is true even if we go back and check the evidence again. No matter how many times we look at a photo, listen to a recording, or read a journal article, it's still always in the *present*. Thus, despite all the physical evidence we may accumulate to give us a picture of the past, we never actually experience it. We only experience things now . . . and now . . . and now—which is why Meister Eckhart says,

> That now in which God made the first man, and the now in which the last man will have his end, and the now in which I am talking, they are all the same in God, and there is not more than the one now.[383]

Conducting this kind of inquiry may convince you intellectually that the past and the future are imaginary, but, as we said before, the cultural and linguistic conditioning which creates and sustains the delusion that these time divisions are real is extremely powerful. So if you are like most seekers, in order to actually change your day-to-day perception about 'when' your life takes place, you need to make a concerted effort to interrupt and detach from your habitual thoughts about the past and future. Here's how Hui-Neng describes it:

> In the thinking faculty, let the past be dead. If we allow our thoughts, past, present and future to become linked up into a series, we put ourselves under restraint. On the other hand, if we never

> let our mind become attached at any time to any thing, we gain emancipation.[384]

As usual, the best way to learn to do this is to begin by training in your formal meditation or prayer practice. And, since the way to stop thoughts from becoming "linked up into a series" is to allow them to self-liberate, all you really need to do is make the following adjustments to the practice of liberating thoughts with which you are already familiar.

Instructions for Liberating Thoughts About Past and Future

STEP ONE: *Begin by Stabilizing Attention*

If you have been practicing choiceless awareness, focus your attention on your breath (or other object) until you have attained some stability. Then, allow your attention to expand into the total field of consciousness-awareness. Spend a few minutes resting in this space of undistracted awareness, without trying to grasp anything or push anything away.

If you have been practicing prayer-in-the-heart, focus attention on your sacred word or prayer, then use it to bring your attention into the space of your heart. Once you feel you are in the Presence of your Beloved, stop saying your word or prayer and spend a few minutes abiding in the vastness of that Presence.

STEP TWO: *Generate Thoughts of the Past*

Now start purposely generating thoughts about the past—your first date, your high school graduation, your wedding day, etc. Make each thought as vivid as possible, and then let them congeal into a little story about the past.

STEP THREE: *Let Thoughts of the Past Self-Liberate*

Just before you become totally lost in these thoughts about the past, recognize that they are actually occurring in the present. Then, let the last thought in the series self-liberate and observe how your attention automatically returns to the present.

STEP FOUR: *Generate Thoughts about the Future*

Now start purposely generating thoughts about the future—a person you expect to see, a place you plan to visit, an item you are going to purchase, etc. Make each of these thoughts as vivid as possible, and then let them congeal into a little story about the future.

STEP FIVE: *Let Thoughts about the Future Self-Liberate*

Just before you become totally lost in these thoughts about the future, recognize that they are actually occurring in the present. Then, let the last thought in the series self-liberate and observe how your attention automatically returns to the present.

STEP SIX: *Let Spontaneous Thoughts about Time Self-Liberate*

Now, relax and just let your thoughts flow spontaneously. Try to identify those thoughts that are about the past, and those that are about the future without, however, losing track of the fact that they are actually occurring in the present. Allow them all to self-liberate as they arise, like drawings on water, while your attention remains rooted in the present.

Liberating Thoughts of Past and Future in Everyday Life

After you have practiced liberating thoughts about the past and the future in your formal meditation or prayer sessions, you should try doing it periodically throughout the day. This is particularly helpful when it comes to breaking the seventh and ninth links (deliberation and rumination) in the chain of conditioning. So, for example, if you find yourself repeatedly replaying some memory from the past, or obsessively worrying about something that might happen in the future, you can snap the spell cast by such thoughts simply by allowing them to self-liberate. If you are a jnani, look directly at whatever thought happens to be running though your mind at the moment and let it dissolve without following it up with another similar thought. If you are a bhakti, offer it to your Beloved with love and devotion. Either way, notice that whatever past or future world your mind has created instantly vanishes, leaving only the pristine present to fill your awareness.

Part Two: *Inquiring into the Present*

In the first part of this chapter, we examined the three divisions of time—past, present, and future—and discovered that the past and future exist only as thoughts in our own minds. Furthermore, we discovered that, like everything else, these thoughts actually occur in the present. But what exactly is this present? Does it have any more reality than the past or future? Let's investigate. Once again, sit quietly for a few minutes and see if you can detect any boundaries which separate this present moment from either future moments or from past moments.

If there are no boundaries, how can you tell where the present begins or ends?

If the present has no boundaries, no beginning and no end, in what sense does it exist? Isn't it just as imaginary as the past and the future?

In fact, this is what the mystics claim: *All* temporal categories—including the present—are mere constructs of our minds. The "one now," which Meister Eckhart talked about, is *not* the same as the "present"—especially when the word *present* is used to designate a particular division of time. The one now which characterizes the Ultimate Nature of Reality is beyond time altogether. Thus, in the Tibetan tradition the time of Primordial Awareness or *rigpa* is often described as "four parts without three." Tsoknyi Rinpoche explains what this means:

> The three here refers to the time of past, time of present, and time of future. When you take those three away from the four parts, what is left is the time of rigpa. What time *is* rigpa? Is it the past? Is it the present? Is it the future? No, it's none of these three. If you want to call rigpa a time, it is actually timelessness. Timelessness is rigpa.[385]

This is the way Rumi expresses it:

> What are past and future and present to the man of No-place, within whom is God's Light?[386]

And Zen master Sengtsan declares,

> The Way is beyond language,
> for in it there is
> no yesterday
> no tomorrow
> no today.[387]

Making a distinction between the *present* (conceived as one of the three divisions of time) and the *now* (which is timeless or eternal) is important, because seekers trying to free themselves from an imaginary past and future often end up trying to cling to a present that is equally unreal. This can happen, for example, during formal meditation or prayer practice. When you experience states of clarity and bliss, or love and devotion, you may start making a subtle effort to hang onto them indefinitely. Or, during everyday life, when you experience moments of true compassion, peace, or joy, you may hear your ego-mind saying things like, "Oh, I wish this could last forever." In order to thoroughly dismantle the delusion of time, then, you must not only be able to liberate thoughts about the past and future. You must also be able to recognize thoughts about the present and allow them to self-liberate as well. Here is how Huang Po describes it:

> When thoughts of the past cannot be taken hold of, that is relinquishment of the past. When thoughts of the present cannot be taken hold of, that is relinquishment of the present. When thoughts of the future cannot be taken hold of, that is relinquishment of the future. This is called utter relinquishment of Triple Time.[388]

What follows are some instructions for recognizing and liberating thoughts about all three divisions of time—past, present, and future—during your formal meditation or prayer practice.

Instructions for Liberating the Three Times

STEP ONE: *Begin by Stabilizing Attention*

If you have been practicing choiceless awareness, focus your attention on your breath (or other object) until you have attained some stability. Then, allow your attention to expand into the total field of consciousness-awareness. Spend a few minutes resting in this space of undistracted awareness, without trying to grasp anything or push anything away.

If you have been practicing prayer-in-the-heart, focus attention on your sacred word or prayer, then use it to bring your attention into the space of your heart. Once you feel you are in the Presence of your Beloved, stop saying your word or prayer and spend a few minutes abiding in the vastness of that Presence.

STEP TWO: *Liberate Thoughts of the Past*

Purposely generate some thoughts of the past. Make them as vivid as possible and then allow them to self-liberate. Notice that as they disappear there is a sense that attention returns to the 'present.'

STEP THREE: *Liberate Thoughts about the Future*

Purposely generate some thoughts about the future. Make these thoughts as vivid as possible and then allow them to self-liberate. Again, notice that as they disappear there is a sense that attention returns to the 'present.'

STEP FOUR: *Liberate Thoughts about the Present*

Now let your thoughts flow freely in this apparent 'present.' Notice that what you call the 'present' is nothing else than the limitless open space of the total field of Consciousness-Awareness through which all phenomena arise and pass in an endless stream of change. Notice that in this stream there is nothing to cling to, and nowhere to stand. So just relax your attention, without any grasping or rejecting. Here are the instructions given by the legendary Tibetan yogi Padmasambhava:

> You should relinquish all notions of the past and abandon all precedents.
> You should cut off all plans and expectations with respect to the future.
> And in the present, you should not grasp (at thoughts that arise)
> But allow (the mind) to remain in a state like the sky.[389]

Deconstructing Time in Your Everyday Life

It is important to remember that thoughts about past, present, and future are not in themselves obstacles. On the contrary, they can be extremely useful. Our ability to reconstruct a past is what allows us to learn from our mistakes. Our ability to envision a future is what allows us to make predictions and formulate plans. Even the concept of a 'present' is useful, not only for practical affairs, but (as we have just seen) for giving spiritual instructions. As with all distinctions, these imaginary time divisions only become obstacles when we take them to be real. So, as a spiritual seeker, it is not that you never want to recall the past, or plan for the future, or pay attention to what is going on in the present. It is only that when you engage in these activities, you want to do so with mindfulness and skill.

For instance, some people are obsessed with thoughts of the past. They get thoroughly absorbed in reliving bygone triumphs, or mentally flagellating themselves over misdeeds committed long ago. But, whether pleasant or painful, indulging in such reminiscences only serves to reinforce the Story of I and distract attention from Reality's true timelessness, which is why an anonymous Sufi shaykh insisted:

> Memory's a veil, and doth with thought unite
> To bind my heart, and hide Thee from my sight.[390]

So whenever you find yourself obsessed by thoughts of the past, allow them to self-liberate. Then practice liberating whatever emotions they evoked, either by freeing that spark of love lying at their root, or by transforming them into appropriate wisdom energies.

Other people compulsively try to anticipate everything that could possibly happen to them in the future. Such anxiety over what *might* come to pass not only generates lots of unnecessary suffering, it chokes off the potential for freedom and spontaneity inherent in the eternal now. For this reason, Jesus told his disciples,

> Do not worry about your life, what you will eat, or about your body, what you will wear. For life is more than food, and the body more than clothing.... Consider the lilies, how they grow: they neither toil nor spin; yet I tell you, even Solomon in all his glory was not clothed like one of these.... And do not keep striving for what you are to eat and what you are to drink, and do not keep worrying. For it is the nations of the world that strive after all these things, and your Father knows that you need them. Instead, strive for his kingdom, and these things will be given to you as well.[391]

If you find yourself obsessing about the future, you can simply let such thoughts self-liberate or offer them as gifts to your Beloved. Then, on those occasions when you do have to make plans, be sure to practice detachment from the results. This is one of the central teachings of the *Bhagavad Gita,* often summarized by the phrase *you have a right to the action but not the fruit.* Here is how Krishna describes it to Arjuna:

> The disciplined man gives up the results of his acts
> and attains perfect peace.
> The undisciplined man acts out of desire; he is
> attached to the results; his acts imprison him.[392]

Finally, although it can be helpful to use the concept of a present to dispel thoughts about the past and future, don't fixate on it. If you want to Realize the Truth, you need to break through the delusion of time altogether. Thus, the Buddha taught,

> Let go of the past.
> Let go of the future.
> Let go of the present.
> Proceed to the opposite shore with a free mind,
> Leaving behind all suffering.[393]

Chapter 27

Avoiding Pitfalls

Unless you reach "destruction of the home," do not think your attainment is sufficient; vow to penetrate all the way through seven, eight, even nine thickets of brambles.

— Hakuin (Buddhist)

If you have come this far, chances are you have tasted at least some of the path's fruits. As we have seen, these may include blissful meditative states, experiences of unconditional love, insights into the true nature of various aspects of Reality, and glimpses of the Beloved. More importantly, such experiences, insights, and glimpses should have begun to transform your life in general by weakening the links in your chain of conditioning, purifying your heart of self-centered desires, and freeing your attention some of the time from its absorption in the Story of I. So even when there are no spiritual fireworks going off, you should be feeling more open, compassionate, and peaceful in everyday situations.

Now, not only are all these developments valuable in their own right, they also indicate that, relatively speaking, you are, indeed, making progress on the path. If you are not careful, however, these same fruits can turn into spiritual pitfalls. So let's take a closer look at some of the most common ones and how to avoid them.

Becoming Attached to the Fruits of Your Practice

First, as you throw off your attachments to worldly pleasures, you must be careful not to form new attachments to spiritual ones. As Javad Nurbakhsh explains, the two kinds of qualities that veil us from the Real are the "light" and the "dark":

> To the darkness belong the attributes of "self". Such qualities are the veils of beginners. To the light, on the other hand, belong the qualities of the heart, which are the veils of the more advanced—those who have surrendered themselves to God to the extent that the veils of their worldly desires and fears have fallen away and only the veils of their spiritual attachments remain.[394]

The "light" qualities he is referring to include those states of clarity and bliss experienced by jnanis, and those raptures of divine love and ecstasy which periodically overwhelm bhaktas. These fruits can become veils because, if you get attached to them, they will produce a subtle shift in your motivation for practice. Instead of trying to dismantle the delusion of self, you will start practicing in order to repeat or maintain these elevated states which will actually reinforce your delusion of self. This is why the *Lankavatara Sutra* says this of the Buddhist seeker:

> He should never let himself rest in nor exert himself in the bliss of the Samadhis.[395]

In fact, some seekers—especially bhaktas—can end up becoming just as hooked on spiritual highs as drug addicts are on physical ones. Here, for example, is what Theophan the Recluse says about the "warmth" that is experienced in advanced stages of prayer-in-the-heart:

> This warmth is full of sweetness and so we long to keep it, both for the sake of the sweetness itself, and because it brings right harmony to everything within. But whoever tries to maintain and increase this warmth for the sake of its sweetness alone, will develop in himself a kind of spiritual hedonism.[396]

If you find yourself becoming attached to these types of experiences, you might want to remember this prayer offered up by St. Catherine of Genoa:

> Lord, Lord, I want no signs from you nor am I looking for intense feelings to accompany your love. . . They get in the way of Pure Love—for under the guise of Pure Love it is those emotional feelings to which the soul becomes attached. Love must be naked.[397]

If you are a jnani, rather than becoming attached to states or experiences, you will be more apt to form attachments to mystical teachings—or, more precisely, to your own understanding of them. This happens because, when you start on the path, the words of the mystics seem quite puzzling and obscure. After a while, however, you begin to comprehend more of what they are saying and may even be able to explain it to others. The danger is it's easy to believe that by continuing to acquire and refine this kind of conceptual knowledge you will come closer to Gnosis. Nothing, however, could be further from the Truth, for as Zen master Dogen writes,

> It is worth noticing that what you think one way or another is not a help for realization.... Realization does not depend on thoughts, but comes forth from beyond them; realization is helped only by the power of realization itself.[398]

It is even possible to become attached to non-conceptual insights. While meditating on impermanence, for instance, you may be graced with a direct insight into the transitory nature of all things. But later, when you try to recall it, you find that what seemed so significant at the time has faded into a hollow abstraction. Why? Because as soon as you had that insight, your thinking mind crammed it into a conceptual box which it could trot out from time to time to admire like some stuffed trophy. No wonder it now seems so lifeless! So, listen to Anandamayi Ma's advice:

> A traveller who is eager to reach his destination quickly, does not look back to see by what road he has come nor does he ponder about what he has seen on the way or what he has gained by it. Exactly like that, thoughts of the past must be cast aside in the aspirant's life.[399]

Genuine insights are windows onto a Reality that is timeless. If you want to see again what you saw before, don't rummage through the vaults of your memory searching for dead images. Look directly into your immediate experience as it unfolds right here and now, for it's only in the here and now that the *living* Truth can be found.

Succumbing to Spiritual Complacency

One of the biggest problems of becoming attached to spiritual insights, states, and experiences is that they can cause you to succumb to self-satisfaction and complacency. This usually occurs when your ego stops resisting the spiritual quest, and, instead, tries to appropriate its fruits for itself. So, for example, if worldly desires no longer bind you as much they once did, you may hear your thinking mind congratulating you on how much detachment you have attained. If you have had some insights into impermanence, your mind will extol the depth of your new-found wisdom. If you have managed to reach some of the deeper states of meditation or prayer-in-the-heart, this same ego mind will tell you that you have now mastered these practices. And, if you have received archetypal visions or dreams, your mind may even whisper that this is a sign you have been singled out for some special destiny, and so you can dispense with spiritual disciplines altogether. It is because of these dangers that Theophan gives us this warning:

> Flee from satiety—the state when the heart says cunningly to itself: Enough! I need nothing more; I have worked hard, I have established order in myself, now I can allow myself a little rest.... The direct effect of satiety is weakening of attention and allowing of exemp-

> tions to oneself. Whoever permits this will begin to slide downhill like a man on a slippery slope. This is the danger. So watch![400]

What you must realize is that this is not the time to rest on your laurels. On the contrary, it is the time to redouble your efforts to root out every last vestige of self-centeredness. In particular, you should be meticulous about keeping precepts and cultivating compassion. Remember, the delusion of self is like a tapestry made up of thousands of individual stitches. Each stitch is a little knotting of desire, aversion, or attachment. The only way to unravel this tapestry is to take it apart stitch by stitch (although, fortunately, undoing one stitch will sometimes release a whole row of them!) If you fail to do this, not only will the existing knots in the tapestry remain, but your self-centered conditioning will keep on creating new ones, hour by hour and day by day. This is why Dilgo Khyentse says,

> Every morning, … pray that throughout the day you will never forget to think of the welfare of others. Every evening, remember all that you have thought and done during the day and determine how much was motivated by selfishness; it is important to look at your most subtle attitudes and intentions before deciding what you should or should not have done. Never think that any tiny act is insignificant just because it is so small, for the least negative action can set off a devastating chain of consequences, in the same way a single minute spark can set fire to an entire forest. Conversely, just as a slight trickle of water quickly fills a large pitcher, when one small positive action is added to many others the accumulated effect soon becomes substantial.[401]

And you will find the exact same teaching in all the great traditions. Here, for example, is what Anandamayi Ma recommends:

> At all times practice patience and self-discipline. Just as when a drop of acid falls into a large quantity of milk, all of it turns sour, so even if a little attachment or anger steals into one's work or service it is very harmful—remember this![402]

This is why Theophan writes,

> Mercilessness towards self, willingness to undertake any service for others, and complete self-surrender to the Lord, abiding in Him in prayer—these are the things which build up spiritual life.[403]

Mistaking Spiritual Experiences for Enlightenment

The most dangerous trap a seeker can fall into is to mistake his or her spiritual experiences for Enlightenment. It cannot be emphasized too much that

*Enlightenment is **not** an experience. Enlightenment **transcends** all experiences,* even the most exalted—which is why Longchen-pa warns,

> If one does not distinguish between experiences and realization,
> He will be deluded by holding onto the experiences as realization.[404]

There are two main reasons why this pitfall is so hazardous. First of all, seekers who fall into it almost always believe now that they are Enlightened, they can give up those practices which eventually *would* lead them to genuine Realization. Worse, they also often feel they are no longer bound by any moral laws and so can do anything they want without having to worry about the consequences. Here is what John Myrdhin Reynolds says about practitioners of the Dzogchen school of Buddhism who succumb to this delusion:

> To jump up from our meditation seat thinking, "Wow, I am in the state! I'm a Mahāsiddha [Enlightened being]!," and then run around doing whatever we like without regard for whom we hurt, exploit or deceive is not Dzogchen, but just plain stupidity. . . .
> The really demonic or perverted view is the self-justifying one that both good and bad actions are empty and meaningless, whereby it does not matter at all what we do since there are no karmic consequences to our actions.[405]

Given the seriousness of this error, the question naturally arises, how can you distinguish between mere experiences and a true Gnostic Awakening? We will have a lot more to say on this subject in the last two chapters. In the meantime, here are three practical criteria which at least can help you determine that what you've experienced is definitely *not* Gnosis.

1. One of the main characteristics of Gnosis is that it admits of no doubt, for as the Upanishads say,

    > When he [Brahman] is seen in his immanence and transcendence, then the ties that have bound the heart are unloosened, the doubts of the mind vanish, and the law of Karma works no more.[406]

    Ibn al-'Arabi agrees:

    > If you know God through God and know all the affairs through Him, you shall have no ignorance, no suspense, no wavering, no doubt.[407]

    Franklin Merrell-Wolff explains why:

    > In contrast to ordinary knowledge, introceptive cognition [Gnosis] is in the form of an identity between the knower and the known. Thus the certainty-destroying factor of distance or difference is eliminated, with the consequence that introceptive cognition is abso-

> lutely certain in its original state [i.e., before it is given conceptual formulation].[408]

Consequently, if doubts arise about whether or not what has occurred is Gnosis, you can be sure that it's not.

2. Sometimes it takes a while for doubts about some exceptionally sublime experience to surface. That's why it's always a good idea to seek confirmation from a teacher you believe is Enlightened. This, however, is not completely fool-proof. For one thing, the teacher may, in fact, *not* be Enlightened and so fail to recognize what has really happened to you. Nevertheless, seeking such confirmation can still be useful, because, regardless of whether or not a teacher is Enlightened, if he or she is able to arouse doubts in your mind, you will know there is more for you to attain. On the other hand, if you still have no doubts after talking to your teacher, it will tend to verify that your Gnosis is genuine.

   This is illustrated by a Zen story of a monk who came to his master claiming to have had satori (Realization). After questioning the monk, the master declared, "That's not satori. You need to meditate more." The student was surprised at this rejection, but because he respected his master so much, he obeyed. However, a few days later he came back to his master and said, "If this isn't satori, you keep your satori and I'll keep this!" Only then, did the master confirm the monk's attainment.

3. Last but not least, when true Gnosis dawns, then the search for happiness, which has driven your life since birth, ends forever. Here's how the Buddha put it:

   > The purpose of the Holy Life does not consist in acquiring alms, honour, or fame, nor gaining morality, concentration, or the eye of knowledge. That unshakable deliverance of the heart: that, verily, is the object of the Holy Life, that is the essence, that is its goal.[409]

   Similarly, Meister Eckhart declares,

   > Truly, if anyone had denied himself and had wholly forsaken himself, nothing could be for him a cross or sorrow or suffering; it would all be a delight to him, a happiness, a joy to his heart.[410]

   And this is the way Lalleshwari describes her Realization:

   > When at last I found Him,
   > I saw that He
   > was not different
   > from me.
   >
   > Then my heart became full,
   > my seeking ended,
   > and my understanding was complete.[411]

So, after attaining what you believe to be Gnosis, if you still find yourself searching for something—whether worldly or spiritual—know that you have not yet arrived at the end of the path. But don't be discouraged. Just keep on looking. Remember what Jesus said:

> Ask, and it will be given to you; search, and you will find; knock, and the door will be opened for you. For everyone who asks receives, and everyone who searches finds, and for everyone who knocks, the door will be opened.[412]

The Way of Selflessness

PART VII: *Contemplating Reality*

Chapter 28

Contemplating the Nature of Objects

> *If you don't wash out the stone and sand, how can you pick out the gold? Lower your head and bore into the hole of open nonreification; carefully seek the heart of heaven and earth with firm determination. Suddenly you will see the original thing; everywhere you meet the source, all is a forest of jewels.*
>
> — Liu I-ming (Taoist)

As we've already said, most of the work of a spiritual path, especially in the beginning stages, consists in removing obstacles. You begin by interrupting your conditioned patterns of behavior. Next you purify your heart of self-centered desires and aversions, and work on abandoning inner and outer attachments. After that, you cultivate compassion for all beings and, if you're a bhakta, love for some form of the Divine. Then, you learn to liberate those thoughts that make up the Story of I, and to transform afflicted emotions into devotion to God or wisdom energies for serving other beings. And while all this brings more freedom and more joy into your life, if you are truly committed to the path, it's still not enough. Always, you long to go further, to penetrate once and for all the Great Mystery.

For jnanis the way to do this is to look more deeply into impermanence. Why? Because the fact that all things are impermanent and subject to change contains a vital clue about their true nature or *emptiness*, as the Buddhists call it. Contemporary Buddhist scholar Gadjin M. Nagao explains the connection:

> An activity becomes possible only when the world is śūnyatā [empty]. It is inconceivable that an activity takes place in a substantive being, for a substantive being is understood to be an eternal, immutable being, and, therefore, could not be active and undergo change. Only when there is no substantiality, that is, when śūnyatā is, can there be change and activity.[413]

And while *emptiness* may be a Buddhist term, you'll find the same teaching in one form or another given by mystics of all the great traditions. Here, for example, is how Meister Eckhart puts it:

> All things are created from nothing; therefore their true origin is nothing, and so far as this noble will inclines toward created things, it flows off with created things toward their nothing.[414]

Likewise, Rumi writes,

> Because of the darkness in your eyes, you imagine that a nothing is a something. Your eyes can be made healthy and illumined with the dust of the King's doorstep![415]

So let's try to get some direct insight into exactly what these mystics are talking about.

Impermanence and Emptiness

Since you have already spent some time contemplating moment-to-moment impermanence both in your formal meditation practice and in everyday life, you should have a pretty good experiential understanding of just how transitory everything that appears in the six fields of consciousness really is. But even though you've come to realize that these appearances are ephemeral, chances are you still feel that you are living in a world of more or less solid objects which exist 'out there'.

For example, if you look at a tree and blink your eyes several times, you can see that the subjective images appearing in your visual field come and go and are, therefore, impermanent. But even when your eyes are closed, and you cannot actually *see* the tree, you are probably convinced that there is some independently existing object still sitting in front of you. Well, when mystics say that the tree's true nature is *empty,* what they mean is that this impression that the tree exists independent of your observation is a delusion. What you take to be an objectively existing tree is nothing more than an idea which exists in your mind. And, of course, this is true not only of trees, but of all the other things which you imagine constitute the real world. They are all equally products of your imagination. This is why Nagarjuna insists,

> Whatever is in the three realms, all that is the construction of the mind. How is it so? It is in accordance with one's thought that one realizes all things.[416]

To understand more precisely what he means, remember what we said in chapter 10: the boundaries which seem to separate one thing from another are created in the third link of the chain of conditioning when mental identification takes place. Whenever a set of phenomena arises in consciousness, our minds automatically try to group them together into an 'object' that can be identified by a name, such as *tree,* which distinguishes it from other sets of phenomena, identified by others names, such as *rock* or *house*. In other words, although it seems as though we are giving names to things that already exist, in reality, the situation is reversed. What we perceive as things are actually created by our naming them. Here's how Chuang Tzu explains it:

> A road is formed (where there was none before) merely by people walking constantly upon it. Likewise, the 'things' are formed by their being designated by this or that particular name.[417]

Of course, the simple act of naming phenomena is not, in itself, a problem. The problem comes when we reify these imaginary names and take them to refer to real objects which exist outside of our minds. Shankara describes how this happens:

> A word, after being heard in speech, is acted on by the mind (and projected) externally elsewhere (as an image). And when it has been seen according to its mental form (as an image), it is ready to be converted (once more) into a word. This whole universe is imagined in just this way on the basis of erroneous ideas.[418]

Now, it is important to remember that when mystics say that objects such as trees are imaginary, they are not denying that various visual and auditory phenomena, which arise with what we call a *tree*, appear in consciousness. But what they are saying is that there is no objectively existing tree out there, standing behind these phenomena. Longchen-pa puts this very succinctly when he writes,

> Although not really existing, things still appear. From their own side, however, (such things) are void by nature.[419]

One way mystics of virtually all traditions have tried to illustrate this "emptiness" of objects is to compare our deluded experience of them to the experiences we have in dreams. While we are dreaming we take the objects that surround us to be real. Only when we wake up do we realize that "from their own side" they were "void" of inherent existence. Now, what mystics claim is that the same thing is also true of the objects we encounter in waking life. Here's Longchen-pa again:

> All (the phenomena) which appear in various (forms) are the same in not existing in (their true) nature. They are like the various dreams which are the same as the state of sleep.[420]

Likewise, Ramana Maharshi declares,

> Waking is long and a dream short; other than this there is no difference. Just as waking happenings seem real while awake, so do those in a dream while dreaming.[421]

Ibn al-'Arabi agrees:

> When a man ascends in the degrees of gnosis, he will come to know through both faith and unveiling that he is a dreamer in the state of ordinary wakefulness and that the situation in which he dwells is a dream.[422]

And Chuang Tzu writes,

> Only when one experiences a Great Awakening does one realize that "reality" is but a Big Dream. But the stupid imagine that they are actually awake.... How deep-rooted and irremediable their stupidity is![423]

As Chuang Tzu indicates, this teaching that there is no fundamental difference between waking and dreaming is extremely difficult for most of us to accept because it runs completely counter to the way we have been conditioned to perceive the world. So, even if you become intellectually convinced that what the mystics say is true, it usually won't change your actual experience of things. To do this, you need to take a much more empirical approach. You need to conduct a series of contemplative experiments which combine the power of undistracted attention with a practice of analytic inquiry to see for yourself if you can find any objects that actually exist 'out there' apart from your own mind.

First, to avoid any semantic confusion, we should define our terms a little more rigorously. From now on when we use the word *phenomenon,* we'll take it to mean whatever actually appears in any of the six fields of consciousness—a sight, sound, bodily sensation, taste, smell, or thought. And when we use the word, *object,* we'll take this to mean something which is supposed to exist objectively, outside of consciousness.

Preparing to Contemplate Objects

In order to conduct these contemplative experiments properly you will need two things. One is an environment where you can be completely alone and free of all external distractions. A retreat setting would be best. If this is not possible, at least try to arrange for extended periods of time in which you won't be interrupted by family, friends, phone calls, or other business.

The second thing you will need is some object to serve as the focus for your contemplations. This should be something you can see, touch, tap (in order to make a sound), smell, and taste. An apple or some other piece of hard fruit would be perfect. If there is no fruit available, you can make do with any hand-sized object—a metal bowl, a small gong, even a rock—providing you don't mind smelling or tasting it. (For the purpose of giving the following instructions, we'll assume you are using an apple.)

In this series there are three parts corresponding to the three types of experiments to be performed—*contemplating the emptiness of objects, contemplating the emptiness of correlations between phenomena,* and *contemplating the inseparability of phenomena and consciousness.* So, let's go through them one at a time.

Part One: *Contemplating the Emptiness of Objects*

In the Bahiya Sutta the Buddha said,

> In what is seen, there is nothing but what is seen;
> in what is heard, there is nothing but what is heard;
> in what is felt, there is nothing but what is felt;
> in what is smelled, there is nothing but what is smelled;
> in what is tasted, there is nothing but what is tasted;
> in what is thought, there is nothing but what is thought.

In other words, he's saying again that there is nothing behind the subjective phenomena which appear in the six fields of consciousness. So, let's check this out and see if it's true. Let's see if we can find any 'object' that exists apart from these subjective phenomena. Get out your apple (or other suitable object), set it down in front of you within easy reach, and assume your usual meditative posture.

Instructions for Contemplating the Emptiness of Objects

STEP ONE: *Entering Spacious-Awareness*

Begin by stabilizing your attention through concentration meditation. Then, allow your attention to expand into the total field of consciousness-awareness. Spend a few minutes resting in this space of undistracted awareness without trying to grasp anything or push anything away.

STEP TWO: *Contemplating What is Seen*

Now gaze directly at the apple in front of you. Notice that what you are seeing is a subjective phenomenon appearing in the visual field of awareness.

Close your eyes. Notice that this visual phenomenon is impermanent. A moment ago it was present, but now it has completely vanished from consciousness.

STEP THREE: *Contemplating What is Heard*

With your eyes still closed, reach out and tap the apple several times with your finger nail. Listen closely to the sounds. Notice that what you are hearing is a series of subjective sound phenomena appearing in the auditory field of awareness. Notice that these sound phenomena are totally *different* from the visual phenomenon which you experienced a few moments ago.

Notice also that all these sound phenomena are impermanent. They appear and disappear in consciousness one after another.

STEP FOUR: *Contemplating What is Felt*

Still keeping your eyes closed, pick up the apple and hold it in the palm of your hand. Notice that what you feel are subjective tactile sensations appearing in the bodily sensation field. Notice that these tactile-sensation phenomena are totally *different* from the sound phenomena and from the visual phenomenon you experienced before.

Put the apple down and notice that these tactile sensation-phenomena are all impermanent and, after a few moments, completely vanish.

STEP FIVE: *Contemplating What is Smelled*

Keeping your eyes closed, pick up the apple again and hold it under your nose. Take a deep breath. Notice that what you experience are subjective aromas appearing in the smell field of awareness. Notice that these aromas are totally *different* from the visual phenomenon, the sound phenomena, and the tactile sensations you previously experienced.

Put the apple down and again notice that these aromatic phenomena are impermanent and vanish away.

STEP SIX: *Contemplating What is Tasted*

With your eyes closed, pick up the apple and take a bite. Chew slowly and notice that, along with the tactile sensations on your tongue, you also experience a continuing cascade of flavors. Notice that these subjective flavors are appearing in the taste field of consciousness, and that they are totally *different* from the visual phenomenon, the sound phenomena, the tactile sensation phenomena, and the smell phenomena which you previously experienced.

Now put the apple down and allow the flavors to vanish from your mouth. Notice that even though these flavors may linger longer than the phenomena which appeared in the other fields of consciousness, eventually they, too, prove to be impermanent and completely disappear.

STEP SEVEN: *Contemplating What is Thought*

As you continue sitting in your meditative posture with your eyes closed, spend a few moments inquiring into what you have experienced so far. So far, you have experienced five very distinct kinds of phenomena—sights, sounds, bodily sensations, smells, and tastes. What's more, all of these phenomena have now passed away, and are non-existent. Therefore, none of these phenomena you have experienced can be said to constitute an inherently existing object called an *apple*.

Nevertheless, you are probably still convinced that there is such an object out there. If this is the case, generate the following thought as forcefully and as vividly as you can: "Even though, right now, I neither see, hear, touch, smell nor taste it, there definitely *is* an objectively existing apple sitting out there in front of me."

Now notice that what you are currently experiencing is not any objectively existing apple, but only the *idea* of an apple. And even though this idea of an apple may trigger memories of the sight, sound, touch, smell, and taste phenomena you previously experienced, the idea itself does not appear in any of these sensory fields. It is a thought phenomenon, appearing in the mental field of awareness, and, as such, it is totally *imaginary*. So, in a certain sense, you *have* found an object called an *apple*, but it only exists in your mind!

Finally, allow the thought of the apple to self-liberate. Notice that, like all the other phenomena you have experienced, it, too, is impermanent and vanishes away.

STEP EIGHT: *Reflecting on What You Have Found*

Up to this point, your investigation of the apple has confirmed what the Buddha said. All you have experienced have been impermanent phenomena arising and passing in the six fields of consciousness. You have not found any inherently existing object apart from, or standing behind, these phenomena. The closest you have come to finding anything called *apple* has been the idea that one exists. In other words, the apple has turned out to be imaginary and empty of any inherent existence.

Part Two: *Contemplating the Emptiness of Correlations*

The main reason it is so difficult to dispel the delusion that there is a world of inherently existing objects out there is that the arising and passing of certain kinds of phenomena seem to be correlated in quite precise and predictable ways. For instance, if you look at your apple, pick it up, and hold it close to your nose, the sights, sensations, and smells you associate with the idea of apple all appear more or less together. Then, if you also tap the apple with your fingernail several times, a series of sound phenomena arise and pass which seem perfectly correlated with the sensations of your tapping. Now, if you stop tapping, put the apple down, and close your eyes, then open your eyes, pick the apple up, and start tapping again, not only will the same set of phenomena appear, but they will appear in exactly the same sequence as they did the first time you performed these actions.

The point is that when we encompass different kinds of transitory phenomena within the concept of apple, we are not doing so arbitrarily. We encircle them within an imaginary boundary based on what appear to be objectively existing correlations. But let's look more closely. Where do these correlations exist? Are they inherent in the phenomena, themselves? Or, like our ideas about objects, are they imaginary creations which exist only in our minds?

In fact, ever since the eighteenth-century philosopher David Hume found the relationship of cause and effect to be based on nothing more than a "mental habit," materialists have been trying unsuccessfully to establish some grounds for believing that correlations between events have an objective reality. The main problem (to put it in a nutshell) is that no matter how many times two or more phenomena appear in what seem to be objectively correlated ways, there is no guarantee that these correlations will hold the next time any of the phenomena appear. The British philosopher Bertrand Russell once illustrated this by way of a witty parable. Imagine, he said, a bunch of chickens born and raised on a farm. Since as far back as any of them can remember, every single morning the chickens have heard the farmer's footsteps approaching their coop, heard the gate being unlatched, and seen the farmer's feet as he enters. This sequence of events has always been followed by the farmer spreading chicken feed on the ground. Consequently, it seems to the chickens that the occurrence of footsteps, gate opening, feet, and food, are part of an unbreakable chain of cause and effect. But then one morning the farmer shows up with an ax.

Most of us have experienced some version of this kind of anomaly in our own lives. For example, once I was leading a retreat at the house of one of my students. During a break I went out to the porch. Across the way in the neighbor's yard there was a shed with a corrugated plastic roof. A large black bird was walking along this roof, making rather loud clicking sounds as its claws struck the plastic surface. Then, suddenly the bird flew off, but the clicking sounds continued! Although the clicking sounds had *seemed* to be caused by the movement of the bird's feet, in reality I had only imagined them to be so.

What such incidents of *cognitive dissonance* (as psychologists call them) reveal is that correlations between phenomena do not inhere in the phenomena, themselves. Rather, they are created by our minds as part of the whole process of naming and then reifying a world of objects. Thus, in the *Lankavatara Sutra* we read this:

> All such notions as causation, succession, atoms, primary elements ... are all figments of the imagination and manifestations of the mind.[424]

But don't take the *Lankavatara Sutra's* word for it. It is possible to catch your own mind in the very act of creating such correlations. To do this, let's try another contemplative experiment. Get out your apple, set it down in front of you, and assume your usual meditative posture.

Instructions for Contemplating the Emptiness of Correlations

STEP ONE: *Entering Spacious-Awareness*

As before, begin by stabilizing your attention through concentration meditation. Then, allow your attention to expand into the total field of consciousness-awareness.

STEP TWO: *Look at the Apple*

Once you have entered spacious awareness, direct your gaze to your apple. Again, notice that what you are seeing is a subjective visual phenomenon appearing in the sight field of awareness.

STEP THREE: *Tap the Apple*

Next, with your eyes still open, slowly reach out and tap the apple several times with your fingernail. Notice that you are now experiencing three kinds of subjective phenomena arising in three different fields of awareness—a sight phenomenon in the visual field, a series of sound phenomena in the auditory field, and a series of sensation phenomena (tappings) in the field of bodily sensations.

STEP FOUR: *Generate a Thought of Causation*

As you continue to tap the apple, vividly generate the thought, "My tapping the apple is *causing* the sounds to appear in the auditory field. Notice that this, in fact, is a thought, appearing in the mental field of awareness, and does not exist in any of the phenomena, themselves—the sight, the sounds, or sensations.

STEP FIVE: *Allow All Thoughts to Self-Liberate*

Finally, let all your thoughts about what's-causing-what to self-liberate. Then allow your attention to expand into the total field of consciousness-awareness and try to experience whatever phenomena arise and pass without generating any new thoughts about them

Part Three: *Contemplating the Inseparability of Phenomena and Consciousness*

Even though you may begin to see that the correlations which seem to exist among phenomena are actually products of your imagination, you probably cannot shake the conviction that there still must be some kind of objective connection between them. How else to account for the fact that our correlations seem to work so much of the time? Well, from a mystic's point of view, it's not that phenomena are connected in some mysterious way. It's that they were never truly separated in the first place! As we've said before, like the waves of an ocean, they are actually inseparable manifestations of an underlying Reality that is fundamentally Non-Dual in nature. Here is how Ibn al-'Arabi puts it:

> There is no ontological named thing (*musammā wujūdī*) except God. He is named by every name, described by every attribute, qualified by every description.... There is nothing in Being/existence but God, while the entities are nonexistent.[425]

So, too, Anandamayi Ma says,

> In the whole universe, in all states of being, in all forms is He. All names are His names, all shapes His shapes, all qualities His qualities, and all modes of existence are truly His.[426]

And John Scotus Eriugena tells us this:

> When we hear that God makes all things we ought to understand nothing else than that God is in all things, that is, that He is the Essence of all things. For only He truly exists by Himself, and He alone is everything which in the things that are is truly said to be.[427]

But if this is true, it means that the distinctions we have been making between the six fields of consciousness are also creations of our own minds. And while they are useful for interrupting the habitual ways in which we draw boundaries and reify objects, in reality, they are no less imaginary. So now it is time to drop even these distinctions and try to contemplate the true inseparability of all phenomena, regardless of what names we give them—sights, sounds, bodily sensations, smells, tastes, or thoughts.

The biggest difficulty for most people in seeing this is that phenomena appear to be separated by time and space. For instance, you might hear a bird call while walking in the park one afternoon. The following day you might stub your toe while getting out of the shower and feel a sharp pain sensation. Now because they happened so far apart, these two phenomena seem entirely distinct. There isn't even any apparent causal connection between them. How, then, can it be, as mystics claim, that they are in some essential way the same?

The key here is to recognize that all phenomena—including the bird sound heard one day, and the pain felt the next—are inseparable from each other, because, again like the phenomena appearing in dreams, they are all inseparable from Consciousness. Jamgon Kongtrul explains it this way:

> The impure phenomena of cyclic life arise within ongoing intrinsic awareness, abide within intrinsic awareness, and are simply the play of intrinsic awareness. They have never existed outside intrinsic awareness, just as dreams never occur except in sleep.[428]

So, too, Shankara writes,

> In the case of dream, there can be no doubt that the mind assumes a mere appearance of duality, while remaining non-dual in its true nature as the Self.... For in dream there are in reality neither the elements which are beheld as objects nor the eyes and other sense organs which "perceive" them. There is nothing but consciousness. And our argument is that it is exactly the same in waking experience too. There, too, the only reality is consciousness, so that from this point of view there is no difference between the states of waking and dream.[429]

In other words, as in dreams, under delusion there appears to be a duality between the phenomena that are experienced and the consciousness that experiences them. In reality, however, the phenomena appearing in consciousness cannot be separated from the consciousness in which they appear. This being the case, we can say that in a certain sense everything that we experience is actually a *form* of Consciousness the way waves are forms of the ocean—or, to use a more modern analogy, the way all the different characters, objects, and environments seen in a movie are, in reality, nothing but forms of light.

Notice that this is true even though we have no trouble distinguishing so-called dream sequences in a movie from waking sequences if the film-makers have provided us with the appropriate clues—strange camera angles, distorted images, jump cuts, slow motion, etc. It is worth noting that film-makers can also hide the fact that we are witnessing a dream sequence by omitting such clues, in which case we only know that what we have been watching is a dream at the end of the sequence when the camera cuts to the dreamer suddenly sitting bolt upright in bed with a startled look on his or her face. This, in fact, mimics what happens in our own so-called 'real' lives when we awaken from an unusually lifelike dream and, for a moment, can't tell which state—dreaming or waking—we're actually in. None of these cinematic tricks, however, alters the fact that, in either case, what we are really seeing are forms of light and nothing else. Likewise, what the mystics claim is that, whether dreaming or awake all we really ever experience are forms of Consciousness.

So let's try to get some actual experience of this by conducting another contemplative experiment. This time, we'll take a clue from something Rumi wrote:

> If we look at the ocean, we find all the waves are in the ocean and that in reality they are all one. But if we look at the waves, we find that they are many in number and separate from one another.[430]

What Rumi is getting at is that habitually our attention focuses on phenomenal forms and we completely ignore that ocean of formless Consciousness out of which they arise. Now, as you go through the steps in the experiment below, try to shift your attention back and forth between the forms of Consciousness and Consciousness Itself and see if you can't get some experiential insight into their inseparability. So, get out your apple once again, set it down in front of you, and assume your usual meditative posture.

Instructions for Contemplating Inseparability

STEP ONE: *Entering Spacious-Awareness*

Begin by stabilizing your attention through concentration meditation. Then, allow your attention to expand into the total field of consciousness-awareness. Spend a few minutes resting in this spacious awareness, without trying to grasp anything or push anything away.

STEP TWO: *Contemplating Sight and Consciousness*

Once you have entered spacious awareness, direct your gaze to the image of your apple. Focus your attention on this image for a while, then close your eyes and focus your attention on the space of consciousness in which it appeared. Do this several times until you get a sense of their inseparability.

STEP THREE: *Contemplating Sound and Consciousness*

With your eyes closed, reach out and tap the apple. Focus your attention on the sound. When the sound is gone, continue focusing your attention on the space in consciousness in which it appeared. Do this several times until you get a sense of their inseparability.

STEP FOUR: *Contemplating Bodily Sensation and Consciousness*

With your eyes closed, pick up the apple and focus your attention on the sensations in your hand. Put the apple down and, as the sensations fade, focus your attention on the space of consciousness in which they appeared until you get some sense of their inseparability.

STEP FIVE: *Contemplating All Phenomena and Consciousness*

Open your eyes and allow your attention to expand until it fills the entire space of consciousness-awareness. Resting in this space, allow whatever phenomena appear to arise and pass away without grasping at them or pushing them away. Then, try to shift the gestalt of the entire field by re-focusing your attention from the phenomena in the foreground of consciousness to the space of consciousness that constitutes their ever-present background. Do this several times until you get a sense of their inseparability.

Gaining Non-conceptual Insights

At the very least, conducting these kinds of contemplative experiments should give you a better intellectual understanding of what the mystics mean when they talk about all things being imaginary, dream-like, and empty of any objective existence. But this is not the same as having a direct, non-conceptual insight like that of the sixteenth-century Confucian sage Kao P'an-lung. Here's how he describes it:

> I saw a saying by [Ch'eng] Ming-tao, ... "The myriad changes all exist within the person; in reality there is not a single thing." Suddenly, I realized this and said, "It really is like this, in reality there is not a single thing!" With this single thought, all entanglements were broken. Suddenly, it was as if a load of a hundred pounds had fallen to the ground in an instant. It was as if a flash of lightning had penetrated the body and pierced the intelligence. Subsequently, I was merged with the Great Transformation until there was no differentiation between Heaven and humanity, exterior or interior.[431]

In order to gain this kind of non-conceptual insight, most seekers need to repeat these experiments numerous times, using a variety of objects, until their attention becomes refined enough to be able to apprehend whatever arises in consciousness *before* the thinking mind has a chance to name and reify it. Shankara calls this *spiritual discrimination* and gives the following advice on how to attain it:

> "The apparent world is caused by our imagination, in its ignorance. It is not real.... It is like a passing dream"—that is how a man should practice spiritual discrimination, and free himself from his consciousness of this objective world.[432]

Likewise, we read this in the *Lankavatara Sutra*:

> The disciple must get into the habit of looking at things truthfully. He must recognize the fact that the world has no self-nature, that it is un-born, that it is like a passing cloud, like an imaginary wheel made by a revolving firebrand, like the [illusory] castle of the Gandharvas, like the moon reflected in the ocean, like a vision, a mirage, a dream.[433]

And the more you get in the habit of seeing things "truthfully," the more it will transform your everyday experience. Instead of living in a world of solid objects which have clear-cut boundaries, you will begin to live in a more fluid world—a world where everything arises and passes away in one continuous flow of empty transformations. Then, even the most mundane forms will become for you increasingly transparent to that Formless Consciousness which does not arise and does not pass away. In other words, you will begin to recognize the positive aspect of emptiness. It's not just that things lack any inherent existence, but, for this very reason, they actually reflect and reveal the Ultimate Reality Itself. As Dudjom Lingpa writes,

> All apparent phenomena are not other than the ground of being but are of one taste with that ground itself, like the reflections of all the planets and stars in the ocean (*gya-tsoi za-kar*) that are not other than the ocean but one taste with the water itself.[434]

A common Hindu analogy for this is to compare the world of objects to a collection of gold figures. Their forms are different, but their essence is the same. So, if you know the essence of one, you know the essence of all. Thus, in the *Chandogya Upanishad*, Svetaketu's sagely father tells him,

> Just as, my dear, by one nugget of gold all that is made of gold is known, the modification being only a name, arising from speech, while the truth is that all is gold.[435]

Similarly, Ibn al-'Arabi says,

> Every name the creatures possess belongs truly (*haqq*) to the Real and metaphorically (*musta'ār*) to the creatures.[436]

The Jnani's Initiation

For most jnanis, attaining a non-conceptual insight into the emptiness of forms constitutes their initiation, because it represents the first real crack in their shell of delusion. Moreover, even though it usually comes considerably later on the path, this kind of insight often surpasses the bhakta's introduction to Ultimate Reality in at least two ways.

First, while the bhakta's initial glimpses are mediated by the experience of a Divine Other who seems to stand apart from the world of forms, the jnani apprehends the inseparability of Formlessness and forms, or, as the Buddhists put it, they see that form *is* emptiness, and emptiness *is* form.

Second, once attained, the jnani's insights tend to be more stable. They do not fluctuate with feelings of proximity to or distance from the Beloved, as is often the case with bhaktas. This is why it is said that, for a seeker who reaches this stage, everything which appears has the potential to be one's teacher. Here is how Longchen-pa, speaking from the point of view of his own Realization, expresses it in terms of the five traditional elements of earth, water, wind, fire, and space:

> I, the creativity of the universe,
> Arise as the teacher, in five forms of pure and total presence.
> Their dimension is the full richness of being.
> Their message is conveyed through their form.
> The teacher teaches its own nature.

The teacher, the dimension of the full richness of being,
Cannot be conceived of in terms of identity or difference.
The five forms of the state of pure and total presence
Show everything to be the truth itself.[437]

Chapter 29

Contemplating the Nature of Self

> *Only come to know the nature of your own mind, in which there is no self and no other, and you will in fact be a Buddha!*
>
> — Huang Po (Buddhist)

Attaining a direct insight into the emptiness of the objects that appear in consciousness gives you only half the picture. In order to have a complete Realization of emptiness, you must also have a direct insight into the emptiness of the subject to consciousness, which is to say, your supposed 'self.' And, if you are a jnani, the way to attain such an insight is very similar to the way you attained direct insights into the emptiness of objects. It is to conduct a series of contemplative experiments in order to see if you can find any real referent for the word *self,* or any real boundary which separates it from the rest of the world.

Since conducting this kind of self-inquiry is a key practice for jnanis in both the Hindu and Buddhist traditions, let's take a brief look at how they go about it. The first step is to determine exactly what it is you believe constitutes your 'self.' In the Hindu view, the experience of being a separate self results from the false identification of the Atman or True Self with a body-mind composed of five *koshas,* or "coverings." Starting from the grossest and ending with the most subtle, these coverings are: 1) the material body; 2) the vital energy or life force; 3) sense perceptions; 4) thoughts; and 5) feelings of bliss. Having ascertained these five coverings, one then conducts a type of inquiry called *neti neti*—which means "not this, not that." By paying close attention to the impermanence of each of the five coverings, the Hindu jnani comes to understand that neither "this" covering nor "that" covering can be the Atman which is identical with Brahman, the Ultimate Changeless Reality. Here's how Shankara describes the process:

> Wrapped in the five coverings.... the Atman remains hidden, as water of a pond is hidden by a veil of scum....
> A man must separate this Atman from every object of experience, as a stalk of grass is separated from its enveloping sheaths.[438]

Buddhists have a slightly different view of what makes up the illusory self. According to them, it is comprised of five *skandhas* or "aggregates." These are: 1) the material body; 2) sensations; 3) perceptions; 4) mental formations; and 5) self-consciousness. Nevertheless, Buddhists conduct essentially the same kind of *neti neti* inquiry as Hindus, and for the same reason. It is to discover that, as the Buddha himself said,

> Whatever there be of bodily form, of feeling, perception, mental formations or [self]-consciousness, whether one's own or external, whether gross or subtle, lofty or low, far or near; one should understand according to reality and true wisdom:—This does not belong to me; this am I not.[439]

Now, the fact that the Hindu and Buddhist traditions have arrived at somewhat different conceptions of what constitutes the separate self is interesting insofar as it shows that the experience of self is not the same for all human beings. It is determined to a large extent by a person's culture. This is why the essential thing is not to learn about Hindu or Buddhist views of the self (unless, of course, you happen to be a Hindu or a Buddhist), but to ascertain as precisely as possible whatever it is *you* identify as comprising your 'self', right here and now.

If you are a Westerner, for example, chances are you identify your 'self' with a body-mind composed of at least four kinds of phenomena: 1) a physical body; 2) thoughts; 3) emotions; and 4) some sort of agent of volition, such as an *ego, soul,* or *spirit.* In any case, these are the categories we will use in giving the following instructions for conducting a self-inquiry. If your own sense of self includes additional or different types of phenomena, simply adjust your inquiry accordingly.

Making Preparations

As with contemplating the emptiness of objects, you need to be able to conduct these experiments in circumstances where there is a minimum of external distractions. Again, being on retreat would provide the best setting, but if this is not possible, at least set aside some time when you won't be disturbed by everyday affairs.

There are two experiments to be conducted: 1) *contemplating the emptiness of self;* and 2) *contemplating the boundary between self and not-self.* The first has four parts, so let's go through them one at a time.

I. Instructions for Contemplating the Emptiness of Self

Part One: *Are You a Physical Body?*

STEP ONE: *Entering Spacious-Awareness*

Begin by stabilizing your attention through concentration meditation. Then, allow your attention to expand into the total field of consciousness-awareness. Spend a few minutes resting in this spacious awareness, without trying to grasp anything or push anything away.

Now, turn your attention to your physical body. Actually, the body is very much like other physical objects that we normally believe exist objectively. So ask yourself this: "Does this body really have any inherent existence?" And to answer this question, you can make the same kind of inquiry as you did in the previous chapter with regard to the apple.

STEP TWO: *Contemplating What is Seen of the Body*

Look at whatever parts of your body are visible—hands, feet, belly, and so on. Notice that all of them are phenomena appearing in the visual field of consciousness. Close your eyes and observe that they are all impermanent and have now completely disappeared from consciousness. Now ask yourself, "Have *I* disappeared?"

The fact that all the visual phenomena which you call your "body" are gone but *you* are still here means that you cannot *be* any of these visual phenomena.

STEP THREE: *Contemplating What Is Heard in the Body*

Now listen to whatever sounds your body may be making—breathing, swallowing, coughing, etc. Again notice that all these sounds appearing in the auditory field of consciousness are impermanent. They come and go, but *you* do not come and go: Therefore you cannot *be* any of these sounds.

STEP FOUR: *Contemplating What is Felt of the Body*

Next, direct your attention to the sensations arising in the bodily-sensation field of consciousness. Beginning at the crown of your head, slowly and carefully move your attention down through your body, scanning various areas—your face, neck, shoulders, arms, chest, stomach, pelvis, legs, feet, and so on.

Notice that your body is not one single sensation, but a mass of individual throbbings and tinglings. Notice also that each of these throbbings and tinglings is impermanent. Since all these bodily sensations come and go, but *you* do not come and go, you can't *be* any of these sensations.

STEP FIVE: *Contemplating What is Smelled/Tasted of the Body*

If there are any bodily odors or tastes present, notice that they, too, are impermanent phenomena which arise in the smell and taste fields of consciousness. Notice that they arise and pass, but *you* do not arise and pass. Therefore you cannot *be* any of these odors or tastes.

STEP SIX: *Contemplating What is Thought of the Body*

Now strongly generate the thought, "There must be a body which is producing all these phenomena that I experience." As with the apple, notice that what you are currently experiencing is only an idea or mental *image* of a body, and apart from this *imaginary* body, no objectively existing 'body' can be found. Moreover, even this image of a body is itself impermanent and passes away when you stop thinking about it. *You*, however, do not pass away, so you cannot *be* this image.

STEP SEVEN: *Reflecting on What You Have Found*

Finally, take a moment to reflect on the fact that, having thoroughly searched the six fields of consciousness, you have failed to find any inherently existing 'body' which you could be. Furthermore, the various phenomena which you did find—sights, sounds, sensations, smells, tastes, and thoughts—were all impermanent and have now vanished away. Therefore, *you*, the one who observed them, cannot *be* any of these phenomena.

Part Two: *Are You Thoughts?*

STEP ONE: *Entering Spacious-Awareness*

Begin by stabilizing your attention through concentration meditation. Then, allow your attention to expand into the total field of consciousness-awareness. Once you have entered a space of undistracted awareness, turn your attention to the mental field of consciousness.

STEP TWO: *Contemplating Thoughts about Others*

Strongly and vividly generate a series of thoughts about people, things, or events other than yourself, such as these:

1. The memory of a friend's face.
2. A verse from a favorite song.
3. A recent event you heard about on the news.
4. Today's date.

Allow each of these thoughts to self-liberate completely before generating the next thought. Observe how impermanent these thoughts actually are. Notice that, while each thought arises and passes away, *you* do not arise and pass away. Therefore, you cannot *be* any of these thoughts.

STEP THREE: *Contemplating Thoughts about Oneself*

Strongly and vividly generate a series of true thoughts about yourself, each coupled with a false thought about yourself:

1. I am a man.

   I am a woman.
2. I am over forty years old.

   I am under forty years old.
3. I am married.

   I am single.
4. I like ice cream.

   I don't like ice cream.

Allow each of these thoughts to self-liberate completely before generating the next thought. Notice that these thoughts about your self, whether true or false, are just as impermanent as any other thoughts. Notice that even the judgment that some of these thoughts are true and some are false is a thought which is impermanent and passes away. In other words, all your thoughts—whether they are about yourself or not, whether they are true or not—arise and pass away. *You*, however, do not arise and pass away. Therefore, you cannot *be* any of these thoughts.

STEP FOUR: *Reflecting on What You Have Found*

Finally, take a moment to reflect on the fact that, having thoroughly examined various kinds of thoughts that appear in the mental field of consciousness, you have failed to find any fixed or permanent thought that could constitute an inherently existing 'self.' Therefore, *you*, the one to whom these thoughts occur, can't *be* any of them

Part Three: *Are You Emotions?*

STEP ONE: *Entering Spacious-Awareness*

Begin by stabilizing your attention through concentration meditation. Then, allow your attention to expand into the total field of consciousness-awareness.

STEP TWO: *Contemplating Unpleasant Emotions*

1. Try to recall some situation or event which caused you to experience some unpleasant emotion, such as anger. Perhaps it was something a colleague at work said, or something hurtful a friend did. Recall this incident as vividly as possible, and then focus your attention on the feeling of anger that arises.
2. Let the memory of the event fade, and try to experience the anger nakedly, without any further judgment, justification, or other mental commentary.
3. Observe that if you refrain from generating more thoughts about the anger, or the situation that gave rise to it, the feeling of anger naturally self-liberates.
4. Notice how impermanent the emotion of anger actually is. It arises and passes away. *You*, however, do not arise or pass away. Therefore, you cannot *be* this anger.

STEP THREE: *Contemplating Pleasant Emotions*

1. Next, try to recall some situation or event which caused you to experience some pleasant emotion, such as joy. This might have been the day of your marriage, the birth of your child, or simply a fun time you had on vacation. Recall this event as vividly as possible and then focus attention on the feeling that arises.
2. Again, let the memory of the event fade, and try to experience the joy nakedly, without any further mental commentary.
3. Observe that if you refrain from generating more thoughts

about the joy, or the situation that gave rise to it, this feeling also naturally self-liberates.

4. Again, notice how impermanent the emotion of joy actually is. It arises and passes away. *You*, however, do not arise or pass away. Therefore, you cannot *be* this joy.

STEP FOUR: *Contemplating the Absence of Emotions*

1. Rest in the space of undistracted awareness without trying to generate any particular thoughts or emotions.
2. If thoughts or emotions do arise, allow them to instantly self-liberate, like drawings on water.
3. Notice those intervals when there are no emotions present in the total field of consciousness-awareness. Simultaneously notice that *you* are still present. Therefore, you cannot *be* your emotions.

STEP FIVE: *Reflecting on What You Have Found*

Finally, take a moment to reflect on the fact that all emotions, whether pleasant or unpleasant, are transitory and impermanent. They come and go like the weather—sometimes it's sunny and bright, sometimes it's dark and stormy, and sometimes the sky is perfectly clear. In any case, *you*, the one who experiences all these emotions, do not come and go. Therefore you cannot *be* any of them.

Part Four: *Are You the Agent of Volition?*

For most people, the hardest aspect of the delusion of self to dispel is the sense of being an agent of volition or self-will—that is, some ego, soul, or spirit who *wills* certain actions and *decides* certain things. For a jnani, the best way to begin overcoming this impression is to observe very carefully the actual process by which actions are initiated and decisions made in order to see if there really is any 'one' who does these things.

So, for example, an excellent place to conduct this kind of inquiry is in a restaurant. Whenever you are trying to decide what to order you can ask yourself, "Who is making this decision?" Then watch closely to see what really happens. If you're reading a menu, words will appear in your visual field, and these words will generate mental images of the dishes they describe. Next, based on these images, conditioned likes and dislikes will arise, and perhaps a certain sorting out process will occur in your thoughts. Then, finally, a decision will be made, but can you find any ego, soul, or spirit, who actually does the deciding?

While everyday situations, such as ordering in a restaurant, provide fertile opportunities for investigating the delusion of self-will, they are usually full of all sorts of extraneous distractions. Therefore, as with other forms of self-inquiry, it is best to start learning how to do this in the context of a formal contemplative experiment. In this case, however, there is one obvious difficulty. When you are sitting in meditation, there are few decisions to make or actions to take. One way to get around this problem is to solicit the help of a sympathetic friend. After you have entered a space of undistracted awareness, ask your friend to instruct you to perform a series of simple tasks, like raising your hand, putting it down, wiggling your toes, closing and opening your eyes, etc. Then, as each instruction is given, make a conscious decision to obey or not to obey. Whatever you actually decide doesn't matter, because either way something will be decided and that is what you want to observe.

If you are on a solo retreat and there is no one available to help, you can try using the written instructions which follow. Be careful, however, not to make any decisions about what you are going to do until *after* you have entered a space of undistracted awareness. The whole point of this practice is to watch what actually happens in the moment in which a decision is made.

STEP ONE: *Entering Spacious-Awareness*

Begin by stabilizing your attention through concentration meditation. Then, allow your attention to expand into the total field of consciousness-awareness.

STEP TWO: *Looking for the 'One' Who Wills Actions*

When you are ready, repeat these simple instructions to yourself, one at a time. After each instruction, make a conscious decision either to obey it, or not to obey it.

1. Raise your right arm.
2. Raise your left arm.
3. If you have raised your right arm, put it down.
4. If you have raised your left arm, put it down.
5. If any arm is still down, raise it.
6. If any arm is still up, put it down.

See if you can observe any ego, soul, or spirit that is *deciding* whether to raise or lower your arms, and then *willing* the action to happen or not to happen.

STEP THREE: *Attending to Thoughts About Will*

If the thought arises "*I* am the one who is deciding to raise or lower my arm," look at this thought carefully. Recognize that it is just a thought. It arises and passes, and, therefore, can't be *you*, the observer of the thought. If the thought arises "But there *must* be some self who is making these decisions and willing these actions," realize that this, too, is just another thought. Like all thoughts, it comes and goes, but *you* do not come and go. Therefore, you cannot *be* this thought.

STEP FOUR: *Looking for Your Ego, Soul, or Spirit*

Finally, to be absolutely sure there is no ego, soul, or spirit that makes decisions and wills actions, you should conduct a very thorough search of all the six fields of consciousness to see if you can find any trace of such an entity.

Systematically focus your attention first in the visual field, then the auditory field, the bodily sense field, the taste field, the smell field, and the mental field. As you proceed, ask yourself very concrete questions, such as these:

1. If my ego, soul, or spirit appears in the visual field, what color is it—red, white, green, blue?
2. If my ego, soul, or spirit appears in the sound field, what kind of sound is it—loud, soft, high, low?
3. If my ego, soul, or spirit appears in the field of bodily sensations, what does it feel like—flat, round, coarse, smooth?
4. If my ego, soul, or spirit appears in the smell or taste fields, what does it smell or taste like—mild or pungent, bitter or sweet?
5. If my ego, soul, or spirit appears in the thought field, is this really my true *self*, or simply an impermanent thought or image which has arisen and will pass away?

STEP FIVE: *Reflecting on What You Have Found*

If you think you have found anything in any of the six fields of consciousness which you can identify as your ego, soul, or spirit, focus your attention directly on that and ask yourself, "If this is really my true self, then *who* is observing it?" Realize that, as Franklin

Merrell-Wolff used to say, whatever object you observe arising *in* consciousness cannot be you, the subject *to* consciousness who is experiencing it.

II. Instructions for Contemplating the Boundary Between 'Self' and 'Not-self'

Despite the fact that upon investigation no permanent referent for the word *self* can be found, most seekers continue to identify with those phenomena which are enclosed within a boundary that defines their body-minds. In other words, even though everything inside this body-mind boundary may be impermanent, the boundary itself still seems very solid and real. But is this true? Does this boundary which distinguishes 'self' from 'not-self' really have an objective existence? Or, like all the boundaries we have encountered thus far, is it, too, imaginary?

Again, the way to find out is to make a contemplative inquiry and try to locate this boundary in your own experience. To aid in this inquiry you will need a knife with a sharp point, which you should place within easy reach before you begin.

STEP ONE: *Entering Spacious-Awareness*

Begin by stabilizing your attention through concentration meditation. Then, allow your attention to expand into the total field of consciousness-awareness.

STEP TWO: *Locating the Boundary of 'Self' in the Visual Field*

Once you have entered spacious-awareness, focus your attention in the visual field of consciousness.

1. Place the knife on the floor or a table just in front of you. Place your right hand next to it.
2. Now, observe how the two phenomena (knife and hand) appear in the visual field of consciousness, side by side. Ask yourself, "On which side of the boundary between my 'self' and 'not-self' does the knife fall, and on which side does the hand fall?"

3. If you answer that the hand falls on the 'self' side, while the knife falls on the 'not-self' side, look again. Can you really see this boundary? Does it actually appear in the visual field? Or is it simply a mental construct?
4. Try to observe the knife and the hand nakedly, without the intervention of any thoughts *about* them. Regarded as pure visual phenomena, are they not completely equal in the way they appear in the visual field of consciousness?

STEP THREE: *Locating the Boundary of 'Self' in the Sound Field*

1. Focus your attention in the sound field of consciousness, and listen to the various phenomena that arise and pass away. Try to identify which sounds come from within the boundary of self—breathing, swallowing, coughing—and which come from outside it—car horns, airplanes, dogs barking.
2. Ask yourself, "Is there anything about the sounds, themselves—loudness, tone, pitch—that mark them as belonging to one side of the boundary or the other?"
3. Try to listen to whatever sounds arise nakedly, without the intervention of thoughts *about* them. Regarded as pure auditory phenomena, are they not completely equal in the way they appear in the sound field of consciousness?

STEP FOUR: *Locating the Boundary of 'Self' in the Field of Bodily Sensations*

1. Now, pick up the knife and lay it flat across your left hand. Focus your attention on the sensation of its weight. Ask yourself, "Does this sensation called *weight* belong to the knife or my hand?" Try to determine on which side of the boundary of 'I' and 'other' the sensation of weight falls.
2. Now pick up the knife with your right hand and very gently touch the point against the palm of your left hand until you feel a slight pressure. Ask yourself, "Does this sensation I call *pressure* belong to the knife or my hand?"
3. Press the knife harder against your left hand until you feel a little pain. Ask yourself, "Does this sensation I call *pain* belong to the knife or my hand?"
4. If you answered that the *weight* and *pressure* belonged to the knife, but that the *pain* belonged to your hand, repeat this experiment, and ask yourself why you attribute some sensations to yourself and some to what is not your self? Do you actually experience a boundary or is it something your thoughts project onto your experience?

5. Finally, repeat this experiment several more times. Try to experience each sensation nakedly, without the intervention of any thoughts about it. Can you experience each sensation as a unitary event—just a phenomenon arising and passing in the sensation field of consciousness, devoid of any inherent distinctions between self and not-self?

STEP FIVE: *Reflecting on What You Have Found*

Your thinking mind has probably come up with quite a few very logical reasons for drawing the boundary of 'self' and 'not-self' where it does. For instance, perhaps it defined those sounds which seem to be correlated with bodily sensations, like breathing or coughing, as being inside the boundary, while those that are not correlated with bodily sensations, like car horns, as being outside it. Similarly, it may have drawn the boundary to include the visual phenomenon of hand, but not the visual phenomenon of knife, because some hand movements can be directly correlated with thoughts, such as, "I am going to will my hand to move," while objects like knives cannot be so correlated. As we saw in the chapter on contemplating objects, however, all such correlations are imaginary. Like boundaries, our mind creates them because they are *useful*. But that does not mean they possess any objective reality.

So the point of these contemplative experiments is not to get rid of boundaries, but to clearly recognize their true nature. Useful or not, they are all constructs of the mind. To the extent that we reify these imaginary boundaries as defining an inherently real self, we fall under delusion. Conversely, to the extent that we realize these boundaries are empty of any inherent reality, we begin to dispel that delusion.

Continuing Self-Inquiry in Everyday Life

As with contemplating the emptiness of objects, if you are like most seekers, you will need to repeat this kind of self-inquiry many times in order to gain a direct insight into the empty nature of the self. This means continuing to practice not only during your formal meditation sessions, but throughout the day in the midst of whatever situations you find yourself—whether you're watching TV, working at your job, or having an argument with your spouse. Here is how eighteenth-century Zen master Hakuin described this practice to a student who asked him, "How can I awaken?"

> What is that which asks such a question? Is it your mind? Is it your original nature? Is it some kind of spirit or demon? Is it inside you? Outside you? Is it somewhere intermediate? Is it blue, yellow, red, or white?
>
> It is something you must investigate and clarify for yourself. You must investigate it whether you are standing or sitting, speaking or silent, when you are eating your rice or drinking your tea. You must keep at it with total, single-minded devotion.[440]

Fear of Selflessness

Full Enlightenment or Gnosis comes about through the complete and unequivocal Realization that 'I' and 'other,' 'self' and 'world,' 'subject' and 'object' are all empty of any inherent existence—that, in Reality, there is nothing but God, Brahman, Buddha-Mind, or Consciousness Itself. Before attaining this Ultimate Realization, however, it is not only possible, but quite common for seekers to gain a partial realization of the emptiness of objects (without the complementary insight into the emptiness of one's self); or, conversely, a partial realization of the emptiness of one's self (without the complementary insight into the emptiness of objects).

Of the two, a realization of the emptiness of one's self is more profound, because it strikes directly at that First Distinction between subject and object which forms the very core of our delusion. Unfortunately, this is also what makes it the more difficult to attain. As we saw in chapter 4, the whole process of building up the delusion of self is actually motivated by an existential fear of discovering that the boundary which defines the self doesn't exist. Consequently, the closer you get to realizing this, the more that original fear is likely to re-emerge. Contemporary Buddhist teacher Ayya Khema explains it this way:

> The fear of annihilation of this supposed person ... may arise particularly when we come near to seeing impermanence in ourselves very strongly. Then there is great fear, even panic, that we may find a truth we don't want to know, namely that this identity, this personality, is a myth. Fear is the first and foremost hindrance to going deeper.[441]

And, of course, this is known in other traditions as well. Shankara, for example, warns,

> On account of the crude conditioning of their minds they will always feel afraid of the unborn principle of Reality, thinking it means their own destruction.[442]

Likewise, while Rumi writes,

> The whole world have taken the wrong way, for
> they fear nonexistence, while it is their refuge.[443]

So what can you do if and when this fear of selflessness arises? First, it is important to remember that the occurrence of fear is actually a good sign, because it indicates you are getting beyond a mere intellectual understanding of emptiness and closer to a direct Realization of it. Second, you can actually incorporate this fear in your inquiry by asking, "To whom is this fear occurring?" Look to see if you can locate any substantial 'self' that is experiencing this feeling. In this way you can transform what first appeared to be an obstacle to your practice into an opportunity for furthering it.

Chapter 30

Contemplating the Nature of God

> *So long as there are the opposites of knowledge and ignorance, in other words distinction and the idea of difference, the Brahman cannot be realized. By merging in the Brahman, all differences dissolve into It and one is forever established in one's true being.*
>
> — Anandamayi Ma (Hindu)

If you are a bhakta, you probably find the kinds of analytic contemplations described in the last two chapters far too mental for your taste. You may even feel that filling your head with a bunch of ideas about emptiness and the Ultimate Nature of Reality actually gets in the way of personally experiencing It. But even though you are a bhakta, you have no doubt formed some image or idea of Who or What this Reality is—a God, Lord, Father, Mother, Lover, Great Spirit, Higher Power, or Friend.

Now, not only is it perfectly natural for your mind to imagine Ultimate Reality in some form, but doing so is essential to the whole bhakti approach. As we heard Krishna tell Arjuna, having some form of the Divine to surrender to makes the spiritual path much easier for most people to travel. When worldly thoughts and desires arise, all a bhakta has to do to dispel them is recall the far more powerful image of his or her Beloved. This is what Rumi is referring to when he writes,

> Other images run before Thy Image, like the minds of prisoners at the cry, "Freedom!"[444]

But then Rumi also goes on to say,

> I am he who carves idols from his Images—but when the time of union comes, then I smash the idols![445]

What he means is that once these Divine forms have served their purpose, they, too, must be surrendered. Why? Because, in reality, God has no form.

God is that formless Radiant Heart which constitutes the core of all things. So, if you want to be united with God as He *truly* is, then you must let go of all your images and ideas—no matter how sublime—and heed Meister Eckhart's advice:

> You should love him [God] as he is a non-God, a nonspirit, a nonperson, a nonimage, but as he is a pure, unmixed bright "One," separated from all duality; and in that One we should eternally sink down, out of "something" into "nothing."[446]

Many bhaktas, however, are extremely reluctant to do this, because the relationship they have established with their Beloved has been a source of such incredible consolation and joy. In fact, some have actually preferred to hang onto this relationship, even though it means sacrificing the possibility of attaining complete Union. Listen, for example, to the famous seventeenth-century Hindu bhakta, Tukaram:

> He who worships God must stand distinct from Him,
> So only shall he know the joyful love of God;
> For if he say that God and he are one,
> That joy, that love, shall vanish instantly away.
>
> Pray no more for utter oneness with God.[447]

It is at this point, then, that the great advantage of the bhakti path—i.e., the unleashing of a spiritual love so overwhelming that it sweeps all other loves before it—turns into a great disadvantage. If you have given up everything for your Beloved, you're going to find it extremely difficult to turn around and give up your Beloved, as well. But this is precisely what is required if you are to complete the journey, for as Ramakrishna says,

> So long as there is still a little ego left, the consciousness that "I am a devotee," God is comprehended as personal, and His form is realized. This consciousness of a separate ego is a barrier that keeps one at a distance from the highest realization.[448]

Moreover, if you fail to attain this "highest realization," you will end up trapped in a spiritual fantasy of your own making, because as Ibn al-'Arabi warns,

> If the lover is not a gnostic, he creates in himself a form by which he becomes enraptured and of which he is enamoured. Hence he only worships and yearns for that which is under his own sway. Nothing can remove him from this station but knowledge.[449]

When Ibn al-'Arabi insists that only "knowledge" can save the lover from this delusion, he is, of course, not referring to any kind of conceptual knowledge. He is referring to a Gnosis of the Divine's true nature which, as we've already said, constitutes the end of the path for both bhaktas and jnanis.

So then how exactly can a bhakta attain Gnosis? Well, Ibn al-'Arabi himself gives us a clue when he writes this of God:

> He is distinguished from his creatures through negation of attributes (*salb*), not affirmation (*ithbāt*).[450]

What Ibn al-'Arabi is suggesting is that to attain a Gnosis of God's true nature a bhakta must proceed by the *via negativa* or way of negation. As you may remember, we mentioned in chapter 2 that the way of negation is used to avoid those philosophical paradoxes which arise when we try to describe the Ultimate Reality in words: Instead of saying what Ultimate Reality is, mystics try to say what It isn't. What we need to do now, however, is translate this philosophical principle into a concrete contemplative practice.

The Way of Negation

Greek and early Christian mystics called this practice of negation, *aphairesis*, or abstraction. Here is how the author of *The Cloud of Unknowing* explains it:

> However much a man may know about every created spiritual thing, his intellect will never be able to comprehend the uncreated spiritual truth which is God. But there is a negative knowledge which does understand God. It proceeds by asserting everything it knows: this is not God, until finally he comes to a point where knowledge is exhausted.[451]

In other words, the way to apprehend God's true nature is not to imagine what He *is*, but to contemplate what He is *not*–i.e., any of the 'things' that appear in Consciousness. Then, when everything that appears in Consciousness has been rejected as being not-God, what's left is God.

Now, if you think this sounds a little like the kind of *neti neti* ("not this, not that") inquiry practiced by jnanis to discover their own true nature, you're right, and for a very good reason. Ultimately, there is no difference between your true nature and God's true nature, for as Anandamayi Ma says,

> To realize the Self is to realize God and to know God is to know one's Self.[452]

Or, as the Sufis put it,

> Whoso knoweth himself, knoweth his Lord.[453]

So it is not surprising that the bhakta's method of contemplating God parallels the jnani's method of contemplating his or her true self. In fact, it is right at this juncture that the two paths start to converge. For just as a jnani who begins by seeking truth must eventually cultivate selfless love and compassion, so a bhakta who longs for unconditional love must eventually seek the truth. Nevertheless, most bhaktas can skip the kind of detailed analysis which jnanis undertake and, instead, proceed directly to emptying their hearts of everything that is not God. Then, as Teresa of Avila declares,

> It is quite certain that, when we empty ourselves of all that is creature and rid ourselves of it for love of God, that same Lord will fill our souls with Himself.[454]

Prayer of Silence

Now, the way to accomplish this is to intensify your practice of prayer-in-the-heart until it carries you to that final stage of mystical prayer which, following the Christians, we are calling silent prayer. This is how Dionysius the Areopagite describes it:

> The higher we soar in contemplation the more limited become our expressions of that which is purely intelligible; even as now, when plunging into the Darkness which is above the intellect, we pass not merely into brevity of speech, but even into absolute silence, of thoughts as well as of words.[455]

And, of course, you'll find the same teaching in other traditions as well. Abdullah Ansari of Herat, for example, puts it more poetically:

> A time will come when the tongue will join the heart,
> the heart will join the soul (jān),
> the soul will join the secret (sirr-consciousness),
> and the secret will join the Truth (Haqq).
>
> The heart will say to the tongue, "Keep silent!"
> The secret will say to the soul, "Keep silent!"
> (And) the (inward) light (nūr) will say to the secret, "Keep silent!"[456]

And here's how the Upanishads explain the way to reach this silence using the mantra *Om*:

> By sound we go to silence. The sound of Brahman is OM. With OM we go to the End: the silence of Brahman.[457]

It is important to note that *silence* here does not mean simply the absence of sound. What Dionysius, Ansari, and the Upanishads are talking about is that Sacred Silence of the Radiant Heart which lies at both the center of the World and of your Self. And the reason *Om* (or any sacred word or prayer) can take you there is because the more fully you concentrate on it, the more you can ignore all the other phenomena arising in Consciousness—including whatever thoughts you have *about* the Divine. Without even the whisper of an idea of your Beloved to cling to, you will be able to descend all the way through your spiritual heart, until you reach the very threshold of the Radiant Heart. Then, if at this point you allow even your sacred word or prayer to self-liberate, you will automatically fall into that Silence where God's true nature stands revealed as Pure Consciousness.

Preparations for Practice

As with contemplating the true nature of objects and self, contemplating God's true nature in silent prayer requires a lot more concentration than most seekers can muster in the midst of a busy work-a-day schedule. Consequently, it is best to begin this practice when you are on retreat. If this is not possible, at least arrange for some extended periods of time at home in which you won't be disturbed by family, friends, phone calls, or other business.

Once you have established a time and place, the next thing you need to do before actually starting your search for Ultimate Reality is to make a firm resolve not to settle for anything less that might appear, no matter how wonderful it seems. This is necessary because, as you enter the deeper regions of your spiritual heart, you are apt to experience visions and revelations coming from those archetypal realms that are inaccessible to ordinary consciousness. Of course, if the purpose of your retreat is to seek guidance from these sources, then you will want to pay very close attention to whatever communications you receive. But if your goal is Gnosis, then you must practice detachment from these kinds of spiritual phenomena, for as St. John of the Cross says,

> Those are decidedly hindered, then, from attainment of this high state of union with God who are attached to any understanding, feeling, imagining, opinion, desire, or way of their own, or to any other of their works or affairs, and know not how to detach and denude themselves of these impediments. Their goal transcends all of this, even the loftiest object that can be known or experienced. Consequently, they must pass beyond everything to unknowing.[458]

To fortify you against even the most powerful distractions, Ibn al-'Arabi recommends making two special retreat vows or "covenants" (as he calls them) before you begin. Here's how he describes them:

> Let your [first] covenant at your entry into retreat be that there is nothing like unto God. And to each form that appears to you in retreat and says "I am God," say: "Far exalted be God above that! You are *through* God" ... Turn your attention from it and occupy yourself with *dhikr* continually.... The second one is that you will not seek from Him in retreat anything other than Himself and that you will not attach your *himma,* the power of the heart's intention, to anything other than Him. And if everything in the universe should be spread before you, receive it graciously—but do not stop there.

> Persist in your quest, for He is testing you. If you stay with what is offered, He will escape you. But if you attain Him, nothing will escape you.[459]

What follows, then, are some specific instructions for advancing all the way from prayer-in-the-heart to the prayer of silence, where it becomes possible to enter the Radiant Heart.

Instructions for Contemplating God in Silence

STEP ONE: *Sink Attention into the Heart*

Begin practicing prayer-in-the-heart as usual by concentrating on your sacred word or prayer and using it to bring your attention down into the space of your physical heart.

STEP TWO: *Purify Your Emotional Heart*

Continue repeating your word or prayer with as much devotion as you genuinely feel. Allow whatever thoughts arise to self-liberate, and transform whatever afflicted emotions you experience into love and longing for the Divine. If at this or any point along the way, your sacred word or prayer starts repeating itself spontaneously, well and good. Be sure, however, to continue concentrating on it just as diligently as before.

STEP THREE: *Enter your Spiritual Heart*

Leaving behind all worldly concerns, sink deeper into that warm clear space of your spiritual heart. If you now feel yourself entering the presence of your Beloved, notice that this is still an *experience,* which comes and goes in time. Therefore, it cannot be that Ultimate Reality which is timeless. Without either grasping at your feeling of being in the Divine Presence, or trying to push it away, continue concentrating on your word or prayer.

STEP FOUR: *Sink Deeper into the Spiritual Heart*

As you move ever deeper into your spiritual heart, various kinds of visions, or other spiritual phenomena may begin to manifest. Remember, if you want to reach the Radiant Heart, you must not dwell on these experiences, no matter how spectacular they seem.

Allow them to self-liberate as you would any other phenomena, neither grasping at nor trying to push them away.

STEP FIVE: *Arriving at the Radiant Heart*

The way you know you have arrived at the entrance to the Radiant Heart is that there will be nothing to hold your attention except your sacred word or prayer. If your word or prayer is repeating itself spontaneously, wait until it ceases spontaneously. If you are still making an effort to repeat it, surrender that effort and allow the repetitions to terminate. Then abide in the Silence of the Radiant Heart with a mind totally undistracted by any phenomena—worldly or spiritual. It is here that a Gnosis of God's true nature becomes possible.

Practicing in Everyday Life

It would be highly unusual for you to attain Gnosis the first few times you try practicing silent prayer. In fact, what you'll probably experience is frustration and disappointment, because as the author of *The Cloud of Unknowing* explains,

> Your senses and faculties will be frustrated for lack of something to dwell on and they will chide you for doing nothing. But never mind. Go on with this nothing, moved only by your love for God....
>
> Don't worry if your faculties fail to grasp it. Actually, that is the way it should be, for this nothingness is so lofty that they cannot reach it. It cannot be explained, only experienced.[460]

So, if you are like most seekers, you will need to repeat this practice many times before tasting its fruits. And not just on retreat, either. When you return to your householder's life, you should adopt contemplating God's true nature as your regular formal practice. Admittedly, this will be a challenge at first, but the more you do it, the easier it will become. In fact, eventually you will even be able to integrate this prayer of silence into your everyday routines. Again, here's how the author of *The Cloud of Unknowing* describes it in *The Book of Privy Counseling*:

> [So] with the help of his grace and the light of the wisdom that comes from this work, remain whole and recollected in the depths of your being as often as you can.

> As I have already explained to you, this simple work is not a rival to your daily activities. For with your attention centered on the blind awareness of your naked being united to God's, you will go about your daily rounds, eating and drinking, sleeping and waking, going and coming, speaking and listening, lying down and rising up, standing and kneeling, running and riding, working and resting. In the midst of it all ... this work will be at the heart of everything you do, whether active or contemplative.[461]

The Fear of God

Just as jnanis can experience a "fear of selflessness" as they get close to a Realization that there is no self, so you, too, may experience what in bhakti traditions is called the "fear of God," as you approach the Radiant Heart. For mystics, however, this is not the same as the fear of being punished for your sins which haunts so many exoteric believers. Rather, as Abdullah Ansari of Herat writes,

> The fear (khawf) of the privileged is awe and veneration (haybat) towards His Majesty (Jalāl —and) not fearing (His) chastisement ('adhāb). Because fearing chastisement is to strive for the self (nafs) in order to protect it, (while) awe and veneration toward (His) Majesty is to glorify God and to forget self (nafs).[462]

Now, the reason this awe is described as "fear" is because, to reach the Radiant Heart, you must pass back through that primordial state of pure subjectivity in which everything but the First Distinction has vanished. In this state the ego intuits that if this last boundary were also to vanish, it would die and be swallowed up in an Ocean of Pure Consciousness. This produces an afflicted emotion which you identify as fear. But because this death of the self is also what you have been longing for all along, if you can focus on the naked energy of that fear, it will transform into inconceivable bliss, This, in turn, will draw you deeper and deeper into the practice, for as the thirteenth-century Hasidic master Eleazar of Worms says:

> When the soul thinks deeply about the fear of God, then the flame of heart felt love bursts in it and the exultation of innermost joy fills the heart.[463]

So don't be afraid of fear. Greet it as a particularly powerful manifestation of the Divine and plough its energy right back into your practice.

Chapter 31

Contemplating Nothing

> *The divine being is equal to nothing, and in it there is neither image nor form.*
>
> — Meister Eckhart (Christian)

If you still have not discovered the true nature of yourself or God, perhaps you are making the same mistake Merrell-Wolff made until the very end of his path. Here's how he describes it:

> It suddenly dawned on me that a common error in meditation—and one which I had been making right along—lay in seeking a subtle object or experience. Now an object or an experience, no matter how subtle, remains a phenomenal time-space existence and therefore is other than the supersensible substantiality [Ultimate Reality]. Thus the consciousness to be sought is a state of pure subjectivity without an object.
>
> ... I saw that genuine Recognition is simply a realization of Nothing, but a Nothing that is absolutely substantial and identical with the SELF.[464]

Of course, Merrell-Wolff was not the only one to make this mistake. In fact, it is probably one of the most common for both jnanis and bhaktas. It is also extremely difficult to detect. Why? Because, under delusion our attention is so thoroughly conditioned to focus on *things*, we find it almost impossible to accept that the Reality we are looking for can only be found where there is *no*-thing. And yet, this is the teaching of all the mystics. Here, for example, is what Longchen-pa says about the true nature of mind:

> [It] has no color, design, and there is nothing to be shown or to find, even if one examines it and searches thoroughly outside, inside, or in between. This not finding (the mind) is a space-like state, clear, equal, free from designation and analysis, and detached from actor and acted upon. It is the vision of the nature of the Ultimate Body.[465]

Likewise, Ibn al-'Arabi writes this of Allah:

> He is not accompanied by thingness, nor do we ascribe it to Him. Such is He , and there is no thing with Him. The negation of thingness from Him is one of His essential attributes.[466]

And Gershom Scholem reports that, according to the Kabbalists,

> Only when the soul has stripped itself of all limitation and, in mystical language, has descended into the depths of Nothing does it encounter the Divine.[467]

Anandamayi Ma sums up all these teachings with this:

> Where nothing is, there is everything. All efforts are for the sake of this realization.[468]

So then how can we actually locate this nothing or, as Merrell-Wolff dubbed it, *Consciousness-without-an-object*? There are a number of ways to do it.

Discovering Nothing at the Time of Death

Virtually all traditions agree that our most profound opportunity to experience Consciousness-without-an-object will come at the time of our physical death. During the death process all those worldly things which normally captivate our attention and distract us from Reality will vanish into oblivion. For this reason, Al-Ghazzali writes of a Sufi's death,

> The barriers which lay between him and his Beloved will now be removed, and he will be free of the obstacles and cares of the world, all of which had distracted him from the remembrance of God.[469]

So, too, God tells this to St. Catherine of Siena:

> After the soul has let go of the body's heaviness, her will is filled. She longed to see me and now she sees me, and in that vision is blessedness.[470]

In the Kabbalist tradition, attaining Gnosis at the time of death is called "receiving the kiss." The anonymous author of *Sefer ha-Zeruf* explains it as follows:

> And this is the secret of the kiss spoken of regarding the patriarchs, of whom it is said that they died with the kiss: that is, that at the moment that they departed they attained the essence of all apprehensions and above all degrees [*ma'alah*], because the interruptions and all the obstacles which are in the world left them, and the intellect returned to cleave to that light which is the [Divine] Intel-

> lect. And when he cleaves in truth that is the true kiss, which is the purpose of all degrees.[471]

Both Hindu and Buddhist traditions envision death as a process in which the body-mind's elemental energies are re-absorbed into that Formless Consciousness out of which they originally emerged. Then, when nothing is left to obstruct it, the pure light of that Consciousness stands perfectly revealed and Enlightenment becomes possible. There is, however, a catch, for as the Tibetan master Bokar Rinpoche tells us,

> When the [last] absorption is complete, we are in the phase of *attainment-clear light* or the *clear light of the fundamental nature of the mind.* In fact, it can only be clear light provided we identify it, otherwise it is simply ignorance or an unconscious darkness.[472]

In other words, if you don't *Recognize* what that Light of Consciousness is—i.e., the true nature of yourself and the world—it will appear to be a blank nothingness and Enlightenment will not occur.

This incidentally is why, even if you have decided *not* to make attaining Enlightenment your priority in this life, it is still important to maintain a minimum level of practice. Unless you have cultivated at least some degree of detachment from your self-centered conditioning, and developed some capacity for surrendering your self-will, then, when the moment of death arrives, chances are you will be too overwhelmed by confusion and fear to take advantage of it.

If, on the other hand, you *have* made Enlightenment your priority in this life, then you certainly don't want to wait for physical death to attain it—nor, of course, do you have to. Once you have reached the more advanced stages of the path, there are a number of ways you can intentionally enter a state of Consciousness-without-an-object. For example, a close approximation of the Nothingness experienced at the time of death can be induced by certain rigorous meditation and/or prayer practices which lead to states of deep absorption or *samadhi*, as they are known in the East.

Discovering Nothing in States of Samadhi

Practices leading to samadhi are similar to the practice of silent prayer discussed in the last chapter, but more intense. In these practices the goal is not merely to enter a state of Silence in which you are able to ignore the contents of consciousness, but to actually suppress them. This is done by withdrawing attention from all six fields of awareness and concentrating it so completely on a series of increasingly subtle meditation objects that eventually nothing else arises. Then, when attention is withdrawn even from the most subtle object, what is left is a state of Consciousness-without-an-object almost as pure as that experienced at the time of death.

In the Hindu tradition engaging in such samadhi-oriented practices is called *Raja-Yoga* and is based on Patanjali's seminal work, *The Yoga-Sutras*. In this ancient manual of instructions, Patanjali distinguishes several types of samadhi. These range from samadhis in which some objects and forms still appear in Consciousness, to the highest samadhi, *asamprajnata-samadhi*, in which no forms or objects appear. Here is how Patanjali explains it:

> The samadhis attained through concentration, first on gross objects (*vitarka*); second on subtle objects (*vicahara*), third on bliss (*ananda*), and fourth on the pure experience of "I" (*asmita*) are called Samprajnata [samadhis].
> There is another type of samadhi which follows the former [Samprajnata] and arises from the practice of concentrating on the absence of all objects. In this samadhi only latent tendencies (*samskara*) remain. This is called *Asamprajnata-samadhi*.[473]

Buddhists have a similar set of practices in which the meditator also concentrates on more and more subtle meditation objects. This leads to eight (or by some accounts nine) states of progressively deeper absorptions called *jhanas* (not to be confused with *jnana*.) These jhanas culminate in a formless state called "neither perception, nor non-perception."

Although most Westerners tend to associate practices leading to states of samadhi with Eastern traditions, similar practices and states are known in the West as well. Here is how Theophan the Recluse describes the most advanced stages of contemplative prayer:

> The state of contemplation is a captivity of the mind and of the entire vision by a spiritual object so overpowering that all outward things are forgotten, and wholly absent from consciousness. The mind and consciousness become so completely immersed in the object contemplated that it is as though we no longer possess them.[474]

In similar fashion, Arthur Green and Barry Holtz write this of the highest stages of Hasidic prayer:

> This emptying the mind of all content, which Hasidic prayer shares with many other meditative techniques, finally leads to that place *within* God known as the "Nothing" or the realm of Primordial Nothingness....
> The worshiper is no longer a separate self, but is fully absorbed, for the moment, in the Nothingness of divinity.[475]

There are, however, two problems with these practices and the states of absorption they produce. First, even the highest samadhis do not themselves constitute Enlightenment.[476] Like the clear light experienced at the time of death, they only provide an *opportunity* for Gnosis. This is an important distinction, because seekers who confuse samadhi with Gnosis can easily end up trying to attain a permanent state of samadhi. Not only is this impossible (because all states are ultimately impermanent), but fixating on samadhi can also become an obstacle, for as Patanjali himself declares,

> Only the yogi who is not attached even to the most elevated states attains, through Gnosis (*sarvatha viveka-khyater*), the "dharma-cloud" samadhi (*dharma-meghah-samadhi*).[477]

Likewise, Buddhists insist that the highest jhana—"neither perception, nor non-perception"—represents not Enlightenment, but only the "peak of cyclic existence." In other words, no matter how sublime this state may seem, it remains within the realm of samsara or delusion. This is why Ayya Khema warns,

> Having come to the experience of 'neither perception nor non-perception', it is easy to imagine that one has reached such a high state of purification and realization that nothing else needs to be done. But that is a misconception, and the Buddha's own example points to the absorptions as a *means* towards insight–wisdom.[478]

The second problem with these practices is that the degree of concentration required to enter the highest states of samadhi makes it difficult for most seekers to master. This is particularly true of householders who have enough trouble entering states of spacious awareness or silent prayer. Consequently, these practices are more suitable for monastics, or, at least, seekers who have the time to go on extended retreats (which is why we will not give any extended instructions here.) There are, however, other ways to access Consciousness-without-an-object which lay practitioners may find more compatible with their busy lifestyles. For instance, every night all of us encounter the Nothingness of Consciousness-without-an-object in dreamless sleep. This is why the Upanishads insist,

> In deep sleep it [the True Self] becomes transparent like water, the witness, one without a second. This is the World of Brahman, Your Majesty This is the supreme attainment.[479]

In fact, the only difference between dreamless sleep and the highest states of samadhi is that normally in dreamless sleep we have no lucidity, whereas when we arrive at consciousness-without-an-object through contemplation we do. To attain Gnosis in a state of dreamless sleep, then, we first need to become lucid. So what methods or techniques can we employ to develop lucidity during sleep?

Discovering Nothing During Sleep

Some traditions, like Tibetan Buddhism, have developed highly complex and detailed practices for cultivating lucidity during both the dreaming and dreamless sleep states. In addition, there have been a number of scientific studies of lucid dreaming and ways to induce it. Here we only have space to present a few of the most basic methods gleaned from these sources. Hopefully, however, they will suffice to at least get you started.

How to Cultivate Lucidity During Sleep

1. Resolve each night before you fall asleep to become lucid in both your dreaming and dreamless sleep states. As with reciting your precepts once a day, if you formulate this intention every night, it will plant a seed deep within your psyche which has the potential to blossom once you are asleep.

2. To become lucid in dreams, choose a dream clue. The way to do this is to recall your most recent dreams or, if you are keeping a dream journal, review your latest entries, and see if you can't find some recurring object or event which could serve as a signal that you are, indeed, dreaming. Try to pick something that is at odds with what you normally experience in waking life. A common example would be walking around naked in public. If this is something you dream of often, fix it firmly in your mind as a potential clue to your state. Then, the next time you notice you are naked in public, it may trigger an awareness that you are in the midst of a dream.

3. If you are a bhakta who has been practicing prayer-in-the-heart, then the easiest way to stay lucid as you fall asleep is simply to continue with this practice. The trick is to apply just enough effort to keep your attention focused on your sacred word or prayer, but no more. Too much effort will prevent you from falling fully asleep. Too little effort, and you won't remain lucid. If you can find exactly the right balance, however, then your prayer will act as a boat, carrying your attention from the land of wakefulness to the isle of dreams.

4. If you are a jnani, you might want to try the following Tibetan technique for staying lucid as you fall asleep. Visualize a white A in the center of your body. Traditional Tibetans, of course, use a Tibetan letter that is the equivalent of our English "A." But what is really important is that the letter correspond to the *Ahhh* sound, which (according to their cosmology) helps balance the body's subtle energies. For this reason, the Tibetans themselves say that using an English "A" will work just as well.[480]

   As with prayer-in-the-heart, it is essential to find just the right amount of effort needed to visualize and hold this white A in the center of your body. Start by generating as clear and as sharp an image of it as you can. Then, when you begin your descent into sleep, gradually relax your effort, but without completely losing sight of the A. In this way, your lucidity will remain unbroken as you pass from the waking state to the dream state.

5. Watch how dream images appear in Consciousness. This is especially suitable for people who have very visual dreams. When you are ready to fall asleep, close your eyes and ignore whatever thoughts are running through your mind. Instead, focus your attention on the inside of your forehead, as though you were looking at a blank movie screen in a dark theater.

   At first, you may see abstract light forms appearing on this screen. But as you begin to drift deeper into sleep, these forms will fade away. Next, the screen itself will disappear and you will be left with the sense that you are staring into a vast, borderless abyss. If you can keep your attention focused on this abyss, after a while you will begin to see hypnagogic images flashing in the darkness–a fragment of a face here, a glimpse of landscape there, perhaps a section of a room or building. The way you can tell that these are genuine dream images, and not just products of your ego-mind, is that they will be exceptionally vivid and will appear spontaneously, without your having to think them up. If you continue to watch these images, they will eventually coalesce into a relatively coherent dream which you can then step into as a lucid participant.

6. Concentrate on the feeling of sleepiness itself. This is a Hindu technique which involves focusing your attention on what in Sanskrit is called the *tamasic* feeling—that heavy, leaden sensation you sometimes have as you fall into a particularly deep slumber. The big drawback to this method is that most people don't experience this heaviness in any pronounced way unless they are physically and mentally exhausted. If you do feel this sensation, however, concentrating your attention on it can be especially effective for maintaining lucidity between the waking state and the onset of dreams.

How to Use Lucidity During Sleep

If you attain enough lucidity to take advantage of them, a number of prime opportunities for Realizing Consciousness-without-an-object open up in the course of an average night. The first occurs during the transition from the waking to dream states. Here's what Rumi says about it:

> If you wonder how the senses come and go,
> Pay attention just before the time of sleep.
> That stage unties all the knots
> And shows the truth.[481]

Likewise, in an ancient Hindu text Shiva tells his consort Devi,

> At the moment of sleep when sleep has not yet come and external wakefulness vanishes, at this point *being* is revealed.[482]

Tibetans recognize this state as being the same as the "clear" or "natural" light which opens up at the time of death. Namkhai Norbu describes it this way:

> That which is called the state of natural light is not a moment or a state in which the mind is functioning. It is the period beginning when you fall asleep and ending when the mind begins to function again....
>
> It has always been considered that it is during this period that the practitioner of Tantra realizes him- or herself.[483]

What these mystics are pointing to is that, for a brief moment during the first transition from the waking state to the dream state, we actually pass through a space of pure Consciousness-without-an-object in which no phenomena arise to distract our attention. But precisely *because* there are no phenomena arising in Consciousness, most people interpret this to be a state of complete *un*-consciousness. Consequently, they lose all awareness of what's happening. If, as at the time of death, you can maintain your awareness during this moment of Nothingness, then there is the possibility of Gnostic Awakening. Lama Gendun Rinpoche gives instructions on how to do this using the syllable *Om* (instead of a white A) as an object of concentration:

> Let the mind remain on this syllable, without wavering or being distracted elsewhere, until you actually lose consciousness and fall asleep.
>
> When this happens you may have the impression that the world outside, all the different manifestations created by the mind, folds up and comes to dissolve in the heart. This is followed by an instant where the mind becomes very dull, without any clarity at all, only complete darkness. At that point the different energies of the mind will enter the central channel and just for a brief instant the clear light of the mind will appear. If we can remain in it without being distracted elsewhere, we will be able to recognize the clear light.[484]

If you miss this initial moment of Nothingness, your next opportunity for spiritual practice will come when you are in the dream state. Whether you enter a dream lucidly, or only become lucid once you are in the middle of it, doesn't matter. What does matter is what you do after you become aware that you are, in fact, dreaming.

Lucid dreaming is often accompanied by the power to control your environment and frequently that is the first thing which occurs to people to try. You might experiment with flying through the air, walking through walls, etc. Worldly people are often tempted to engage in illicit activities which they would be too afraid to carry out in waking life. Doing such things, however, is a big mistake, because whether you are awake or dreaming, the moral law still holds—*Self-centered actions produce suffering; selfless actions lead to happiness.* So if you want to play with transforming your dream environment, go right ahead. But make sure you do it with a compassionate motivation that seeks the good of the whole.

The most profound way to take advantage of lucid dreaming, however, is not to manipulate your environment, but to use it to try to gain a direct insight into the empty nature of things. Namkhai Norbu explains this as follows:

> If, while dreaming, you are not only aware of dreaming, but also conscious that all vision is an illusion, you penetrate to the Void at its heart. Thus a dream can be transformed into knowledge of emptiness, *shunyata*.[485]

One way to do this is to purposefully intensify the sensory aspects of your dream surroundings, so that you experience them as vividly and concretely as possible. If you find yourself walking through a forest, for instance, stop and examine the color of the trees, their trunks, and the different hues of their leaves. Next, listen to the sounds of the wind rustling in the branches, the birds chirping, insects humming. Take a deep breath and smell whatever fragrances are wafting through the air. Then, reach out your hand and touch the bark of the nearest tree, carefully noting its texture and solidity. Finally, spend a few minutes contemplating how 'objective' and 'real' all these dream objects seem in spite of the fact that you know they lack any existence apart from the Consciousness in which they are appearing. Once you have experienced this for yourself, even if only in the context of a dream, you will know experientially what the mystics mean when they talk about "emptiness," or "the void," or the fact that everything is but a manifestation of Consciousness Itself.

After contemplating the emptiness of your dream world, the next thing you can try to do is let the dream completely dissolve. If you manage to accomplish this while maintaining your lucidity, you will again enter a state of dreamless sleep, where nothing is manifesting and, thus, have another prime opportunity to attain Gnosis.

If you lose lucidity during this transition, you will get one final chance to experience Nothingness just after the last dream of the night has faded away, but before the waking world re-appears. This moment of Nothingness is the hardest to catch, because usually, by the time you become aware of what is happening, the First Distinction between 'I' and 'other' has already been drawn. Consequently, even though no objects have yet arisen, there still exists that primordial sense of a subject *to* Consciousness, around which the whole Story of I will reconstitute itself as you continue to move into the waking state. What you must attempt to do, then, is to let your attention slip back into that Pure Consciousness which abides eternally prior to all forms of distinctions. This is a bit tricky, but certainly worth a try.

Although cultivating lucidity during sleep is easier for most seekers than attaining deep states of samadhi, it can still be quite a challenge. Again, this is especially true for householders, whose busy lives tend to leave them too tired to practice at night. If this happens to you, don't be discouraged, for as Ramana Maharshi says,

> *Susupti* [pure consciousness of dreamless sleep] does exist in your waking state also. You are in *susupti* even now.... There is no real going in and coming out of it.[486]

In other words, the Nothingness you are looking for is identical with that very Consciousness which underlies all circumstances and all states–even deluded ones, as indicated by this exchange between Zen master, Huang Po, and one of his students:

> [*Student*]: At this moment, while erroneous thoughts are arising in my mind, where is the Buddha?
> [*Huang Po*]: At this moment you are conscious of those erroneous thoughts. Well, your consciousness is the Buddha![487]

This is why (in principle at least) Enlightenment can occur anytime, anywhere. All that is really required is that one stops paying attention to things and, instead, pays attention to the Consciousness in which they appear. And, in fact, this is precisely how Merrell-Wolff attained his Recognition:

> I had never found it possible to completely silence thought. So it occurred to me that success might be attained simply by a discriminative isolation of the subjective pole of consciousness, with the focus of consciousness placed upon this aspect, but otherwise leaving the mental processes free to continue in their spontaneous functioning—they, however, remaining in the periphery of the attentive consciousness. Further, I realized that subjective consciousness without an object must appear to the relative consciousness to have objects. Hence Recognition did not, of itself, imply a new experiential content in consciousness.... This was the final turn of the Key that opened the Door. I found myself identical with the Voidness, Darkness, Silence, but realized them as utter, though ineffable, Fullness.[488]

Turning Attention Back To Its Source

Now, this maneuver of turning attention back to its Source, which Merrell-Wolff so fortuitously stumbled on, is actually well-known in the mystical traditions. Ramana Maharshi, for example, used to tell this to his disciples:

> If the mind is turned in, toward the Source of illumination, objective knowledge ceases, and the Self alone shines as the Heart.[489]

Here's how Dogen describes it:

> *Stop* the intellectual practice of investigating words and chasing after talk; *study* the backward step of turning the light and shining it back.

> Body and mind will drop away of themselves, and your original face will appear.[490]

And Christian mystic St. Basil puts it this way:

> A mind undistracted by external things and not dispersed through the senses among worldly things, returns to itself.[491]

But while this turning attention back to its Source does not require the seeker be in any special state, it still calls for a degree of concentration that can completely ignore the seemingly endless stream of phenomena which ordinarily captivates our attention. Fortunately for seekers who lack this ability, there is yet another method for discovering the Nothingness of Consciousness Itself—one which actually makes use of phenomena. This will be the subject of our next chapter.

Chapter 32

Returning to the Source

Form comes out from Formlessness: Then it returns, for unto Him we are returning.

— Rumi (Muslim)

All the methods we have discussed so far for contacting that Space of Nothingness in which Gnosis becomes possible depend either on suppressing or ignoring the phenomena that appear in Consciousness. But if, instead, you focus your attention on any particular one—and keep it there—that phenomenon will eventually lead you back to the Consciousness out of which it emerged. Here's how Lao Tzu describes it:

I do my utmost to attain emptiness;
I hold firmly to stillness.
The myriad creatures all rise together
And I watch their return.
The teaming creatures
All return to their separate roots.
Returning to one's roots is known as stillness.
This is what is meant by returning to one's destiny.
Returning to one's destiny is known as the constant.
Knowledge of the constant is known as discernment.[492]

This is what makes it possible for Zen students to Wake Up at the whack of a master's stick; or by witnessing a candle being blown out; or on hearing a bird cry. The instant any of these phenomena vanish, Consciousness-without-an-object stands revealed. In order to notice this, however, the student's mind must be completely undistracted. Then, if he or she Realizes this Space to be the Ultimate Nature of everything, Gnosis dawns. This is why, upon receiving a kick from his master, Zen student Shui-liao attained Enlightenment and exclaimed,

> How wonderful! How marvelous! A hundred thousand meditations and infinite sublime principles are discerned at once, right at their source, on the tip of a single hair![493]

But, of course, Zen practitioners are not the only ones who know the value of following phenomena back to their Source. Listen, for example, to the way Gershom Scholem sums up the teachings of the fourteenth-century Kabbalist Rabbi Joseph ben Shalom of Barcelona:

> In every transformation of reality, in every change of form, or every time the stature of a thing is altered, the abyss of nothingness is crossed and for a fleeting mystical moment becomes visible.[494]

Since this is true of all phenomena whatsoever, if you are a jnani who has been using your breath as an object of concentration, you may want to take note of this instruction given by Shiva to his consort Devi:

> When breath is all out (up) and stopped of itself, or all in (down) and stopped—in such universal pause, one's small self *vanishes*. This is difficult only for the impure.[495]

And if you are a bhakta who has been using a sacred word or prayer as an object of concentration, you may find this teaching of Ramana Maharshi's interesting:

> When a mantra is repeated, if one watches the Source from which the mantra sound is produced the mind is absorbed in That.[496]

In other words, it turns out that many "beginning" concentration practices, which use objects like the breath or a mantra, can actually carry you straight to Enlightenment. For the majority of seekers, however, the type of phenomena which will prove most effective in leading attention back to its Source is *thought*.

Following Thoughts Back to Their Source

The reason that it's more effective to follow a thought than other kinds of phenomena is because thought alone creates distinctions and, thus, can delude us. Consequently, if we follow other phenomena to their Source and thoughts are still present, we can still be deceived. If, on the other hand, we follow a thought, then even if other phenomena are present, for that instant in which the thought has vanished, no delusion can occur. This is why Ramana Maharshi suggested a form of self-inquiry that terminates with the specific thought "Who am I?" Here's how he describes it:

> When other thoughts arise, one should not pursue them, but should inquire: "To whom did they arise?" It does not matter how many thoughts arise. As each thought arises, one should inquire with dili-

> gence, "To whom has this thought arisen?" The answer that would emerge would be "To me." Thereupon if one inquires "Who am I?," the mind will go back to its source, and the thought that arose will become quiescent. With repeated practice in this manner, the mind will develop the skill to stay in its source.... The thought "who am I?" will destroy all other thoughts, and, like the stick used for stirring the burning pyre, it will itself in the end get destroyed. Then, there will be Self-realization.[497]

In other words, if you use the thought "Who am I?" to drive out all other thoughts, and then allow *that* thought to vanish, the underlying Consciousness-without-an-object will become apparent. And yet, truly speaking, you don't even need to engage in this kind of highly formalized inquiry. Following *any* thought back to its Source will do the trick. Gendun Rinpoche explains how it works:

> This perception of the essence of mind takes place when all previous thoughts have come to a stop and the next thought has not yet appeared. The mind is in the spontaneous present, its own reality. It is the mind which sees its own essence, and this is what we call primordial wisdom.[498]

Three Pointers for Practice

So now we've really come full circle, for those very thoughts, which you used to view as your worst enemies, turn out to be your greatest allies ... *if*, that is, you know how to make use of them. This, according to the Dzogchen school of Tibetan Buddhism, requires being able to do three things.

The first is to clearly recognize when a thought is present in Consciousness. If you have been practicing meditation or mystical prayer on a regular basis, this should not be difficult. Second, you must be able to allow whatever thought you are watching to self-liberate *without a trace.* The reason this is so important is that if there is even the faintest echo of a thought left over for attention to latch onto, you will continue to be distracted from the pure Nothingness of Consciousness-without-an-object. John Myrdhin Reynolds describes how these two steps work together:

> First we recognize each thought as a thought, seeing its real face nakedly (*gcer mthong*), without conceptions or the activity of the intellect intervening.... But simultaneously with this recognition (*ngos bzung*), we allow the thought to self-liberate by itself, dissolving into its original condition of emptiness and pure potentiality without leaving a trace behind. Thus, this recognition and this liberation must occur together.[499]

But even for veteran meditators, letting thought dissolve without a trace is easier said than done. For one thing, under normal circumstances, the interval between two thoughts is so short we usually aren't aware that it exists. And even if we do manage to glimpse this interval, our attention is actually conditioned to skip over it in its eagerness to grasp onto whatever new thoughts are coming over the horizon. As a result, most seekers find that, in the beginning at least, once the thought they are following self-liberates, they have to make a very slight but distinct effort to hold back the next thought until the present thought has had a chance to totally disappear. To use a rather crude analogy, this is like being a traffic cop who steps into a busy intersection and raises his hand in order to halt the flow of cars long enough for the one that is currently passing through the intersection to completely clear it.

One way to tell when a thought has truly *vanished without a trace* is that you will experience a moment of utter stupidity, as is the case when you suddenly forget the name of one friend you're about to introduce to another. Normally, when this happens you feel something has gone terribly wrong and you start searching your mind for the missing information. But this state of mental blankness is precisely where following a thought until it self-liberates is *supposed* to lead. So instead of frantically trying to fill this gap, just relax into it.

This brings us to the third and last thing you must do in order to successfully follow thought back to its Source—which is actually a *non*-doing. The instant the thought you have been watching completely disappears, you must surrender all effort. This includes not only the effort to hold thoughts back, but also whatever effort you have been making to meditate with an undistracted mind. Why? Because at this point the effort itself will become a distraction.

Now this surrendering all effort to meditate, for which Dzogchen is so famous, emphatically does not mean that it is okay to just sit around being distracted. On the contrary, it means that you have to be such an accomplished meditator that you no longer *need* to make any effort to remain undistracted. This is why Tsoknyi Rinpoche gives us this warning:

> There is some risk of misunderstanding this matter, if you only get half the message, the nonmeditation part, and you miss the first part, which is to remain undistracted. It would be easy then to simply not meditate! But that wouldn't make any sense. People who are already not meditating are constantly being carried away by the three poisons of attachments, aversion, or dullness. That is not meditating at all, so if one is told "don't meditate" in that situation, that makes no sense at all....
>
> Remain without even an atom of focus being meditated upon,
> and without being distracted for even an instant. [That is] undistracted nonmeditation.[500]

In point of fact, even advanced meditators find that initially they can only do this for very short periods of time. Tsoknyi Rinpoche elaborates as follows:

> First, when recognizing mind essence, there is a sense of seeing that it is no-thing. Then that seeing is allowed to continue. That is the training. After a while, it slips away and we get distracted. At some

> point we notice that we've gotten distracted, and remind ourselves to look once more. This reminding is the utilizing, through which we again recognize.[501]

So let's summarize these three points and incorporate them into a set of formal instructions for following thought back to its Source.

Instructions for Following Thought Back to Its Source

STEP ONE: *Entering Spacious-Awareness*

If you are a jnani, concentrate your attention on your breath (or other meditation object) until you have attained some stability. Then, allow your attention to expand into the total field of consciousness-awareness. Spend a few minutes resting in this spacious-awareness without trying to grasp anything or push anything away.

If you are a bhakta, concentrate your attention on your sacred word or prayer, then use it to bring your attention all the way down into your spiritual heart. As you continue repeating your word or prayer, spend a few minutes resting in that place of Silence.

STEP TWO: *Allowing Thoughts to Self-liberate*

If you are resting in spacious-awareness, become aware of the stream of thoughts continually arising and passing in Consciousness. Either wait until a particularly vivid thought appears and let it self-liberate, or purposely generate one by asking, "To whom are these thoughts occurring?" If your thinking mind answers, "To me," then ask, "Who am I?" and allow this last thought to self-liberate.

If you have been repeating a sacred word or prayer, notice that it, too, is a thought and allow it to self-liberate.

STEP THREE: *Allowing a Thought to Vanish without a Trace*

As the thought, word, or prayer self-liberates follow it with undivided attention until it has vanished without a trace. Hold back the next thought or repetition until you become fully aware of the Nothingness revealed by the last thought's absence.

STEP FOUR: *Surrendering All Effort*

The instant you become aware of this Nothingness, surrender all effort. Just continue abiding in this Consciousness-without-an-object until you once again become distracted. Then, repeat steps two through four.

Do this in as relaxed and effortless way as possible. The depth of clarity of your awareness of Consciousness-without-an-object is far more important than the number of times it happens, so pace yourself accordingly.

STEP FIVE: *Practicing Between Sessions*

Once you can allow thought to vanish without a trace easily and frequently, you should abandon the distinction between formal and informal practice. Whenever you become aware you have been distracted by idle thoughts, fantasies, or daydreams, simply allow the last thought in your mind to self-liberate. Follow as it vanishes without a trace. Then surrender all effort and relax into the Nothingness of Consciousness-without-an-object that stands revealed. This is something you can do in any situation, whether you are at home or at work, alone or with friends, walking, eating, even while you fall asleep. Since thoughts are always with you, there's no need to wait for any special time or place to follow them back to their Source.

Recognizing Consciousness Itself

Experiencing the Nothingness between the arising and passing of phenomena does not automatically guarantee you will become Enlightened. As we said, Enlightenment comes only with the Realization that this Space of Nothingness is that Consciousness which constitutes the Ultimate Reality of all things, including your 'self.' But precisely because Consciousness is *not* a thing, recognizing its true nature is difficult, even when you are staring It right in the face. Here is how the thirteenth-century Christian mystic St. Bonaventure puts it:

> Our mind, accustomed to the darkness of beings and the images of the things of sense, when it glimpses the light of the supreme Being, seems to itself to see nothing. It does not recognize that this very darkness is the supreme illumination of our mind.[502]

Nor is there any way you can force this Recognition to occur, for as the Buddhist *Awakening of Faith Sutra* says,

> The thing called Enlightenment is nothing that can be attained by practising, nor can it be created by human hands.[503]

The reason Enlightenment cannot be "created by human hands" is because it always happens spontaneously, or, in theistic terms, by grace. All you can do is to spend as much time as possible hanging out in this Nothingness. So take the advice of the author of *The Cloud of Unknowing*:

> In the beginning ... this darkness and this cloud will remain between you and your God. You will feel frustrated, for your mind will be unable to grasp him, and your heart will not relish the delight of his love. But learn to be at home in this darkness.[504]

Then, as Zen master Suzuki Roshi says,

> There is always the possibility of understanding as long as we exist in the utter darkness of the sky, as long as we live in emptiness.[505]

Surrender All Seeking

Perhaps the most difficult thing about learning to *live in emptiness* is that you must stop looking for something more. There is nothing more! You have arrived—you just don't know it yet! This is why Abdullah Ansari of Herat writes,

> To find You involves neither time (hangām) nor means (sabab);
> the one who is dependent on seeking (talab) is veiled (mahjūb).
> To seek You is a remnant of separation and dispersion:
> You are before everything,
> (so) what (would it mean) to seek You?[506]

Similarly, Huang Po says this of those who are looking for Enlightenment:

> By their very seeking they lose it, for that is using the Buddha to seek for the Buddha and using mind to grasp Mind.[507]

In other words, seeking God is distracting you from God! Seeking Enlightenment is distracting you from Enlightenment! What, then, should you do? Tsoknyi Rinpoche gives this advice:

> We need to be resting on nothing, like a bird soaring in the sky. There is space above, there is space below, there is space in front, behind, and to both sides, and the bird is not dwelling on anything whatsoever. It is soaring in mid-air. That is the way to sit. Do not

> lean forward into something, do not lean back into something that you rest on, do not settle down on your seat either. Be suspended in mid-air, with space above, below and on all sides. As a matter of fact, your very being is space as well; it is no different from space.[508]

And this applies not only to your formal practices, but to all your endeavors, whether worldly or spiritual, for as Meister Eckhart says,

> Honor belongs to God. Who are those who honor God? Those who have wholly gone out of themselves, and who do not seek for what is theirs in anything, whatever it may be, great or little, who are not looking beneath themselves or above themselves or beside themselves or at themselves, who are not desiring possessions or honors or ease or pleasure or profit or inwardness or holiness or reward or the kingdom of heaven, and who have gone out from all this, from everything that is theirs, these people pay honor to God, and they honor properly, and they give him what is his.[509]

Here's how Lao Tzu sums up this end-stage teaching:

> In the pursuit of learning one knows more everyday;
> in the pursuit of the way one does less every day.
> One does less and less until one does nothing at all,
> and when one does nothing at all there is nothing that is undone.[510]

This does not mean, of course, that you cease to engage in any of your normal physical or mental activities. What it does mean is that you surrender every last vestige of your own will, so that all of your actions arise as spontaneous expressions of the Tao (as Lao Tzu would say), or in obedience to the Divine Will (as bhaktas would put it). Beyond this there is nothing more for you to do.

The Way of Selflessness

Part VIII: *End of the Way*

Chapter 33

Kenosis

> *I traveled a long way seeking God,*
> *but when I finally gave up and turned back,*
> *there He was, within me!*
>
> — Lalleshwari (Hindu)

When you begin a spiritual path, it is only natural to assume that if you submit to its disciplines and master its practices, eventually it will lead you to Gnosis. But strictly speaking this is not true. Strictly speaking, the spiritual path can never lead you to Gnosis. And this holds whether we are using the pronoun *you* to refer to your deluded self or to your True Self.

If *you* refers to your deluded self, then you can never attain Gnosis, because that 'you' doesn't exist. As Abdullah Ansari of Herat writes,

> There is no seeker, no sought, no receiving of information, no inquiry, no definition, and no description. He (God) is everything in everything.[511]

If, on the other hand, *you* refers to your True Self, then that *You* can never attain Gnosis, because that *You* has never lost it. Here's how Huang Po puts it:

> You have always been one with the Buddha, so do not pretend you can ATTAIN to this oneness by various practices.[512]

Likewise, Ramana Maharshi says,

> In a sense, speaking of Self-realization is a delusion. It is only because people have been under the delusion that the non-Self is the Self and the unreal the Real that they have to be weaned out of it by the other delusion called Self-realization; because actually the Self always is the Self and there is no such thing as realizing it. Who is to realize what and how, when all that exists is the Self and nothing but the Self?[513]

But if this is really true—if following a spiritual path can never lead you to Gnosis—then what has been the point of undertaking all these arduous disciplines and practices? Well, there are two answers to this question.

First, as we have been saying all along, a spiritual path is designed to interrupt and destroy the Story of I and the delusion of self upon which it is based so you can uncover that First Distinction between 'subject' and 'object' and Realize it's imaginary. And, if you, yourself, have been walking this path, you know from your own experience that it does, indeed, work—at least, up to a point. By engaging in various practices you *have* been able to weaken your conditioning, dissolve your attachments, liberate your thoughts, purify your emotions, and transform your desires. You also know that the more you succeed in this, the more the Love, Bliss, and Beauty, which is inherent in Consciousness Itself, starts to shine through in your life. This, in turn, brings about a crucial psycho-spiritual transformation. Whereas, in the beginning you regarded your self as your most prized possession, by the end you come to feel that it is a horrendous burden. Consequently, by the time you finally do arrive back at that First Distinction, your only question is, "How can I destroy this as well?" So, rather than resist the sacrifice of the self, which Gnosis demands, spiritual practices prepare you to actually welcome it.

It is precisely here, however, just when you feel truly ready for Enlightenment, that all your practices suddenly seem to fail, and you run into the kind of impasse that *The Cloud of Unknowing* author warns us about:

> Long after you have successfully forgotten every creature and its works, you will find that a naked knowing and feeling of your own being still remains between you and your God. And believe me, you will not be perfect in love until this, too, is destroyed.[514]

Now the reason breaking through this last barrier is so difficult is that whatever effort you make to destroy your sense of self actually ends up re-enforcing it. Why? Because, as we said in chapter 6, all your efforts are produced by self-will, and self-will is born of seeking, and seeking is what perpetuates the delusion of self. And yet, if you attempt to cease your efforts, surrender your will, and stop seeking, then you encounter what we called the *paradox of practice*—i.e., you are making an effort to cease efforts, willing to surrender your will, and seeking not to seek—which only serves to maintain the illusion that there is, in fact, some 'self' performing these activities.

So then what can you do to break out of this bind? The answer is that *you* can't do anything. Why? Because seeking was not something you chose to do in the first place. It was an automatic response to the suffering you experienced when you lost your Original Happiness. Nevertheless, a way out does, in fact, exist—which brings us to the second reason for engaging in spiritual practices.

If you have been following this path, then you will have found that, along with reversing your attitude towards your self, it has worked another, equally crucial transformation, which we have already mentioned: Instead of being a worldly seeker intent on attaining all sorts of worldly goals, the path has converted you into a spiritual seeker intent on attaining only one goal—Gnosis. And if this conversion is complete, then you will have *no choice* but to continue seeking Gnosis in every way possible, even if this means attempting to do the *impossible*—to practice not practicing, to will to surrender your will, and to seek to stop seeking—until all your efforts are utterly exhausted and you reach the true end of the path, which is not Gnosis but *kenosis*.

Attaining Kenosis

Kenosis is a Greek word which means "to be empty." Here we are using it in a mystical sense to refer to a state of *self*-emptiness. As such, kenosis may be seen as the complement of Consciousness-without-an-object, for just as Consciousness-without-an-object is characterized by the absence of any objects, kenosis is characterized by the absence of anything that could be called a subject or self. This includes not only those ordinary thoughts and emotions that make up the Story of I, but even the most subtle movements of seeking, effort, and will. When all of these have been completely stilled, kenosis is reached. Here is how Anandamayi describes it:

> No matter what anyone's line of approach, at first there is torment and perplexity; one is unable to find. After that comes a state of suspense—emptiness as it were; one cannot penetrate within, neither does one derive satisfaction from worldly enjoyment.[515]

And, as mystics of all traditions testify, this state of kenosis is the indispensable prerequisite for Gnosis. Why? Because, as Suzuki Roshi says,

> True existence comes from emptiness and goes back again into emptiness. We have to go through the gate of emptiness.[516]

Brother Lawrence explains it in more bhakti terms:

> Your heart must be empty of all other things because God desires to possess it exclusively, and he cannot possess it exclusively without first emptying it of everything other than himself.[517]

Merrell-Wolff says the same thing using the language of a jnani:

> He who has thus become as nothing in his own right then is prepared to become possessed by wisdom herself. The completeness of self-emptying is the precondition to the realization of unutterable Fullness.[518]

And yet to say that entering kenosis is a prerequisite for Gnosis seems merely to push the problem back a step without really solving it. For if we now ask how we can attain *kenosis*, we appear to be faced with the same paradox as before—namely, that any effort we make to empty ourselves of self actually insures that the delusion of self will continue. But, while this is certainly true, there is still one way in which kenosis *can* be attained, and that is by trying and *failing* to attain Gnosis. Nor should this entirely surprise us, because, again as we have already seen, each stage of our practice has unfolded according to this very same pattern—i.e., making an effort ends in exhaustion, exhaustion forces us to surrender, and surrender opens us to a grace which leads us further along the path. Well, the same principle applies to the end of the path, for as Ramana Maharshi says,

> *Sadhanas* [practices] are needed so long as one has not realized it. They are for putting an end to obstacles. Finally there comes a stage when a person feels helpless notwithstanding the *sadhanas*. He is unable to pursue the much-cherished *sadhana* also. It is then that God's power is realized. The Self reveals itself.[519]

In other words, ultimately, the path self-destructs—in both meanings of the term: It destroys itself, and, in the process, it also destroys the delusion that there has been any 'self' traveling it. Then, and only then, can Gnosis dawn.

So let's take a last look at the two major approaches we have been tracking—that of the jnani and that of the bhakta—and see how this actually works out for each of them.

How Jnanis Fail

If you are a jnani, your main practice has been to conduct an inquiry in the hope that someday you will come to know the Truth of who you really are. What this inquiry ends up giving you, however, is not knowledge of who you are, but of who you are *not*—i.e., you are not a body, not thoughts, not emotions, not volitions, not an ego, soul, or spirit. And if you continue your inquiry beyond this point, you literally find nothing because, as we've said repeatedly, your True Self is Consciousness, and Consciousness is not a thing. But perhaps by now you, yourself, are convinced that this is, indeed, the case—there is nothing to find and nothing to know. And yet even coming to this conclusion is deceptive, because *thinking* that you don't know can make it seem like you have understood some kind of truth after all, be it only a negative one. But as Menahem Nahum says,

> The end of knowledge is the awareness that we do not know.... If, however, he thinks that he knows some particular thing, he has not attained to wisdom at all.[520]

In other words, when you *really* don't know, it means you don't even know that you don't know! This is why Ibn al-'Arabi declares,

> [True] guidance means being guided to bewilderment, that he might know that the whole affair [of God] is perplexity.[521]

Similarly, the twelfth-century Zen master Ta-hui advises:

> Do not let go of your perplexity, for that is where the intellect cannot operate and thought cannot reach; it is the road through which discrimination is cut and theorizing is ended.[522]

Anandamayi Ma agrees:

> To feel fatigued, exhausted, because one has not found Him is a very good sign indeed. It indicates that one is nearing the purification of one's heart and mind.[523]

In order to reach this state of complete unknowing, however, you must push your inquiry to the limit by continuing to ask, "Who is it that doesn't know? Who is it that is perplexed? Who is it that is bewildered?" And you must keep on following these thoughts back to their Source, until your thinking mind is so utterly exhausted that it simply refuses to function anymore. When this happens you will have no choice *but* to surrender. And, if your surrender is total, you will have, willy-nilly, entered kenosis, which is the gateway to Gnosis. Here is how Hakuin describes a seeker who has reached this state:

> His normal processes of thought, perception, consciousness, and emotion will cease, he will reach the limits of words and reason. He will resemble an utter fool, as everything, including his erstwhile determination to pursue the Way, disappears and his breath itself hangs almost suspended.... this is the occasion when the tortoise shell is about to crack, the phoenix about to break free of its egg.[524]

How Bhaktas Fail

If you are a bhakta, your main practice has been devotion to some form of the Divine. Inspired by the fire of love and longing which devotion aroused, you hoped to attain union with your Beloved. But when you went to look for the Reality behind this form, you, too, found nothing. If, however, you are a true lover, you will continue searching for this Reality by every means possible. Finally, when all your efforts are exhausted, like your jnani cousins you will fall into a state of kenosis. Sufis call this final stage *fana*, which means "the passing away of the self." Then, as Abdullah Ansari of Herat explains, when all else is annihilated, God alone remains:

> God, the Most Exalted, is, and nothing else.
> (For in this state)
>   attachments ('alāyiq) are severed,
>   secondary causes (asbāb) are destroyed, (and)

conventions and norms (rusūm) are nullified.
Limits (hudūd) are shattered.
understandings (fuhūm) are wrecked, (and)
histories (tārīkh) are obliterated.
Signs (īshārāt) are extinct,
allusions ('ibārāt) are effaced, (and)
expressions (khabar) are negated.
And God, the One and Unique, abides by Himself, eternally Subsistent.[525]

St. John of the Cross called kenosis the "dark night of the spirit." Here's how he describes it:

> The spiritual and sensual desires are put to sleep and mortified, so that they can experience nothing, either Divine or human; the affections of the soul are oppressed and constrained, so that they can neither move nor find support in anything; the imagination is bound and can make no useful reflection; the memory is gone; the understanding is in darkness, unable to understand anything, and hence the will likewise is arid and constrained and all the faculties are void and useless ... [526]

But then he goes on to say that this dark night is a necessary precondition for attaining Union with God:

> For in such a way does this dark night of contemplation absorb and immerse the soul in itself, and so near does it bring the soul to God, that it protects and delivers it from all that is not God. For this soul is now, as it were, undergoing a cure, in order that it may regain its health—its health being God Himself.[527]

So it is to kenosis that the spiritual path actually leads, and it doesn't matter how you get there, whether as a jnani or a bhakta. What *does* matter (whether you are a jnani or a bhakta), however, is that during the course of your journey you put all your eggs in one basket, and burn all your bridges behind you, so that there is no possibility of turning back. If you only get temporarily stuck, and think, "Oh well, this spiritual stuff isn't working out, maybe I'll go back to school and become a dentist," you haven't reached true kenosis. In true kenosis all your faculties—intellectual, psychological, and spiritual—are rendered powerless, your desires and aversions dry up, and your will is utterly stymied. Above all, every form of seeking for worldly *and* spiritual things comes grinding to a halt.

Kenosis as Spiritual Death

Once you have entered kenosis, something very profound begins to happen. Having been deprived of anything whatsoever to do, the ego-self starts to undergo that *spiritual death* reported by mystics of all the great traditions. Here, for example, is what the *Lankavatara Sutra* says about what Enlightenment entails:

> There has been an inconceivable transformation-death (*acintya-parinama-cyuti*) by which the false imagination of his particularised individual personality has been transcended by a realisation of his oneness with the universalized mind of Tathagatahood, from which realisation there will be no recession.[528]

Likewise, after comparing a seeker to a silkworm which transforms into a butterfly, Teresa of Avila tells her students this:

> But note very carefully, daughters, the silkworm has of necessity to die; and it is this which will cost you most.[529]

So, too, Menahem Nahum writes,

> He who wants to draw the true life of God into him ... must first put to death his natural self, which has been with him since birth.[530]

Why should this kind of death be necessary? Rumi explains it this way:

> With God, two I's cannot find room. You say "I" and He says "I." Either you die before Him, or let Him die before you ... But since it is impossible for Him to die, you die, so that He may manifest Himself to you and duality may vanish.[531]

From the point of view of Gnosis, of course, no one actually dies, because there is no 'one' there to begin with. And yet, from the point of view of the poor seeker, this 'death' can seem very real, indeed. This is especially true of bhaktas, for whom kenosis is often preceded by feelings of abandonment and heart-break far more devastating than those felt by people who have lost human lovers. Listen to how Mira Bai describes her experience:

> Strange is the path
> When you offer your love....
> If you want to offer love
> Be prepared to cut off your head
> And sit on it.
> Be like the moth,
> Which circles the lamp and offers its body.
> Be like the deer, which, on hearing the horn,
> Offers its head to the hunter....

Be like the fish,
Which yields up its life
When separated from the sea.[532]

But even jnanis can feel that they are on the brink of an actual death. Thus, Hakuin describes someone who has reached the final stage of Zen practice this way:

> Like a man hanging over a precipice he is completely at a loss what to do next. Except for occasional feelings of uneasiness and despair, it is like death itself.[533]

For some, kenosis may last only for a moment or two. This is what happened to Merrell-Wolff, who gives the following account of what transpired just prior to his Realization:

> The final thought before the 'breakthrough' was the very clear realization that *there was nothing to be attained....* I am already That which I seek, and therefore, there is nothing to be sought. By the very seeking I hide Myself from myself. Therefore, abandon the search and expect nothing. This was the end of the long search. I died, and in the same instant was born again. Spontaneity took over in place of the old self-determined effort.[534]

It is even possible (though not very common) for kenosis to be experienced as a state of perfect contentment. This can happen because when you are truly content inside, then no matter what your outer circumstances are, you still feel that there is nothing lacking. And, if there is nothing lacking, there is nothing to be desired, and if there is nothing to be desired, there is nothing to seek. Hence, there is no need for you to make any effort or exercise your will. As Rumi puts it,

Learn from the Prophet an alchemy: Whatever God
gives you, be content.
At the very moment you become content in affliction,
the door of paradise will open.[535]

But however kenosis is reached, the essential factor is, as we said, that all seeking—even for Enlightenment—must come to an end. Then, with nothing to distract it, attention collapses back into that infinite ocean of Consciousness-without-an-object-*and*-without-a-subject from which it arose. And it is here, in this space devoid of any distinctions, that Gnosis dawns. Here's how Lalleshwari describes it:

There all words and thoughts,
as well as Shiva and Shakti, become quiet.
Neither silence nor yogic postures

enable you to enter there.
In that state there is no knowledge,
no meditation, no Shiva or Shakti.
All that remains is That.
O Lallī, you are That.
Attain That.[536]

Chuang Tzu puts it this way:

> Be content to go along [with things] and forget about change and then you can enter the mysterious oneness of Heaven.[537]

Likewise, Suzuki Roshi says,

> If you want to understand it, you cannot understand it. When you give up trying to understand it, true understanding is always there.[538]

And Rumi writes,

> When the heart was annihilated within Him, He remained; then it understood the object of His words: "I Myself am the seeker and the Sought."[539]

Chapter 34

Gnosis

Awareness itself is (self-)liberated by means of Awareness, like water dissolving into water. One's own nature (simply) encounters itself; but its essence transcends all expression (in words); it is like space dissolving into space.

— Garab Dorje (Buddhist)

A Warning about Words

Words are indispensable to anyone walking a spiritual path. Without them there would be no way to receive teachings or instructions. But when it comes to trying to talk about the end of the path—Gnosis and its fruits—words are totally inadequate. The main reason, as we've already seen, is that words create distinctions, and distinctions create dualities. But the Reality disclosed by Gnosis is non-dual. As the *Lankavatara Sutra* declares,

> Words and sentences are produced by the law of causation and are mutually conditioning,—they cannot express highest Reality. Moreover, in highest Reality there are no differentiations to be discriminated and there is nothing to be predicated in regard to it.[540]

But there is another reason words fail. The grammatical structure of our language requires positing a 'self' to act as the subject of experience, but what Gnosis reveals is that no such self exists. Therefore, saying something like "Enlightened beings continue to experience emotions," is false—not because Enlightened beings do *not* experience emotions, but because there are no beings—Enlightened or otherwise—to experience anything.

A third reason words fail when talking about Gnosis is because one of the most common ways we have of describing unfamiliar things is by making use of comparisons. So, for example, if you want to tell someone who has never had a mango what it tastes like you might say, "Well, it tastes a little like a peach, only tarter." But the Reality which Gnosis discloses is not *like* anything. Consequently, there is nothing to compare it to. Ibn al-'Arabi explains it this way:

> The gnostics know, but what they know cannot be communicated. It is not in the power of the possessors of this most delightful station, higher than which there is no station among the possible things, to coin a word which would denote what they know. There is only what He has sent down [in the Qur'an]—His words, "Nothing is like Him" (Koran 42:11).[541]

Despite these difficulties, however, it is important to say *something* about Gnosis, if only to dispel a few of the most prevalent misconceptions of what it actually entails. And, while we will try to use words as precisely as possible, Teresa of Avila's disclaimer must always be born in mind:

> All I say falls short of the truth, which is indescribable.[542]

How Gnosis Happens

As we saw in the last chapter, Gnosis always dawns in a state of kenosis when all distinctions temporarily disappear. Then, with nothing to distract it, attention returns to its Source in that Consciousness which is the Ultimate Reality underlying all things. If Consciousness Recognizes Itself as such, the door to Enlightenment flies open and Gnosis dawns. Here's how Dionysius the Areopagite describes what happens to the Christian mystic:

> It [the Divine Presence] breaks forth, even from that which is seen and that which sees, and plunges the mystic into the Darkness of Unknowing, whence all perfection of understanding is excluded, and he is enwrapped in that which is altogether intangible and noumenal, being wholly absorbed in Him who is beyond all, and is none else (whether himself or another); and through the inactivity of all his reasoning powers is unity by his higher faculty to Him who is wholly unknowable; and thus by knowing nothing he knows That which is beyond his knowledge.[543]

Similarly, Zen master Yun-man says,

> The time will come when your mind will suddenly come to a stop like an old rat who finds himself in a *cul-de-sac*. Then there will be a plunging into the unknown with the cry, "Ah, this!"[544]

As both Dionysius and Yun-man indicate, Gnosis always happens suddenly. Many mystics compare it to a flash of light. For example, here again is Ramana Maharshi's description of his Realization:

> It flashed through me vividly as living truth which I perceived directly, almost without thought-process.[545]

So, too, the eleventh-century Sufi Abu al-Qasim al-Qushayri writes,

> Sufism is a blazing lightning bolt.[546]

The reason Gnosis always happens suddenly, never in a gradual manner, is simple. The world of delusion unfolds in time, while the Reality which Gnosis reveals is Eternal, and there is no way to get from time to Eternity gradually through time. Here's how Huang Po explains it:

> Past, present and future are meaningless. So those who seek the Way must enter it with the suddenness of a knife-thrust.[547]

Realizing the True Nature of the Subject

So what exactly *does* Gnosis reveal in this sudden burst of illumination? Well, first and foremost, as we have been saying all along, Gnosis Reveals that the distinction between subject and object is unreal. This Realization instantly destroys the experience of being a separate self. So, for example, this is the way Shankara describes his Enlightenment:

> My mind fell like a hailstone into the vast expanse of Brahman's ocean. Touching one drop of it, I melted away and became one with Brahman.[548]

Chuang Tzu says much the same of the Taoist sage:

> To him there is no north or south—in utter freedom he dissolves himself in the four directions and drowns himself in the unfathomable. To him there is no east or west—he begins in the Dark Obscurity and returns to the Great Thoroughfare.[549]

Perhaps no one expresses it more beautifully than Rumi:

> Footprints come to the Ocean's shore.
> Therein, no trace remains.[550]

Once the experience of being a separate self has been obliterated, the way is open for a radical shift of identity. Instead of being a particular body-mind, you Realize your true nature is none other than that Ultimate Reality indicated by whatever term your tradition employs. Thus, being a Buddhist, Hui-Neng declares,

> Our very self-nature is Buddha, and apart from this nature there is no other Buddha.[551]

Meister Eckhart gives this account of his "breaking-through":

> I am so changed into him [God] that he produces his being in me as one, not just similar. By the living God this is true! There is no distinction.[552]

Here's what Abraham Abulafia writes about the end of the Kabbalist path:

> Now he is no longer separated from his Master, and behold he is his Master and his Master is he; for he is so intimately adhering to Him ... that he cannot by any means be separated from Him, for he is He.[553]

And the Upanishads say simply,

> In truth who knows God becomes God.[554]

Now to non-gnostics nothing is more shocking than this claim of identity with the Divine. Some, like Jesus of Nazareth and the great tenth-century Persian Sufi, Mansur Al-Hallaj, were executed for uttering such "blasphemies." What is usually missed, however, is that when Gnostics say, "I am God," they are not referring to their ego-selves. In fact, as Rumi explains, they are actually denying that their ego-selves exist:

> People imagine that it is a presumptuous claim [*Ana 'l-Haqq* "I am God"], whereas it is really a presumptuous claim to say *Ana 'l'abd* "I am the slave of God": and *Ana 'l-Haqq* "I am God" is an expression of great humility. The man who says *Ana 'l'abd* "I am the slave of God" affirms two existences, his own and God's, but he that says *Ana 'l-Haqq* "I am God" has made himself non-existent and has given himself up and says "I am God," *i.e.*, "I am naught, He is all: there is no being but God's."[555]

But as profound as this Realization of one's identity with the Ultimate Reality is, it still does not constitute full Gnosis. For full Gnosis, something more is required.

Realizing the True Nature of Objects

As we have also said, full Gnosis involves a Realization of the emptiness of both subject *and* objects. This usually happens as kenosis starts to pass and various phenomena make their appearance once again. Rather than being perceived as inherently existing 'things', however, the phenomena are now Recognized as forms of Consciousness Itself. Here's how Jamgon Kongtrul describes it:

> Liberation as the [primordial buddha] occurs in the following way: The instant the ground's manifestations arise, one does not apprehend them as something else but rather recognizes them as one's own inner radiance. Consequently, the movement [of constructive thoughts] ceases in itself: at the first instant [of movement], the recognition that the manifestations are inner radiance causes realization to dawn. This realization defines the difference [between liberation and deception].
> Immediately thereafter, deception is dispelled and pristine wisdom unfolds. At this point the ground fully develops into the result [i.e., awakening]. This is re-enlightenment, the realization of primordial enlightenment within one's own nature.[556]

This Buddhist insistence on the two-fold nature of Enlightenment is also mirrored in the teachings of mystics of theistic traditions who maintain that complete Gnosis involves not only a Realization that the Divine *transcends* all forms, but that It is also *immanent* in them as their essence. Just listen, for example, to Ibn al-'Arabi:

> When full gnosis dawns upon a man, he possesses it both in qualitylessness and qualitiedness. He realises God to be immanent in all forms of elements; and no form remains whose reality is not considered by him to be the reality of God. And this realization gives him perfect gnosis.[557]

So, too, the Christian mystic Nicholas of Cusa writes,

> O how exalted You are above all things, O Lord! And at the same time how lowly you are because You are present in all things![558]

The thirteenth-century Kabbalist Joseph Gikatila agrees:

> He [God] fills everything and He *is* everything.[559]

When giving accounts of their own Awakenings, however, many if not most Gnostics make no distinction between a Realization of the true nature of the subject and the true nature of objects. Instead, these two Realizations are fused into a single, all-encompassing Enlightenment, as this poem by Dogen so eloquently illustrates:

> An explosive shout cracks the great empty sky.
> Immediately clear self-understanding.
> Swallow up buddhas and ancestors of the past.
> Without following others, realize complete penetration.[560]

One reason for this is that, from the point of view of Gnosis, no distinctions—including those between different kinds of Realization—actually exist.

It is only when we try to analyze what has occurred from the point of view of delusion that speaking this way makes any sense.

Realizing the Identity of Subject and Objects

In particular, distinguishing between two Realizations—or perhaps more accurately between two *aspects* of Realization—helps us understand how it is possible to attain a genuine Gnostic Flash which, nevertheless, falls short of complete Enlightenment. This happens if in a moment of kenosis a seeker Realizes that Consciousness Itself is the Ultimate Reality, but then, when phenomena reappear, fails to Realize that they, too, are manifestations of that Consciousness. In such cases, the mind once again creates and reifies that First Distinction between 'subject' and 'objects'. As a result, the returning phenomena seem to constitute a separate world of 'things' which obscures the non-dual Reality that has been apprehended. If, on the other hand, no reification takes place, then you automatically Realize that the subject *to* Consciousness is identical with the objects arising *in* Consciousness, and this, as Huang Po says, is what constitutes full Enlightenment:

> A perception, sudden as blinking, that subject and object are one, will lead to a deeply mysterious wordless understanding; and by this understanding you will awake to the truth of Zen.[561]

This is how the fourteenth-century Christian mystic John Ruysbroeck puts it:

> What we are, that we behold; and what we behold, that we are; for in this pure vision we are one life and one spirit with God.[562]

And Ibn al-'Arabi writes this of the Gnostic:

> He sees only God as being that which he sees, perceiving the seer to be the same as the seen.[563]

It is worth reiterating that the Realization of this identity between subject and object is not just an intellectual conclusion one arrives at as a result of Gnosis. As Huang Po says, it entails an actual transformation of *perception*. When you look at the world, it no longer appears to exist outside your 'self'. Of course, you can still mentally distinguish your arm from, say, the branch of a tree. But, at the same time, it is also crystal clear that all such distinctions are imaginary. Here's the way Anandamayi Ma explains it:

> What does *Ātmā darśana*, direct perception of That mean? Seer-seeing-seen … these three are realized as modifications created by the mind, superimposed on the one all-pervading Consciousness.[564]

But even if you Realize that there is no real distinction between subject and object, you are not yet completely out of the woods. There are still three misapprehensions which must be avoided if Gnosis is to "stick." Otherwise, what you will end up with is not full Enlightenment, but only a Gnostic episode which, although longer lasting than a Gnostic flash, will in the end prove just as ephemeral. The first of these misapprehensions involves bliss, the second emotions, and the third Realization Itself. So let's look at them one at a time.

Misapprehending Bliss

In chapter 27, we saw how seekers can succumb to a kind of spiritual hedonism by becoming attached to the bliss generated by meditative and devotional practices. Something similar can befall a newly awakened Gnostic, only to an even greater degree. This occurs because the Realization that there is no self to undergo suffering and death almost always unleashes a current of bliss more powerful than anything ever before experienced. Here, for example, is how Shankara describes what happened to him:

> The ego has disappeared. I have realized my identity with Brahman and so all my desires have melted away. I have risen above my ignorance and my knowledge of this seeming universe. What is this joy I feel? Who shall measure it? I know nothing but joy, limitless, unbounded![565]

Likewise, Longchen-pa exclaims,

> Ah Ho! In the perception which is natural and pure from the beginning,
> Arises the wonderful Intrinsic Awareness that makes one laugh.
> There is no duality of mind and its object, and the perceiver is void in essence.[566]

And Rumi writes this of his Awakening:

> I have become senseless, I have fallen into selflessness—in absolute selflessness how joyful I am with Self![567]

Now the problem is not that this bliss is so powerful. The problem is that it can dominate the contents of Consciousness for weeks, or months, or even years to come. If this happens, there is the danger of subtly mistaking the bliss which Gnosis has generated for Gnosis Itself. Then, when the bliss starts to wears off (as eventually it must), the thought will arise, "Uh-Oh, *I* am losing my Enlightenment!" If, in this moment, there is even the slightest reification of such a thought, grasping will take place, followed by more thoughts like, "How can I get my Enlightenment back?"—all of which will once again coalesce into the story of some 'I' who is sliding back into delusion.

One reason seekers fall into this trap is that they have not clearly understood certain teachings—particularly those found in the Eastern traditions—

concerning the relationship between Gnosis and Bliss. Buddhists, for example, often characterize Enlightenment as a "union of emptiness and bliss," which suggests that Gnosis and bliss are identical. In similar fashion, Hindus describe Brahman as *Sat-Chit-Ananda*—Being-Consciousness-Bliss—which also suggests that Ultimate Reality and bliss are somehow synonymous. But as we've seen, Buddhists also warn against becoming attached to the bliss generated by meditation, while Hindus insist that certain kinds of bliss are actually obstacles to Realizing one's identity with Atman, the True Self. Thus, Shankara gives this warning:

> The "covering of bliss" is that covering of the Atman which catches a reflection of the blissful Atman itself. Nevertheless, this covering is a creation of our ignorance.[568]

To avoid any confusion about these teachings, what we need to do is distinguish between two types of bliss: the manifest bliss experienced by a body-mind, and the unmanifest or innate bliss inherent in Consciousness Itself. So what is the difference?

Manifest bliss, no matter how sublime, is still an emotion and, therefore, by nature impermanent. But the unmanifest or innate bliss of Consciousness Itself is not an emotion. It refers to Consciousness's capacity to create this whole world of changing forms, while itself remaining Unchanging and Formless. As such, Consciousness is ever-blissful, because nothing can threaten It. Consequently, there is a total absence of that existential fear which colors all of deluded life. Here's how Longchen-pa explains it:

> It is as if, seeing the army of *māyā* one is taken in, but
> By knowing the reality there is no fear....
> Then there is no other peace to be accomplished.
> (It is as if) being frightened of one's own forces (mistaking them for) others',
> Later, by recognizing them, one is relieved....
> There is no end of satisfaction in happiness and peace.[569]

And upon attaining her own Enlightenment, Lalleshwari composed these verses:

> Birth and death
> do not exist in Shiva,
> just as rising and setting
> do not exist in the sun.
> O Lallī, you existed before;
> you exist now;
> you will exist hereafter.
>
> O Lallī, you are Shiva.
> Shiva, You are Lallī.[570]

If you can discriminate between these two types of bliss, you will be able to enjoy the manifest bliss produced by Realization, without becoming attached to it. Then, when it begins to fade, you will be able to let it completely self-liberate.[573] And precisely because you haven't tried to grasp at it, even when manifest bliss returns again and fades again, you will never mistake it for that unmanifest bliss which is inseparable from Consciousness Itself.

Misapprehending Emotion

The second error seekers make is based on a similar misapprehension of the true nature of emotions. In chapter 25 we saw how all emotions—including so-called negative or afflicted ones—can be transformed into wisdom energies. Not every teacher or teaching, however, makes this clear. As a result, some seekers become convinced that afflicted emotions are *inherently* impure. Consequently, they end up cultivating detachment, not in order to liberate such emotions, but to eradicate them. Seekers who take this kind of ascetic approach can still attain an initial Realization, but their ascetic attitude will often prove to be an obstacle to attaining full Enlightenment.

The reason this happens is because the manifest bliss generated by Realization usually overrides all other emotions for quite some time—especially afflicted ones. Now, if you are someone who has been striving to conquer your emotions, you're apt to mistake their temporary suspension for some kind of permanent victory. Consequently, when an emotion like anger or lust finally does resurface, your thinking mind will interpret this, like the fading of manifest bliss, to mean you are losing your Enlightenment. If you then allow such thoughts to become reified, and try to get rid of the emotion, you will once again get caught up in the Story of I and the delusion of self.

The way to avoid this is simply to purify whatever emotion arises. As we described in chapter 25, let all thoughts about the emotion self-liberate, and then see which of the wisdom energies it transforms into. This is how Longchenpa summarizes the practice:

> Especially when a thought of desire flickers in one, although it is an ordinary emotional defilement, by recognizing it and contemplating on it, it arises as blissful without apprehensions. That is the Discriminative Primordial Wisdom. Hatred arising toward an object is ordinary anger. By recognizing it, it arises as clarity, free from concepts. It is Mirror-like Primordial Wisdom. The arising of unknowing is ignorance. By recognizing it, it arises as natural clarity with no concepts. It is the ultimate sphere primordial wisdom. Boasting that I am better than others is ordinary pride. By recognizing it, one realizes non-duality and equalness. It is the Primordial Wisdom of Equanimity. The arising of competitive thought is ordinary jealousy. By recognizing it, it is cleansed as free from partiality. It is the Primordial Wisdom of Accomplishment. In awareness, although the effect (*rTsal*) of not recognizing (the intrinsic awareness) itself arises

> as the five poisons, when it is recognized, the poisons arise as the power or the play of the five primordial wisdoms.[572]

There is, however, a big difference between doing this before you attained Realization and doing it afterwards. Before, you had to make an effort to remain undistracted long enough to recognize a particular emotion's wisdom energy. Now all it takes is a glance and you will perceive it spontaneously. Why? Because now everything is seen with the Eye of Gnosis.

Misapprehending Realization

The last thing you must avoid is misapprehending Realization Itself as being some sort of fixed state. This happens when your thinking mind generates thoughts such as, "This is IT! I have finally attained Realization! Now I am an Enlightened Being, a Gnostic!" Again, the problem is not that such thoughts arise. If you've become familiar with mystical teachings and their vocabularies, thoughts like this almost certainly will. Again, the problem comes when you reify the thought's contents, because, as we have said over and over, Gnosis is not a state and there is no one to be in it. This is why Ibn al-'Arabi writes,

> The people of perfection have realized all stations and states and passed beyond these to the station above both majesty and beauty, so they have no attribute and no description.... The root of this knowledge of Allah is the station reached ultimately by the gnostics, that is, "no station."[573]

So, too, Shankara says,

> There is neither birth nor death, neither bound nor aspiring soul, neither liberated soul nor seeker after liberation—this is the ultimate and absolute truth.[574]

Chuang Tzu puts it this way:

> Being unified, you have no liking. Being transmuted, you have no fixity.[575]

And Longchen-pa declares,

> Since there is no bondage or liberation, there is no going, coming, or dwelling.[576]

So, just as all efforts to practice must finally be relinquished in order to attain Realization, Realization Itself must be relinquished in order for Gnosis to fully inform your life. Here's how Dogen expresses it:

> If you release the inconceivable practice, the original realization fills your hands; if you become free from the original realization, the inconceivable practice is upheld with your whole body.[577]

But how exactly do you "become free from the original realization?" One way is to try the following:

1. Purposely generate the thought, "I am Enlightened!" Make it as vivid as possible, and then let it completely self-liberate back into the Ocean of Consciousness from which it arose.
2. Next, generate the opposite thought, "I am *not* Enlightened!" Again, make it as vivid as possible, and then let it completely self-liberate into that same Ocean of Consciousness.
3. Repeat this slowly and deliberately several times.
4. As you do so, notice that, in Reality, there is no difference whatsoever between these two thoughts. Both are imaginary; both arise and pass without altering the nature of Consciousness even by a hair. When it is absolutely clear that all thoughts about Realization are just that--*thoughts and nothing else*—then, as Dogen also says,

> No trace of realization remains, and this no-trace continues endlessly.[578]

Then, and only then will you be completely free of all goals, all struggles, all destinies.

Chapter 35

Life After Gnosis

Ecstasy is akin to passing-away (zawāl), while gnosis is stable and does not pass away.

— Abu Bakr al-Kalabadhi (Muslim)

Some teachers deny that Gnosis can ever be permanent. Sooner or later, they say, the delusion of self returns and with it the need for more practice. This view stems from the testimony of mystics who, having themselves never attained more than a Gnostic flash or episode, come to the conclusion that this must be true for everybody else as well. But this is not the case. There are plenty of fully Awakened Gnostics, both ancient and modern, who bear witness to the possibility of Waking Up once and for all. For example, when Ramana Maharshi was asked to describe Gnosis, he replied,

> It is the firm and effortless abidance in the Self in which the mind which has become one with the Self does not subsequently emerge again at any time.[579]

And listen to what Rumi says of Sufis who have attained Union with the Divine:

> The limit of the travelers is union. But what could be the limit of those in union?—that is, that union which cannot be marred by separation. No ripe grape ever again becomes green, and no mature fruit ever again becomes raw.[580]

Meister Eckhart agrees:

> When the Kingdom appears to the soul and it is recognized, there is no further need for preaching or instruction: it is learned enough and has at once secured eternal life.[581]

So, too, Tsoknyi Rinpoche says, in no uncertain terms,

> When and how one achieves liberation is an individual thing. But once you see through to the very root cause of confusion and are totally free from it, falling back is not possible. It is important to know this.[582]

According to these Gnostics, then, the delusion of self can, indeed, be completely destroyed. And once this has happened, there is no more need to walk a spiritual path or undertake any practices. Of course, you may *choose* to continue meditating or to engage in prayer, for a number of reasons. If, for instance, you've become a teacher, you may want to expand your repertoire of skillful means, or track the experiences of your students, or simply set a good example. But once you are fully Awake, you no longer have anything 'personal' to gain from such practices. Thus, Shankara says this of the seeker who has attained Liberation:

> He no longer needs sacred places, moral disciplines, set hours, postures, directions or objects for his meditation. His knowledge of Atman depends on no special circumstances or conditions.[583]

Longchen-pa puts it this way:

> In the rootless mind, pure from the beginning,
> There is nothing to do and no one to do it—how satisfying![584]

Likewise, Rumi writes,

> In the everlasting Presence, you are the Witness and the Witnessed!
> You laugh at the Path, the traveler, migration, and journeying![585]

Nothing to Attain

One reason that full Gnosis cannot be lost is because it includes that Realization that nothing was attained. Your true nature has always been Consciousness Itself, and always will be. This is why, when his disciple Subhuti asked the Buddha what he acquired through his Enlightenment, the Buddha answered,

> Through the Consummation of Incomparable Enlightenment I acquired not even the least thing; wherefore it is called "Consummation of Incomparable Enlightenment."[586]

Similarly, Menahem Nahum writes this of the Hasidic seeker:

> The further he goes and the closer he brings himself to God's service, the more ever higher levels, filled with the presence of the *shekhinah,* appear before him. The intensity of that presence increases as he continues to reach upward. But finally he must realize that he has in fact attained nothing at all.[587]

And Anandamayi Ma declares,

> "Nothing has happened"—to be able to understand this is very fortunate. If you can understand that nothing has happened, you have indeed been blessed with inner vision.[588]

For this reason, some Gnostics prefer to speak of Enlightenment not in terms of something new being attained, but of something which once was, ceasing—i.e., the experience of being a self. But as Ibn al-'Arabi says, from the point of view of the Absolute, even this is going too far:

> Most of 'those who know God' (*al 'urraf*) make a ceasing of existence and the ceasing of that ceasing a condition of attaining the knowledge of God, and that is an error and a clear oversight. For the knowledge of God does not presuppose the ceasing of existence nor the ceasing of that ceasing. For things have no existence, and what does not exist cannot cease to exist. For the ceasing to be implies the positing of existence, and that is polytheism. Then if thou know thyself without existence or ceasing to be, then thou knowest God; and if not, then not.[589]

Nevertheless, from a relative point of view, when we compare life after Gnosis to life lived under delusion, we can say that Gnosis certainly does bear fruit—in fact, infinite fruits which transform life in radical and unimaginable ways. And although these fruits are in Reality indivisible, for the sake of discussion, we can classify them into five basic varieties: the fruit of Freedom, the fruit of Happiness, the fruit of Love, the fruit of Truth, and the fruit of Perfection. So let's take a look to see if we can get some inkling of how Enlightenment actually revolutionizes a Gnostic's day-to-day experience.

The Fruit of Freedom

As we've said repeatedly, the fundamental thing Gnosis does is to free us from the delusion of being separate selves and show us our True Identity as Consciousness Itself. The destruction of the delusion of self, however, does not mean the elimination of all those patterns of conditioning we lump together as "personality." It is only patterns of *self-centered* conditioning that are terminated. Many others remain the same. If, for instance, as a child you were conditioned to speak English, you will continue to speak English once you have Awakened. And, if your favorite dish before Enlightenment was lasagna, chances are it will remain so afterwards. In fact, Gnostics can display as many different kinds of personality traits as deluded people. Listen, for example, to how Chuang Tzu describes an Enlightened Sage:

> Sometimes he is coldly relentless like autumn; sometimes he is warmly amiable like spring. Joy and anger come and go as naturally as the four seasons do in Nature. Keeping perfect harmony with all

> things (which endlessly go on being 'transmuted' into one another) he does not know any limit.[590]

So, too, Shankara writes this of a Realized Being:

> Sometimes he appears to be a fool, sometimes a wise man. Sometimes he seems splendid as a king, sometimes feeble-minded. Sometimes he is calm and silent. Sometimes he draws men to him, as a python attracts its prey. Sometimes people honor him greatly, sometimes they insult him. Sometimes they ignore him. That is how the illumined soul lives, always absorbed in the highest bliss.[591]

This is why people who have only casual contact with Gnostics often do not notice anything special about them. Outwardly, they can appear perfectly ordinary. And why not? When you have no 'self,' there is no reason to show off or draw attention to yourself. Thus, Ibn al-'Arabi says this of Sufis who have reached the highest level of attainment:

> They do not distinguish themselves from the faithful who perform God's obligations by any extra state whereby they might be known. They walk in the markets, they speak to the people, and none of God's creatures see any of them distinguishing himself from the common people by a single thing.[592]

This totally unpretentious attitude is also expressed in a Zen commentary on post-Enlightenment life as depicted in the famous Ox Herding Pictures:

> Inside my gate, a thousand sages do not know me. The beauty of my garden is invisible. Why should one search for the footprints of the patriarchs? I go to the market place with my wine bottle and return home with my staff. I visit the wineshop and the market, and everyone I look upon becomes enlightened.[593]

But even though certain so-called personal characteristics may persist, without a sense of 'self' no identification with them can take place. For this reason, both the Hindu and Buddhist traditions compare a Gnostic's personality to a piece of rope which has been placed on a bed of hot coals. As Ramana Maharshi describes it,

> This ego is harmless; it is merely like the skeleton of a burnt rope—though with a form, it is useless to tie up anything.[594]

Nor, as we saw in the last chapter, does being free of self mean being free of emotions. While purely self-reflexive emotions—loneliness, humiliation, guilt, resentment—do, indeed, disappear, what we might call *primary* or *biological* emotions continue to arise in response to whatever circumstance naturally trigger them. But, as we also saw in the last chapter, far from causing the Gnostic suffering, even so-called negative emotions are recognized for what they truly are—wisdom energies to be enjoyed and used.

To get some idea of how it is possible to enjoy a negative emotion, consider what happens when people go to the movies. One of the main goals of the movie-maker is to arouse an audience's emotions—and not just pleasant ones either. Horror movies arouse fear, revenge movies anger, tear-jerkers sadness, etc. Moreover, the commercial success of movies proves that we humans not only want to experience such emotions, we are actually willing to pay good money for the opportunity to do so! And yet when it comes to what passes for 'real' life, these same emotions cause us untold misery. So what's the difference?

The difference, of course, is that in the movies we know that none of the events we see on the screen are really happening. The entire show is an imaginary creation. But this is precisely what Gnosis reveals about all of life. This whole cosmos is, in Reality, one Great Epic, written and directed by Consciousness who also plays all the parts. Here's how Longchen-pa puts it:

> All that is has me—universal creativity, pure and total presence—as its root.
> How things appear is my being,
> How things arise is my manifestation.
> Sounds and words heard are my messages expressed in sounds and words.
> All the capacities, forms, and pristine awareness of the buddhas,
> The bodies of sentient beings, their habituations, and so forth;
> All environments and their inhabitants, life forms, and experiences,
> Are the primordial state of pure and total presence.[595]

John Scotus Eriugena explains it this way:

> We ought not to understand God and the creature as two things distinct from one another, but as one and the same. For both the creature, by subsisting, is in God; and God, by manifesting Himself, in a marvellous and ineffable manner creates Himself in the creature, the invisible making Himself visible and the incomprehensible comprehensible and the hidden revealed and the unknown known.... So it is from Himself that God takes the occasions of His theophanies, that is, of his divine apparitions, since all things are from Him and through Him and in Him and for Him.[594]

This is also why Anandamayi Ma insists,

> Where man is ever pure, enlightened, free, eternal, there again all God's numberless names, forms, attributes are eternally real. There the nature of the name, the nature of the form and the diverse waves

> of divine moods, inspirations and raptures stand revealed. In Him should one become engrossed, lost, affixed, immersed, stripped of everything, and then this whole world will be seen as the outer expression of the inner Reality, as the One Himself, the field of His creative activity.[597]

And Ibn al-'Arabi says this of Allah:

> He has no other becoming except mine.[598]

The Fruit of Happiness

One of the most radical effects of Gnosis is that it puts an end to that search for happiness which has motivated virtually all our actions since birth. Why? Because, as Ramana Maharshi explains,

> Having realized the Self, nothing remains to be known, because it is perfect Bliss, it is the All.[599]

Here's how Nagarjuna puts it:

> With the realization of the excellent taste of this *prājña*, one realizes a permanent fulfillment (of the heart), and there is no more hankering left.[600]

Writing from a Christian point of view, Teresa of Avila declares,

> The desires of these souls are no longer for consolations or favors, for they have with them the Lord Himself and it is His Majesty Who now lives in them.[601]

In fact, and even more profoundly, the Gnostic is not only freed from seeking happiness, but from all activity. This, of course, does not mean that the body-mind ceases to carry out its normal functions, only that there is no longer any 'doer' of them. Listen, for instance, to what Hakuin says of Zen practitioners before and after they have attained *kensho* (Enlightenment):

> When a person who has not experienced *kenshō* reads the Buddhist scriptures, questions his teachers and fellow monks about Buddhism, or engages in religious disciplines, it is all unenlightened activity, and it demonstrates abundantly that he is still trapped within samsara. He tries constantly to remain detached in thought and deed, but all the while his thoughts and deeds remain attached. He endeavors to be doing nothing all day long, and all day long he is busily doing.
>
> But let this same person experience *kenshō*, and everything changes. Now, though he is constantly thinking and acting, it is all totally

> free and unattached. Although he is engaged in activity around the clock, that activity is, as such, nonactivity. This great change is the result of *kenshō*.[602]

The reason Hakuin says a Gnostic's activity is "nonactivity" is because it does not originate in any self. In this sense, it is no different from the falling rain, or the whispering wind, or the shining stars. All these things happen effortlessly, as spontaneous manifestations of Buddha-Mind. And, of course, the same is true of Gnostics who express themselves in more theistic terms. They, too, insist that they are not the agents of their actions: It is God who performs them. Thus Abu Bakr al-Kalabadhi says,

> The condition of union means, that God controls me, not I myself, in my actions; for God exists, not I.[603]

Comparing union with the Divine to a marriage in which the soul is the bride and Christ the bridegroom, St. John of the Cross writes,

> In this awakening of the bridegroom in the perfect soul, everything that occurs and is caused is perfect, for he [God] is the cause of it all.[604]

Or, as Lalleshwari sings,

> Shiva sees through your eyes.
> Shiva hear through your ears.
> Shiva speaks with your tongue.
> Shiva makes your breath move in and out
> and digests your food when you eat.[605]

But then the question arises, why should Buddha-Mind, God, or Consciousness Itself do anything at all—especially if It is already completely Happy? Answering this brings us to the third fruit of Gnosis, Love.

The Fruit of Love

In the beginning of this book, we saw how many of the great traditions describe the creation of the cosmos as being motivated by an over-flowing of that Love and Bliss inherent in Consciousness Itself. To illustrate this further, mystics often compare the relationship between Consciousness and the world to that of artists and their works. Among the followers of Shiva, for example, the world is Shiva's Dance. Tibetans say whatever forms appear in any field of consciousness are the ornaments of Primordial Awareness. Christian mystics have referred to God as the Supreme Architect, Author, or Geometer. For Jews the universe is God's Language, formed out of the letters of the Torah; for Sufis it is God's Writing produced by His Pen. What all these images and metaphors are meant to convey is that, like any true artist, Consciousness creates the Cosmos, not in order to *get* something, but in order to *express* something—and that is pure, selfless Love. This includes the actions of the Gnostics which are actually God's actions born out of this Love. Here's how Ibn al-'Arabi describes it:

> The lover has no free disposal (*tasarruf*) except in that for which God disposes him. His love has put him at a loss to desire anything other than what is desired for him. In actual fact the reality refuses anything but that. Everything that appears from the lover is God's creation, and the lover is the object of the act (*maf'ūl*), not the agent (*fā'il*). Hence he is the locus within which affairs take place, so he is obliterated in affirmation [of his being a "lover"].[606]

Moreover, this same selfless Love that motivates all the Gnostic's actions automatically turns into compassion whenever suffering is encountered. Why? Huang Po gives us a clue:

> The One Mind alone is the Buddha, and there is no distinction between Buddha and sentient things.[607]

In other words, just because there really is no difference between a Gnostic and any other being, even though the Gnostic experiences no *personal* suffering, in a certain sense he or she actually experiences *all* the suffering of *all* the beings in the *entire* universe! It is only natural, then, that the desire to alleviate suffering wherever it is found should arise, for as Ramana Maharshi says,

> All that one gives to others one gives to one's self. If this truth is understood who will not give to others? [608]

The Fruit of Truth

The fourth fruit of Gnosis is Truth. In the Hindu and Buddhist traditions, this is called *omniscience*. Now, normally, we think that if someone were omniscient, they would possess a complete conceptual map of everything in the universe, past, present, and future. While some Hindu and Buddhist believers do, indeed, believe that Enlightenment confers such knowledge, this is not what Gnostics themselves claim. What Gnostics *do* claim is that, since everything shares the same nature, if you have Gnosis of the true nature of any *one* thing, you will have Gnosis of the true nature of everything. Thus, Zen master Dogen writes,

> To penetrate one thing is to penetrate myriad things.[609]

Here's how Ibn al-'Arabi puts it:

> [The gnostics] never cease witnessing forms within themselves and outside themselves, and that is nothing but the self-disclosure of the Real.[610]

And Meister Eckhart says this of the Gnostic:

> To him God shines in all things; for everything tastes to him of God, and God forms himself for the man out of all things.[611]

If Gnostics sometimes seem unusually prescient about certain everyday matters, it is not because their heads are stuffed full of conceptual knowledge. On the contrary, it is because they recognize that all conceptual knowledge is imaginary, and so have no attachment to any particular idea, theory, or system. And it is precisely because they always start from this space of absolute mental ignorance, that, when faced with new problems, they are free to entertain new and creative ideas without having to conform to preconceived notions of what is 'real' or 'true.' This, as Jamgon Kongtrul writes, is what constitutes the basis of the Buddha's skillful means:

> The omniscient Victorious One did not view any aspect of either the environment or the inhabitants of our world-system as ultimately real. Therefore, his teaching is not one that, based on a belief in a single view, sets forth a particular system as the only valid one. Instead, the Buddha spoke in response to the various levels and capabilities, interests, and dispositions of those to be guided [to enlightenment].[612]

Fruit of Perfection

The last and perhaps greatest fruit of Gnosis is the Realization that this whole world, which under delusion appears to be filled with so much ugliness, conflict, anguish, and pain, is, in Reality, that Lost Paradise you have been searching for all along. This is why, according to the Gospel of Thomas, when Jesus was asked when the Kingdom would come, he replied,

> It will not come by watching for it. It will not be said, 'Look, here it is,' or 'Look, there it is.' Rather, the father's kingdom is spread out upon the earth, and people do not see it.[613]

Tibetans call this *Dzogchen* which means "The Great Perfection" and it refers both to the practice of undistracted non-meditation (discussed in chapter 32) *and* the True Nature of the Reality that this practice discloses. Here's how Tsoknyi Rinpoche explains it:

> When we vividly see and experience the actual purity of everything as it is, then the perfection of the development stage is that the entire environment, whatever is perceived, is seen as it really is, a pure land, a buddhafield. There is no impurity, no concreteness, apprehended anywhere. In actuality, your experience is in such a way that whatever used to be an object of distraction has now become a play of the innate nature.[614]

In Hinduism this "play of the innate nature" is called *Lila*—the Play of God—which even includes the whole drama of falling under delusion, enduring all its sufferings, and Waking up to Reality once again. Thus, Lalleshwari sings,

> O Lallī, Creation and sustenance,
> dissolution, concealment, and grace
> are God's Divine play.[615]

What's more, once the true nature of the Cosmos is apprehended, it can be appreciated in its entirety—again, much the way we appreciate a really fine movie. Even though it may contain scenes of sorrow that make us weep, or scenes of violence that arouse our fear, we nevertheless understand that these things are just as necessary to the transcendent perfection of the drama as scenes of humor, tranquility, and joy. And so it is with the world when seen through the eye of Gnosis, which is why God tells St. Catherine of Siena this:

> With my wisdom I have organized and I govern all the world with such order that nothing is lacking and nothing could be added to it.[616]

This is also why Ibn al-'Arabi writes,

> As for the idea that one might remove the bad from the Cosmos of created being, such a thing is not possible, since the Mercy of God inheres in both the good and the bad.[617]

And Chuang Tzu says,

> There is nothing that is not 'right'. Whether a stalk of grain or a great pillar, whether a leper or a (beautiful lady like) Hsi Shih, however, strange, bizarre, ugly and grotesque things may be, the Way makes them all one.[618]

And Huang Po insists,

> That which is before you is it, in all its fullness, utterly complete. There is naught besides.[619]

We have naught else to say, except that, if you still haven't attained Gnosis, you might try one last practice. Sit in a comfortable position and read the following instructions, but make no effort to comply with them. If your attention wants to go where these instructions point, it will; if it doesn't, it won't—it has nothing to do with you.

Instructions for Effortless Contemplation

1. Without fixing your attention on anything in particular, just consider this:

    Is there consciousness of sights?
    Is there consciousness of sounds?
    Is there consciousness of sensations?
    Is there consciousness of desires, aversions, emotions?
    Is there consciousness of thoughts?

    This very Consciousness, which is here right now,
    is that eternal, self-luminous Reality
    you have been striving to Realize all along.

    However, since this Consciousness is already here,
    your striving is unnecessary.

2. Let all thoughts *about* your experience self-liberate, and simply observe as follows:

    See how phenomena arise in Consciousness.
    Since whatever arises is already present,
    how can it be avoided?

    See how phenomena pass in Consciousness.
    Since whatever has passed is no longer present,
    how can it be grasped?

    See how everything arises without the least obstruction.
    Since nothing obstructs phenomena,
    there are no obstacles to be removed.

    See how everything passes without the least hindrance.
    Since everything is self-liberating,
    there is nothing to be set free.

    Relax into this effortless contemplation of how things actually are.

3. Without making any adjustments, continue to observe as follows:

Although you say, "Forms arise in Consciousness,"
can you really separate Consciousness from its
forms? Is not Consciousness like an ocean,
and the forms its waves?

Because Consciousness and its forms are ultimately
inseparable, duality never existed:
How then can it be transcended?

Although you say, "I am aware of such-and-such object,"
can you truly distinguish between your self and
the object? Where does your 'self' end and
the 'object' begin?

Because subject and object are, in reality,
indistinguishable, delusion never originated.
How then can it be dispelled?

4. ***Look!*** Reality is staring you right in the face:

You say, "I cannot surrender my self,"
but there is no self to surrender.

You say, "I have not attained Enlightenment,"
but there is not the slightest thing to attain.

You say, "I am ignorant of my true nature,"
but how can this be? What else is there besides
this infinite, eternal, non-dual field of
Consciousness-and-form which is already present,
right here and now … and now …. and now…

Therefore, drop all striving for attainment
and just be what you are!

Endnotes

1 *The Upanishads*, trans. Juan Mascaró, reprint (New York: Penguin Books, 1983), 81.

2 A.G. Ravan Farhadi, *'Abdulālh Ansārī of Herāt (1006-1089 C.E.): An Early Sufi Master* (Richmond, Surry: Curzon Press, 1996), 71.

3 St. Teresa of Avila, *Interior Castle*, trans. and ed. E. Allison Peers (Garden City, NY: Doubleday & Compnay, Inc., Image Books, 1961), 214-215.

4 Dudjom Lingpa, *Buddhahood Without Meditation: A Visionary Account Known As Refining Apparent Phenomena (Nang-jang)*, trans. Richard Barron (Junction City, CA: Padma Publishing, 1994), 157.

5 R.W.J. Austin, trans., *Ibn al-'Arabi: The Bezels of Wisdom* (New York: Paulist Press, 1980), 25.

6 William Johnston, ed., *The Cloud of Unknowing and the Book of Privy Counseling* (Garden City, NY: Double-day & Company, Inc , Image Books, 1973), 171.

7 Swami Prabhavananda and Chris-topher Isherwood, *Shankara's Crest-Jewel of Discrimination*, 3rd ed. (Hollywood: Vedanta Press, 1978), 112.

8 Joel Morwood, *Naked Through the Gate* (Eugene, OR: Center for Sacred Sciences, 1985), 239.

9 Franklin Merrell-Wolff, *The Philosophy of Consciousness Without an Object: Reflections on the Nature of Transcen-dental Philosophy*, pbk. ed. (New York: Julian Press, 1973), 44.

10 Jn 8:31-34 (New Revised Standard Version).

11 Jn 4:13-14 (NRSV).

12 Suzanne Noffke, trans., *Catherine of Siena: The Dialogue* (New York: Paulist Press, 1980), 292.

13 Edmund Colledge and Bernard McGinn, trans., *Meister Eckhart: The Essential Sermons, Commentaries, Treatises, and Defense* (New York: Paulist Press, 1981), 179.

14 Brother Lawrence, *The Practice of the Presence of God: Writings and Conversations*, trans. Salvatore Sciubra (Washington, DC: ICS Publications, 1994), 61.

15 Michel Chodkiewicz, *Seal of the Saints: Prophethood and sainthood in the doctrine of Ibn 'Arabi*, trans. Liadain Sherrard (Cambridge: Islamic Texts Society, 1993), 167.

16 Moshe Idel, *The Mystical Experience in Abraham Abulafia* (Albany, NY: State University of New York Press, 1988), 144.

17 *The Upanishads*, Mascaró, 86.

18 Burton Watson, trans., *Chuang Tzu: Basic Writing* (New York: Columbia University Press, 1964), 41-42.

19 Prabhavananda and Isherwood, *Crest-Jewel of Discrimination*, 77.

20 Bokar Rinpoche, *Chenrezig Lord of Love: Principles and Methods of Deity Meditation*, French trans., François Jacqumart, English trans., Christiane Buchet, ed., Dan Jorgensen (San

Francisco: ClearPoint Press, 1991), 14-15.

21 Johnston, *The Cloud of Unknowing*, 103.

22 Javad Nurbakhsh, *In the Tavern of Ruin: Seven Essays on Sufism* (London: Khaniqahi-Nimatullahi Publications, 1978), 103.

23 K. Venkata Ramanan, *Nāgārjuna's Philosophy: As Presented in The Maha-Prajñāpāramitā Śāstra*, reprint ed. (Delhi: Motilal Banarsidass, 1978), 107.

24 Prabhavananda and Isherwood, *Crest-Jewel of Discrimination*, 60.

25 William C. Chittick, *The Sufi Path of Love: The Spiritual Teachings of Rumi* (Albany, NY: State University of New York Press, 1983), 149.

26 Walpola Rahula, *What the Buddha Taught*, rev, ed. (New York: Grove Press, 1974), 51.

27 Prabhavananda and Isherwood, *Crest-Jewel of Discrimination*, 64.

28 Austin, *The Bezels of Wisdom*, 25.

29 Cited in Evelyn Underhill, *Mysticism: A Study in the Nature and Development of Man's Spiritual Consciousness* (New York: New American Library, 1974), 200.

30 Prabhavananda and Isherwood, *Crest-Jewel of Discrimination*, 90.

31 Bokar Rinpoche, *Death and the Art of Dying in Tibetan Buddhism*, French trans., François Jacqumart, English trans., Christiane Buchet, ed., Jennifer Pessereau (San Francisco: ClearPoint Press, 1993), 75.

32 Nurbakhsh, *In the Tavern of Ruin*, 98.

33 *The Upanishads*, Mascaró, 101.

34 Dudjom, *Buddhahood Without Meditation*, 113.

35 Dudjom, *Buddhahood Without Meditation*, 111.

36 D.C. Lau, trans. *Lao Tzu: Tao Te Ching* (New York: Penguin Books, 1963), 57.

37 Jn 10:30 (NRSV).

38 Colledge and McGinn, *Meister Eckhart*, 188.

39 Colledge and McGinn, *Meister Eckhart*, 205.

40 Austin, *The Bezels of Wisdom*, 151.

41 William C. Chittick, *The Sufi Path of Knowledge* (Albany: State University of New York Press, 1989), 64.

42 Dwight Goddard, ed., *A Buddhist Bible* (Boston: Beacon Press, 1970), 292.

43 Prabhavananda and Isherwood, *Crest-Jewel of Discrimination*, 71.

44 Colledge and McGinn, *Meister Eckhart*, 227.

45 Chittick, *The Sufi Path of Love*, 183.

46 Goddard, *A Buddhist Bible*, 292-293.

47 Chittick, *The Sufi Path of Love*, 272.

48 Nr. Godalming, (Surrey, UK: The Shrine of Wisdom, 1965), 24. Dionysius the Areopagite, *Mystical Theology and the Celestial Hierarchies*, trans. Editors of the Shrine of Wisdom, 2nd ed.

49 Lama Yeshe, *Introduction to Tantra: A Vision of Totality*, comp. and ed. Jonathan Landaw (Boston: Wisdom Publications, 1987), 77.

50 Prabhavananda and Isherwood, *Crest-Jewel of Discrimination*, 111.

51 S.A.Q. Husaini, *The Pantheistic Monism of Ibn al-'Arabi*, 2nd ed. (Lahore: Sh. Muhammad Ashraf, 1979), 69.

52 Dionysius the Areopagite, *The Divine Names,* trans. Editors of the Shrine of Wisdom, 2nd ed. (Nr. Godalming, Surrey, UK: The Shrine of Wisdom, 1957), 14-15—italics mine.

53 Prabhavananda and Isherwood, *Crest-Jewel of Discrimination*, 75.

54 Chittick, *The Sufi Path of Knowledge*, 327.

55 Chittick, *The Sufi Path of Knowledge*, 7.

56 Vernon J. Bourke, ed., *The Essential Augustine*, 2nd ed. (Indianapolis: Hack-

ett Publishing Company, 1974), 97.

57 Dudjom, *Buddhahood Without Meditation*, 91.

58 John Blofeld, trans. *Zen Teachings of Huang Po: On the Transmission of Mind* (New York: Grove Press, Inc., 1959), 29.

59 The reason Buddhist positive terms for the Ultimate Reality are usually translated by expressions such as "Pristine Awareness" and "One Mind," rather than "Consciousness," is because it has become a convention among Buddhist translators to reserve the word consciousness for other Buddhist terms, such as the Skt. vijñāna, which refer to the kind of dualistic awareness we experience under delusion. So, don't be confused, then, when you read in English versions of Buddhists texts that consciousness is not ultimately real, but a derived phenomenon. What they are really talking about is subject-object consciousness. We, however, are using consciousness in a much broader sense to refer to the sheer fact of awareness—whether or not there are any objects to be aware of, or any subject to be aware of them.

60 Sri Anandamayi Ma, *Mātri Vāni, vol. 2*, trans, Atmananda, compl. Sister Uma, 2nd ed. (Calcutta: Shree Shree Ababdanayee Charitable Society, 1993), 136-137.

61 Tsultrim Allione, *Women of Wisdom* (London: Routledge & Kegan Paul, 1984), 218.

62 *The Upanishads*, Mascaró, 111. The Sanskrit word Mascaró translates as *joy* is *ananda*, which is traditionally translated as *bliss*. For consistency's sake, I have substituted *bliss* for *joy*.

63 Austin, *The Bezels of Wisdom*, 257.

64 Dionysius, *The Divine Names*, 40.

65 *The Upanishads*, Mascaró, 52.

66 Goddard, *A Buddhist Bible*, 311.

67 Chittick, *The Sufi Path of Knowledge*, 111.

68 Kieran Kavanaugh, ed., *John of the Cross: Selected Writings* (New York: Paulist Press, 1987), 67.

69 Ramanan, *Nāgārjuna's Philosophy*, 161-162.

70 Husaini, *The Pantheistic Monism of Ibn al-'Arabi*, 53-54.

71 Jasper Hopkins, *Nicholas of Cusa's Dialectical Mysticism: Text, Translation, and Interpretive Study of De Visione Dei* (Minneapolis, MN: The Arthur J. Banning Press, 1985), 161.

72 *The Dhammapada: The Path of Truth*, trans. The Venerable Balangoda Ananda Maitreya, rev. Rose Kramer (Novato, CA: Lotsawa, 1988), 19.73 Prabhavananda and Isherwood, *Crest-Jewel of Discrimination*, 75.

74 Goddard, *A Buddhist Bible*, 317.

75 Idel, *Abraham Abulafia*, 130—This quote actually comes from a collection of anonymous Kabbalist writings. In attributing it to Abulafia I am following Idel's opinion.

76 Mahmud Shabistari, *The Secret Garden*, trans. John Pasha (New York: E.P. Dutton & Co., Inc., 1974), 26.

77 Swami Muktananda, *Lalleshwari: Spiritual Poems by a Great Siddha Yogini* (New York: SYDA Foundation, 1981), 54.

78 Chittick, *The Sufi Path of Love*, 222.

79 Venerable Lama Lodö, *Bardo Teachings: The Way of Death and Rebirth*, rev. ed. (San Francisco: KDK Publications, 1982), 7-8.

80 Prabhavananda and Isherwood, *Crest-Jewel of Discrimination*, 33.

81 Colledge and McGinn, *Meister Eckhart*, 203.

82 *The Upanishads*, Mascaró, 83.

83 Johnston, *The Cloud of Unknowing*, 169.

[84] Abū Bakr al-Kalābādhī, *The Doctrine of the Sūfīs*, trans. A.J. Arberry, reprint ed. (Lahore: Sh. Muhammad Ashraf, 1983), 130.

[85] *The Upanishads*, Mascaró, 52.

[86] Idel, *Abraham Abulafia*, 176n336.

[87] Chittick, *The Sufi Path of Love*, 59.

[88] Johnston, *The Cloud of Unknowing*, 173.

[89] Prabhavananda and Isherwood, *Crest-Jewel of Discrimination*, 82.

[90] Bokar Rinpoche, *Chenrezig Lord of Love*, 47.

[91] Cited in Nurbakhsh, *In the Tavern of Ruin*, 16.

[92] John Scotus Eriugena, *Periphyseon (The Division of Nature)*, trans. John O'Meara (Washington, DC: Dumbarton Oaks, 1987), 568-569.

[93] Chittick, *The Sufi Path of Knowledge*, 375.

[94] Gershom G. Scholem, *Major Trends in Jewish Mysticism* (New York: Schocken Books, 1961), 20.

[95] Liu I-ming, *Awakening to the Tao*, trans. Thomas Cleary (Boston: Shambhala, 1988), 100.

[96] Noffke, *Catherine of Siena*, 157.

[97] *The Upanishads*, Mascaró, 85.

[98] Suzanne Segal, *Collision with the Infinite: A Life Beyond the Personal Self* (San Diego, CA: Blue Dove Press, 1996), 12-13.

[99] Rex Warner, trans. The Confessions of Saint Augustine (New York: The New American Library, Mentor-Omega Books, 1963), 149, 154.

[100] Lau, *Lao Tzu: Tao Te Ching*, 58, 139.

[101] Merrell-Wolff, *The Philosophy of Consciousness Without an Object*, 178.

[102] Swami Prabhavananda, trans.*Narada's Way of Divine Love: The Bhakti Sutras*, pbk. ed. (Hollywood: Vedanta Press, 2000), 47.

[103] Mt 22:37-38 (NRSV)

[104] Idel, *Abraham Abulafia*, 142.

[105] al-Kalābādhī, *The Doctrine of the Sūfīs*, 78.

[106] Sometimes called *contemplative prayer*, especially in the Christian and Jewish traditions.

[107] A.J. Alston, trans., *The Devotional Poems of Mīrābāī* (Delhi: Motilal Banarsidass, 1980), 99.

[108] Anandamayi Ma, *Mātri Vāni, vol. 2*, 138.

[109] Arthur Green, trans. *Menahem Nahum of Chernobyl: Upright Practices, The Light of the Eyes* (New York: Paulist Press, 1982), 125.

[110] Raymond B. Blakney, trans., *Meister Eckhart: A Modern Translation* (New York: Harper & Row , Publishers, Harper Torchbooks, 1941), 123.

[111] Ramana Maharshi, *The Spiritual Teaching of Ramana Maharshi* (Boston: Shambhala, 1988), 17-18.

[112] Watson, *Chuang Tzu,* 26.

[113] Goddard, *A Buddhist Bible*, 38.

[114] Noffke, *Catherine of Siena*, 292.

[115] Arthur Green and Barry Holtz, eds. and trans., *Your Word Is Fire: The Hasidic Masters on Contemplative Prayer* (Woodstock, VT: Jewish Lights Publishing, A Jewish Lights Classic Reprint, 1993), 58.

[116] Chittick, *The Sufi Path of Love*, 188.

[117] Simone Weil, *Waiting For God*, trans. Emma Craufurd (New York: Harper & Row, Publishers, Perennial Library, 1973), 197.

[118] Mt 6:24 (NRSV).

[119] *The Dhammapada,* Maitreya, 95.

[120] *The Upanishads*, Mascaró, 58.

[121] Chittick, *The Sufi Path of Love*, 32.

[122] Serge Hughes, trans., *Catherine of Genoa: Purgation and Purgatory, The Spiritual Dialogue* (New York: Paulist Press, 1979), 85.

[123] Goddard, *A Buddhist Bible*, 56.

[124] Muktananda, *Lalleshwari*, 7.

[125] Longchen Rabjam, *The Practice of Dzogchen*, trans. Tulku Thondup, ed. Harold Talbott, 3rd ed. (Ithaca, NY: Snow Lion Publications, 2002), 265.

[126] Ramana, *The Spiritual Teaching of Ramana Maharshi,* 42-43.

[127] Green and Holtz, *Your Word Is Fire*, 56.

[128] Goddard, *A Buddhist Bible*, 524.

[129] Alston, *The Devotional Poems of Mīrābāī*, 99.

[130] Colledge and McGinn, *Meister Eckhart*, 294.

[131] Sri Anandamayi Ma, *Mātri Vāni, vol. 1*, trans, Atmananda, 5th ed. (Calcutta: Shree Shree Ababdanayee Charitable Society, 1982), 63—my italics.

[132] *The Dhammapada,* Maitreya, 103.

[133] Huston Smith, *The World's Religions* (New York: HarperCollins Publishers, HarperSanFrancisco, 1991), 102-103.

[134] Igumen Chariton of Valamo compl., *The Art of Prayer: An Orthodox Anthology*, trans. E. Kadloubovsky and E.M. Palmer, ed. Timothy Ware, reprint (London: Faber and Faber, 1985), 209.

[135] Shamar Rinpoche, *A Change of Expression* and Lama Gendun Rinpoche, *Working With Emotions*, trans. Anila Rinchen Palmo (Saint-Léon-sur-Vézère, France: Editions Dzambala, 1992), 12.

[136] Anandamayi Ma, *Mātri Vāni, vol. 1,* 12-13.

[137] Anandamayi Ma, *Mātri Vāni, vol. 2,* 149.

[138] *The Bhagavad Gita*, trans. Juan Mascaró, reprint (New York: Penguin Books, 1987), 59.

[139] *The Bhagavadgītā*, trans. Kees Bolle (Berkeley, CA: University of California Press, 1979), 45.

[140] Rahula, *What the Buddha Taught*, 32.

[141] *The Upanishads*, Mascaró, 59.

[142] Chittick, *The Sufi Path of Love*, 323.

[143] Teresa of Avila, *Interior Castle,* 65.

[144] Kazuaki Tanahashi, ed., *Moon in a Dewdrop: Writings of Zen Master Dōgen* (San Francisco: North Point Press, 1985), 40.

[145] Arthur Osborne, *Ramana Maharshi and the Path of Self-Knowledge* (London: Rider, Century Paperback, 1987), 142.

[146] Chittick, *The Sufi Path of Knowledge*, 92.

[147] Chariton of Valamo, *The Art of Prayer*, 133.

[148] Writings from the Philokalia on Prayer of the Heart, trans. E. Kadloubovsky and G.E.H. Palmer (London: Faber and Faber, 1951), 179-180.

[149] Tanahashi, ed., *Moon in a Dewdrop*, 34.

[150] Chittick, *The Sufi Path of Love*, 123.

[151] *The Upanishads*, Mascaró, 58.

[152] Osborne, *Ramana Maharshi*, 140.

[153] As the story goes, one night when Prince Gautama, the about-to-become Budha, was meditating under a Bo tree he had a series of revelations. During the first watch he recalled all his own past lives. During the second watch he arrived at a profound understanding of how the law of karma determines the types of rebirth a being experiences. During the third watch he arrived at an equally profound understanding of cyclic existence and how to liberate oneself from it. Not until he saw the morning star during the fourth watch, however, did his mind suddenly open up, allowing him to attain full Enlightenment.

[154] Chariton of Valamo, *The Art of Prayer*, 268-269.

[155] Mir Valiuddin, *Contemplative Disciplines in Sufism*, ed. Gulshan Khakee (London: East-West Publications, 1980), 147.

[156] Carl Bielefeldt, *Dōgen's Manuals of Zen Meditation* (Berkeley, CA: University of California Press, 1988), 184.

[157] Anandamayi Ma, *Mātri Vāni, vol. 2,* 172.

[158] Ramana, *The Spiritual Teaching of Ramana Maharshi,* 65.

[159] Teresa of Avila, *Interior Castle*, 185-186.

[160] Tsoknyi Rinpoche, *Carefree Dignity: Discourse on Training in the Nature of Mind*, comp. and trans. Erik Pema Kunsang and Marcia Binder Schmidt, ed. Kerry Moran (Hong Kong: Rangjung Yeshe Publications, 1998), 177.

[161] Edith Hamilton and Huntington Cairns, eds., *The Collected Dialogues* of Plato (Princeton, NJ: The Princeton University Press, Bollingen Series LXXI, 1980), 24.

[162] Lk 6:46 (NRSV).

[163] Cited in Gadjin M. Nagao, *Mādhyamika and Yogācāra: A Study of Mahāyāna Philosophies*, ed. and trans. Leslie S. Kawamura (Albany, NY: State University of New York Press, 1991), 36.

[164] Lk 22:27 (NRSV).

[165] Osborne, *Ramana Maharshi*, 143.

[166] Idel, *Abraham Abulafia*, 118-119.

[167] R.W.J. Austin, trans., *Sufis of Andalusia: The Rūh al-quds and al-Durrat al-fākhirah of Ibn 'Arabi* (Berkeley, CA: University of California Press, 1977), 22-23.

[168] R.M. French, trans., *The Way of a Pilgrim and The Pilgrim Continues His Way* (New York: Ballantine Books, 1974), 16.

[169] Swami Sivananda Radha, *Realities of the Dreaming Mind* (Spokane, WA: Timeless Books, 1994), 151.

[170] Radha, *Realities of the Dreaming Mind,* 152.

[171] Chittick, *The Sufi Path of Knowledge*, 124.

[172] Tenzin Wangyal Rinpoche, *The Tibetan Yogas of Dream and Sleep* (Ithaca, NY: Snow Lion Publications, 1998), 70-71.

[173] Joan Halifax, *Shamanic Voices: A Survey of Visionary Narratives* (New York: E.P, Dutton, 1979), 67.

[174] Longchen Rabjam, *The Practice of Dzogchen*, 149.

[175] Moshe Idel, *Kabbalah: New Perspectives* (New Haven, CT: Yale University Press, 1988), 83.

[176] Morwood, *Naked Through the Gate*, 35.

[177] Cited in David Kinsely, *The Goddesses' Mirror: Visions of the Divine from East and West* (Albany, NY: State University of New York Press, 1989), 238.

[178] Namkai Norbu, *Dream Yoga and the Practice of Natural Light*, ed. Michael Katz (Ithaca, NY: Snow Lion Publications, 1992), 62— *trechod* and *togel* are two very advanced Dzogchen practices found in Tibetan Buddhism.

[179] Idel, *Abraham Abulafia*, 15.

[180] John C. Lamoreaux, *The Early Muslim Tradition of Dream Interpretation* (Albany, NY: State University of New York Press, 2002), 65

[181] Lamoreaux, *The Early Muslim Tradition of Dream Interpretation*, 65.

[182] Norbu, *Dream Yoga* 55-56

[183] Halifax, *Shamanic Voices*, 69.

[184] *The Bhagavadgītā*, Bolle, 73

[185] Longchen Rabjam, *The Practice of Dzogchen*, 340.

[186] Scholem, *Major Trends in Jewish Mysticism*, 136.

[187] Chittick, *The Sufi Path of Knowledge*, 158-159.

[188] Ibn 'Arabi, *Journey to the Lord of Power: A Sufi Manual on Retreat*, comm.
'Abdul-Karim Jili, trans. Rabia Terri Harris (New York: Inner Traditions International, 1981), 30.

[189] Gen Lamrimpa, *Calming the Mind: Tibetan Buddhist Teachings on Cultivat-*

ing Meditative Quiescence, trans. B. Alan Wallace, ed. Hart Sprager, 2nd ed. (Ithaca, NY: Snow Lion Publications, 1995), 33.

[190] James R. Walker, *Lakota Belief and Ritual*, eds. Raymond J. DeMallic and Elaine A. Jahner (Lincoln, NB: University of Nebraska, Bison Books, 1991), 85, 86.

[191] *The Dhammapada,* Maitreya, 68.

[192] Chittick, *The Sufi Path of Love*, 173.

[193] Hughes, *Catherine of Genoa*, 80.

[194] Thubten Chodron, *Taming the Monkey Mind*, reprint (Tyrone Press, 1992), vi.

[195] *The Upanishads*, Mascaró, 88.

[196] Edward B. Pusey, trans., *The Confessions of Saint Augustine* (New York: Random House, The Modern Library, 1940), 251.

[197] Goddard, *A Buddhist Bible*, 55, 56.

[198] *The Bhagavadgītā*, Bolle, 73.

[199] Underhill, *Mysticism*, 313.

[200] Goddard, *A Buddhist Bible*, 523.

[201] Gen Lamrimpa, *Calming the Mind*, 33-34.

[202] Lati Rinbochay and Denma Lochö Rinbochay, *Meditative States in Tibetan Buddhism: The Concentrations and Formless Absorptions*, trans. Leah Zahler and Jeffrey Hopkins (London: Wisdom Publications, 1983), 74.

[203] Joseph Goldstein, "Mindfulness, & Compassion, Wisdom, Three Means To Peace," *Shambhala Sun*, March 2004,

[204] Muktananda, *Lalleshwari*, 71.

[205] Watson, *Chuang Tzu*, 95.

[206] Goddard, *A Buddhist Bible*, 299.

[207] Anandamayi Ma, *Mātri Vāni, vol. 2,* 57.

[208] Allione, *Women of Wisdom*, 113-114.

[209] Watson, *Chuang Tzu*, 103.

[210] Mt 6:19 (NRSV).

[211] Goddard, *A Buddhist Bible*, 52.

[212] Venerable Mahasi Sayadaw, *Practical Insight Meditation: Basic and Progressive Stages*, Tans. U Pe Thin and Myanaug U Tin (Kandy, Sri Lanka: Buddhist Publication Society, 1980), 25.

[213] Dilgo Khyentse, *The Heart Treasure of the Enlightened Ones: The Practice of View, Meditation, and Action*, trans. The Padmākara Translation Group (Boston: Shambhala, 1992), 102.

[214] Kavanaugh, *John of the Cross*, 64.

[215] Merrell-Wolff, *The Philosophy of Consciousness Without an Object*, 22.

[216] There are some forms of chronic depression—especially those associated with conditions like bi-polar disorder—which appear to have a predominantly biological basis not connected with spiritual practices. Seekers who think they may suffer from these kinds of depression should definitely seek medical treatment.

[217] Weil, *Waiting For God*, 210-211.

[218] *The Bhagavad Gita*, Mascaró, 96.

[219] Ps. 42:1-3 (NRSV).

[220] Charles Upton, *Doorkeeper of the Heart: Versions of Rabi'a* (Putney, VT: Threshold Books, 1988), 52.

[221] Swami Ghananda and Sr. John Stewart-Wallace, eds., *Women Saints East and West* (Hollywood: Vedanta Press, 1979), 32.

[222] Johnston, *The Cloud of Unknowing*, 172,

[223] *Mother As Seen By Her Devotee*, 3rd ed. (Calcutta: Shree Shree Anandmayee Charitable Society, 1976), 141.

[224] Claude Addas, *Quest for Red Sulphur: The Life of Ibn 'Arabi*. trans. Peter Kingsley (Cambridge: Islamic Texts Society, 1993), 36.

[225] Weil, *Waiting For God*, 24.

[226] Leo Tolstoy, Confession, trans. David Patterson (New York: W. W. Norton and Company, 1983), 74-75.

[227] Javad Nurbakhsh, *In the Paradise of the Sufis*, 2nd ed. (New York: Khaniqahi-Nimatullahi Publications, 1979), 42.

[228] Muktananda, *Lalleshwari*, 12.

[229] Chariton of Valamo, *The Art of Prayer*, 182.

[230] Dilgo Khyentse, *The Heart Treasure of the Enlightened Ones*, 77.

[231] Mt 15:19-20 (NRSV).

[232] Elizabeth T. Gray, Jr., trans. *The Green Sea of Heaven: Fifty* ghazals *from the Díwán of Háfiz* (Ashland, OR: White Cloud Press, 1995), 83.

[233] Cited in Dionysius, *Mystical Theology*, 71.

[234] Ramana, *The Spiritual Teaching of Ramana Maharshi,* 91.

[235] Chittick, *The Sufi Path of Love*, 211.

[236] Green and Holtz, *Your Word Is Fire*, 69.

[237] Louis Jacobs, *Hasidic Thought* (New York: Behrman House, Inc, 1976), 63-64.

[238] Johnston, *The Cloud of Unknowing*, 92.

[239] Muktananda, *Lalleshwari*, 9, 11.

[240] Chariton of Valamo, *The Art of Prayer*, 86.

[241] Ibn 'Arabi, *Journey to the Lord of Power*, 31.

[242] Chariton of Valamo, *The Art of Prayer*, 131.

[243] Green and Holtz, *Your Word Is Fire*, 37.

[244] Johnston, *The Cloud of Unknowing*, 56.

[245] Chariton of Valamo, *The Art of Prayer*, 61.

[246] *The Upanishads*, Mascaró, 88.

[247] Valiuddin, *Contemplative Disciplines in Sufism* , 65.

[248] Nurbakhsh, *In the Paradise of the Sufis*, 36.

[249] Chariton of Valamo, *The Art of Prayer*, 182-183.

[250] Chariton of Valamo, *The Art of Prayer*, 113.

[251] Nurbakhsh, *In the Paradise of the Sufis*), 39.

[252] Anandamayi Ma, *Mātri Vāni, vol. 2,* 190.

[253] Green and Holtz, *Your Word Is Fire*, 59.

[254] Chariton of Valamo, *The Art of Prayer*, 94.

[255] Chariton of Valamo, *The Art of Prayer*, 129.

[256] Chariton of Valamo, *The Art of Prayer*, 98.

[257] Anandamayi Ma, *Mātri Vāni, vol. 2,* 85.

[258] Green, *Menahem Nahum of Chernobyl*, 41.

[259] Brother Lawrence, *The Practice of the Presence of God*, 97.

[260] Chariton of Valamo, *The Art of Prayer*, 77.

[261] Anandamayi Ma, *Mātri Vāni, vol. 2,* 64.

[262] Chittick, *The Sufi Path of Love*, 153.

[263] French, *The Way of a Pilgrim*, 8-9.

[264] French, *The Way of a Pilgrim*, 9-10.

[265] Valiuddin, *Contemplative Disciplines in Sufism*, 81.

[266] Valiuddin, *Contemplative Disciplines in Sufism*, 81.

[267] French, *The Way of a Pilgrim*, 15, 16.

[268] Muktananda, *Lalleshwari*, 11.

[269] Chariton of Valamo, *The Art of Prayer*, 84.

[270] Chittick, *The Sufi Path of Knowledge*, 220.

[271] Hughes, *Catherine of Genoa*, 79.

[272] Green and Holtz, *Your Word Is Fire*, 83.

[273] Chittick, *The Sufi Path of Love*, 187-188.

[274] Anandamayi Ma, *Mātri Vāni, vol. 2,* 127.

[275] Hughes, *Catherine of Genoa*, 116-117.

[276] Alston, *The Devotional Poems of Mīrābāī*, 76-77.

[277] Brother Lawrence, *The Practice of the Presence of God*, 52-53.

[278] Shaykh Muhammad Hisham Kabbani, *Angels Unveiled: A Sufi Perspective* (Chicago: KAZI Publications, Inc., 1995), 199.

[279] Anandamayi Ma, *Mātri Vāni, vol. 2,* 145.

[280] Bokar Rinpoche, *Chenrezig Lord of Love*, 24.

[281] Austin, *The Bezels of Wisdom*, 165, 255.

[282] Noffke, *Catherine of Siena*, 114.

[283] Upton, *Doorkeeper of the Heart*, 43.

[284] Al-Ghazzali, *The Alchemy of Happiness*, trans. Claud Field, reprint (Lahore: Sh. Muhammad Ashraf, 1987), 23.

[285] Longchen Rabjam, *The Practice of Dzogchen*, 219.

[286] Chariton of Valamo, *The Art of Prayer*, 191.

[287] If you want to withhold your taxes as an act of protest, because you believe the government is engaged in some sort of exceptionally grievous activity, then you should do so openly and be willing to accept the consequences.

[288] Teresa of Avila, *Interior Castle*, 229.

[289] *The Bhagavadgītā*, Bolle, 149.

[290] Qur'an 4:36

[291] Jamgon Kongtrul, *The Great Path of Awakening: A Commentary on the Mahayana Teaching of the Seven Points of Mind Training*, trans. Ken McLeod (Boston: Shambhala, 1987), 47.

[292] Teresa of Avila, *Interior Castle*, 117.

[293] Leonard Lewisohn, *The Heritage of Sufism*, Vol. 1 (Oxford: Oneworld Publications, 1999), xxv.

[294] Noffke, *Catherine of Siena*, 292.

[295] Lodö, *Bardo Teachings*, 57.

[296] Anandamayi Ma, *Mātri Vāni, vol. 1,* 40.

[297] Rick Fields, *How the Swans Came to the Lake: A Narrative History of Buddhism in America*, 3rd ed. (Boston: Shambhala Publications, Inc., 1992), 181.

[298] *The Dhammapada,* Maitreya, 2.

[299] Lk 6:27-28 (NRSV).

[300] Anandamayi Ma, *Mātri Vāni, vol. 2,* 162.

[301] Kongtrul, *The Great Path of Awakening)*, 18.

[302] *The Dhammapada,* Maitreya, 1.

[303] Sallie B. King, trans., *Passionate Journey: The Spiritual Autobiography of Satomi Myōdō* (Boston: Shambhala Publications, Inc., 1987), 45.

[304] Kavanaugh, *John of the Cross*, 195.

[305] Longchenpa, *You Are the Eyes of the World*, trans. Kennard Lipman and Merrill Peterson (Novato, CA: Lotsawa, 1987), 34.

[306] Chittick, *The Sufi Path of Love*, 217.

[307] Noffke, *Catherine of Siena*, 280.

[308] Anandamayi Ma, *Mātri Vāni, vol. 2,* 156.

[309] 1 Jn 4:7-8 (NRSV).

[310] Cited in Ben Zion Bokser, trans., *The Talmud: Selected Writings* (New York: Paulist Press, 1989), 44.

[311] Cited in Nurbakhsh, *In the Tavern of Ruin*, 91.

[312] Chariton of Valamo, *The Art of Prayer*, 243-244.

[313] *Matri Darshan: A photo-album about Shri Anandamayi Ma*, Eng. trans. Atmananda, English-German-French ed. (Westerkappeln, West Germany: Mangalan Verlag S. Schang, 1988). There are no page numbers, but this quote occurs on the third page, counting from the beginning of the actual text.

[314] Anandamayi Ma, *Mātri Vāni, vol. 1,* 130.

[315] Chariton of Valamo, *The Art of Prayer*, 122.

[316] Brother Lawrence, *The Practice of the Presence of God*, 97.

[317] Chariton of Valamo, *The Art of Prayer*, 236.

[318] As always, your eagerness to serve must be tempered by the demands of justice. If, for example, the law or contractual agreements require your employer to pay overtime, you cannot undercut your fellow workers hard-won gains by giving away your own labor for free. Still, you should be on the lookout for opportunities to be extra helpful to your boss and co-workers alike.

[319] *The Bhagavad Gita*, Mascaró, 63.

[320] Green, *Menahem Nahum of Chernobyl*, 105-106.

[321] Nurbakhsh, *In the Paradise of the Sufis*, 95.

[322] Ramana, *The Spiritual Teaching of Ramana Maharshi*, 56.

[323] Brother Lawrence, *The Practice of the Presence of God*, 59.

[324] Chariton of Valamo, *The Art of Prayer*, 117.

[325] Alan Wallace, *A Passage from Solitude: Training the mind in a Life Embracing the World* (Ithaca, NT: Snow Lion Publications, 1992), 63.

[326] Green, *Menahem Nahum of Chernobyl*, 33.

[327] Rahula, *What the Buddha Taught*, 31.

[328] *The Bhagavadgītā*, Bolle, 187.

[329] Goddard, *A Buddhist Bible*, 33.

[330] Valiuddin, *Contemplative Disciplines in Sufism*, 22.

[331] W. Montgomery Watt, *The Faith and Practice of Al-Ghazzali*, reprint (Lahore: Sh. Muhhamd Ashraf, 1963), 56-57.

[332] Watt, *The Faith and Practice of Al-Ghazzali*, 57, 58.

[333] Kongtrul, *The Great Path of Awakening*), 19.

[334] Anandamayi Ma, *Mātri Vāni, vol. 1*, 45-46.

[335] Paravahera Vajiranāna Mahāthera, *Buddhist Meditation in Theory and Practice*, 3rd ed. (Kuala Lumpur, Malaysia: Buddhist Missionary Society, 1987), 177, 178, 180.

[336] Al-Ghazzālī, *The Remembrance of Death and the Afterlife* (Cambridge: The Islamic Texts Society, 1989), 28.

[337] Idel, *Abraham Abulafia*, 120. Abulafia's description is remarkably reminiscent of many shamanic initiation ceremonies—see Mircea Eliade, *Shamanism: Archaic Techniques of Ecstasy*, trans. Willard R. Trask (Princeton, NJ: Princeton University Press, Bollingen series LXXVI, 1974).

[338] Noffke, *Catherine of Siena*, 112.

[339] Prabhavananda and Isherwood, *Crest-Jewel of Discrimination*, 33.

[340] Bourke, *The Essential Augustine*, 174.

[341] Osborne, *Ramana Maharshi*, 18-19.

[342] Chittick, *The Sufi Path of Love*, 92.

[343] Noffke, *Catherine of Siena*, 292.

[344] Shamar and Gendun, *A Change of Expression* and *Working With Emotions*, 20.

[345] Chittick, *The Sufi Path of Love*, 154.

[346] Muktananda, *Lalleshwari*, 72.

[347] *The Dhammapada*, Maitreya, 29.

[348] Cited in Michaela Özelsel, *Forty Days: The Diary of a Traditional Solitary Sufi Retreat*, trans. Andy Gaus (Brattleboro, VT: Threshold Books, 1996), 26.

[349] Chariton of Valamo, *The Art of Prayer*, 136.

[350] Chittick, *The Sufi Path of Knowledge*, 252.

[351] Goddard, *A Buddhist Bible*, 329.

[352] Pusey, *The Confessions of Saint Augustine*, 167—italics added.

[353] Norbu, *Dream Yoga*, 81 —*Ekajati* is a fierce female Tibetan deity.

[354] *An Epistle of Stirrings*, cited in Johnston, *The Cloud of Unknowing*, 22-23—my rendering into modern English.

[355] Nurbakhsh, *In the Paradise of the Sufis*, 22.

[356] John Myrdhin Reynolds, trans., *Self-Liberation Through Seeing With Naked Awareness* (Barrytown, NY: Station Hill Press, 1989), 67.

[357] Chariton of Valamo, *The Art of Prayer*, 253.

[358] Dilgo Khyentse, *The Heart Treasure of the Enlightened Ones*, 107-108.

[359] Dilgo Khyentse, *The Heart Treasure of the Enlightened Ones*, 108.

[360] It should be noted that it *is* possible to generate and hold stationary visual images in the mind, such as mandalas or icons (used in some concentration practices), but this is not the same as trying to hold onto those verbal thoughts and fluid images which constitute our mental stories.

[361] Cited in Sogyal Rinpoche, *The Tibetan Book of Living and Dying*, eds. Patrick Gaffney and Andrew Harvey (New York: Harper Collins Publishers, Harper San Francisco, 1992), 166.

[362] Green and Holtz, *Your Word Is Fire*, 15.

[363] Cited in Prabhavananda, *Narada's Way of Divine Love*, 62.

[364] Johnston, *The Cloud of Unknowing*, 151.

[365] John Myrdhin Reynolds, trans. *The Golden Letters* (Ithaca, NY: Snow Lion Publications, 1996), 115.

[366] Blofeld, *Zen Teachings of Huang Po*, 63.

[367] Shamar and Gendun, *A Change of Expression* and *Working With Emotions* 6.

[368] Green and Holtz, *Your Word Is Fire*, 15-16

[369] Prabhavananda, *Narada's Way of Divine Love*, 137.

[370] Eriugena, *Periphyseon*, 107-108.

[371] Shamar and Gendun, *A Change of Expression* and *Working With Emotions* 38.

[372] Keith Dowman, *Sky Dancer: The Secret Life and Songs of the Lady Tsogyel* (London: Routledge & Kegan Paul, 1984), 46.

[373] Dowman, *Sky Dancer*, 45.

[374] Dowman, *Sky Dancer*, 46.

[375] Dowman, *Sky Dancer*, 46-47.

[376] Dowman, *Sky Dancer*, 47.

[377] This, in fact, is the purpose of Zen koan practice, as Zen scholar D.T. Suzuki explains,

> The koan given to the uninitiated is intended "to destroy the root of life", "to make the calculating mind die", "to root out the entire mind that has been at work since eternity", etc. This may sound murderous, but the ultimate intent is to go beyond the limits of intellection, and these limits can be crossed over only by exhausting oneself once for all, by using up all the psychic powers at one's command. (Suzuki, *Zen Buddhism*, 138.)

[378] A.J. Alston, trans., *Śankara on the Creation: A Śankara Source-Book* vol 2, 2nd ed. (London: Shanti Sadan, 2004), 256.

[379] Ramanan, *Nāgārjuna's Philosophy*. 200.

[380] Husaini, *The Pantheistic Monism of Ibn al-'Arabi*, 123.

[381] Cited in Alexandre Koyré, *From the Closed World to the Infinite Universe*, pbk. ed. (Baltimore, MD: The Johns Hopkins University Press, 1968), 161.

[382] Palle Yougrau, *A World Without Time: The Forgotten Legacy of Gödel and Einstein*, pbk. ed. (New York: Basic Books, 2006), 112.

[383] Colledge and McGinn, *Meister Eckhart*, 179.

[384] Goddard, *A Buddhist Bible*, 524.

[385] Tsoknyi Rinpoche, *Carefree Dignity*, 203.

[386] Chittick, *The Sufi Path of Love*, 277.

[387] Sengtsan, *hsin hsin ming*, trans. Richard B. Clarke (Buffalo, NY: White Pine Press, 1984) no page numbers.

[388] Blofeld, *Zen Teachings of Huang Po*, 49-50.

[389] Reynolds, *Self-Liberation Through Seeing With Naked Awareness*, 18.

[390] Cited in al-Kalābādhī, *The Doctrine of the Sūfīs*, 107.

[391] Lk 12:22-31 (NRSV).

[392] *The Bhagavadgītā*, Bolle, 65.

[393] *The Dhammapada,* Maitreya, 93-94.

[394] Nurbakhsh, *In the Tavern of Ruin*, 55.

[395] Goddard, A Buddhist Bible, 323. p. 277.

[396] Chariton of Valamo, *The Art of Prayer*, 160.

[397] Hughes, *Catherine of Genoa*, 122.

[398] Tanahashi, ed., *Moon in a Dewdrop*, 161-162.

[399] Anandamayi Ma, *Mātri Vāni, vol. 2*, 154.

[400] Chariton of Valamo, *The Art of Prayer*, 208.

[401] Dilgo Khyentse, *The Heart Treasure of the Enlightened Ones*, 99-100.

[402] Anandamayi Ma, *Mātri Vāni, vol.2*, 231-232.

[403] Chariton of Valamo, *The Art of Prayer*, 244.

[404] Longchen Rabjam, *The Practice of Dzogchen*, 329.

[405] Reynolds, *Self-Liberation Through Seeing With Naked Awareness*, 67.

[406] *The Upanishads*, Mascaró, 79.

[407] Husaini, *The Pantheistic Monism of Ibn al-'Arabi*, 151.

[408] Franklin Merrell-Wolff, *Transformations in Consciousness: The Metaphysics and Epistemology* (Albany, NY: State University of New York Press, 1995), 197-198.

[409] Goddard, *A Buddhist Bible*, 59-60.

[410] Colledge and McGinn, *Meister Eckhart*, 230.

[411] Muktananda, *Lalleshwari*, 43.

[412] Mt 7:7-8 (NRSV).

[413] Nagao, *Mādhyamika and Yogācāra*, 43.

[414] Colledge and McGinn, *Meister Eckhart*, 184.

[415] Chittick, *The Sufi Path of Love*, 24.

[416] Ramanan, *Nāgārjuna's Philosophy,* 71.

[417] Toshihiko Izutsu, *Sufism and Taoism: A Comparative Study of Key Philosophical Concepts* (Berkeley, CA: University of California Press, 1984), 364.

[418] Alston, *Śankara on the Creation*, 161.

[419] Long-ch'en Rab-jam-pa, *The Four-Themed Precious Garland: An Introduction to Dzog Ch'en*, comm., Dudjom Rinpoche and Beru Khyentze Rinpoche, trans. and ed. Alexander Berzin (Haramsala: Library of Tibetan Works and Archives, 1979), 44.

[420] Longchen Rabjam, *The Practice of Dzogchen*, 276.

[421] Ramana, *The Spiritual Teaching of Ramana Maharshi,* 10.

[422] Chittick, *The Sufi Path of Knowledge*, 120.

[423] Izutsu, *Sufism and Taoism,* 481.

[424] Goddard, *A Buddhist Bible*, 314.

[425] Chittick, *The Sufi Path of Knowledge*, 95.

[426] Anandamayi Ma, *Mātri Vāni, vol. 1,* 131.

[427] Eriugena, *Periphyseon*, 116.

[428] Jamgön Kongtrul Lodrö Tayé, *Myriad Worlds: Buddhist Cosmology in Abhidharma, Kálacakra and Dzog-chen*, trans. and ed. The International Translation Committee of Kunkhyab Chöling (Ithaca, NY: Snow Lion Publications, 1995), 215.

[429] Alston, *Śankara on the Creation*, 247.

[430] Cited in Valiuddin, *Contemplative Disciplines in Sufism*, 142.

[431] Rodney L. Taylor, *The Religious Dimensions of Confucianism* (Albany, NY: State University of New York Press, 1990), 62.

[432] Prabhavananda and Isherwood, *Crest-Jewel of Discrimination*, 73.

[433] Goddard, *A Buddhist Bible*, 320-321.

[434] Dudjom, *Buddhahood Without Meditation*, 27-29.

[435] *The Upanishads*, trans. Swami Nikhilananda, abridged edition (New York: Bell Publishing Company, 1962), 327.

[436] Chittick, *The Sufi Path of Knowledge*, 43.

[437] Longchenpa, *You Are the Eyes of the World*, 37-38.

[438] Prabhavananda and Isherwood, *Crest-Jewel of Discrimination*, 56-57.

[439] Goddard, *A Buddhist Bible*, 27.

[440] Norman Waddell, trans., *The Essential Teachings of Zen Master Hakuin* (Boston: Shambhala Publications, Inc., 1994), 61.

[441] Ayya Khema, *When the Iron Eagle Flies: Buddhism for the West* (New York: Penguin Books, ARKANA, 1991), 77-78.

[442] Alston, *Śankara on the Creation*, 227.

[443] Chittick, *The Sufi Path of Love*, 175.

[444] Chittick, *The Sufi Path of Love*, 263.

[445] Chittick, *The Sufi Path of Love*, 266.

[446] Colledge and McGinn, *Meister Eckhart*, 208.

[447] Cited in Huston Smith, *The World's Religions*, 33.

[448] Cited in Prabhavananda, *Narada's Way of Divine Love*, 14.

[449] Chittick, *The Sufi Path of Knowledge*, 380-381.

[450] Chittick, *The Sufi Path of Knowledge*, 345.

[451] Johnston, *The Cloud of Unknowing*, 139.

[452] Anandamayi Ma, *Mātri Vāni, vol. 2,* 205.

[453] This is a favorite Sufi *hadith*.

[454] Teresa of Avila, *Interior Castle*, 216.

[455] Dionysius, *Mystical Theology*, 14.

[456] Farhadi, *'Abdulālh Ansārī of Herāt*, 110.

[457] *The Upanishads*, Mascaró, 102.

[458] Kavanaugh, *John of the Cross*, 86-87.

[459] Ibn 'Arabi, *Journey to the Lord of Power*, 32.

[460] Johnston, *The Cloud of Unknowing*, 136.

[461] Johnston, *The Cloud of Unknowing*, 162-163.

[462] Farhadi, *'Abdulālh Ansārī of Herāt*, 96.

[463] Scholem, *Major Trends in Jewish Mysticism*, 95.

[464] Merrell-Wolff, *The Philosophy of Consciousness Without an Object*, 36-37.

[465] Longchen Rabjam, *The Practice of Dzogchen*, 295.

[466] Chittick, *The Sufi Path of Knowledge*, 88.

[467] Scholem, *Major Trends in Jewish Mysticism*, 25.

[468] Anandamayi Ma, *Mātri Vāni, vol. 2,* 147.

[469] Al-Ghazzālī, *The Remembrance of Death and the Afterlife*, 124.

[470] Noffke, *Catherine of Siena*, 92.

[471] Cited in Idel, *The Mystical Experience in Abraham Abulafia* (Albany, 183-184.)

[472] Bokar Rinpoche, *Death and the Art of Dying,* 22.

[473] Yoga-Sutras 1.17-18—my renditions.

[474] Chariton of Valamo, *The Art of Prayer*, 64.

[475] Green and Holtz, *Your Word Is Fire*, 14.

[476] *Samadhi* literally means "placing together." This *does* suggest a Gnosis) which abolishes the distinction between subject and object that is the goal of all mystical traditions. However, in both the Hindu and Buddhist tradi-

tions it has commonly come to refer to various meditative states—especially when qualified by an adjective such as *samyaka* in *samyakasamadhi* ("perfect concentration"). Therefore, we must rely on the context or qualifiers to tell us exactly what is intended by the term: Is it being used to mean an on-going Gnosis of Reality, or some profound but nevertheless ephemeral condition?

[477] Yoga-Sutras 4.29–my rendition.

[478] Khema, *When the Iron Eagle Flies*, 147–italics added.

[479] *The Upanishad*, Nikhilananda, 231.

[480] See Namkhai Norbu, *Dream Yoga and the Practice of Natural Light,* 2nd ed.(Ithaca, NY: Snow Lion Publications, 2002), 56.

[481] Mevlana Jalaluddin Rumi, *Magnificent One: Selected new verses from Divan-i Kebir*, trans. Nevit Oguz Ergin (Burdett, NY: Larson Publications, 1993), 47.

[482] Paul Reps, comp., *Zen Flesh, Zen Bones* (Rutland, VT: Charles E. Tuttle Company, Inc., 1957), 201.

[483] Norbu, *Dream Yoga,* 46.

[484] Shamar and Gendun, *A Change of Expression* and *Working With Emotions,* 43.

[485] Norbu, *Dream Yoga,* 58-59.

[486] Ramana, *The Spiritual Teaching of Ramana Maharshi,* 59.

[487] Blofeld, *Zen Teachings of Huang Po*, 80-81.

[488] Merrell-Wolff, *The Philosophy of Consciousness Without an Object*, 36-37.

[489] Ramana, *The Spiritual Teaching of Ramana Maharshi,* 50.

[490] Bielefeldt, *Dōgen's Manuals of Zen Meditation*, 176.

[491] *Writings from the Philokalia*, Kadloubovsky and Palmer, 195.

[492] Lau, *Lao Tzu: Tao Te Ching*, 72.

[493] Thomas Cleary, *Kensho: The Heart of Zen* (Boston: Shambhala Publications, Inc. 1997), 27.

[494] Scholem, *Major Trends in Jewish Mysticism*, 217.

[495] Reps, *Zen Flesh, Zen Bones*, 194.

[496] Osborne, *Ramana Maharshi*, 95.

[497] Ramana, *The Spiritual Teaching of Ramana Maharshi,* 5—I have reversed the order of the last sentence.

[498] Shamar and Gendun, *A Change of Expression* and *Working With Emotions,* 36.

[499] Reynolds, *The Golden Letters*, 112.

[500] Tsoknyi Rinpoche, *Carefree Dignity*, 119-120, 130.

[501] Tsoknyi Rinpoche, *Carefree Dignity*, 69.

[502] Ewert Cousins, trans., *Bonaventure: The Soul's Journey into God, The Tree of Life, The Life of St. Francis* (New York: Paulist Press, 1978) 96-97.

[503] Goddard, *A Buddhist Bible*, 370.

[504] Johnston, *The Cloud of Unknowing*, 48-49.

[505] Shunryu Suzuki, *Zen Mind, Beginner's Mind*, ed. Trudy Dixon, pbk. ed. (New York: Weatherhill, Inc., 1973), 85.

[506] Farhadi, *'Abdulālh Ansārī of Herāt*, 130.

[507] Blofeld, *Zen Teachings of Huang Po*, 29.

[508] Tsoknyi Rinpoche, *Carefree Dignity*, 122.

[509] Colledge and McGinn, *Meister Eckhart*, 185.

[510] Lau, *Lao Tzu: Tao Te Ching*, 109.

[511] Farhadi, *'Abdulālh Ansārī of Herāt,* 13-15 [no page 14].

[512] Blofeld, *Zen Teachings of Huang Po*, 79.

[513] Arthur Osborne, ed., *The Teachings of Ramana Maharshi: In His Own Words*, reprint ed. (London: Century, 1987), 175.

[514] Johnston, *The Cloud of Unknowing*, 103.

[515] Anandamayi Ma, *Mātri Vāni, vol. 2,* 112.

[516] Suzuki, *Zen Mind, Beginner's Mind,* 110.

[517] Brother Lawrence, *The Practice of the Presence of God*, 57.

[518] Merrell-Wolff, *The Philosophy of Consciousness Without an Object*, 178.

[519] Ramana Maharshi, *Talks With Ramana Maharshi: On Realizing Abiding Peace and Happiness*, 2nd rev, ed. (Carlsbad, CA: InnerDirections Publishing, 2001), 497.

[520] Green, *Menahem Nahum of Chernobyl*, 82.

[521] Austin, *The Bezels of Wisdom*, 254.

[522] Cited in Robert E. Buswell, Jr., *Tracing Back the Radiance: Chinul's Korean Way of Zen* (Honolulu: University of Hawaii Press, 1991), 184.

[523] Anandamayi Ma, *Mātri Vāni, vol. 2,* 30.

[524] Waddell, *The Essential Teachings of Zen Master Hakuin*, 70-71.

[525] Farhadi, *'Abdulālh Ansārī of Herāt*, 72.

[526] St. John of the Cross, *Dark Night of the Soul*, trans. and ed. E. Allison Peers, 3rd rev. ed. (Garden City, NY: Doubleday & Company, Inc. Image Books, 1959), 150-151.

[527] John of the Cross, *Dark Night of the Soul*, 155.

[528] Goddard, *A Buddhist Bible*, 341.

[529] Teresa of Avila, *Interior Castle*, 113.

[530] Green, *Menahem Nahum of Chernobyl*, 150.

[531] Chittick, *The Sufi Path of Love*, 191.

[532] Alston, *The Devotional Poems of Mīrābāī*, 114.

[533] D.T. Suzuki, *Zen Buddhism*, ed. William Barrett (Garden City, NY: Doubleday & Company, Inc., Doubleday Anchor Books, 1956), 148.

[534] Merrell-Wolff, *The Philosophy of Consciousness Without an Object*, 81n9.

[535] Chittick, *The Sufi Path of Love*, 293-294.

[536] Muktananda, *Lalleshwari*, 84.

[537] Watson, *Chuang Tzu*, 85.

[538] Suzuki, *Zen Mind, Beginner's Mind*, 131.

[539] Chittick, *The Sufi Path of Love*, 210.

[540] Goddard, *A Buddhist Bible*, 287.

[541] Chittick, *The Sufi Path of Knowledge*, 354.

[542] Teresa of Avila, *Interior Castle*, 198.

[543] Dionysius, *Mystical Theology,* 11.

[544] Suzuki, *Zen Buddhism*, 142.

[545] Osborne, *Ramana Maharshi*, 19.

[546] Carl W. Ernst, Ph.D., *The Shambhala Guide to Sufism* (Boston: Shambhala Publications, Inc., 1997), 23.

[547] Blofeld, *Zen Teachings of Huang Po*, 110-111.

[548] Prabhavananda and Isherwood, *Crest-Jewel of Discrimination*, 113.

[549] Watson, *Chuang Tzu*, 108-109.

[550] Cited in Nurbakhsh, *In the Tavern of Ruin*, 11.

[551] Goddard, *A Buddhist Bible*, 514.

[552] Colledge and McGinn, *Meister Eckhart*, 188.

[553] Scholem, *Major Trends in Jewish Mysticism*, 140-141.

[554] *The Upanishads*, Mascaró, 81.

[555] Reynold A, Nicholson, trans., *Rumi: Poet and Mystic* (London: Unwin Paperbacks, Mandala Books, 1978), 184.

[556] Jamgön Kongtrul, *Myriad Worlds*, 211.

[557] S.A.Q. Husaini, *Ibn al-'Arabi: The Great Muslim Mystic and Thinker*, reprint ed. (Lahore: Sh. Muhammad Ashraf, 1977), 68.

[558] Hopkins, *Nicholas of Cusa's Dialectical Mysticism*, 185.

[559] Scholem, *Major Trends in Jewish Mysticism*, 222.

[560] Tanahashi, ed., *Moon in a Dewdrop*, 218.

[561] Blofeld, *Zen Teachings of Huang Po*, 92.

[562] Cited in Dionysius, *Mystical Theology*, 71.

[563] Austin, *The Bezels of Wisdom*, 235.

[564] Anandamayi Ma, *Mātri Vāni, vol. 2,* 138.

[565] Prabhavananda and Isherwood, *Crest-Jewel of Discrimination*, 113.

[566] Longchen Rabjam, *The Practice of Dzogchen*, 338.

[567] Chittick, *The Sufi Path of Love*, 174.

[568] Prabhavananda and Isherwood, *Crest-Jewel of Discrimination*, 66.

[569] Longchen Rabjam, *The Practice of Dzogchen*, 320.

[570] Muktananda, *Lalleshwari*, 81.

[571] Some seekers who have a Gnostic Awakening only Realize its full significance *after* the manifest bliss disappears. For an example of this, see Merrell-Wolff's *Pathways Through to Space*, in which he describes his thirty-three-day period of Awakening which began with what he termed a "Nirvanic Realization" and culminated in the "High Indifference."

[572] Longchen Rabjam, *The Practice of Dzogchen*, 315.

[573] Chittick, *The Sufi Path of Knowledge*, 376.

[574] Prabhavananda and Isherwood, *Crest-Jewel of Discrimination*, 127.

[575] Izutsu, *Sufism and Taoism* 341.

[576] Longchen Rabjam, *The Practice of Dzogchen*, 317.

[577] Tanahashi, ed., *Moon in a Dewdrop*, 152.

[578] Tanahashi, ed., *Moon in a Dewdrop*, 70.

[579] Ramana, *The Spiritual Teaching of Ramana Maharshi*, 34.

[580] Chittick, *The Sufi Path of Love*, 247.

[581] Blakney, *Meister Eckhart*, 130.

[582] Tsoknyi Rinpoche, *Carefree Dignity*, 61.

[583] Prabhavananda and Isherwood, *Crest-Jewel of Discrimination*, 120.

[584] Longchen Rabjam, *The Practice of Dzogchen*, 325.

[585] Chittick, *The Sufi Path of Love*, 291.

[586] *The Diamond Sutra and The Sutra of Hui Neng*, trans. A. F. Price and Wong Mou-Lam (Boulder CO: Shambhala Publications, Inc., 1969), 61.

[587] Green, *Menahem Nahum of Chernobyl*, 76.

[588] Anandamayi Ma, *Mātri Vāni, vol. 2,* 139.

[589] Ibn 'Arabi, *Whoso Knoweth Himself...* trans. T.H. Weir (Northleach Cheltenham, UK: Beshara Publications, 1976), 5.

[590] Izutsu, *Sufism and Taoism,* 454.

[591] Prabhavananda and Isherwood, *Crest-Jewel of Discrimination*, 122-123.

[592] Chittick, *The Sufi Path of Knowledge*, 374.

[593] Reps, *Zen Flesh, Zen Bones*, 186.

[594] Ramana, *The Spiritual Teaching of Ramana Maharshi*, 59.

[595] Longchenpa, *You Are the Eyes of the World*, 32.

[596] Eriugena, *Periphyseon*, 305.

[597] Anandamayi Ma, *Mātri Vāni, vol. 2,* 175.

[598] Austin, *The Bezels of Wisdom*, 95.

[599] Ramana, *The Spiritual Teaching of Ramana Maharshi*, 77.

[600] Ramanan, *Nāgārjuna's Philosophy,* 119.

[601] Teresa of Avila, *Interior Castle*, 221.

[602] Waddell, *The Essential Teachings of Zen Master Hakuin*, 27.

[603] al-Kalābādhī, *The Doctrine of the Sūfīs*, 130.)

[604] Kavanaugh, *John of the Cross*, 315.

[605] Muktananda, *Lalleshwari*, 11.

[606] Chittick, *The Sufi Path of Knowledge*, 114.

[607] Blofeld, *Zen Teachings of Huang Po*, 29.

[608] Ramana, *The Spiritual Teaching of Ramana Maharshi*, 8.

[609] Tanahashi, ed., *Moon in a Dewdrop*, 134.

[610] Chittick, *The Sufi Path of Knowledge*, 366.

[611] Colledge and McGinn, *Meister Eckhart*, 253.

[612] Jamgön Kongtrul, *Myriad Worlds*, 166.

[613] Marvin Meyer, trans., *The Gospel of Thomas: The Hidden Sayings of Jesus* (New York: HarperSanFrancisco, 1992), 65.

[614] Tsoknyi Rinpoche, *Carefree Dignity*, 185.

[615] Muktananda, *Lalleshwari*, 79.

[616] Noffke, *Catherine of Siena*, 287.

[617] Austin, *The Bezels of Wisdom*, 279.

[618] Izutsu, *Sufism and Taoism,* 364.

[619] Blofeld, *Zen Teachings of Huang Po*, 35.

Quotation Index

Subject Index

I

J

N

O

P

Q

R

S

T